A Framework for International Business

S. Tamer Cavusgil

Gary Knight

John R. Riesenberger

PEARSON

Boston Columbus Indianapolis New York San Francisco Upper Saddle River
Amsterdam Cape Town Dubai London Madrid Milan Munich Paris Montréal Toronto
Delhi Mexico City São Paulo Sydney Hong Kong Seoul Singapore Taipei Tokyo

Editorial Director: Sally Yagan
Acquisitions Editor: Brian Mickelson
Director of Editorial Services:
    Ashley Santora
Director of Marketing: Maggie Moylan
Senior Marketing Manager: Nikki Ayana Jones
Marketing Assistant: Ian Gold
Senior Managing Editor: Judy Leale
Sr. Production Project Manager/Supervisor:
    Lynn Savino Wendel
Senior Operations Supervisor: Arnold Vila

Operations Specialist: Cathleen Petersen
Creative Director: Jayne Conte
Cover Designer: Bruce Kenselaar
Cover Illustration: Fotolia: Le monde
    selon toi © CARRÉ PIXEL
Full-Service Project Management: Danielle
    Urban, Integra Chicago
Composition: Integra Chicago
Printer/Binder: STP Courier
Cover Printer: STP Courier
Text Font: 10/12, Garamond

Credits and acknowledgments borrowed from other sources and reproduced, with permission, in this textbook appear on the appropriate page within text.

Library of Congress Cataloging-in-Publication Data
Cavusgil, S. Tamer.
    Framework of international business/S. Tamer Cavusgil, Gary Knight, John Riesenberger.
        p. cm.
    ISBN 978-0-13-212282-5—ISBN 978-0-13-212288-7
    1. International business enterprises—Management.   I. Knight, Gary A.
    II. Riesenberger, John R., 1948–   III. Title.
    HD62.4.C388 2012
    658'.049—dc23

                                                                2011035443

10 9 8 7 6 5 4 3 2 1

ISBN 10:   0-13-212282-0
ISBN 13: 978-0-13-212282-5

BRIEF CONTENTS

CONTENTS

PREFACE

A *Framework for International Business* provides students and practicing managers with a concise but thorough review of essential international business management concepts and techniques. The insights we gained from comprehensive research and discussions with hundreds of practitioners, students, and faculty have been instrumental in refining the pedagogical approach incorporated herein.

This book captures the *new realities* in international business as practiced today. These include global sourcing, the impact of technological advances on globalization, the globalization of finance, emerging markets, the success of the smaller firm in international markets, and corporate social responsibility. Emerging markets receive special attention. Brazil, China, India and other high-growth, high-potential countries have sprung to the forefront of cross-border business with rapid industrialization, privatization, and modernization.

Large multinational enterprises (MNEs) historically have played the most important role in international business. Today, however, the field is characterized increasingly by additional important players. Thus, we provide a balanced coverage of MNEs, small and medium-sized enterprises (SMEs), and 'born global' firms. In addition, managers are increasingly aware of their role as good corporate citizens. Corporate social responsibility—ethical conduct, local relevance, and sustainability— figures prominently in the book.

Suggested uses of this book vary. Many colleagues will adopt it as the basic textbook for the international business course, supplementing it with extra cases or applied exercises. Others adopt it with complementary textbooks in courses that blend several topics (such as international business and management) or in specialized courses (such as "International Business for Entrepreneurial Firms"). Because this Framework contains a practical and up-to-date review of essential international business concepts and techniques, practicing managers also find it useful for refreshing their knowledge.

SPECIAL FEATURES

Many practitioners now have international business responsibilities, so this book is intended for all students of management and strategy, not just those who are or will be international specialists. The international business environment is experiencing rapid change with the impact of the global financial crisis, economic volatility, and rapidly changing dynamics among firms conducting business in advanced economies, emerging markets, and developing economies. Accordingly, in this book we emphasize the following changes and environmental factors:

1. *Ethics and corporate social responsibility* are increasingly recognized as key issues in international business. Hence, we address ethical conduct in various chapters.
2. We include nearly 100 *exhibits* that provide the latest data and thinking on key issues.

3. We provide *balanced geographical coverage* of companies and issues, from developing to advanced economies, with particular emphasis on emerging markets.

4. We provide 26 videos produced during 2010, 2011, and 2012 developed to support the specific major themes of the book.

5. We make every effort to provide *current content* in light of changing environmental conditions and the focus of new, emerging topics in international business.

INSTRUCTOR'S RESOURCE CENTER

At www.pearsonhighered.com, instructors can access a variety of print, digital, and presentation resources available with this text in downloadable format. Registration is simple and gives you immediate access to new titles and new editions. As a registered faculty member, you can download resource files and receive immediate access and instructions for installing course management content on your campus server. The following supplements are available for download to adopting instructors:

- Instructor's Manual
- Test Item File
- TestGen Test Generating Software
- Power Points
- Videos on DVD

In addition, we provide the following supplements:

CourseSmart eTextbooks were developed for students looking to save on required or recommended textbooks. Students simply select their eText by title or author and purchase immediate access to the content for the duration of the course using any major credit card. With a CourseSmart eText, students can search for specific keywords or page numbers, take notes online, print out reading assignments that incorporate lecture notes, and bookmark important passages for later review. For more information or to purchase a CourseSmart eTextbook, visit www.coursesmart.com

ACKNOWLEDGMENTS

Our Reviewers

Through three drafts of the manuscript, we received guidance and insights at several critical junctures from many trusted reviewers who provided specific recommendations on how to improve and refine the content, presentation, and organization. Their contributions were invaluable in crystallizing our thinking. We extend our gratitude to:

Anil Agarwal, *University of Arizona*

Raj Aggarwal, *University of Akron*

Richard Ajayi, *University of Central Florida*

Hamid Ali, *Chicago State University*

Allen Amason, *University of Georgia*

Gary Anders, *Arizona State University*

Mathias Arrfelt, *Arizona State University*

Bulent Aybar, *Southern New Hampshire University*

Nizamettin Aydin, *Suffolk University*

Peter Banfe, *Ohio Northern University*

Eric Baumgardner, *Xavier University*

Mack Bean, *Franklin Pierce University*

Lawrence Beer, *Arizona State University*

Dan Bello, *Georgia State University*

Enoch Beraho, *South Carolina State University*

David Berg, *University of Wisconsin–Milwaukee*

Jean Boddewyn, *Baruch College, City University of New York*

Jacobus Boers, *Georgia State University*

Henry Bohleke, *Owens Community College Santanu Borah, University of Northern Alabama*

Darrell Brown, *Indiana University Purdue University Indianapolis*

Linda Brown, *Scottsdale Community College*

David Bruce, *Georgia State University*

Diana Bullen, *Mesa Community College Kirt Butler, Michigan State University*

Michael Campo, *Regis University Tom Cary, City University, Seattle*

Pedro Carrillo, *Georgia State University*

Kalyan Chakravarty, *California State University, Northridge*

Aruna Chandra, *Indiana State University*

Kent Cofoid, *Seminole State College*

Tim Curran, *University of South Florida*

Madeline Calabrese Damkar, *California State University-East Bay*

Donna Davisson, *Cleveland State University*

Seyda Deligonul, *St. John Fisher College*

Peter Dowling, *La Trobe University, Australia*

Juan España, *National University*

Bradley Farnsworth, *University of Michigan*

Aysun Ficici, *Southern New Hampshire University*

John Finley, *Columbus State University*

Ian Gladding, *Lewis University*

Jorge Gonzalez, *University of Texas–Pan American*

Max Grunbaum Nagiel, *Daytona State College*

Tom Head, *Roosevelt University*

Bruce Heiman, *San Francisco State University*

David Hrovat, *Northern Kentucky University*

Douglas Johansen, *Jacksonville University*

Paul Jones, *Regis University*

Ali Kara, *Pennsylvania State University–University Park*

Daekwan Kim, *Florida State University*

Konghee Kim, *St. Cloud State University*

Ahmet Kirca, *Michigan State University*

Leonard Kloft, *Wright State University*

Anthony Koh, *University of Toledo*

Stephanie Kontrim-Baumann, *Missouri Baptist University*

Tatiana Kostova, *University of South Carolina*

Chuck Kwok, *University of South Carolina*

Ann Langlois, *Palm Beach Atlantic University*

Romas Laskauskas, *Stevenson University*

Yikuan Lee, *San Francisco State University*

Bijou Lester, *Drexel University*

Phil Lewis, *Eastern Michigan University*

Bob McNeal, *Alabama State University, Montgomery*

Minghua Li, *Franklin Pierce University*

Janis Miller, *Clemson University*

Barbara Moebius, *Waukesha County Technical College*

Bruce Money, *Brigham Young University*

Bill Murray, *University of San Francisco*

Matthew B. Myers, *University of Tennessee*

Kuei-Hsien Niu, *Sacramento State University*

Bernard O'Rourke, *Caldwell College*

Braimoh Oseghale, *Fairleigh Dickinson University*

Jeffrey W. Overby, *Belmont University*

Susan Peterson, *Scottsdale Community College*

Iordanis Petsas, *University of Scranton*

Zahir Quraeshi, *Western Michigan University*

Roberto Ragozzino, *University of Central Florida*

Brandon Randolph-Seng, *Texas Tech University*

Michelle Reina, *Wisconsin Lutheran College*

Michael Rubach, *University of Central Arkansas*

Hakan Saraoglu, *Bryant University*

Jeff Sarbaum, *University of North Carolina at Greensboro*

Carol Sanchez, *Grand Valley State University*

Deepak Sethi, *Old Dominion University*

Karen Sneary, *Northwestern Oklahoma State University*

Kurt Stanberry, *University of Houston–Downtown*

John Stanbury, *George Mason University*

William Streeter, *Olin Business School, Washington University in Saint Louis*

Philip Sussan, *University of Central Florida*

Charles Ray Taylor, *Villanova University*

Deanna Teel, *Houston Community College*

Gladys Torres Baumgarten, *Ramapo College of New* Jersey

Kimberly Townsend, *Syracuse University*

Marta Szabo White, *Georgia State University*

Focus Group Participants

We were also fortunate that so many colleagues generously gave their time and offered perspectives on our teaching resources. We met with these colleagues in person, tele-conferenced with them, or otherwise received their input. The insights and recommendations of these educators were instrumental in the design and format of this book and supplements. We extend our gratitude and thanks to the following reviewers and colleagues:

David Ahlstrom, *The Chinese University of Hong Kong*

Yusaf Akbar, *Southern New Hampshire University*

Victor Alicea, *Normandale Community College*

Gail Arch, *Curry College*

Anke Arnaud, *University of Central Florida*

Choton Basu, *University of Wisconsin–Whitewater*

Eric Baumgardner, *Xavier University*

Mark Bean, *Franklin Pierce College*

Enoch Beraho, *South Carolina State University*

Paula Bobrowski, *Auburn University*

Teresa Brosnan, *City University, Bellevue*

Darrell Brown, *Indiana University Purdue University-Indianapolis*

Nichole Castater, *Clark Atlanta University*

Aruna Chandra, *Indiana State University*

Mike C.H. (Chen-Ho) Chao, *Baruch College, City University of New York*

David Chaplin, *Waldorf College*

Dong Chen, *Loyola Marymount University*

Chen Oi Chin, *Lawrence Technological University*

Patrick Chinon, *Syracuse University*

Farok J. Contractor, *Rutgers University*

Christine Cope Pence, *University of California, Riverside*

Angelica Cortes, *University of Texas–Pan American*

Wade Danis, *University of Victoria*

Michael Deis, *Clayton State University*

Les Dlabay, *Lake Forest College*

Gary Donnelly, *Casper College*

Gideon Falk, *Purdue University–Calumet*

Marc Fetscherin, *Rollins College*

Charles Fishel, *San Jose State University*

Frank Flauto, *Austin Community College*

Georgine K. Fogel, *Salem International University*

Frank Franzak, *Virginia Commonwealth University*

Debbie Gilliard, *Metropolitan State College*

Robert Goddard, *Appalachian State University*

Andy Grein, *Baruch College, City University of New York*

Andrew C. Gross, *Cleveland State University*

David Grossman, *Goucher College*

Seid Hassan, *Murray State University*

Xiaohong He, *Quinnipiac University*

Wei He, *Indiana State University*

Christina Heiss, *University of Missouri–Kansas City*

Pol Herrmann, *Iowa State University*

Guy Holburn, *University of Western Ontario*

Anisul Islam, *University of Houston–Downtown*

Basil Janavaras, *Minnesota State University*

Raj Javalgi, *Cleveland State University*

Ruihua Jiang, *Oakland University*

Yikuan Jiang, *California State University–East Bay*

James Kennelly, *Skidmore College*

Ken Kim, *University of Toledo*

Leonard Kloft, *Wright State University*

Anthony C. Koh, *The University of Toledo*

Ann Langlois, *Palm Beach Atlantic University*

Michael La Rocco, *University of Saint Francis*

Romas A. Laskauskas, *Villa Julie College*

Shaomin Li, *Old Dominion University*

Ted London, *University of Michigan*

Peter Magnusson, *Saint Louis University*

Charles Mambula, *Suffolk University*

David McArthur, *Utah Valley State College*

Ofer Meilich, *Bradley University*

Lauryn Migenes, *University of Central Florida*

Mortada Mohamed, *Austin Community College*

Robert T. Moran, *Thunderbird School of Global Management*

Carolyn Mueller, *Stetson University*

Kelly J. Murphrey, *Texas A&M University*

Lilach Nachum, *Baruch College, CUNY*

William Newburry, *Florida International University*

Stanley Nollen, *Georgetown University*

Augustine Nwabuzor, *Florida A&M University*

Bernard O'Rourke, *Caldwell College*

David Paul, *California State University–East Bay*

Christine Pence, *University of California Riverside*

Heather Pendarvis-McCord, *Bradley University*

Kathleen Rehbein, *Marquette University*

Liesl Riddle, *George Washington University*

John Rushing, *Barry University*

Mary Saladino, *Montclair State University*

Carol Sanchez, *Grand Valley State University*

Camille Schuster, *California State University–San Marcos*

Eugene Seeley, *Utah Valley State College*

Deepak Sethi, *Old Dominion University*

Mandep Singh, *Western Illinois University*

Rajendra Sinhaa, *Des Moines Area Community College*

John E. Spillan, *Pennsylvania State University–DuBois*

Uday S. Tate, *Marshall University*

Janell Townsend, *Oakland University*

Sameer Vaidya, *Texas Wesleyan University*

Robert Ware, *Savannah State University*

Marta Szabo White, *Georgia State University*

Steve Williamson, *University of North Florida*

Lynn Wilson, *Saint Leo University*

Attila Yaprak, *Wayne State University*

Rama Yelkur, *University of Wisconsin-Eau Claire*

Minyuan Zhao, *University of Michigan*

Christopher Ziemnowicz, *Concord University*

Our Colleagues, Doctoral Students, and Practitioners

Numerous individuals have contributed to our thinking over the years. Through conversations, conferences, seminars, and writings, we have benefited enormously from the views and experience of international business educators and professionals from around the world. We also have had many rich conversations with the doctoral students we have mentored over the years. Their names appear below if they have not been previously mentioned above. Directly or indirectly, their thoughtful ideas and suggestions have made a significant impact on the development of this book. Our appreciation goes to many individuals, including:

John Abbott, *The Upjohn Company*

Billur Akdeniz, *University of New Hampshire*

Catherine N. Axinn, *Ohio University*

Nizam Aydin, *Suffolk University*

Ted Bany, *The Upjohn Company*

Christopher Bartlett, *Harvard Business School*

Simon Bell, *University of Melbourne*

Daniel C. Bello, *Georgia State University*

Muzaffer Bodur, *Bogazici University*

Jacobus Boers, *Georgia State University*

Nakiye Boyacigiller, *Sabanci University*

John Brawley, *The Upjohn Company*

David Bruce, *Georgia State University*

Pedro Carrillo, *Georgia State University*

Erin Cavusgil, *University of Michigan–Flint*

Brian Chabowski, *University of Tulsa*

Emin Civi, *University of New Brunswick, St. John, Canada*

Tevfik Dalgic, *University of Texas at Dallas*

Guillermo D'Andrea, *Universidad Austral–Argentina*

Fernando Doria, *Georgia State University*

Rick Della Guardia, *The Upjohn Company*

Angela da Rocha, *Universidad Federal do Rio de Janeiro, Brazil*

Deniz Erden, *Bogazici University*

Felicitas Evangelista, *University of Western Sydney, Australia*

Cuneyt Evirgen, *Sabanci University*

Carol Finnegan, *University of Colorado at Colorado Springs*

Richard Fletcher, *University of Western Sydney, Australia*

Harold Fishkin, *The Upjohn Company*

Michael Fishkin, *Stony Brook University*

Esra Gencturk, *Ozyegin University*

Pervez Ghauri, *Kings College London*

Tracy Gonzalez-Padron, *University of Colorado at Colorado Springs*

Bill Hahn, *Science Branding Communications*

Tomas Hult, *Michigan State University*

Destan Kandemir, *Bilkent University*

Yener Kndogan, *University of Michigan–Flint*

George Kaufman, *The Upjohn Company*

Ihsen Ketata, *Georgia State University*

Irem Kiyak, *Michigan State University*

Tunga Kiyak, *Michigan State University*

Phillip Kotler, *Northwestern University*

David Kuhlmeier, *Valdosta State University*

Denis LeClerc, *Thunderbird School of Global Management*

Tiger Li, *Florida International University*

Karen Loch, *Georgia State University*

Mushtaq Luqmani, *Western Michigan University*

Robert McCarthy, *The Upjohn Company*

Ellen Miller, *The Upjohn Company*

Myron Miller, *Michigan State University (ret.)*

Vincent Mongello, *The Upjohn Company*

Robert T. Moran, *Thunderbird School of Global Management*

G. M. Naidu, *University of Wisconsin–Whitewater*

John R. Nevin, *University of Wisconsin–Madison*

Gregory Osland, *Butler University*

Aysegul Ozsomer, *Koc University*

Ed Perper, *Science Branding Communications*

Morys Perry, *University of Michigan–Flint*

Alex Rialp, *Universidad Autónoma de Barcelona, Spain*

Tony Roath, *University of Oklahoma*

Carol Sanchez, *Grand Valley State University*

Michael Savitt, *The Upjohn Company*

Peter Seaver, *The Upjohn Company*

Linda Hui Shi, *University of Victoria*

Rudolf R. Sinkovics, *The University of Manchester*

Carl Arthur Solberg, *Norwegian School of Management, Norway*

Elif Sonmez-Persinger, *Eastern Michigan University*

Douglas Squires, *The Upjohn Company of Canada*

Barbara Stoettinger, *Wirtschaftsuniversität Wein, Austria*

Detmar Straub, *Georgia State University*

Berk Talay, *University of New Hampshire*

Cherian Thachenkary, *Georgia State University*

David Tse, *University of Hong Kong*

Mithat Uner, *Gazi University*

Nukhet Vardar, *Yeditepe University*

Marta Szabo White, *Georgia State University*

Fang Wu, *University of Texas–Dallas*

Shichun (Alex) Xu, *University of Tennessee*

Goksel Yalcinkaya, *University of New Hampshire*

Attila Yaprak, *Wayne State University*

Ugur Yavas, *East Tennessee State University*

Sengun Yeniyurt, *Rutgers University*

Poh-Lin Yeoh, *Bentley College*

Eden Yin, *University of Cambridge*

William Youngdahl, *Thunderbird School of Global Management*

Chun Zhang, *University of Vermont*

Shaoming Zou, *University of Missouri*

Our Prentice Hall Team

This book would not have been possible without the tireless efforts of many dedicated professionals at our publisher, Pearson Education. We are especially grateful to Sally Yagan, Editorial Director; Brian Mickelson, Acquisitions Editor; Nikki Jones, Marketing Manager; Ian Gold, Marketing Assistant; and Lynn Savino Wendel, Production Project Manager. Our appreciation goes to many other individuals at Pearson, including: Linda Albelli, Stephen Deitmer, Jerome Grant, Patrice Jones, Judy Leale, Patrick Leow, Ben Paris, and Ashley Santora.

At home, we extend thanks to the following:
S. Tamer Cavusgil—I want to thank my wife, Judy, and my children, Erin and Emre, for their encouragement and frank comments.

Gary Knight—I thank my wife, Mari, for her patience, intellect, and adventurous spirit. I also thank my parents, Bill and Audrey, for their excellent example and support.

John Riesenberger—This book is dedicated to my parents, Richard and Marie Riesenberger for their example, many sacrifices and love. To my wife and best friend, Pat, for her enthusiasm and loving support. To my daughters, Christine and Jennifer, and their husbands Byron and Martin, of whom I am so very proud and thankful. To my amazing grandchildren—Ryan, Paige, and Ethan—the future of the New Realities.

Foundation Concepts

What Is International Business?

LEARNING OBJECTIVES
In this chapter, you will learn about:

1. What is international business?

2. What are key concepts in international trade and investment?

3. How does international business differ from domestic business?

4. What motivates firms to go international?

5. Market globalization: An organizing framework

6. Regional integration and economic blocs

WHAT IS INTERNATIONAL BUSINESS?

International business refers to the performance of trade and investment activities by firms across national borders. Because it emphasizes crossing national boundaries, we also refer to international business as *cross-border business*. Firms organize, source, manufacture, market, and conduct other value-adding activities on an international scale. They seek foreign customers and engage in collaborative relationships with foreign business partners. While international business is performed mainly by individual firms, governments and international agencies also undertake international business activities.[1] Firms and nations exchange many physical and intellectual assets, including products, services, capital, technology, know-how, and labor. In this book, we are mainly concerned with the international business activities of the individual firm.

While internationalization of the firm refers to the tendency of companies to systematically increase the international dimension of their business activities, the **globalization of markets** refers to the ongoing economic integration and growing interdependency of countries worldwide. Globalization is associated with the internationalization of countless firms and dramatic growth in the volume and variety of cross-border transactions in goods, services, and capital flows. It has led to widespread diffusion of products, technology, and knowledge worldwide.

The globalization of markets is evident in several related trends. First is the unprecedented growth of international trade. In 1960, cross-border trade was modest—about $100 billion per year. Today, it accounts for a substantial proportion of the world economy, amounting to some $13 trillion annually—that is, $13,000,000,000,000! Second, trade between nations is accompanied by substantial flows of capital, technology, and knowledge. Third is the development of highly sophisticated global financial systems and mechanisms that facilitate the cross-border flow of products, money, technology, and knowledge. Fourth, globalization has brought about a greater degree of collaboration among nations through multilateral regulatory agencies such as the World Trade Organization (WTO; www.wto.org) and the International Monetary Fund (IMF; www.imf.org).

Globalization both compels and facilitates expansion abroad. A few decades ago, international business was largely the domain of large, multinational companies. Recent developments have created a more level playing field that allows all types of firms to benefit from active participation in international business, even service companies in such industries as banking, engineering, insurance, and retailing.

As a result, the global economy is more integrated than ever, and economic problems spread quickly across porous national borders. The financial crisis that began in 2008 in the United States and moved to other countries, triggered a severe global *recession*, a condition in which national economies undergo a sustained period of negative growth.[2] Canada's recession resulted largely from its intense trading relationship with the United States. Mexico's exports to the United States declined substantially, worsening Mexico's already high unemployment rate. Job losses also ensued in Japan and other Asian countries as exports to the United States fell sharply. The economies of both China and India, the world's most populous countries, slowed significantly due to the crisis. In short, integration and interdependency of national economies quickly spread the crisis throughout the world.

WHAT ARE THE KEY CONCEPTS IN INTERNATIONAL TRADE AND INVESTMENT?

The most conventional international business transactions are international trade and investment. **International trade** refers to an exchange of products and services across national borders. Trade includes both products (merchandise) and services (intangibles). Exchange can occur through **exporting**, an entry strategy that relies on the sale of products or services to customers located abroad, from a base in the home country or a third country. Exchange also can take the form of **importing** or **global sourcing**—the procurement of products or services from suppliers located abroad for consumption in the home country or a third country. While exporting represents the outbound flow of products and services, importing is an *inbound* activity. Both finished products and intermediate goods, such as raw materials and components, are subject to importing and exporting.

International investment refers to the transfer of assets to another country or the acquisition of assets in that country. These assets include capital, technology, managerial talent, and manufacturing infrastructure. Economists refer to such assets as *factors of production*. Trade implies that products and services cross national borders. By contrast, investment implies the firm itself crosses borders to secure ownership of assets located abroad.

The two essential types of cross-border investment are international portfolio investment and foreign direct investment. **International portfolio investment** refers to the passive ownership of foreign securities such as stocks and bonds for the purpose of generating financial returns. It does not entail active management or control over these assets. The foreign investor has a relatively short-term interest in the ownership of these assets. **Foreign direct investment (FDI)** is an internationalization strategy in which the firm establishes a physical presence abroad through acquisition of productive assets such as capital, technology, labor, land, plant, and equipment. It is a foreign-market entry strategy that gives investors partial or full ownership of a productive enterprise typically dedicated to manufacturing, marketing, or management activities. Investing such resources abroad is generally for the long term and requires extensive planning.

The Nature of International Trade

Exhibit 1.1 contrasts the growth of total world exports and the growth of total world *gross domestic product (GDP)* since 1970. GDP is the total value of products and services produced in a country over the course of a year. Following a 27-year boom, world trade declined in 2009 due to the global recession. The hardest-hit imports were consumer goods, cars, and car parts.[3] Overall, however, export growth has outpaced the growth of domestic production during the past few decades, illustrating the fast pace of globalization. In fact, during this period, world exports grew more than thirtyfold, while world GDP grew only tenfold. To illustrate this point, consider the journey of a shirt sold in France. Initially, the cotton to produce the shirt is exported from the United States to China. After the shirt is manufactured in China, it is exported to France. Eventually, after the French owner discards her used shirt, it is exported once again and sold on the used-clothing market in Africa. In total, the value generated in exporting the shirt greatly exceeds the cost to produce it.

Much of the difference in growth between exports and GDP arises because advanced (or developed) economies such as Britain and the United States now source many of the products they consume from low-cost manufacturing locations such as China and Mexico. For example, although the United States once produced most of the products it consumed, today it depends much more on imports.

The United States is the leading country in terms of the absolute volume, in total dollars, of merchandise trade worldwide. Other leading trading countries in absolute volume terms include Germany, China, and Japan. However, when expressed as a percentage of each nation's GDP, Belgium is the world leader, in which international trade equates to about 171 percent of its GDP. It is followed by the Netherlands (138 percent) and Germany (72 percent). The United States obtains only 23 percent of its GDP from

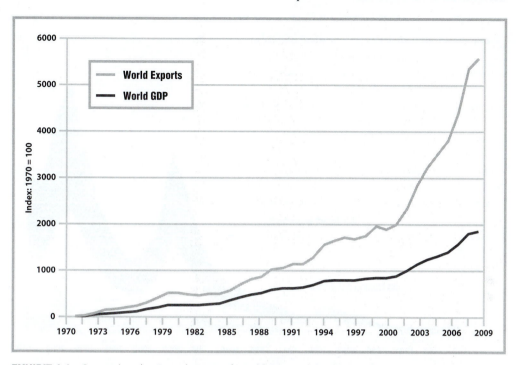

EXHIBIT 1.1   Comparing the Growth Rates of World GDP and World Exports.   *Source:* World Investment Report 2009 (New York: United Nations, 2008), retrieved from http://www.unctad.org, June 4, 2010; World Trade Organization, World Trade Report 2009 (Geneva, Switzerland: WTO Publications, 2009), retrieved from http://www.wto.org, June 4, 2010; and International Monetary Fund, World Economic Outlook, (Washington, DC: IMF database 2010), retrieved from http://www.imf.org, June 4, 2010.

international trade. These percentages show that some economies are very dependent on international trade relative to the value of all goods and services they produce domestically.

The Nature of International Investment

Of the two types of investment flows between nations—portfolio investment and foreign direct investment—we are concerned primarily with FDI, because it is the ultimate stage of internationalization, is practiced by the firms most active internationally, and encompasses the widest range of international business involvement. Companies usually engage in FDI for the long term and retain partial or complete ownership of the assets they acquire.

Firms undertake FDI in foreign countries for a variety of strategic reasons, including to (1) set up manufacturing or assembly operations or other physical facilities, (2) open a sales or representative office or other facility to conduct marketing or distribution activities, or (3) establish a regional headquarters. In the process, the firm establishes a new legal business entity, subject to the regulations of the host government in the country where the entity is established.

Exhibit 1.2 illustrates that the dollar volume of FDI has grown immensely since the 1980s, especially into advanced economies such as Japan, Europe, and North America. FDI inflows were interrupted in 2001 as investors panicked following the

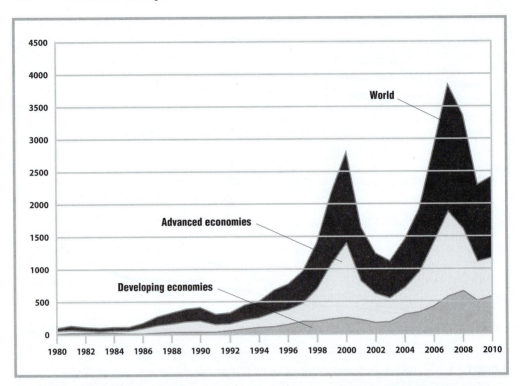

EXHIBIT 1.2 Foreign Direct Investment (FDI) Inflows into World Regions (in Billions of U.S. Dollars per Year).   *Sources:* OECD, *OECD International Direct Investment Statistics 2011*, Organization for Economic Co-operation and Development; International Monetary Fund, *Coordinated Direct Investment Survey*, International Monetary Fund, Washington, 2010; UNCTAD, *World Investment Report 2011*, United Nations; World Bank, *World Bank Development Indicators 2011*, World Bank.

September 11 terrorist attacks in the United States. The inflows were interrupted again in 2008 by the global recession. But the overall trend remains strong and growing over time. Particularly significant is the growth of FDI into *developing economies*, which are nations with lower incomes, less-developed industrial bases, and less investment capital than the advanced economies. Most of the developing economies are located in parts of Africa, Asia, and Latin America. Despite lower income levels, they collectively comprise a substantial and growing proportion of international trade and investment.

Services as Well as Products

Historically, international trade and investment were mainly the domain of companies that make and sell products—tangible merchandise such as clothing, computers, and cars. Today, firms that produce *services* (intangibles) are key international business players as well. Services are deeds, performances, or efforts performed directly by people working in banks, consulting firms, hotels, construction companies, retailers, and countless other firms in the services sector. For example, if you own a house, your mortgage may be underwritten by the Dutch bank ABN Amro. Perhaps you eat lunch in a cafeteria owned by the French firm Sodexo, which manages the food and beverage operations on numerous university campuses.

International trade in services accounts for about one-quarter of all international trade and in recent years has been growing faster than products trade. The leading countries in total volume terms in international services trade include the United States, Germany, the United Kingdom, and Japan. However, as a percentage of each nation's GDP, the Netherlands, the United Kingdom, Spain, and Germany are the world leaders. As with products, larger advanced economies account for the greatest proportion of world services trade. Services typically comprise more than two-thirds of the GDPs of these countries. Although services trade is growing rapidly, the value of merchandise trade is still much larger. One reason is that, compared to merchandise goods, services face greater challenges and barriers in cross-border trade.

There are numerous industries in the services sector with strong potential for internationalization. The giant Internet retailer eBay earned nearly $9 billion in 2009, of which more than 50 percent came from international sales. The company expects most future revenue growth will come from abroad. When developing its business in India, eBay acquired the Mumbai-based e-retailer Baazee. This acquisition followed eBay's expansion into China, Korea, and Europe.[4] In terms of the volume of trade, the most important service sectors in international business include banking and finance, construction and engineering, education, publishing, entertainment, information services, professional business services, transportation, travel, and tourism.

The internationalization of banks and the massive flow of money across national borders into pension funds and portfolio investments have led to the emergence and growth of capital markets worldwide. In developing economies, banks and other financial institutions have been fostering economic activity by increasing the availability of local investment capital, which stimulates the development of financial markets and encourages locals to save money.[5]

HOW DOES INTERNATIONAL BUSINESS DIFFER FROM DOMESTIC BUSINESS?

Firms that engage in international business operate in environments characterized by unique economic conditions, national culture, and legal and political systems. For example, the economic environment of Colombia differs sharply from that of Germany. The legal environment of Saudi Arabia does not resemble that of Japan. The cultural environment of China is very distinct from that of Kenya. The firm finds itself in unfamiliar surroundings and encounters many *uncontrollable variables*—factors over which management has little control. These factors introduce new or elevated business risks.

The Four Risks in Internationalization

Internationalizing firms are routinely exposed to four major types of risk, as illustrated in Exhibit 1.3: cross-cultural risk, country risk, currency risk, and commercial risk. The firm must manage these risks to avoid financial loss or product failures.

Cross-cultural risk arises from differences in language, lifestyles, mind-sets, customs, and religion and occurs when a cultural misunderstanding puts some human value at stake. Values unique to a culture tend to be long-lasting and transmitted from one generation to the next. They can influence the mind-set and work style of employees and the shopping patterns of buyers. In addition to facilitating communication,

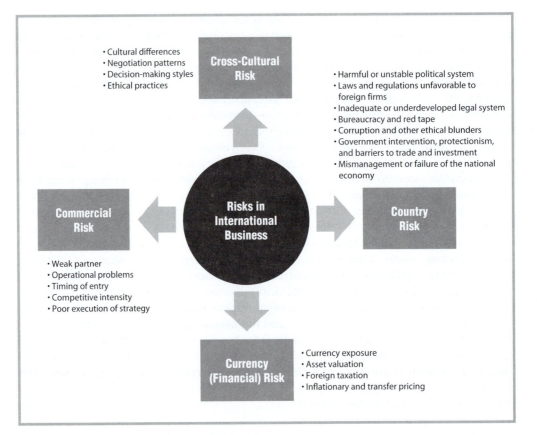

EXHIBIT 1.3   The Four Risks of International Business.

for instance, language is a window on people's value systems and living conditions. Language challenges can impede effective communication and cause misunderstandings, inappropriate business strategies, and ineffective customer relationships.

Country risk (also known as *political risk*) refers to the potentially adverse effects on company operations and profitability caused by developments in the political, legal, and economic environment in a foreign country, including the possibility of foreign government intervention in firms' business activities. For example, governments may restrict access to markets, impose bureaucratic procedures on business transactions, and limit the amount of income that firms can bring home from foreign operations. The degree of government intervention in commercial activities varies from country to country. Singapore and Ireland are characterized by substantial economic freedom, while the Chinese and Russian governments regularly intervene in business affairs.[6]

Currency risk (also known as *financial risk*) refers to the risk of adverse fluctuations in exchange rates. Fluctuation is common for *exchange rates*—the value of one currency in terms of another. Currency risk arises because international transactions are often conducted in more than one national currency. For example, when

U.S. fruit processor Graceland Fruit Inc. exports dried cherries to Japan, it is normally paid in Japanese yen. The cost of importing parts or components used in manufacturing finished products can increase dramatically if the value of the currency in which the imports are denominated rises sharply. Inflation and other harmful economic conditions experienced in one country may have immediate consequences for exchange rates due to the interconnectedness of national economies.

Commercial risk refers to the firm's potential loss or failure from poorly developed or executed business strategies, tactics, or procedures. Managers may make poor choices in such areas as the selection of business partners, timing of market entry, pricing, creation of product features, and promotional themes. While such failures also exist in domestic business, the consequences are usually more costly abroad due to regulations that protect local firms. Marketing inferior or harmful products, falling short of customer expectations, or failing to provide adequate customer service may damage the firm's reputation and profitability. Commercial risk is also often affected by currency risk, because fluctuating exchange rates can affect various types of business deals.

The four types of international business risks are omnipresent; the firm may encounter them around every corner. Although they cannot be avoided, they can be anticipated and managed. Experienced international firms constantly assess their environments and conduct research to anticipate potential risks, understand their implications, and take proactive action to reduce their effects.

Today, manufacturing firms source from a large selection of suppliers located around the world. Supply lines for automobiles, computers, and countless other consumer and industrial goods are spread out across the globe, creating much complexity for managers of multinational firms.

Global commerce exposes firms to interruptions arising from events that originate far away. For example, the massive earthquake that struck Japan in 2011 affected supply lines worldwide. Major automakers were unable to obtain the parts they need to build cars. Firms that sell consumer products suffered significant business declines in the months following the quake. The luxury goods retailer Coach closed 20 of its 165 stores in Japan, and Tiffany shuttered some of its outlets. Civil unrest was also a problem in 2011. The civil war that broke out in Libya interrupted the country's oil output of more than 1.5 million barrels per day. When Egypt experienced unrest during the spring of 2011, management at global firms worried the crisis would affect cargo transportation through the Suez Canal, one of the world's top shipping corridors. Most managers ignore or underestimate the likelihood of exposure to global risk.

Who Participates in International Business?

What types of organizations are active in international business? Among the most important are *focal firms*, the companies that directly initiate and implement international business activity. Two critical focal firms in international business are the multinational enterprise and the small and medium-sized enterprise.

A **multinational enterprise (MNE)** is a large company with substantial resources that performs various business activities through a network of subsidiaries and affiliates located in multiple countries. MNEs carry out research and development (R&D), procurement, manufacturing, and marketing activities wherever in the world the firm can reap the most advantages. In addition to a home office or headquarters, the typical MNE owns a worldwide network of subsidiaries and collaborates with numerous suppliers and independent business partners abroad (sometimes termed *affiliates*).

Consider the world's largest MNEs, drawn from the Global 500 list published annually by *Fortune* magazine. The United States is home to 140 of the top 500 MNEs. Japan is the headquarters of 68 of the top 500 firms. Several European countries also host numerous top firms. Collectively, the European Union countries have more top 500 firms than the United States. Canada and Australia have 14 and 9, respectively. China, India, and other emerging market countries have begun to produce firms in the top 500 group, led by China, which has 37 of the companies. The "new global challenger" firms from emerging markets are fast becoming key contenders in world markets. The Mexican firm Cemex is one the world's largest cement producers. In Russia, Lukoil has big ambitions in the global energy sector. China Mobile dominates the cell phone industry in Asia.

International business is not solely the domain of large, resourceful MNEs. Many **small and medium-sized enterprises (SMEs)** participate as well. As defined in Canada and the United States, an SME is a company with fewer than 500 employees. In the European Union, SMEs are defined as firms with fewer than 250 employees. SMEs tend to have smaller market share and limited managerial and other resources. They primarily use exporting to expand internationally. However, in most nations, they constitute the great majority of all firms. In some countries—for example, Italy, South Korea, and China—SMEs contribute roughly 50 percent of total national exports.[7] One type of contemporary international SME is the **born global firm**, a young entrepreneurial company that initiates international business activity very early in its evolution, moving rapidly into foreign markets.[8]

Nongovernmental Organizations (NGOs)

Much cross-border activity is conducted by *nonprofit organizations*, such as charitable groups and *nongovernmental organizations (NGOs)*. They pursue special causes and serve as advocates for the arts, education, politics, religion, and research, operating internationally either to conduct their activities or to raise funds. The Bill and Melinda Gates Foundation and the British Wellcome Trust both support health and educational initiatives. CARE is an international nonprofit organization dedicated to reducing poverty. Many MNEs operate charitable foundations that support various initiatives. GlaxoSmithKline (GSK), the giant pharmaceutical firm, operates a number of small country-based foundations in Canada, France, Italy, Romania, and Spain.

WHAT MOTIVATES FIRMS TO GO INTERNATIONAL?

There are multiple motives for international expansion. Nine specific ones are:

1. *Seek opportunities for growth through market diversification.* Many firms, such as Gillette, Siemens, Sony, and Biogen, derive more than half their sales from international markets.

2. *Earn higher margins and profits.* Less intense competition abroad, combined with strong market demand, mean companies such as bathroom fixture manufacturer American Standard can command higher margins than in their home markets.

3. *Gain new ideas about products, services, and business methods.* The experience of doing business abroad helps firms acquire new knowledge for improving organizational effectiveness and efficiency, such as the just-in-time inventory techniques refined by Toyota in Japan.

4. *Better serve key customers that have relocated abroad.* When Nissan opened its first factory in the United Kingdom, many Japanese auto parts suppliers followed, establishing their own operations there.

5. *Be closer to supply sources, benefit from global sourcing advantages, or gain flexibility in product sourcing.* Companies in petroleum, mining, and forestry industries establish international operations where raw materials are located. Dell Computer has assembly facilities in Asia, Europe, and the Americas that allow it to outperform competitors and skillfully manage exchange rate fluctuations.

6. *Gain access to lower-cost or better-value factors of production.* Some Taiwanese computer manufacturers established subsidiaries in the United States to access low-cost capital. More commonly, firms venture abroad in search of skilled or low-cost labor.

7. *Develop economies of scale in sourcing, production, marketing, and R&D.* On a per-unit-of-output basis, the greater the volume of production, the lower the total cost. Economies of scale also exist in R&D, sourcing, marketing, distribution, and after-sales service.

8. *Confront international competitors more effectively or thwart the growth of competition in the home market.* Caterpillar's entry into Japan just as its main rival in the earthmoving equipment industry, Komatsu, was getting started in the early 1970s hindered Komatsu's international expansion for at least a decade.

9. *Invest in a potentially rewarding relationship with a foreign partner.* Black and Decker entered a joint venture with Bajaj, an Indian retailer, to position itself for expected long-term sales in the huge Indian market. The French computer firm Groupe Bull partnered with Toshiba in Japan to gain insights for developing the next generation of information technology.

MARKET GLOBALIZATION: AN ORGANIZING FRAMEWORK

Let's turn our focus from the individual firm to the nation. As mentioned earlier, globalization of markets refers to the ongoing economic integration and growing interdependency of countries worldwide. Exhibit 1.4 presents an organizing framework for examining market globalization. The exhibit makes a distinction among: (1) drivers or causes of globalization, (2) dimensions or manifestations of globalization, (3a) societal consequences of globalization, and (3b) firm-level consequences of globalization. In the exhibit, the double arrows illustrate the interactive nature of the relationship between market globalization and its consequences. As market globalization intensifies, individual firms respond to the challenges and new advantages that it brings. However, keep in mind that firms do not expand abroad solely as a reaction

1 DRIVERS OF MARKET GLOBALIZATION

- Worldwide reduction of barriers to trade and investment
- Market liberalization and adoption of free markets
- Industrialization, economic development, and modernization
- Integration of world financial markets
- Advances in technology

2 DIMENSIONS OF MARKET GLOBALIZATION

- Integration and interdependence of national economies
- Rise of regional economic integration blocs
- Growth of global investment and financial flows
- Convergence of buyer lifestyles and preferences
- Globalization of production activities
- Globalization of services

3a SOCIETAL CONSEQUENCES OF MARKET GLOBALIZATION

- Contagion: Rapid spread of financial or monetary crises from one country to another
- Loss of national sovereignty
- Offshoring and the flight of jobs
- Effect on the poor
- Effect on the natural environment
- Effect on national culture

3b FIRM-LEVEL CONSEQUENCES OF MARKET GLOBALIZATION: INTERNATIONALIZATION OF THE FIRM'S VALUE CHAIN

- Countless new business opportunities for internationalizing firms
- New risks and intense rivalry from foreign competitors
- More demanding buyers who source from suppliers worldwide
- Greater emphasis on proactive internationalization
- Internationalization of firm's value chain

EXHIBIT 1.4 The Drivers and Consequences of Market Globalization.

to market globalization. They also internationalize proactively in order to pursue new markets, find lower-cost inputs, or obtain other advantages. Often adverse conditions in the home market, such as regulation or declining industry sales, push firms to boldly venture abroad. Firms that do so tend to be more successful in global competition than those that engage in international business as a reactive move.

Drivers of Market Globalization

Various trends have converged in recent years as causes of market globalization. Five are particularly notable:

   1. *Worldwide reduction of barriers to trade and investment.* Tariffs on the import of automobiles, industrial machinery, and countless other products have declined nearly to zero in many countries, encouraging freer international exchange of goods and services. Falling trade barriers, facilitated by the WTO, are also associated with the emergence of regional economic integration blocs, a key dimension of market globalization.

2. *Market liberalization and adoption of free markets.* The collapse of the Soviet Union's economy in 1989, demolition of the Berlin Wall that same year, and China's free-market reforms all smoothed the integration of former command economies into the global economy. East Asian economies from South Korea to Malaysia, Indonesia, and India had already embarked on ambitious market-based reforms. Along with privatization of state-owned industries in many countries, these events opened roughly one-third of the world to freer international trade and investment.

3. *Industrialization, economic development, and modernization.* Rapidly developing economies in Asia, Latin America, and Eastern Europe are becoming sophisticated competitive producers and exporters of premium products such as electronics, computers, and aircraft.[9] Economic development is enhancing standards of living and discretionary income in emerging markets. Perhaps the most important measure of economic development is *gross national income (GNI)* per head.[10] The adoption of modern technologies, improvement of living standards, and adoption of modern legal and banking practices are increasing the attractiveness of emerging markets as investment targets.

4. *Integration of world financial markets.* The integration of world financial markets via a network of international commercial banks makes it possible for internationally active firms to raise capital, borrow funds, pay suppliers, collect from customers, and engage in foreign currency transactions. The Society for Worldwide Interbank Financial Telecommunication (SWIFT) network connects more than 7,800 financial institutions in some 200 countries.

5. *Advances in technology.* Technological advances are a remarkable facilitator of cross-border trade and investment. These include discoveries and new capabilities in information technology, communications, manufacturing, and transportation. Note that technological advances have made international operations affordable for all types of firms. The cost of international communications has plummeted over time, just as the number of Internet users has grown dramatically.

Societal Consequences of Market Globalization

Major advances in living standards have been achieved in virtually all countries that have opened their borders to increased trade and investment. Nevertheless, the transition to an increasingly single, global marketplace poses challenges to individuals, organizations, and governments. Low-income countries have not been able to integrate with the global economy as rapidly as others, and poverty remains a major problem. Let's turn to some of the unintended consequences of globalization.

LOSS OF NATIONAL SOVEREIGNTY *Sovereignty,* the ability of a nation to govern its own affairs, is a fundamental principle that underlies global relations. One country's laws cannot be applied or enforced in another country. Globalization can threaten national sovereignty in various ways. For example, large multinationals can exert considerable influence on governments by making campaign contributions or lobbying for, say, devaluation of the home currency, which gives them greater price competitiveness in export markets.

OFFSHORING AND THE FLIGHT OF JOBS   *Offshoring* is the relocation of manufacturing and other value-chain activities to cost-effective locations abroad. It has resulted in job losses in numerous mature economies. The first wave of offshoring began in the 1960s and 1970s with the shift of U.S. and European manufacturing of cars, electronics, textiles, and toys to cheap-labor locations such as Mexico and Southeast Asia. The next wave began in the 1990s with the exodus of service-sector jobs in credit card processing, software code writing, accounting, health care, and banking services.

EFFECT ON THE POOR   MNEs are often criticized for paying low wages, exploiting workers, and employing child labor. In 2010, the International Labor Organization (www.ilo.org) reported there are approximately 153 million children aged 5–14 at work around the world.

Labor exploitation and sweatshop conditions are major concerns in many developing economies.[11] Nevertheless, studies suggest that banning products made using child labor may produce unintended negative consequences such as loss of wages and reduced living standards.[12] Legislation passed to reduce child labor in the formal economic sector (the sector regulated and monitored by public authorities) may have little effect on jobs in the informal economic sector, sometimes called the *underground economy.* In the face of persistent poverty, abolishing formal sector jobs does not ensure that children leave the workforce and go to school.

In many developing countries, work conditions tend to improve over time. The growth of the footwear industry in Vietnam translated into a fivefold increase in wages. While still low by advanced economy standards, increasingly higher wages are improving the lives of millions of workers and their families. For most countries, globalization tends to support a growing economy. Evidence also suggests that countries that liberalize international trade and investment enjoy faster per-capita economic growth. During the 1990s, for example, developing economies that sought integration with the rest of the world grew their per-capita GDP much faster than non-integrating developing economies.

EFFECT ON THE NATURAL ENVIRONMENT   Globalization can harm the environment by promoting increased manufacturing and economic activity that result in pollution, habitat destruction, and deterioration of the ozone layer. For example, economic development in China is attracting much inward FDI and stimulating the growth of numerous industries. However, the construction of factories, infrastructure, and modern housing can spoil previously pristine environments. In Eastern China, growing industrial demand for electricity led to construction of the Three Gorges Dam, which flooded agricultural lands and permanently altered the natural landscape.

As globalization stimulates rising living standards, however, people focus increasingly on improving their environment. Over time, governments pass legislation that promotes improved environmental conditions. For example, Japan endured polluted rivers and smoggy cities in the early decades of its economic development following World War II. But as their economy grew, the Japanese passed tough environmental standards to restore natural environments.

Evolving company values and concern for corporate reputations also lead most firms to reduce or eliminate practices that harm the environment.[13] Benetton in Italy (clothing), Alcan in Canada (aluminum), and Kirin in Japan (beverages) are examples of firms that embrace practices that protect the environment, often at the expense of profits.[14] Conservation Coffee Alliance, a consortium of companies, has committed approximately $2 million to environmentally friendly coffee cultivation in Central America, Peru, and Colombia.

EFFECT ON NATIONAL CULTURE   Market liberalization leaves the door open to foreign companies, global brands, unfamiliar products, and new values. Consumers increasingly wear similar clothing, drive similar cars, watch the same movies, and listen to the same recording stars. Advertising leads to the emergence of societal values modeled on Western countries, especially the United States. Global media have a pervasive effect on local culture, gradually shifting it toward a universal norm. At the same time, the flow of cultural influence often goes both ways. Advanced Fresh Concepts is a Japanese company that is transforming fast food by selling $250 million worth of sushi and other Japanese favorites in supermarkets throughout the United States every year.[15]

Although some tangibles are becoming more universal, people's behaviors and mind-sets remain stable over time. Religious differences are as strong as ever. Language differences are steadfast across national borders. As globalization tends to standardize superficial aspects of life across national cultures, people resist these forces by insisting on their national identity and taking steps to protect it. For example, in Belgium, Canada, and France, laws were passed to protect national language and culture.

REGIONAL INTEGRATION AND ECONOMIC BLOCS

Regional economic integration has been a distinct dimension of market globalization and deserves additional discussion. Also known as *regional integration,* **regional economic integration** refers to the growing economic interdependence that results when two or more countries within a geographic region form an alliance aimed at reducing barriers to trade and investment. Since the end of World War II, most nations have sought to cooperate, with the aim of achieving some degree of economic integration. More than 50 percent of world trade today takes place under some form of preferential trade agreement signed by groups of countries. Two of the best-known examples of such integration are the European Union (EU) and the North American Free Trade Agreement (NAFTA) area.

Nations seek at least four objectives in pursuing regional integration.[16]

- *Expand market size.*   Regional integration greatly increases the scale of the marketplace for firms inside the economic bloc.
- *Achieve scale economies and enhanced productivity.*   Expansion of market size within an economic bloc gives member country firms the opportunity to increase the scale of operations in both production and marketing, gaining greater concentration and increased efficiency.
- *Attract direct investment from outside the bloc.*   Foreign firms prefer to invest in countries that are part of an economic bloc because factories they build there receive preferential treatment for exports to all member countries within the bloc.

• ***Acquire stronger defensive and political posture.*** One goal of regional integration is to strengthen member countries relative to other nations and world regions.

Regional integration results from the formation of a **regional economic integration bloc**, or simply, an economic bloc. This refers to a geographic area that consists of two or more countries that agree to pursue economic integration by reducing tariffs and other restrictions to the cross-border flow of products, services, capital, and, in more advanced stages, labor. (In this book, we use the term *bloc* instead of *block*.) At a minimum, the countries in an economic bloc become parties to a **free trade agreement**, a formal arrangement between two or more countries to reduce or eliminate tariffs, quotas, and other barriers to trade in products and services. The member nations also undertake cross-border investments within the bloc.

More advanced economic blocs, such as the EU, permit the free flow of capital, labor, and technology among their member countries. The EU is also harmonizing monetary policy (to manage the EU money supply and currency values) and fiscal policy (to manage government finances, especially tax revenues), and gradually integrating the economies of its member nations. Reaching agreement on free trade is much easier in negotiations among a handful of countries than among all the nations in the world. This helps explain why there are hundreds of trade blocs in existence today.

Levels of Regional Integration

Regional integration allows distinct national economies to become economically linked and interdependent through greater cross-national movement of products, services, and factors of production. It also allows member states to use resources more productively and achieve greater output than they could individually.

Exhibit 1.5 identifies five possible levels of regional integration. They progress from a low level—the free trade area—to the most advanced form—the political union, which no countries have yet achieved.

The **free trade area** is the simplest and most common arrangement, in which member countries agree to gradually eliminate formal barriers to trade in products and services within the bloc, while each member country maintains an independent international trade policy with countries outside the bloc. NAFTA (the United States, Mexico, and Canada) is an example. The free trade area emphasizes the pursuit of comparative advantage for a group of countries rather than for individual states. Governments may impose local content requirements, which specify that producers located within the member countries provide a certain proportion of products and supplies used in local manufacturing.

The **customs union** is the second level of regional integration, similar to a free trade area except that member states harmonize their external trade policies and adopt *common* tariff and nontariff barriers on imports from nonmember countries. An exporter outside MERCOSUR, an economic bloc in Latin America, for example, faces the *same* tariffs and nontariff barriers when trading with *any* MERCOSUR member country. Member countries must agree on the level of tariff and on how to distribute proceeds among themselves.

In the third stage of regional integration, member countries establish a **common market** (also known as a single market), in which trade barriers are reduced or

Level of Integration	Free Trade Area	Customs Union	Common Market	Economic and (sometimes) Monetary Union	Political Union
Members agree to eliminate tariffs and non-tariff trade barriers with each other but maintain their own trade barriers with non-member countries. Examples: NAFTA, EFTA, ASEAN, Australia and New Zealand Closer Economic Relations Agreement (CER)	■	■	■	■	■
Common external tariffs Example: MERCOSUR		■	■	■	■
Free movement of products, labor, and capital Example: Pre-1992 European Economic Community			■	■	■
Unified monetary and fiscal policy by a central authority Example: The European Union today exhibits common trade, agricultural, and monetary policies				■	■
Perfect unification of all policies by a common organization;submersion of all separate national institutions Example: Remains an ideal; yet to be achieved					■

EXHIBIT 1.5 Five Potential Levels of Regional Integration among Nations (For example, a customs union has the features of a free trade area, plus common external tariffs). *Source:* Bela Balassa, *The Theory of Economic Integration* (Santa Barbara, CA: Greenwood Press Reprint, 1982). Jaime De Melo and Arvind Panagariya, *New Dimensions in Regional Integration* (Cambridge: Cambridge University Press, 1996); Rolf Mirus and Nataliya Rylska, *Economic Integration: Free Trade Areas vs. Customs Unions* (Edmonton, Alberta: Western Centre for Economic Research, 2001); Bela Balassa, *The Theory of Economic Integration* (Homewood, IL: Richard D. Irwin, 1961); Joseph S. Nye. (1968), "Comparative Regional Integration: Concept and Measurement," *International Organization,* 22(4), pp. 855–880.

removed, common external barriers are established, and products, services, and *factors of production* (such as capital, labor, and technology) are allowed to move freely among the member countries. Like a customs union, a common market also establishes a common trade policy with nonmember countries. The EU is a common market. It has gradually reduced or eliminated restrictions on immigration and the cross-border flow of capital. A worker from an EU country has the right to work in other EU countries, and EU firms can freely transfer funds among their subsidiaries within the bloc.

Common markets require substantial cooperation on labor and economic policies, and benefits to individual members can vary. Skilled labor may go where wages are higher, and investment capital may flow to where returns are greater. In the EU, for example, workers from Poland and the Czech Republic have flowed into Germany because they can earn substantially higher wages there than at home.

An **economic union** is the fourth stage of regional integration, in which member countries enjoy all the advantages of early stages but also strive to have common fiscal and monetary policies. At the extreme, each member country adopts identical tax rates. The bloc aims for standardized monetary policy, which requires establishing fixed exchange rates and free convertibility of currencies among the member states, in addition to allowing the free movement of capital. This standardization helps eliminate discriminatory practices that might favor one member state over another.

The EU has made great strides toward achieving an economic union. For example, sixteen member countries have established a *monetary union* in which a single currency, the euro, is now in circulation. Monetary union and the euro have greatly increased the ease with which European financial institutions establish branches across the EU and offer banking services, insurance, and savings products and have eased investment and trading for firms doing business within the bloc.

Economic union member countries strive to eliminate border controls, harmonize product and labeling standards, and establish regionwide policies for energy, agriculture, and social services. An economic union also requires its members to standardize laws and regulations regarding competition, mergers, and other corporate behaviors, including licensing of professionals, so that a doctor or lawyer qualified in one country can practice in any other country.

The Leading Economic Blocs

Examples of regional integration can be found on all continents.

The European Union (EU). The EU, summarized in Exhibit 1.6, is the world's most integrated economic bloc. Over time, the EU has taken the following steps on its path to becoming a full-fledged economic union:

- *Market access.* Tariffs and most nontariff barriers have been eliminated for trade in products and services. Rules of origin favor manufacturing that uses parts and other inputs produced in the EU.
- *Common market.* Barriers to the cross-national movement of production factors— labor, capital, and technology—have been removed. An Italian worker now has the right to get a job in Ireland, and a French company can invest freely in Spain.
- *Trade rules.* The member countries have largely eliminated customs procedures and regulations, which streamlines transportation and logistics within Europe.
- *Standards harmonization.* The EU is harmonizing technical standards, regulations, and enforcement procedures that relate to products, services, and commercial activities.

In the long run, the EU is seeking to adopt common fiscal, monetary, taxation, and social welfare policies. The 2002 introduction of the euro eliminated exchange rate risk and forced member countries to improve their fiscal and monetary policies. Since 2004, twelve new states have joined the EU, and the recent addition of Bulgaria and Romania brought the number of member countries to twenty-seven. Most new members are important, low-cost manufacturing sites for EU firms.[17]

In addition to the European Union, several other trading blocs are notable.

European Free Trade Association (EFTA). EFTA (www.efta.int), was established in 1960 by Austria, Britain, Denmark, Norway, Portugal, Sweden, and Switzerland. Some eventually left EFTA to join the EU; current EFTA members are Iceland, Liechtenstein, Norway, and Switzerland.

North American Free Trade Agreement (NAFTA). Consisting of Canada, Mexico, and the United States, NAFTA launched in 1994. It is the most significant economic bloc in the Americas and comparable to the EU in size (see

Members	Population (millions)	GDP (U.S.$, billions, PPP terms)	GDP per Capita (U.S.$; PPP terms)	Exports as a Percentage of GDP
Austria	8	$329	$39,647	29%
Belgium	11	390	36,322	52
Bulgaria	8	94	12,900	24
Cyprus	1	23	28,381	7
Czech Republic	10	266	25,754	44
Denmark	5	210	38,208	26
Estonia	1	28	20,754	36
Finland	5	194	36,844	29
France	63	2,125	34,262	17
Germany	83	2,919	35,552	26
Greece	11	343	30,661	3
Hungary	10	199	19,900	42
Ireland	4	189	42,780	53
Italy	57	1,821	30,705	17
Latvia	2	40	17,800	21
Lithuania	3	64	18,855	36
Luxembourg	0.5	40	81,730	28
Malta	0.4	10	23,908	44
The Netherlands	17	675	40,434	44
Poland	38	669	17,560	24
Portugal	11	236	22,264	18
Romania	22	272	12,200	22
Slovakia	5	120	22,242	51
Slovenia	2	58	29,894	38
Spain	45	1,400	30,757	16
Sweden	9	346	37,526	30
United Kingdom	61	2,231	36,570	14
	Total: 493	Total: $15,291		

EXHIBIT 1.6 Key Features of the European Union Member Countries, 2009. *Source:* International Monetary Fund at www.imf.org and European Union at http://europa.eu.

www.nafta-sec-alena.org). Its passage was smoothed by the existence of the *maquiladora* program, under which, since the 1960s, U.S. firms have been allowed to locate manufacturing facilities in an area just south of the border and access low-cost labor and other advantages in Mexico without having to pay significant tariffs.

El Mercado Comun del Sur (MERCOSUR). Established in 1991, MERCOSUR (the "Southern Common Market") is the strongest economic bloc in South America (see www.mercosur.int).

The Caribbean Community (CARICOM). Composed of roughly twenty-five member and associate member states around the Caribbean Sea, CARICOM was established in 1973 to lower trade barriers and institute a common external tariff (see www.caricom.org).

Comunidad Andina de Naciones (CAN). Long called the Andean Pact, CAN was established in 1969. Its main members are Bolivia, Colombia, Ecuador, and Peru (see www.comunidadandina.org).

Association of Southeast Asian Nations (ASEAN). ASEAN was created in 1967 with the goal of maintaining political stability and promoting regional economic and social development among its members (see www.aseansec.org). Many tariffs were reduced to less than 5 percent, but further regional integration has been slowed by large economic differences among member countries.

Asia Pacific Economic Cooperation (APEC). APEC incorporates twenty-one nations on both sides of the Pacific, including Australia, Canada, Chile, China, Japan, Mexico, Russia, and the United States (see www.apec.org).

Australia and New Zealand Closer Economic Relations Agreement (CER). In 1966, Australia and New Zealand reached a free trade agreement that removed 80 percent of tariffs and quotas between them, but it was relatively complex and bureaucratic. In 1983, the CER sought to accelerate free trade, leading to further economic integration of the two nations. The bloc gained importance when Australia and New Zealand lost their privileged status in the British market as Britain joined the EU.

Management Implications of Regional Integration

Regional economic integration suggests several implications for management.

1. *Internationalization by firms inside the economic bloc.* Initially, regional integration pressures or encourages companies to internationalize into neighboring countries within the bloc. The elimination of trade and investment barriers also presents new opportunities to source input goods from foreign suppliers within the bloc. Internationalizing into neighboring, familiar countries also provides the firm with the skills and confidence to further internationalize to markets outside the bloc.

2. *Rationalization of operations.* Instead of viewing the bloc as a collection of disparate countries, managers can develop strategies and value-chain activities suited to the region as a whole, rather than to individual countries. *Rationalization* is the process of restructuring and consolidating company operations following regional integration to reduce redundancy and costs, and increase the efficiency of operations.

3. *Mergers and acquisitions.* The formation of economic blocs also leads to mergers and acquisitions (M&A), sometimes due to rationalization. For example, development of the EU encouraged two giant engineering firms, Asea AB of Sweden and Brown, Boveri & Co. of Switzerland, to merge to form Asea Brown Boveri (ABB). The merger allowed the new firm to increase its R&D activities and pool greater capital funding for major projects, such as construction of power plants and large-scale industrial equipment.

4. *Regional products and marketing strategy.* It is easier and much less costly to make and sell a few product models rather than dozens. An economic bloc facilitates the standardization of products and streamlining of marketing activities because, in more advanced stages of regional integration, the member countries tend to harmonize product standards and commercial regulations.[18]

5. *Internationalization by firms from outside the bloc.* The most effective way for a foreign firm to enter an economic bloc is to establish a physical presence there via foreign direct investment. By building a production facility, marketing subsidiary, or regional headquarters anywhere inside a bloc, the outsider gains access to the entire bloc and to advantages enjoyed by local firms based inside the bloc.

Summary

International business refers to the performance of trade and investment activities by firms across national borders. **Globalization of markets** is the ongoing economic integration and growing interdependency of countries worldwide. International business is characterized by international trade and investment. International trade typically refers to exporting and importing. **Exporting** is the sale of products or services to customers located abroad, from a base in the home country or a third country. **Importing** or **global sourcing** refers to procurement of products or services from foreign suppliers for consumption in the home country or a third country. **International investment** refers to international transfer or acquisition of ownership in assets. Through **foreign direct investment**, the firm establishes a physical presence abroad through acquisition of productive assets such as capital, technology, labor, land, plant, and equipment.

International firms are constantly exposed to four major types of risk that must be managed. **Cross-cultural risk** refers to a situation or event where some human value is put at stake due to a cultural misunderstanding. **Country risk** refers to the potentially adverse effects on company operations and profitability caused by developments in the political, legal, and economic environment in a foreign country. **Currency risk** refers to the risk of adverse fluctuations in exchange rates. **Commercial risk** arises from the possibility of a firm's loss or failure from poorly developed or executed business strategies, tactics, or procedures.

A key participant in international business is the **multinational enterprise (MNE)**, a large company with many resources whose business activities are performed by a network of subsidiaries located in multiple countries. Also active in international business are **small and medium-sized enterprises (SMEs)**, companies with 500 or fewer employees.

Companies internationalize for various reasons. These include the ability to increase sales and profits, better serve customers, access lower-cost or superior production factors, optimize sourcing activities, develop economies of scale, confront competitors more effectively, develop rewarding relationships with foreign partners, and gain access to new ideas for creating or improving products and services.

Market globalization can be viewed in terms of its drivers, dimensions, societal consequences, and firm-level consequences.

As market globalization intensifies, firms are compelled to respond to challenges and exploit new advantages. Many firms internationalize proactively as a strategic move.

Under **regional economic integration**, groups of countries form alliances to promote free trade, cross-national investment, and other mutual goals. This integration results from **regional economic** **integration blocs** (or economic blocs), in which member countries agree to eliminate tariffs and other restrictions on the cross-national flow of products, services, capital, and, in more advanced stages, labor, within the bloc. At minimum, the countries in an economic bloc become parties to a **free trade agreement**, which eliminates tariffs, quotas, and other trade barriers.

Key Terms

born global
   firm *10*
country risk *8*
commercial risk *9*
common market *16*
cross-cultural risk *7*
customs union *16*
currency risk *8*
economic union *17*
exporting *3*

foreign direct investment
   (FDI) *4*
free trade agreement *16*
free trade area *16*
globalization of markets *3*
global sourcing *3*
international business *2*
international investment *4*
international portfolio
   investment *4*

international trade *3*
importing *3*
multinational enterprise
   (MNE) *9*
small and medium-sized
   enterprises (SMEs) *10*
regional economic
   integration *15*
regional economic
   integration blocs *16*

Endnotes

1. We use the term *international business* to refer to the cross-border business activities of individual firms, while economists use *international trade* to refer to aggregate cross-border flows of products and services between nations. While international business describes an enterprise-level phenomenon, international trade describes the macrophenomenon of aggregate flows between nations.

2. Dave Shellock, "Signs of Deepening Recession Dent Confidence," *Financial Times,* February 14, 2009, p. 14; Gabriele Parussini, "World News: Euro-Zone Economic Outlook Darkens," *Wall Street Journal,* January 17, 2009, p. A7.

3. "Numbers: International Trade Hits a Wall," *Business Week.* January 26/February 2, 2009, p. 15.

4. Nick Wingfield, "eBay Sets Sights on Indian Market with Acquisition," *Wall Street Journal,* June 23, 2004, p. A3.

5. "Desert Song," *Economist,* October 7, 2004, p. 88; "News: The Banker Country Awards 2007," *The Banker,* December, 2007, p. 1.

6. Marc A. Miles et al., *2008 Index of Economic Freedom* (Washington, DC: The Heritage Foundation).

7. Organisation for Economic Co-operation and Development, *Globalization and Small and Medium Enterprises (SMEs)* (Paris: OECD, 1997).

8. Gary Knight and S. Tamer Cavusgil, "Innovation, Organizational Capabilities, and the Born-Global Firm," *Journal of International Business Studies* 35, no. 2 (2004): 124–41; Patricia McDougall, Scott Shane, and Benjamin Oviatt, "Explaining the Formation of International

New Ventures: The Limits of Theories from International Business Research," *Journal of Business Venturing* 9, no. 6 (1994): 469–87; OECD (1997).

9. Marcos Aguiar et al., The New Global Challengers: How Top 100 Rapidly Developing Economies Are Changing the World, Boston Consulting Group, May 25, 2006.

10. GNI refers to the total value of goods and services produced within a country after taking into account payments made to, and income received from, other countries.

11. Tara Radon and Martin Calkins, "The Struggle Against Sweatshops: Moving Toward Responsible Global Business," *Journal of Business Ethics* 66, no. 2–3 (2006): 261–69.

12. S. L. Bachman, "The Political Economy of Child Labor and Its Impacts on International Business," *Business Economics* (July 2000): 30–41.

13. Martin Wolf, *Why Globalization Works* (New Haven, CN: Yale University Press, 2004).

14. Michael Smith, "Trade and the Environment," *International Business* 5, no. 8 (1992): 74.

15. "Rise of the Sushi King," *Business 2.0*, December 1, 2004, p. 80.

16. Marcos Aguiar et al., The New Global Challengers: How Top 100 Rapidly Developing Economies are Changing the World, Boston Consulting Group, May 25, 2006.

17. "Transformed: EU Membership has Worked Magic in Central Europe," *Economist*, June 25, 2005, pp. 6–8.

18. Subhash Jain and John K. Ryans, "A Normative Framework for Assessing Marketing Strategy Implications of Europe 1992," in *Euromarketing*, E. Kaynak and P. Ghauri, eds. (New York: International Business Press, 1994).

Theories of International Trade and Investment

LEARNING OBJECTIVES
In this chapter, you will learn about:

1. The theories that explain international trade and investment

2. The reasons why nations trade

3. The ways nations can enhance their competitive advantage

4. Why and how firms internationalize

5. The ways internationalizing firms can gain and sustain competitive advantage

In this chapter, we explain why nations and firms trade and invest internationally.[1] We explain why such participation allows nations to acquire and sustain comparative advantage and why it enables firms to acquire and sustain competitive advantage in the global marketplace. We address such questions as:

- What is the underlying economic rationale for international business activity?
- Why does trade take place?
- What are the gains from trade and investment?

WHAT THEORIES EXPLAIN INTERNATIONAL TRADE AND INVESTMENT?

For centuries, scholars have offered theories and economic rationale for international trade and investment. **Comparative advantage** describes superior features of a country that provide unique benefits in global competition, typically derived from either natural endowments or deliberate national policies. Also known as *country-specific advantage*, comparative advantage includes inherited resources, such as labor, climate, arable land, and petroleum reserves, such as those enjoyed by the Gulf nations. Other types of comparative advantages are acquired over time, such as innovative capacity and widely available venture capital.

Competitive advantage describes organizational assets and competencies that are difficult for competitors to imitate and thus help firms enter and succeed in foreign markets. These competencies take various forms, such as specific knowledge, capabilities, superior strategies, or close relationships with suppliers. Competitive advantage is also known as *firm-specific advantage*.

Scholars and managers often use the term *competitive advantage* to refer to the advantages possessed by nations as well as individual firms. We adopt this convention as well.

Exhibit 2.1 categorizes leading theories of international trade and investment into two broad groups. The first group includes nation-level theories. These are classical theories that have been advocated since the sixteenth century. They address two questions: (1) *Why* do nations trade? (2) *How* can nations enhance their competitive advantage?

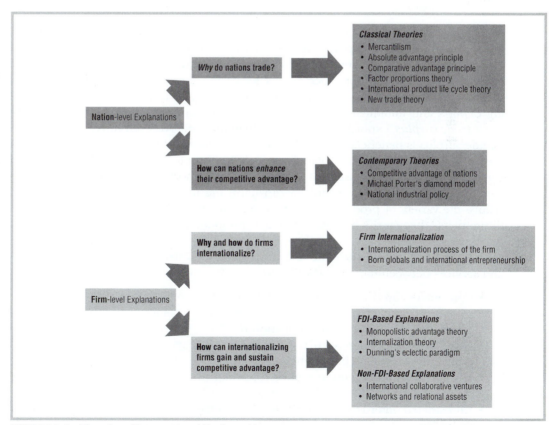

EXHIBIT 2.1   Theories of International Trade and Investment.

The second group includes firm-level theories. These are contemporary theories of how firms can create and sustain superior organizational performance. Firm-level explanations address two additional questions: (3) *Why* and *how* do firms internationalize? (4) *How* can internationalizing firms gain and sustain competitive advantage?

We organize the remainder of our discussion according to the four fundamental questions.

WHY DO NATIONS TRADE?

Without international trade, most nations would be unable to feed, clothe, and house their citizens at current levels. Even resource-rich countries like the United States would suffer. Coffee and sugar would be luxury items. Without petroleum-based energy sources, vehicles would stop running, freight would not be delivered, and homes would go unheated in winter. In short, not only do nations, companies, and citizens benefit from international trade, but modern life is virtually impossible without it. Six classical perspectives explain the underlying rationale for trade among nations: mercantilism, absolute advantage, comparative advantage, factor proportions theory, international product life cycle theory, and new trade theory. Let's examine these in turn.

MERCANTILISM   In the 1500s, European states received payment for exports and paid for imports in gold, so exports increased their gold stock while imports reduced it. Thus, European governments saw exports as good and imports as bad. Because the nation's power and strength increase as its wealth increases, **mercantilism** argues that national prosperity results from a positive balance of trade achieved by maximizing exports and minimizing imports. Mercantilism explains why nations attempt to run a *trade surplus*, exporting more goods than they import. Even today many believe a trade surplus is beneficial, a view known as *neo-mercantilism*. Labor unions (which seek to protect home-country jobs), farmers (who want to keep crop prices high), and certain manufacturers (those that rely heavily on exports) all tend to support neo-mercantilism. However, mercantilism can harm the interests of importing firms and reduce the variety of products available to consumers. Taken to an extreme, mercantilism invites "beggar thy neighbor" policies, promoting the benefits of one country at the expense of others.

By contrast, **free trade**—the relative absence of restrictions to the flow of goods and services between nations—should produce the following outcomes:

- Consumers and firms can more readily buy the products they want.
- Imported products are usually cheaper than domestically made products because access to low-cost production results in lower prices.
- Lower-cost imports reduce the expenses of firms, which raises their profits (which may translate into higher wages for workers).
- Lower-cost imports tend to reduce consumer prices, which helps increase living standards.
- Unrestricted international trade tends to increase overall prosperity in poor countries.

ABSOLUTE ADVANTAGE PRINCIPLE In 1776, Scottish political economist Adam Smith attacked the mercantilist view by suggesting nations benefit most from free trade. Relative to others, each country is more efficient in the production of some products and less efficient in the production of others. Smith's **absolute advantage principle** states that a country can consume more at lower cost by producing primarily those products in which it has an absolute advantage or that it can produce using fewer resources than another country. By trying to minimize imports, a country wastes national resources in the production of goods it is not suited to produce efficiently, reducing its wealth while enriching a limited number of individuals and interest groups. Each country thus increases its welfare by specializing in the production of certain products, exporting them, and then importing other products in which it lacks advantages.

Exhibit 2.2 illustrates the absolute advantage principle. Consider two nations, France and Germany, engaged in a trading relationship. France has an absolute advantage in the production of cloth, and Germany has an absolute advantage in the production of wheat. Assume labor is the only factor of production used in making both goods. (Firms employ *factors of production*—for example, labor, capital, technology, and natural resources—to produce goods and services.) In Exhibit 2.2, it takes an average worker in France 30 days to produce one ton of cloth and 40 days to produce one ton of wheat. It takes an average worker in Germany 100 days to produce one ton of cloth and 20 days to produce one ton of wheat.

France has an absolute advantage in the production of cloth, since it takes only 30 days of labor to produce one ton compared to 100 days for Germany. Germany has an absolute advantage in the production of wheat, since it takes only 20 days to produce one ton compared to 40 days for France. If both France and Germany were to specialize, exchanging cloth and wheat at a ratio of one-to-one, France could employ more of its resources to produce cloth and Germany could employ more of its resources to produce wheat. According to Exhibit 2.2, France can import one ton of wheat in exchange for one ton of cloth, thereby "paying" only 30 labor-days for one ton of wheat. If France had produced the wheat itself, it would have used 40 labor-days, so it gains 10 labor-days by engaging in trade. In a similar way, Germany gains from trade with France.

Each country benefits by specializing in producing the product in which it has an absolute advantage and securing the other product through trade. In this way, each employs its labor and other resources more efficiently and, consequently, increases its standard of living. To employ a more contemporary example, Japan has no natural

	One Ton of	
	Cloth	Wheat
France	30	40
Germany	100	20

EXHIBIT 2.2 Example of Absolute Advantage (Labor Cost in Days of Production for One Ton).

holdings of oil, but it manufactures some of the world's best automobiles. Saudi Arabia produces much oil, but lacks a substantial car industry. Given this state of resources, it is wasteful for each country to attempt to produce both oil and cars. By trading with each other, Japan and Saudi Arabia employ their respective resources more efficiently in a mutually beneficial relationship. Japan gets oil that it refines to power cars, and Saudi Arabia gets the cars its citizens need. By extending this example, we see that freely trading countries achieve substantial gains from trade. Brazil can produce coffee more cheaply than Germany; Australia can produce wool more cheaply than Switzerland; Britain can provide financial services more cheaply than Zimbabwe; and so forth.

While the concept of absolute advantage provided perhaps the earliest sound rationale for international trade, later studies revealed that a country benefits from international trade even when it *lacks* an absolute advantage. This line of thinking led to the principle of *comparative advantage.*

COMPARATIVE ADVANTAGE PRINCIPLE   British political economist David Ricardo explained in 1817 that what matters is not the absolute cost of production, but rather the *relative efficiency* with which the two countries can produce the products. Hence, the **comparative advantage principle** states that it can be beneficial for two countries to trade without barriers as long as one is *relatively* more efficient at producing goods or services needed by the other. The principle of comparative advantage provides the most important rationale for international trade.

To illustrate, let's modify the example of France and Germany. As shown in Exhibit 2.3, suppose now that Germany has an absolute advantage in the production of both cloth and wheat. That is, in labor-per-day terms, Germany can produce *both* cloth and wheat in fewer days than France. Based on this new scenario, you might initially conclude that Germany should produce all the wheat and cloth it needs and not trade with France at all. However, even though Germany can produce both items more cheaply than France, it is still beneficial for Germany to trade with France.

How can this be true? The answer is that rather than the absolute cost of production, it is the *ratio of production costs* between the two countries that matters most. In Exhibit 2.3, Germany is comparatively more efficient at producing cloth than wheat: It can produce three times as much cloth as France (30/10), but only two times as much wheat (40/20). Thus, Germany should devote all its resources to producing cloth and import all the wheat it needs from France. France should specialize in producing wheat and import all its cloth from Germany. Both countries then can each produce and consume relatively more of the goods they desire for a given level of labor cost.

| | One Ton of ||
	Cloth	Wheat
France	30	40
Germany	10	20

EXHIBIT 2.3   Example of Comparative Advantage (Labor Cost in Days of Production for One Ton).

Another way to understand comparative advantage is to consider *opportunity cost*, the value of a foregone alternative activity. In Exhibit 2.3, if Germany produces 1 ton of wheat, it forgoes 2 tons of cloth. However, if France produces 1 ton of wheat, it forgoes only 1.33 tons of cloth. Thus, France should specialize in wheat. Similarly, if France produces 1 ton of cloth, it forgoes 0.75 ton of wheat. But if Germany produces 1 ton of cloth, it forgoes only 0.5 ton of wheat. Thus, Germany should specialize in cloth. The opportunity cost of producing wheat is lower in France, and the opportunity cost of producing cloth is lower in Germany.[2]

While a nation might have sufficient production factors to provide every kind of product and service, it cannot produce each with equal facility. The United States could produce all the car batteries its citizens need, but only at high cost. This occurs because batteries require much labor to produce, and wages in the United States are relatively high. By contrast, producing car batteries is a reasonable activity in China, where wages are lower. It is advantageous, therefore, for the United States to specialize in a product such as patented medications, the production of which more efficiently employs the country's abundant supply of knowledge workers and technology in the pharmaceutical industry. The United States is better off exporting medications and importing car batteries from China. The comparative advantage view is optimistic because it implies that a nation need not be the first-, second-, or even third-best producer of particular products to benefit from international trade. Indeed, it is generally advantageous for *all* countries to participate in international trade.

Initially, adherents of the comparative advantage principle focused on the importance of *inherited* or *natural resource advantages*, such as fertile land, abundant minerals, and favorable climate. Thus, because South Africa has extensive mineral deposits, it produces and exports diamonds. Because Argentina has much agricultural land and a suitable climate, it grows and exports wheat. However, countries also can create or *acquire* comparative advantages. For example, following World War II, Japanese companies such as Hitachi, Panasonic, and Sony systematically invested massive resources to acquire the knowledge and skills needed to become world leaders in consumer electronics. Today, Japan accounts for approximately half the industry's total world production, including digital cameras, flat-screen TVs, and personal computers.

LIMITATIONS OF EARLY TRADE THEORIES   While the concepts of absolute advantage and comparative advantage provide the rationale for international trade, they failed to account for some complicating factors.

- Traded goods are not just commodities; many are complex products characterized by strong branding and differentiated features.
- International transportation is often costly.
- Government restrictions such as tariffs (taxes on imports), import barriers, and regulations can hinder international trade.
- Large-scale production may bring about scale economies, and therefore lower prices.
- Governments may target and invest in certain industries, build infrastructure, or provide subsidies to boost the competitive advantages of home-country firms.
- Many services, such as banking and retailing, cannot be traded in the usual sense and must be internationalized via foreign direct investment.

- Modern telecommunications and the Internet facilitate global trade in some services at very low cost.
- Many firms are highly entrepreneurial and innovative, or have access to exceptional human talent that they employ to develop superior business strategies.

Next we discuss additional theories that have been introduced in view of the above factors.

FACTOR PROPORTIONS THEORY   In the 1920s, two Swedish economists, Eli Heckscher and his student, Bertil Ohlin, proposed the *factor proportions theory,* sometimes called the *factor endowments theory.*[3] This view rests on two premises: (1) products differ in the types and quantities of factors (labor, capital, and natural resources) required for their production; and (2) countries differ in the type and quantity of production factors they possess. Thus, each country should export products that intensively use relatively abundant factors of production and import goods that intensively use relatively scarce factors. For example, the United States produces and exports capital-intensive products, such as commercial aircraft; Russia produces and exports land-intensive products, such as wheat; and China produces and exports labor-intensive products, such as home appliances. Factor proportions theory differs from earlier theories by emphasizing that, in addition to differences in production efficiency, differences in the *quantity* of factors of production also determine international trade patterns. The abundance of a given factor of production, say labor, leads to a *per-unit-cost advantage.*

The theory suggests that because the United States has abundant capital, it should be an exporter of capital-intensive products. However, Russian-born economist Wassily Leontief's 1950s analysis, termed the *Leontief paradox,* revealed that the United States often exported labor-intensive goods and imported more capital-intensive goods than the theory should predict. One explanation is that, in Leontief's time, U.S. labor was relatively more productive than labor elsewhere in the world. Perhaps the main contribution of the Leontief paradox is its suggestion that international trade is complex and cannot be fully explained by a single theory.

INTERNATIONAL PRODUCT LIFE CYCLE THEORY   In 1966, professor Raymond Vernon developed the *international product life cycle (IPLC) theory,* which described how each product and its manufacturing technologies go through three stages of evolution: introduction, maturity, and standardization.[4]

In the introduction stage, a new product typically originates in an advanced economy, such as televisions in the United States, and enjoys a temporary monopoly. As the product enters the maturity phase, the product's inventors mass-produce it and seek to export it to other advanced economies. Gradually, however, manufacturing becomes more routine and foreign firms begin producing the product, ending the inventor's monopoly power. In the standardization phase, mass production can be accomplished in low-income countries using cheaper inputs and low-cost labor and, eventually, the country that invented the product becomes a net importer. Today nearly all TVs sold in the United States are imported from China, Mexico, and other lower-cost producers. In effect, exporting the product causes its underlying technology to become widely known and standardized around the world. IPLC theory illustrates that national advantages are dynamic; they do not last forever. The IPLC has become much shorter as new products such as smart phones and tablet computers diffuse much more quickly around the world.

HOW CAN NATIONS ENHANCE THEIR COMPETITIVE ADVANTAGE?

The most advantaged nations today possess national competitive advantage. It is maximized when numerous industries collectively possess firm-level competitive advantages *and* the nation itself has comparative advantages that benefit those particular industries. This is illustrated in Exhibit 2.4. Many governments create policies designed to encourage competitive advantage, often by developing world-class business sectors and prosperous geographic regions.

Three key modern perspectives that help explain the development of national competitive advantage are the competitive advantage of nations, the diamond model, and national industrial policy.

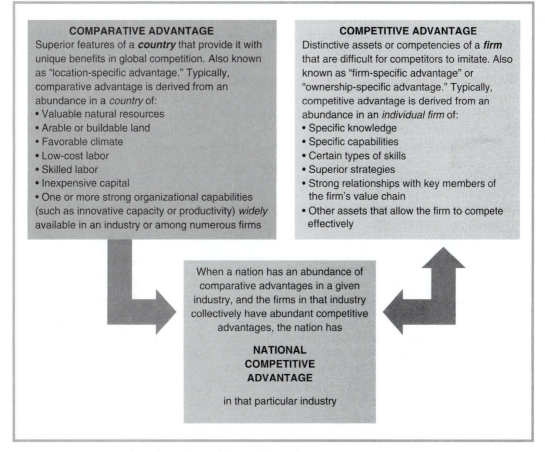

EXHIBIT 2.4 Comparative Advantage and Competitive Advantage.

The Competitive Advantage of Nations

In 1990, Michael Porter proposed that the competitive advantage of a nation depends on the collective competitive advantages of its firms.[5] Over time, the nation's competitive advantages tend to drive the development of new firms and industries with these same competitive advantages. For example, Britain achieved a substantial national competitive advantage in the prescription drug industry due to its first-rate pharmaceutical firms, including GlaxoSmithKline and AstraZeneca.

At both the firm and national levels, competitive advantage and technological advances grow out of *innovation*.[6] Companies develop new products, new production processes, new approaches to marketing, new ways of organizing or training, and so forth. Through research and development (R&D), firms sustain innovation (and by extension, competitive advantage) by continually finding better products, services, and ways of doing things.[7] Among the industries most dependent on technological innovation are biotechnology, information technology, new materials, pharmaceuticals, robotics, medical equipment, fiber optics, and various electronics-based industries.

Most top European, Japanese, and U.S. firms spend half or more of their total R&D in countries other than where they are headquartered. Why? First, they can gain access to gifted engineers and scientists located around the world. Second, they can cut costs by hiring lower-paid engineers and scientists abroad. Third, by relocating R&D abroad, the firms can gain insights into target markets during the product development process.[8] This explains why Europe and the United States are also popular sites for foreign R&D, as firms seek to understand and create new products for the world's most lucrative markets.

The more innovative firms a nation has, the stronger its competitive advantage. Innovation also promotes *productivity*, the value of the output produced by a unit of labor or capital. The more productive the firms in a nation are, the more efficiently the nation uses its resources, and the higher its long-run standard of living and per-capita income growth. In recent years, South Korea and the United States have been among the world's most productive nations. Productivity increased substantially with the widespread introduction of information and communications technologies in the 1990s.

The Diamond Model

Porter developed the *diamond model*, proposing that competitive advantage at both the company and the national level originates from the presence and quality of four major elements:[9]

1. *Firm strategy, structure, and rivalry* refer to the nature of domestic rivalry and conditions in a nation that determine how firms are created, organized, and managed. The presence of strong competitors for market share, human talent, and technical and quality leadership in a nation helps create national competitive advantage.

2. *Factor conditions* describe the nation's position in factors of production, such as labor, capital, natural resources, and know-how. Consistent with factor proportions theory, each nation has a relative abundance of certain factor endowments, which helps determine the nature of its national competitive advantage.

3. *Demand conditions* refer to the nature of home-market demand for specific products and services. The presence of highly demanding customers pressures firms to innovate faster and produce better products.

4. *Related and supporting industries* refer to the presence of clusters of suppliers, competitors, and complementary firms that excel in particular industries. The resulting business environment supports the founding of particular types of firms.

Industrial cluster refers to a concentration of businesses, suppliers, and supporting firms in the same industry at a particular geographic location, characterized by a critical mass of human talent, capital, or other factor endowments. Examples include the fashion industry in northern Italy, the pharmaceutical industry in Switzerland, and the footwear industry in Vietnam.

Today, the most important sources of national advantage are the *knowledge and skills* possessed by individual firms, industries, and countries. For instance, Silicon Valley, California, and Bangalore, India, have emerged as leading-edge business clusters because of the availability of specialized talent. Some even argue that knowledge is now the only source of sustainable long-run competitive advantage. If correct, then future national wealth will go to those countries that invest the most in R&D, education, and infrastructure that support knowledge-intensive industries.

National Industrial Policy

Porter's diamond model implies that any country, regardless of its initial circumstances, can attain economic prosperity by systematically cultivating new and superior factor endowments. Nations can develop these endowments, typically in collaboration with the private sector, through proactive **national industrial policy** to develop or support high value-adding industries which generate superior corporate profits, higher worker wages, and tax revenues. Progressive nations increasingly favor knowledge-intensive industries such as IT, biotechnology, medical technology, and financial services. These industries also lead to the development of supplier and support companies that further enhance national prosperity.

National industrial policies typically include:

- Tax incentives to encourage citizens to save and invest, which provides capital for public and private investment.
- Sound fiscal and monetary policies, such as low-interest rates, that ensure a stable business environment and available capital.
- Rigorous higher-educational systems that ensure a steady stream of competent workers in the sciences, engineering, and business administration.
- Development and maintenance of strong national infrastructure in areas such as IT, communication systems, and transportation.
- Creation of strong legal and regulatory systems to ensure citizens are confident about the soundness and stability of the national economy.[10]

WHY AND HOW DO FIRMS INTERNATIONALIZE?

In the 1960s scholars began to develop theories about the managerial and organizational aspects of company internationalization. Let's review these next.

Internationalization Process of the Firm

The *internationalization process model* was developed in the 1970s to describe how companies expand abroad. According to this model, internationalization takes place in incremental stages over a long time.[11] Typically, firms start without much analysis or planning and begin to export, the simplest form of international activity, and as they acquire experience and information about foreign markets they progress to foreign direct investment (FDI), the most complex. The gradual and incremental nature of internationalization often results from managers' uncertainty and uneasiness about how to proceed, because they lack information on foreign markets and experience with cross-border transactions.[12]

BORN GLOBALS AND INTERNATIONAL ENTREPRENEURSHIP   Recently scholars have questioned the slow and gradual process proposed by the internationalization process model.[13] Despite the scarcity of resources that characterize most new businesses, *born global firms* internationalize early in their evolution. Indeed, current trends suggest that early internationalizing firms will gradually become the norm in international business. Among the reasons are the growing intensity of international competition, the integration of world economies under globalization, and advances in communication and transportation technologies that make international trade easier. The born global phenomenon has given rise to a new field of scholarly inquiry, *international entrepreneurship*.[14]

HOW CAN INTERNATIONALIZING FIRMS GAIN AND SUSTAIN COMPETITIVE ADVANTAGE?

So important is the rise of the multinational enterprise (MNE) that it ranks with the development of electric power or the invention of the aircraft as one of the major events of modern history. Let's examine MNEs and their internationalization processes in more detail.

FDI-Based Explanations

FDI stock refers to the total value of assets that MNEs own abroad via their investment activities. Exhibit 2.5 shows the total stock of inward FDI, and Exhibit 2.6 shows the total stock of outward FDI. MNEs invest millions abroad every year to establish and expand factories and other facilities. While historically most of the world's FDI was invested both by and in Western Europe, North America, and Japan, in recent years MNEs have invested heavily in emerging markets, such as China, Mexico, Brazil, and Eastern Europe.[15]

FDI is such an important entry strategy that scholars provide three alternative theories of how firms can use it to gain and sustain competitive advantage: the monopolistic advantage theory, internalization theory, and Dunning's eclectic paradigm. These theoretical perspectives are summarized in Exhibit 2.7 and described on page 37–38.

MONOPOLISTIC ADVANTAGE THEORY   Monopolistic advantage refers to resources or capabilities owned by a company that few other firms have and that it can leverage

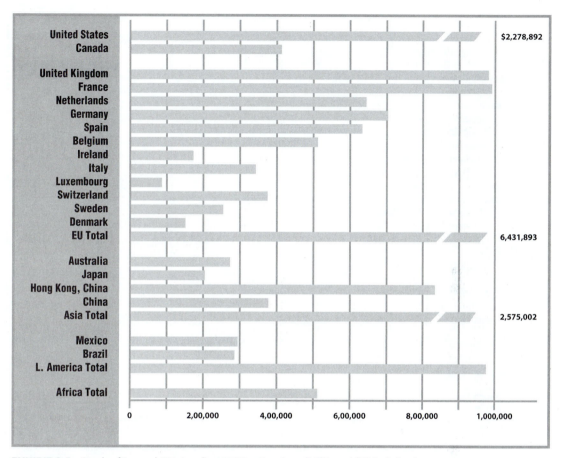

EXHIBIT 2.5   Stock of Inward FDI: Leading FDI Destinations (Millions of U.S. dollars).   *Source:* UNCTAD, "Annex Table B.2. FDI Stock, by Region and Economy, 1990, 2000, 2010," *World Investment Report 2009* (New York: United Nations, 2009) p. 251, retrieved from http://unctad.org/en/docs/wir2009_en.pdf, June 4, 2010.

to generate profits and other returns. Monopolistic advantage theory suggests that firms which use FDI as an internationalization strategy must own or control certain resources and capabilities not easily available to competitors, such as a proprietary technology or a brand name. Such a monopolistic advantage helps firms internationalize and succeed in foreign markets.[16]

INTERNALIZATION THEORY   Scholars have investigated the benefits that MNEs derive from internationalizing via FDI. For example, when Procter & Gamble entered Japan, management initially considered exporting, which would have required contracting with an independent Japanese distributor to warehouse and market P&G's soap, diapers, and other products. Ultimately, P&G instead chose to enter Japan via FDI, through which it established its own marketing subsidiary in Tokyo. P&G benefited from this arrangement through its ability to better control how its products were marketed in Japan and to minimize the risk its proprietary knowledge would be dissipated to potential Japanese competitors.

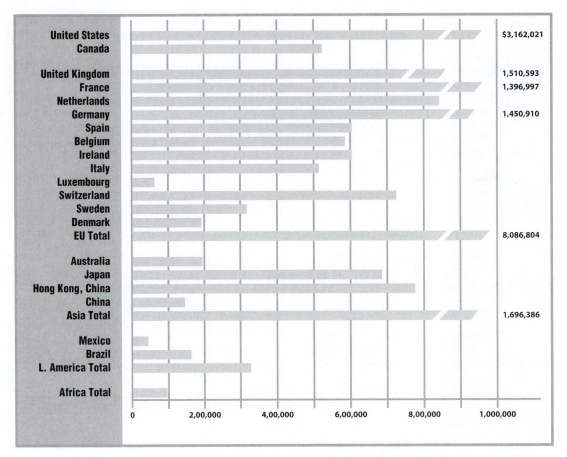

EXHIBIT 2.6   Stock of Outward FDI: Top Sources of Outward FDI (Millions of U.S. dollars).   *Source:* UNCTAD, "Annex Table B.2. FDI Stock, by Region and Economy, 1990, 2000, 2010," *World Investment Report 2009* (New York: United Nations, 2009) p. 251), retrieved from http://unctad.org/en/docs/wir2009_en.pdf, June 4, 2010.

Internalization theory explains the process by which firms acquire and retain one or more value-chain activities inside the firm. Internalization helps minimize the disadvantages of dealing with external partners and gives the firm greater control over its foreign operations. By internalizing key activities, the MNE bypasses the bottlenecks and costs of interfirm exchanges of goods, materials, and workers. In this way, the firm *replaces* business activities performed by independent suppliers in external markets with business activities it performs itself. Another key reason companies internalize certain value-chain functions is to control proprietary knowledge critical to the development, production, and sale of their products and services. For example, Intel tends to internalize production of its leading-edge computer chips, to prevent potential competitors from gaining access to its latest technology.[17]

DUNNING'S ECLECTIC PARADIGM   Professor John Dunning proposed the *eclectic paradigm* as a framework for determining the extent and pattern of the value-chain

Theory	Key Characteristics	Benefits	Examples
Monopolistic Advantage Theory	The firm controls one or more resources, or offers relatively unique products and services that provide it a degree of monopoly power relative to foreign markets and competitors.	The firm can operate foreign subsidiaries more profitably than the local firms that compete in their own markets.	The European pharmaceutical Novartis earns substantial profits by marketing various patent medications through its subsidiaries worldwide.
Internalization Theory	The firm acquires and retains one or more value-chain activities within the firm.	• Minimizes the disadvantages of relying on intermediaries, collaborators, or other external partners. • Ensures greater control over foreign operations, helping to maximize product quality, reliable manufacturing processes, and sound marketing practices. • Reduces the risk that knowledge and proprietary assets will be lost to competitors.	The Japanese MNE Toshiba: • Owns and operates factories in dozens of countries to manufacture laptop computers. • Controls its own manufacturing processes, ensuring quality output. • Ensures its marketing activities are carried out per headquarters's plan. • Retains key assets within the firm, such as leading-edge knowledge for producing the next generation of laptops.
Dunning's Eclectic Paradigm	• *Ownership-specific advantages*: The firm owns knowledge, skills, capabilities, processes, or physical assets. • *Location-specific advantages*: Factors in individual countries provide specific benefits, such as natural resources, skilled labor, low-cost labor, and inexpensive capital. • *Internalization advantages*: The firm benefits from internalizing foreign manufacturing, distribution, or other value-chain activities.	Provides various advantages relative to competitors, including the ability to own, control, and optimize value-chain activities—R&D, production, marketing, sales distribution, after-sales service, as well as relationships with customers and key contacts—performed at the most beneficial locations worldwide.	The German MNE Siemens: • Owns factories at locations worldwide that provide optimal access to natural resources, as well as skilled and low-cost labor. • Leverages the knowledge base of its employees in 190 countries. • Internalizes a wide range of manufacturing activities in categories such as lighting, medical equipment, and transportation machinery.

EXHIBIT 2.7   Theoretical Perspectives on Why Firms Choose FDI.

operations that companies own abroad. It specifies three conditions that determine whether a company will internationalize via FDI:

1. The MNE must possess *ownership-specific advantages* relative to other firms in the market—that is, knowledge, skills, capabilities, key relationships, and other assets that allow it to compete effectively in foreign markets. These assets amount to the firm's competitive advantages. The notion of ownership-specific advantages is related to monopolistic advantage theory.

2. The firm must have access to *location-specific advantages,* the comparative advantages available in individual foreign countries, such as natural resources, skilled labor, low-cost labor, and inexpensive capital.

3. The MNE must have *internalization advantages,* benefits it derives from internalizing foreign-based manufacturing, distribution, or other stages in its value chain. When profitable, the firm will transfer its ownership-specific advantages across national borders *within* its own organization rather than dissipating them to independent, foreign entities, such as distributors and other autonomous intermediaries abroad.[18]

Non-FDI-Based Explanations

In the 1980s, firms began to recognize the importance of collaborative ventures and other flexible non-FDI entry strategies.

INTERNATIONAL COLLABORATIVE VENTURES   A collaborative venture is a form of co-operation between two or more firms. There are two major types: (1) equity-based *joint ventures* that result in the formation of a new legal entity, and (2) non-equity-based *strategic alliances* in which firms partner temporarily to work on projects related to R&D, design, manufacturing, or any other value-adding activity. In both cases, collaborating firms pool resources and capabilities and share risks to carry out activities that each might be unable to perform on its own.[19]

NETWORKS AND RELATIONAL ASSETS   Networks and relational assets represent the economically beneficial long-term *relationships* the firm undertakes with other business entities, such as manufacturers, distributors, suppliers, retailers, consultants, banks, transportation suppliers, governments, and any other organization that can provide needed capabilities. Firm-level relational assets represent a distinct competitive advantage in international business. Japanese *keiretsu,* complex groupings of firms with interlinked ownership and trading relationships that foster interfirm organizational learning, are their predecessors.[20] Like the keiretsu, networks are neither formal organizations with clearly defined hierarchical structures nor impersonal, decentralized markets.

Summary

The basis for trade is specialization. Each nation specializes in producing certain goods and services and then trades with other nations to acquire those goods and services in which it is not specialized.

Absolute advantage principle argues that a country benefits by producing only those products in which it has absolute advantage or can produce using fewer resources than another country. The principle of **comparative advantage** contends that countries should specialize and export those goods in which they have a relative advantage compared to other countries. Nations benefit by trading with one another. Comparative advantage is based on *natural advantages* and *acquired advantages.* **Competitive advantage** derives from distinctive assets or competencies of a firm—such as cost, size, or innovation strengths—that are difficult for competitors to replicate or imitate. The collective competitive advantages of many firms give rise to competitive advantage in the nation as a whole. *Factor proportions theory* holds that nations specialize in the production of goods and services whose factors of production they hold in abundance.

Porter's diamond model specifies the four conditions in each nation that give rise to national competitive advantages: *firm strategy, structure, and rivalry; factor conditions; demand conditions;* and *related and supporting industries.* An **industrial cluster** is a concentration of companies in the same industry in a given location that interact closely with one another, gaining mutual competitive advantages. **National industrial policy** refers to efforts by governments to direct national resources to developing expertise in specific industries.

MNEs have value chains that span geographic locations worldwide. FDI means that firms invest at various locations to establish factories, marketing subsidiaries, or regional headquarters. *Monopolistic advantage theory* describes how companies succeed internationally by developing resources and capabilities that few other firms possess. Internalization is the process of acquiring and maintaining one or more value-chain activities inside the firm to minimize the disadvantages of subcontracting these activities to external firms, such as independent intermediaries. **Internalization theory** explains the tendency of MNEs to internalize value-chain stages when it is to their advantage.

The *eclectic paradigm* argues the internationalizing firm should possess certain internal competitive advantages, called *ownership-specific advantages, location-specific advantages,* and *internalization advantages.* Many companies engage in international *collaborative ventures,* interfirm partnerships that give them access to assets and other advantages held by foreign partners.

Key Terms

absolute advantage
   principle *27*
comparative advantage
   principle *28*

comparative advantage *24*
competitive advantage *25*
free trade *26*
industrial cluster *33*

internalization theory *36*
mercantilism *26*
national industrial
   policy *33*

Endnotes

1. We thank Professor Attila Yaprak, Wayne State University, and Professor Heechun Kim, Georgia State University, for their helpful comments on this chapter.
2. David Ricardo, *Principles of Political Economy and Taxation* (London: Everyman Edition, 1911; first published in 1817).
3. John Romalis, "Factor Proportions and the Structure of Commodity Trade," *The American Economic Review* 94, no. 1 (2004): 6–97.
4. Raymond Vernon, "International Investment and International Trade in the Product Cycle," *Quarterly Journal of Economics* 80 (May 1966): 190–207.
5. Michael Porter, *The Competitive Advantage of Nations* (New York: Free Press, 1990).
6. Mourad Dakhli and Dirk De Clercq, "Human Capital, Social Capital, and Innovation: A Multi-Country Study," *Entrepreneurship and Regional Development* 16, no. 2 (2004): 107–28.

7. Richard Nelson and Sidney Winter, *An Evolutionary Theory of Economic Change* (Cambridge, MA: Belknap Press, 1982).

8. Barry Jaruzelski and Kevin Dehoff, "Beyond Borders: The Global Innovation 1000," *Strategy+Business* 53 (2008): 52–67.

9. Porter (1990).

10. Clyde Prestowitz, *Trading Places* (New York: Basic Books, 1989); Lester Thurow, *Head to Head: The Coming Economic Battle among Japan, Europe, and America* (New York: William Morrow, 1992).

11. Warren Bilkey, "An Attempted Integration of the Literature on the Export Behavior of Firms," *Journal of International Business Studies* 9 (Summer 1978): 3–46; S. Tamer Cavusgil, "On the Internationalization Process of Firms," *European Research* 8, no. 6 (1980): 27–81; Jan Johanson and Jan-Erik Vahlne, "The Internationalization Process of the Firm—A Model of Knowledge Development and Increasing Foreign Commitments," *Journal of International Business Studies* 8 (Spring/Summer 1977): 2–32.

12. Ibid

13. G. Knight and S. T. Cavusgil, "The Born Global Firm: A Challenge to Traditional Internationalization Theory," in *Advances in International Marketing* 8, ed. S. T. Cavusgil and T. Madsen (Greenwich, CT: JAI Press, 1996): 11–26.

14. S. T. Cavusgil and Gary Knight, *Born Global Firms: A New International Enterprise,* New York: Business Expert Press, 2009; Gary Knight and S. T. Cavusgil, "Innovation, Organizational Capabilities, and the Born-Global Firm," *Journal of International Business Studies* 35, no. 2 (2004): 12–41; Benjamin Oviatt and Patricia McDougall, "Toward a Theory of International New Ventures," *Journal of International Business Studies* 25, no. 1 (1994): 4–64; Michael Rennie, "Born Global," *McKinsey Quarterly,* no. 4 (1993): 4–52.

15. UNCTAD, *World Investment Report,* United Nations, New York, 2008, retrieved from http://www.unctad.org.

16. Stephen Hymer, *The International Operations of National Firms* (Cambridge, MA: MIT Press, 1976).

17. Peter Buckley and Mark Casson, *The Future of the Multinational Enterprise* (London: MacMillan, 1976); John Dunning, "The Eclectic Paradigm of International Production: A Restatement and Some Possible Extensions," *Journal of International Business Studies* 19 (1988): 1–31.

18. Dunning (1988); John Dunning, *International Production and the Multinational Enterprise* (London: Allen and Unwin, 1981).

19. Bruce Kogut, "Joint Ventures: Theoretical and Empirical Perspectives," *Strategic Management Journal* 9 (1988): 319–332; P. Rajan Varadarajan and Margaret H. Cunningham, "Strategic Alliances: A Synthesis of Conceptual Foundations," *Journal of the Academy of Marketing Science* 23 (1995): 282–296.

20. James Lincoln, Christina Ahmadjian, and Eliot Mason, "Organizational Learning and Purchase-Supply Relations in Japan," *California Management Review* 40, no. 3 (1998): 244–264.

Dell's work-flow connection with Visa, a global financial services facilitator, and releases the order into Dell's production system. Tom's order is processed at the Dell notebook factory in Malaysia, where workers access the product's thirty key components from nearby suppliers. Shipping is handled via air transport. For example, Dell charters a China Airlines 747 that flies from Malaysia to Nashville, Tennessee, six days a week. Each jet carries 25,000 Dell notebooks that together weigh more than 100,000 kilograms, or 220,000 pounds. The total supply chain for Tom's computer, including multiple tiers of suppliers, encompasses about 400 companies in Asia, Europe, and the Americas.

FOCAL FIRMS IN INTERNATIONAL BUSINESS

Focal firms are the most prominent international players. Let's examine each in detail.

The Multinational Enterprise

An MNE is a large company with substantial resources that performs various business activities through a network of subsidiaries and affiliates located in multiple countries. Examples include well-known companies such as Nestlé, Sony, Unilever, Nokia, Ford, Barclays, ABB, and Shell Oil. MNEs are best known for their foreign direct investment (FDI) activities and derive much of their total sales and profits, often more than half, from international operations. Exhibit 3.1 displays a sample of MNEs and their diverse industries. Note that, due to the global financial crisis and worldwide recession, the market value of sectors in the exhibit has declined recently.

Some focal firms operate in the services sector, including HSBC in banking, CIGNA in insurance, Bouygues in construction, Accor in hospitality, Disney in entertainment, Nextel in telecommunications, and Best Buy in retailing. Although retailers are usually classified as intermediaries, some large ones such as IKEA, Walmart, and Gap are considered focal firms. Internet-mediated businesses like Netflix and Amazon that deliver knowledge-based offerings such as music, movies, and software online have joined the ranks of global focal firms.

In developing countries and centrally planned economies, some focal firms are partly or wholly owned by the government. Lenovo Group is China's leading computer maker. It owns the former PC business of IBM and is about 25 percent government-owned.

Small and Medium-Sized Enterprises

As defined in Canada and the United States, SMEs are manufacturers or service providers with fewer than 500 employees (fewer than 250 as defined in Europe). SMEs now make up the majority of companies active in international business. They are usually less bureaucratic, more adaptable, and more entrepreneurial than larger firms and are often the basis for innovation in national economies.

With limited financial and human resources, SMEs usually choose exporting as their main strategy for entering foreign markets. Thus, most leverage the services of intermediaries and facilitators to succeed abroad. Smaller firms also rely on information and communications technologies that allow them to identify global market niches and efficiently serve specialized buyer needs. As a result, they are gaining equal footing with large multinationals in marketing sophisticated products around the world.

Sector	2010 Market Value (US $ billions)	Percentage of World Total	Representative Firms
Financial Services	$3,554	17.3%	Capital One, Danske Bank, Mitsui Sumitomo Bank
Energy	2,436	11.9	Mobil, Total, China Oilfield Services
Industrials	2,265	11.0	Landstar Systems, Shenzhen Expressway, Haldex
Technology	2,226	10.8	Microsoft, Oracle, Hoya, Taiwan Semiconductor Manufacturing
Consumer Staples	2,213	10.7	Procter & Gamble, Unilever, China Mengniu Dairy, Honda
Consumer Discretionary	2,162	10.5	Coach, Adidas, Salomon, Matsushita Electric
Health Care	2,150	10.5	GlaxoSmithKline, Novartis, Baxter International
Materials	1,618	7.9	Dow Chemical, Alcan, Vitro SA
Communication Services	1,014	4.9	AT&T, China Mobile, Royal KPN
Utilities	898	4.3	Duke Energy, Empresa Nacional de Electricidad SA, Hong Kong and China Gas, Ltd.
TOTAL	**16,211**	**100.0**	

EXHIBIT 3.1 Typical Multinational Enterprises as Focal Firms (ranked by industry sector Size).
Source: Fortune, "Fortune Global 500", Industries, 2010, accessed at http://money.cnn.com/magazines/fortune/; FTSE, "FTSE Global Sector Index Series," accessed at http://www.ftse.com; MSCI, "MSCI Global Sector Indices", accessed at http://www.msci.com; S&P Global 1200, 2010, accessed at www.standardandpoors.com

Born Global Firms

Born global firms represent a relatively new breed of international SME—those that undertake early and substantial internationalization to a dozen or more countries within a few years of their founding. Some successful born globals grow large enough to become large multinational firms. For instance, just four years after its founding, QualComm began exporting to Europe and soon followed with market entry into Brazil, China, India, Indonesia, and Japan. Its founders were entrepreneurs who, from the beginning, made little distinction between domestic and foreign markets. Technological prowess and managerial vision were strong factors driving international success early after the firm's founding.[1]

INTERNATIONAL ENTRY STRATEGIES OF FOCAL FIRMS

One way to analyze focal firms in international business is in terms of the entry strategies they use to expand abroad. Both MNEs and SMEs often rely on contractual relationships such as franchising and licensing.

A Framework for Classifying International Entry Strategies

Exhibit 3.2 shows the array of foreign market entry modes that focal firms use and the foreign partners they seek. The first column lists three categories of international business transactions: (1) transactions that involve the trade of products, (2) transactions that involve contractual exchange of services or intangibles, and (3) transactions based on investing equity ownership in foreign-based enterprises.

The second column in Exhibit 3.2 identifies the types of focal firms engaged in international business. Some focal firms are manufacturers that produce tangible products to sell in foreign markets. Trading companies are brokers of goods and services. Service providers are firms in the services sector, such as insurance companies and hotel chains. The second column also identifies firms that license various types of intellectual property, including patents and know-how. A **licensor** is a firm that enters a contractual agreement with a foreign partner to allow the partner the right to use certain intellectual property for a specified period in exchange for royalties or other compensation. A **franchisor**, essentially a sophisticated licensor, is a firm that grants another the right to use an entire business system in exchange for fees, royalties, or other forms of compensation. **Turnkey contractors** are focal firms or a consortium of firms that plan, finance, organize, manage, and implement all phases of a construction, design, or engineering project and then hand it over to a foreign customer after training local personnel.

The third column in Exhibit 3.2 identifies the foreign market entry strategies that companies employ. When the nature of the business is dealing in intangibles, such as professional services, a focal firm such as a bank, ad agency, or market research firm may enter into agency relationships with a foreign partner. Licensing and franchising are common in the international transfer of intangibles. A franchisor makes a contract with a foreign franchisee; a supplier of expertise makes a contract with a foreign client, and so forth.

In undertaking international business, the focal firm has the option of serving customers either through foreign investment or by relying on the support of independent intermediaries located abroad. In the former case, the firm will set up *company-owned* manufacturing and distribution facilities abroad. The fourth column in Exhibit 3.2 identifies the location of major activities. For example, most exporters carry out major activities—manufacturing, marketing, and sales—in their home country; they

Nature of International Transaction	Types of Focal Firm	Foreign Market Entry Strategy	Location of Major Activities	Typical Foreign Partners
Trade of products	Small manufacturer	Exporting	Home country	Distributor, agent, or other independent representative
	Large manufacturer	Exporting	Mainly abroad	Company-owned office or subsidiary
	Manufacturer	Importing (e.g., sourcing)	Home	Independent supplier
	Importer	Importing	Home	Trader or manufacturer
	Trading company	Exporting and Importing	Home	Trader or manufacturer
Contractual exchange of services or intangibles	Service provider	Exporting	Usually abroad	Agent, branch, or subsidiary
	Supplier of expertise or technical assistance	Consulting services	Abroad (temporarily)	Client
	Licensor with patent	Licensing	Home	Licensee
	Licensor with know-how	Licensing (technology transfer)	Home	Licensee
	Franchisor	Franchising	Home	Franchisee
	Service contractor	Management/Marketing service contracting	Abroad	Business owner or sponsor
	Construction/engineering/ design/architectural firm	Turnkey contracting or build-own-transfer	Abroad (temporarily)	Project owner
	Manufacturer	Non-equity, project-based, partnerships	Home or abroad	Manufacturer
Equity ownership in foreign-based enterprises	MNE	FDI via greenfield investment	Abroad	None
	MNE	FDI via acquisition	Abroad	Acquired company
	MNE	Equity joint venture	Abroad	Local business partner(s)

EXHIBIT 3.2   International Business Transactions, Types of Focal Firms, and Foreign Market Entry Strategies.

produce goods at home and ship them to customers abroad. MNEs and other large firms, however, tend to carry out major activities in multiple countries; they produce goods and sell them to customers primarily located abroad.

The last column in Exhibit 3.2 identifies the nature of the foreign partner, to whom the focal company delegates significant activities including marketing, distribution, sales, and customer service. MNEs now tend to delegate certain noncore functions to outside vendors, a practice known as *outsourcing*. Nike maintains its design and marketing operations within the firm but outsources production to independent suppliers located abroad.

Entry Modes Other than Trade and Investment

Some focal firms expand into foreign markets by entering into contractual relationships, such as licensing and franchising, with foreign partners. Licensing allows companies to internationalize rapidly while remaining in their home market. For instance, Anheuser-Busch signed a licensing agreement with the Japanese beer brewer Kirin, under which Kirin produces and distributes Budweiser beer in Japan. The agreement has substantial potential, given Japan's $30 billion-a-year beer market.[2]

Like licensors, the franchisor remains in its home market and permits its foreign partners to carry out activities in *their* markets. The franchisor, such as Subway, Curves, or Pizza Hut, assists the franchisee in setting up its operation and then maintains ongoing control over aspects of the franchisee's business, such as operations, procurement, quality control, and marketing. The franchisee benefits by gaining access to a proven business plan and substantial expertise.

Turnkey contractors specialize in international construction, engineering, design, and architectural projects, typically for airports, hospitals, factories, power plants, oil refineries, campuses, and upgrades to public transportation such as bridges, roadways, and rail systems. In a typical turnkey contract, the contractor plans, finances, organizes, manages, and implements all phases of a construction project, providing hardware and know-how to produce what the project sponsor requires. Hardware includes buildings, equipment, and inventory that comprise the tangible aspects of the system. Know-how is the knowledge about technologies, operational expertise, and managerial skills that the contractor transfers to the customer during and after completing the project.[3]

An increasingly popular type of turnkey contract in the developing economies is the *build-own-transfer* venture. In this arrangement, the contractors acquire an ownership stake in the facility for a period of time until it is turned over to the client. The contractors also provide ongoing advice, training, and assistance in navigating regulatory requirements and obtaining needed approvals from government authorities. At some point after a successful period of operation, the contractors divest their interest in the project.[4]

An *international collaborative venture* is a cross-border business alliance in which partnering firms pool their resources to create a new venture, sharing the associated costs and risks. A middle ground between exporting and FDI, collaborative arrangements help the focal firm increase international business, compete more effectively with rivals, take advantage of complementary technologies and expertise, overcome trade barriers, connect with customers abroad, configure value chains more effectively, and generate economies of scale in production and marketing.

Joint ventures (JVs) and project-based, nonequity ventures are both examples of international collaborative ventures. A **joint venture partner** is a focal firm that creates and jointly owns a new legal entity through equity investment or pooling of assets. Partners form JVs to share costs and risks, gain access to needed resources, gain economies of scale, and pursue long-term strategic goals. For example, Hitachi formed a joint venture with MasterCard to promote a smart card system for banking and other applications. The Japanese electronics giant invested $2.4 million to take an 18 percent stake in the JV, established in San Francisco.[5]

Partners in a **project-based, nonequity venture** are focal firms that collaborate to undertake a given project with a relatively narrow scope and well-defined timetable, but without creating a new legal entity. In contrast to JVs, which involve equity investment by the parent companies, project-based partnerships are less formal, short-term, nonequity ventures. The partners pool their resources and expertise for a limited time to perform some mutually beneficial task, such as joint R&D or marketing, but do not form a new enterprise.[6]

DISTRIBUTION CHANNEL INTERMEDIARIES IN INTERNATIONAL BUSINESS

A worldwide survey by *McKinsey Quarterly* found that MNE executives are particularly concerned about the capabilities needed to manage global supply chains and distribution channels, as well as the recruitment and retention of skilled personnel in individual foreign markets.[7] These findings emphasize the importance of intermediaries in international business.

Intermediaries range from large international companies to small, highly specialized operations. Techdata (www.techdata.com) is a large distributor of laptops, peripherals, and other IT products that it buys from manufacturers and resells to thousands of retailers in 100 countries worldwide.

For most exporters, relying on an independent foreign distributor is a low-cost way to enter foreign markets. There are three major categories of intermediaries: (i) those based in the foreign target market, (ii) those based in the home country, and (iii) those that operate via the Internet. Let's examine each type.

Intermediaries Based in the Foreign Market

Most intermediaries are based in the exporter's target market. They provide a multitude of services, including conducting market research, appointing local agents or commission representatives, exhibiting products at trade shows, arranging local transportation for cargo, and clearing products through customs. Intermediaries also orchestrate local marketing activities, including product adaptation, advertising, selling, and after-sales service. Many finance sales and extend credit, facilitating prompt payment to the exporter. In short, intermediaries based in the foreign market can function like the exporter's local partner, handling all needed local business functions.

A **foreign distributor**, also called a *merchant distributor,* is a foreign market–based intermediary that works under contract for an exporter and takes title to and distributes the exporter's products in a national market or territory, often also performing marketing functions such as sales, promotion, and after-sales service. It also typically maintains substantial physical resources and provides financing, technical support, and after-sales service for the product, relieving the exporter of these functions abroad. For consumer goods, the distributor usually sells to retailers. For industrial goods, the distributor sells to other businesses and/or directly to end users.

An **agent** is an intermediary (often an individual or a small firm) that handles orders to buy and sell commodities, products, and services in international business transactions under contract and for a commission. Also known as a *broker*, an agent may act for either buyer or seller but does not assume title or ownership of the goods. Agents are common in the international trade of commodities, especially agricultural goods and base minerals. In the services sector, agents often transact sales of insurance and securities.

A **manufacturer's representative** is an intermediary contracted by the exporter to represent and sell its merchandise or services in a designated country or territory. Manufacturer's representatives in essence act as contracted salespersons, but usually with broad powers and autonomy. They do not take title to the goods they represent and are most often compensated by commission. Manufacturer's representatives do not maintain physical facilities, marketing, or customer support capabilities, so these functions must be handled primarily by the exporter.

In consumer markets, the foreign firm must get its products to end users through *retailers* located in the foreign market. A retailer represents the last link between distributors and retail consumers. Dealing directly with foreign-based retailers is efficient because it results in a much shorter distribution channel and reduced channel costs.

Intermediaries Based in the Home Country

Some intermediaries are domestically based. Wholesaler *importers* bring in products or commodities from foreign countries for sale in the home market, re-export, or use in the manufacture of finished products. Manufacturers also import a range of raw materials, parts, and components used in the production of higher value-added products. They may also import a complementary collection of products and services to supplement or augment their own product range.

For exporting firms that prefer to minimize the complexity of selling internationally, a **trading company** serves as an intermediary that engages in import and export of a variety of commodities and agricultural goods, products, and services. A trading company assumes the international marketing function on behalf of producers, especially those with limited international business experience. Large trading companies operate much like agents, coordinating sales of countless products in markets worldwide. Typically, they are high-volume, low-margin resellers compensated by profit margins added to what they sell.

Mitsubishi, Mitsui, Marubeni, Sumitomo, Sinochem, and Samsung are among the largest trading companies in the world. They tend to be high-volume, low-margin resellers dealing largely in commodities such as grains, minerals, and metals. Five of the top ten trading companies are based in Japan where they are known as *sogo shosha,* and have long played a critical role in external trade. Trading companies are also common in China, South Korea, India, and Europe.[8]

A domestically based intermediary is the **export management company (EMC)**, which acts as an export agent on behalf of a (usually inexperienced) client company. In return for a commission, an EMC finds export customers on behalf of the client firm, negotiates terms of sale, and arranges for international shipping. While typically much smaller than a trading company, some EMCs have well-established networks of foreign distributors in place that allow exported products immediate access to foreign markets. EMCs are often supply-driven, visiting the manufacturer's facilities regularly to learn about new products and even to develop foreign market strategies. But because of the indirect nature of the export sale, the manufacturer runs the risk of losing control over how its products are marketed abroad, with possible negative consequences for its international image.

Online Intermediaries

Some focal firms use the Internet to sell products directly to customers rather than going through traditional wholesale and retail channels. By eliminating traditional intermediaries, companies can sell their products more cheaply and faster. This benefits SMEs in particular because they usually lack the often substantial resources needed to undertake conventional international operations.

Countless online intermediaries broker transactions between buyers and sellers worldwide. Emergent technologies offer—and sometimes require—new roles that intermediaries have not taken previously. Many traditional retailers establish Web sites or link with online service providers to create an electronic presence. The electronic sites of retailers such as Tesco (www.tesco.com) and Walmart (www.walmart.com) complement existing physical distribution infrastructure and bring more customers into physical outlets.

FACILITATORS IN INTERNATIONAL BUSINESS

The third category of participant in international business is facilitators, independent individuals or firms that assist the internationalization and foreign operations of focal firms and make it possible for transactions to occur efficiently, smoothly, and in a timely manner. Facilitators include banks, international trade lawyers, freight forwarders, customs brokers, and consultants. Their number and role have grown due to the complexity of international business operations, intense competition, and technological advances. Facilitators provide many useful services, from conducting market research to identifying potential business partners and providing legal advice. They rely heavily on information technology and the Internet to carry out their facilitating activities.

An important facilitator of international trade is the **logistics service provider**, a transportation specialist that arranges for physical distribution and storage of products on behalf of focal firms, also controlling and managing information between the point-of-origin and the point-of-consumption.

Countless international manufacturers use *common carriers*, companies that own the ships, trucks, airplanes, and other transportation equipment they use to transport goods around the world. Common carriers play a vital role in international business and global trade. Most exporters use the services of freight forwarders because they are a critical facilitator in international business. Usually based in major port cities, freight forwarders arrange international shipments for the focal firm to a foreign entry port, and even to the buyer's location in the target foreign market. They are experts on transportation methods and documentation for international trade.

Governments typically charge tariffs and taxes and devise complex rules for the import of products into the countries they govern. **Customs brokers** (or *customs house brokers)* are specialist enterprises that arrange clearance of products through customs on behalf of importing firms. They are to importing what freight forwarders are to exporting. They prepare and process required documentation and get goods cleared through customs in the destination country. Usually the freight forwarder, based in the home country, works with a customs house broker based in the destination country in handling importing operations.

Banks are critical to international business, but are often reluctant to extend credit to SMEs, as these smaller firms usually lack substantial collateral and they experience a higher failure rate than large MNEs. In the United States, smaller firms can turn to the *Export Import Bank* (Ex-IM Bank; www.exim.gov), a federal agency that assists exporters in financing sales of their products and services in foreign markets. In other countries, particularly in the developing world, governments provide financing at favorable rates even to foreign firms, often through public development banks and agencies, to finance the construction of infrastructure projects such as dams and power plants. Governments in Australia, Britain, Canada, Ireland, France, and numerous other countries similarly provide financing to MNEs for the construction of factories and other large-scale operations in their countries.

Focal firms and other participants also use the services of *international trade lawyers* to help navigate international legal environments. The best lawyers are knowledgeable about their client's industry, the laws and regulations of target nations, and the most appropriate means for international activity in the legal/regulatory context.

Insurance companies provide coverage against commercial and political risks. Losses tend to occur more often in international business because of the wide range of natural and human-made circumstances to which the firm's products are exposed as they make their way through the value chain.

International business *consultants* advise internationalizing firms on various aspects of doing business abroad and alert them to foreign market opportunities. Consultants help companies improve their performance by analyzing existing business problems and helping management develop future plans. Particularly helpful are *tax accountants*, who can advise companies on minimizing tax obligations resulting from multicountry operations. *Market research firms* are a potential key resource for identifying and targeting foreign buyers. They possess or can gain access to information on markets, competitors, and the methods of international business.

GOVERNMENTS IN INTERNATIONAL BUSINESS

Governments exist at the local, provincial, national, and supranational levels to make and enforce laws and regulations and provide essential economic security by devising fiscal and monetary policies. Recently, many governments have developed new legislation aimed at protecting the natural environment. For example, the U.S. and European governments are cooperating to develop policies to cut carbon dioxide emissions. Multilateral environmental regulations are deemed necessary to address climate-related phenomena, which can lead to harmful cross-national events such as crop failures and business calamities.[9]

Increasingly, governments also regulate markets. During the recent global financial crisis, governments moved to stimulate national economies, through such programs as the Economic Stimulus Act in the United States, the European Union stimulus plan, and the Economic Stimulus Plan in China.[10] In some cases, important companies were nationalized. For example, the governments of Belgium, Luxembourg, and the Netherlands took control of Fortis, a large bank services company that faced financial ruin. In the United States, the U.S. Treasury took partial ownership of General Motors.

Central banks are the monetary authorities in each country that issue currency and regulate national money supplies. Australia, Canada, China, Indonesia, the United States, and numerous European countries cut bank interest rates and injected billions into national money supplies. The European Central Bank (www.ecb.int) devised new banking regulations with the goal of averting future crises.[11]

At the G-20 summit in London in 2009, heads of state announced a range of synchronized policy initiatives intended to revive the global economy, stimulate employment, reform national financial systems, and improve the International Monetary Fund and other global institutions.[12] Officials from various countries coordinated efforts to restore international growth by providing more credit and liquidity in world banking systems. Several governments advocated creating a new, global currency to replace the U.S. dollar as the favored currency in international business.[13]

Governments participate in international business by investing in other economies. The trend is best exemplified by the **sovereign wealth funds (SWFs)**, state-owned investment funds that undertake systematic, global investment activities to generate income or achieve policy objectives, such as reviving a collapsed economy.[14] While SWFs have been around for decades, their numbers increased dramatically in the 2000s. Many are based in oil-producing countries and originated from massive commodity sales.

Summary

International business transactions require the participation of numerous focal firms, intermediaries, facilitators, and governments. A **focal firm** is the initiator of an international business transaction that conceives, designs, and produces the offerings for customers worldwide. A **distribution channel intermediary** is a specialist firm that provides a variety of logistics and marketing services for focal firms as part of the international supply chain, both in the home country and abroad. A **facilitator** is a firm or individual with special expertise such as legal advice, banking, and customs clearance that assists focal firms in the performance of international business transactions.

Focal firms, intermediaries, and facilitators all make up participants in global value chains. The value chain is the complete business system of the focal firm, comprising all the focal firm's activities, including R&D, sourcing, production, marketing, and distribution. Channel intermediaries and facilitators support the focal firm by performing value-adding functions. In focal firms that export, most of the value chain is concentrated in the home country. In highly international firms, value-chain activities may be performed in various countries.

Focal firms include MNEs, large global corporations such as Sony and Ford. MNEs operate in multiple countries by setting up factories, marketing subsidiaries, and regional headquarters. SMEs, small and medium-sized enterprises, are now the majority of internationally active firms.

Focal firms include a **licensor**, a firm that enters a contractual agreement with a foreign partner that allows the latter the right to use certain intellectual property for a specified period in exchange for royalties or other compensation. A **franchisor** is a firm that grants another the right to use an entire business system in exchange for fees, royalties, or other forms of compensation. A **turnkey contractor** is a focal firm or a consortium of firms that plans, finances, organizes, manages, and implements all phases of a project and then hands it over to a foreign customer. A **joint venture partner** is a focal firm that creates and jointly owns a new legal entity through equity investment or pooling of assets. **Project-based, nonequity venture partners** are focal firms that collaborate through a project with a relatively narrow scope and a well-defined timetable, without creating a new legal entity.

Distribution channel intermediaries move products and services across national borders and eventually to end users. They perform key downstream functions in the target market on behalf of focal firms, including marketing. A **foreign distributor** is a foreign market-based intermediary that works under contract for an exporter and takes title to and distributes the exporter's products in a market abroad, often performing marketing functions such as sales and after-sales service. An **agent** is an intermediary that handles orders to buy and sell commodities, products, and services in international transactions for a commission. A **manufacturer's representative** is an intermediary contracted by the exporter to represent and sell its offerings in a designated country or territory.

Facilitators assist with international business transactions. A **logistics service provider** is a transportation specialist that arranges physical distribution and storage of products on behalf of focal firms, also controlling information between the point of origin and the point of consumption. A **freight forwarder** arranges international shipping on behalf of exporting firms, much like a travel agent for cargo. A **customs broker** is a specialist that arranges clearance of products through customs on behalf of importing firms. Other facilitators include *banks, lawyers, insurance companies, consultants*, and *market research firms*.

Governments make and enforce laws and regulations and provide essential economic security by devising fiscal and monetary policies. Among various important government entities are *central banks* and **sovereign wealth funds**.

Key Terms

agent *48*
born global firms *44*
customs brokers *50*
distribution channel intermediary *41*
export management company (EMC) *49*
facilitator *42*
focal firm *41*

foreign distributor *48*
franchisor *45*
freight forwarder *42*
government *42*
joint venture partner *47*
licensor *45*
logistics service provider *50*

manufacturer's representative *48*
project-based, nonequity venture *47*
sovereign wealth funds (SWFs) *52*
trading company *49*
turnkey contractors *45*

Endnotes

1. Farok Contractor, Chin-Chun Hsu, and Sumit Kundu, "Explaining Export Performance: A Comparative Study of International New Ventures in Indian and Taiwanese Software Industry," *Management International Review* 45, no. 3 (2005): 83-110.

2. Y. Ono, "Beer Venture of Anheuser, Kirin Goes Down Drain on Tepid Sales," *Wall Street Journal,* November 3, 1999, p. A23.

3. W. Alsakini, K. Wikstrom, and J. Kiiras, "Proactive Schedule Management of Industrial Turnkey Projects in Developing Countries," *International Journal of Project Management* 22, no. 1 (2004): 75-82; Christian Hicks and Tom McGovern, "Product Life Cycle Management in Engineer-to-Order Industries," *International Journal of Technology Management* 48, no. 2 (2009): 153-61.

4. Engineering News-Record, "The Top 225 International Contractors," August 18, 2008, p. 32.

5. "Hitachi Ltd.: Joint Venture to Promote Smart-Card Operating System," *Wall Street Journal*, November 26, 2005, p. A9.

6. D. Kealey, D. Protheroe, D. MacDonald, and T. Vulpe, "International Projects: Some Lessons on Avoiding Failure and Maximizing Success," *Performance Improvement* 45, no. 3 (2006): 38-47; H. Ren, B. Gray, K. Kim, "Performance of International Joint Ventures: What Factors Really Make a Difference and How?" *Journal of Management* 35, no. 3 (2009): 805-814.

7. "Managing Global Supply Chains," *McKinsey Quarterly*, July 2008, http://www.mckinsey quarterly.com.

8. S. Tamer Cavusgil, Lyn S. Amine, and Robert Weinstein, "Japanese Sogo Shosha in the U.S. Export Trading Companies," *Journal of the Academy of Marketing Science* 14, no. 3 (1986): 21–32.

9. Andrew Rettman, "EU Welcomes New U.S. CO^2-Reduction Plan," *Business Week*, April 2, 2009, http://www.businessweek.com.

10. Dave Shellock, "Signs of Deepening Recession Dent Confidence," *Financial Times*, February 14, 2009, p. 14; Gabriele Parussini, "World News: Euro-Zone Economic Outlook Darkens," *Wall Street Journal*, January 17, 2009, p. A7.

11. Chris Giles, "Big Ideas Fail to Mop up Europe's Current Mess," *Financial Times*, February 26, 2009, p. 2.

12. Stanley Reed, "G-20 Summit: Thorny Issues, a Soothing Outcome?" *Business Week*, 2009, http://www.businessweek.com.

13. Harvey Morris, "Dollar Reserve Reform Urged," *Financial Times*, March 27, 2009, p. 7.

14. "Sovereign-Wealth Funds," *Economist*, May 24, 2007, p. 54; "Capital Markets," *Economist*, January 17, 2008, p. 62; Nuno Fernandes and Arturo Bris, "Sovereign Wealth Revalued," *Financial Times*, February 12, 2009, http:// www.ft.com.

Culture and Ethics in International Business

LEARNING OBJECTIVES
In this chapter, you will learn about:

1. Culture and cross-cultural risk

2. Interpretations of culture

3. Overcoming cross-cultural risk: Managerial guidelines

4. Ethics in international business

5. Corporate social responsibility

6. A framework for making ethical decisions

CULTURE AND CROSS-CULTURAL RISK

Culture is the learned, shared, and enduring orientation patterns in a society. People demonstrate their culture through values, ideas, attitudes, and behaviors. In international business, we step into cultural environments characterized by unfamiliar languages and unique value systems, beliefs, behaviors, and norms. Often, these differences get in the way of straightforward communication, representing one of the four risks associated with international business that we introduced in Chapter 1. **Cross-cultural risk** is a situation or event in which a cultural misunderstanding puts some human value at stake.

Unlike political, legal, and economic systems, culture has proven difficult to identify and analyze, but its effects on international business are profound and broad. Its effect on value-chain activities, such as product and service design, marketing and sales, is substantial. For example, red is beautiful to the Russians but it symbolizes mourning in South Africa. Packaging products in groups of four or nine is considered bad luck in Japan. Items such as pens are universally acceptable business gifts, but chrysanthemums are associated with funerals in many countries.

Cross-cultural risk is exacerbated by **ethnocentric orientation**—the use of our own culture as the standard for judging others. Most of us are raised in a single culture; we have a tendency to view the world primarily from our own perspective. Ethnocentric tendencies are widespread and entail the belief that one's own race, religion, or ethnic group is somehow superior to others. **Polycentric orientation**, in contrast, refers to a host-country mind-set in which the manager develops a strong affinity for the country in which she or he conducts business. **Geocentric orientation** refers to a global mind-set in which the manager is able to understand a business or market without regard to country boundaries. Geocentric tendencies are like a cognitive orientation that combines an openness to, and awareness of, diversity across cultures.[1] Managers with a geocentric orientation make a deliberate effort to develop skills for successful social behavior with members of other cultures.[2] They adopt new ways of thinking, learn to analyze cultures, and avoid the temptation to judge different behavior as somehow inferior.[3]

Although many values are universal and globalization is encouraging cultural convergence, cultural differences remain a feature of international business. Managers should develop an appreciation and sensitivity for cultural differences. Those with cross-cultural savvy perform better in managing employees, marketing products, and interacting with customers and business partners. Companies have much to gain from bridging the cultural divide.

Key Concepts of Culture

American anthropologist Melville Herskovits defined culture as "the human made part of the environment."[4] Geert Hofstede, a well-known Dutch organizational anthropologist, views culture as a "collective mental programming" of people.[5] The "software of the mind," or how we think and reason, differentiates us from other groups. Such intangible orientations shape our behavior.

Some cultures are relatively complex. Some impose many norms, rules, and constraints on social behavior, while others impose very few. Some are more individualistic, while others are more collectivist. Culture captures how the members of the society live—for instance, how they feed, clothe, and shelter themselves. It also explains how they behave toward each other and in groups. Finally, it defines their beliefs and values and the way they perceive the meaning of life.

Now that we have an idea what culture is, let's also define what it is *not*. Culture is:

• *Not right or wrong.*   Culture is relative; there is no cultural absolute. People of different nationalities simply perceive the world differently. Each culture has its own notions of acceptable and unacceptable behavior.

• *Not about individual behavior.*   Culture is about groups. It refers to a collective phenomenon of shared values and meanings. Thus, while culture defines the collective behavior of each society, individuals often behave differently.

• *Not inherited.* Culture is derived from the social environment. People are not born with a shared set of values and attitudes. Children gradually acquire specific ways of thinking and behaving as they are raised in a society.

SOCIALIZATION AND ACCULTURATION   The process of learning the rules and behavioral patterns appropriate to one's society is called **socialization**. It is cultural learning and provides the means to acquire cultural understandings and orientations shared by a particular society. Socialization is a subtle process: We adapt our behavior unconsciously and unwittingly.

Acculturation is the process of adjusting and adapting to a culture *other than one's own*. People who live in other countries for extended periods, such as expatriate workers, usually experience acculturation.

THE MANY DIMENSIONS OF CULTURE   Anthropologists use the iceberg metaphor to understand the many dimensions of culture, some subtle and some not so subtle. Above the surface certain characteristics are visible, but below, unseen to the observer, is a massive base of assumptions, attitudes, and values that strongly influence decision making, relationships, conflict, and other dimensions of international business. While we are conditioned by our own cultural idiosyncrasies, we are usually unaware of the nine-tenths of our cultural makeup that exists below the surface. In fact, we are often not aware of our own culture unless we come in contact with another one.

NATIONAL, PROFESSIONAL, AND CORPORATE CULTURE   While cultural idiosyncrasies influence international business, we cannot attribute all difficulties to differences in national culture. Employees are socialized into three cultures: *national culture, professional culture*, and *corporate culture*.[6] Working effectively within these overlapping cultures is challenging. The influence of professional and corporate culture tends to grow as people are socialized into a profession and workplace.

Most companies have a distinctive set of norms, values, and modes of behavior that distinguish them from other organizations. Such differences are often as distinctive as national culture, so that two firms from the same country, such as conservative Lloyds of London and edgy Virgin Airways, can have vastly different organizational cultures. To what extent, then, is a particular behavior attributable to national culture? In global companies with a strong organizational culture, it is hard to determine where the corporate influence begins and the national influence ends. Thus, attributing all differences to national culture is simplistic.

Cultural Metaphors and Idioms

Scholars have offered several analytical approaches to gaining deeper insights into the role of culture in international business. Let's examine cultural metaphors and idioms.

Professor Martin Gannon offered a particularly insightful analysis of cultural orientations.[7] In his view, a **cultural metaphor** refers to a distinctive tradition or institution strongly associated with a particular society. It is a guide to deciphering people's attitudes, values, and behavior. For example, the Swedish *stuga* (cottage or summer home) is a cultural metaphor for Swedes' love of nature and desire for individualism through self-development. Other examples of cultural metaphors include the Japanese garden (tranquility), the Turkish coffeehouse (social interaction), the Israeli kibbutz (community), and the Spanish bullfight (ritual). The Brazilian concept of *jeito* or *jeitinho Brasileiro* refers to an ability to cope with the challenges of daily life through creative problem solving or manipulating the arduous bureaucracy of the country. In the Brazilian context, manipulation, smooth talking, and patronage are not necessarily viewed negatively, because individuals resort to these methods to conduct business.

An **idiom** is an expression whose symbolic meaning is different from its literal meaning. For example, "to roll out the red carpet" in English is to extravagantly welcome a guest—no red carpet is actually used. In Spanish, the idiom "*no está el horno para bolos*" literally means "the oven isn't ready for bread rolls." But the phrase is understood as "the time isn't right." In Japan, the phrase "the nail that sticks out gets hammered down" refers to the importance of group conformity. In the United States, the idiom "necessity is the mother of invention" relates to Americans' penchant for resourcefulness.

The Role of Culture in International Business

Effective handling of the cross-cultural interface is a critical source of a firm's competitive advantage. In addition to developing empathy and tolerance toward cultural differences, managers should acquire substantial factual knowledge about the beliefs and values of foreign counterparts. Cross-cultural proficiency is paramount in many managerial tasks, including:

- Developing products and services
- Preparing advertising and promotional materials
- Preparing for overseas trade fairs and exhibitions
- Screening and selecting foreign distributors and other partners
- Communicating and interacting with foreign business partners
- Negotiating and structuring international business ventures
- Interacting with current and potential customers from abroad

Consider how cross-cultural differences may complicate company activities.

Developing products and services.   Cultural differences in language, religion, lifestyle, and other factors typically drive firms to adapt their offerings abroad.

Organizational structure.   Depending on cultural norms, firms may be characterized by substantial bureaucracy, or a centralized or decentralized structure.

Teamwork.   Firms employ multinational teams to accomplish managerial goals, but may fall short if there is much cultural misunderstanding.

Pay-for-performance system.   Such systems vary, especially between Western firms and those in Asia.

Lifetime employment.   Internationally, Western managers often struggle to motivate employees who expect to remain employed despite the quality of their work.

Union–management relationships.   Union membership and the nature of relations with management vary greatly around the world.

Attitudes toward ambiguity.   If you're not comfortable working with minimum guidance or taking independent action, then you may not fit well into some cultures.

INTERPRETATIONS OF CULTURE

Culture has been the subject of study by anthropologists and other social scientists for centuries. Initially, let's examine the nature of context in national cultures.

Low- and High-Context Cultures

Renowned anthropologist Edward T. Hall made a distinction between cultures he characterized as "low context" and "high context."[8] **Low-context cultures** rely on elaborate verbal explanations, putting great emphasis on spoken words. As Exhibit 4.1 shows, the low-context countries tend to be in northern Europe and North America, which have long traditions of rhetoric, placing central importance on delivering verbal messages. Communication is direct and explicit, and meaning is straightforward. For example, in negotiations U.S. managers typically come to the point and stay focused on the objective. Low-context cultures tend to value expertise and performance. They conduct negotiations as efficiently as possible, and use specific, legalistic contracts to conclude agreements.

By contrast, **high-context cultures** such as those of Japan and China emphasize nonverbal messages and view communication as a means to promote smooth, harmonious relationships. They prefer an indirect and polite face-saving style that emphasizes a mutual sense of care and respect for others. This helps explain why Japanese people hesitate to say "no" when expressing disagreement. They are more likely to say "it is different," an ambiguous response. Negotiations tend to be slow and ritualistic, and agreement is founded on trust.

The notion of high- and low-context cultures plays a role even in communications between people who speak the same language. British managers sometimes complain that presentations by U.S. managers are too detailed. Everything is spelled out, even when meanings seem obvious.

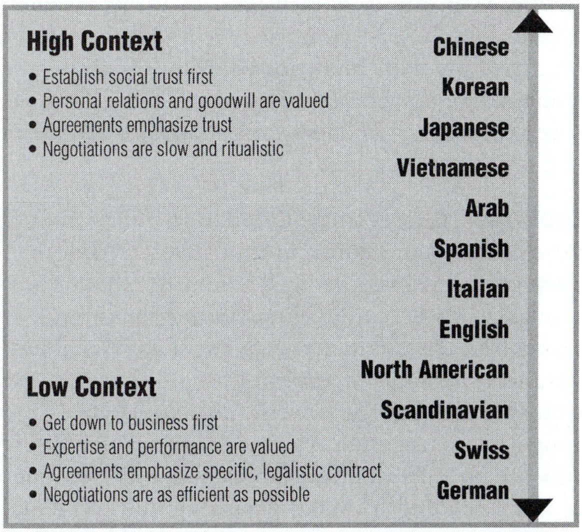

High Context
- Establish social trust first
- Personal relations and goodwill are valued
- Agreements emphasize trust
- Negotiations are slow and ritualistic

Chinese
Korean
Japanese
Vietnamese
Arab
Spanish
Italian
English
North American
Scandinavian
Swiss
German

Low Context
- Get down to business first
- Expertise and performance are valued
- Agreements emphasize specific, legalistic contract
- Negotiations are as efficient as possible

EXHIBIT 4.1   Hall's High- and Low-Context Typology of Cultures.   *Source:* From Edward T. Hall, *Beyond Culture,* copyright © 1976, 1981 by Edward T. Hall. Used by permission of Doubleday, a division of Random House, Inc. For on line information about other Random House, Inc. books and authors, see the Internet Web Site at http://www.randomhouse.com.

Hofstede's Research on National Culture

Dutch anthropologist Geert Hofstede collected data on the values and attitudes of 116,000 employees at IBM Corporation who represented a diverse set of nationality, age, and gender traits. Hofstede's investigation led him to delineate four independent dimensions of national culture, described next.[9]

INDIVIDUALISM VERSUS COLLECTIVISM   **Individualism versus collectivism** refers to whether a person functions primarily as an individual or as part of a group. In individualistic societies, ties among people are relatively loose, and each person tends to focus on his or her own self-interest. These societies prefer individualism over group conformity. Competition for resources is the norm, and those who compete best are rewarded financially. Australia, Canada, the United Kingdom, and the United States tend to be strongly individualistic societies. In collectivist societies, by contrast, ties among individuals are more important than individualism. Business is conducted in the context of a group in which others' views are strongly considered. The group is all-important, as life is fundamentally a cooperative experience. Conformity and compromise help maintain group harmony. China, Panama, and South Korea are examples of strongly collectivist societies.

POWER DISTANCE   **Power distance** describes how a society deals with the inequalities in power that exist among people. In societies with *low* power distance, the gaps between the powerful and weak are minimal. In Denmark and Sweden, for example, governments institute tax and social welfare systems that ensure their nationals are relatively equal in terms of income and power. The United States also scores relatively low on power distance. By contrast, societies where *high* power distance prevails are typically indifferent to inequalities and allow them to grow over time. There are substantial gaps between the powerful and the weak. Guatemala, Malaysia, the Philippines, and several Middle East countries are examples of countries that exhibit high power distance. In firms with high power distance, autocratic power is focused at the top and senior managers grant little autonomy to lower-level employees. In firms with low power distance, managers and subordinates are relatively equal and cooperate to achieve organizational goals.

UNCERTAINTY AVOIDANCE   **Uncertainty avoidance** refers to the extent to which people can tolerate risk and uncertainty in their lives. People in societies with *high* uncertainty avoidance create institutions that minimize risk and ensure financial security. Companies emphasize stable careers and produce many rules to regulate worker actions and minimize ambiguity. Managers may be slow to make decisions as they investigate the nature and potential outcomes of several options. Belgium, France, and Japan are countries that score high on uncertainty avoidance.

Societies scoring low on uncertainty avoidance socialize their members to accept and become accustomed to uncertainty. Managers are entrepreneurial and relatively comfortable taking risks, tending to make decisions quickly. People accept each day as it comes and take their jobs in stride because they are less concerned about ensuring their future. They tend to tolerate behavior and opinions different from their own because they do not feel threatened by them. India, Ireland, Jamaica, and the United States are leading examples of countries with low uncertainty avoidance.

MASCULINITY VERSUS FEMININITY   **Masculinity versus femininity** refers to a society's orientation based on traditional male and female values. Masculine cultures tend to value competitiveness, assertiveness, ambition, and the accumulation of wealth. They are characterized by men and women who are assertive and focused on career and earning money and may care little for others. Typical examples include Australia and Japan. The United States is a moderately masculine society. Hispanic cultures are relatively masculine and display a zest for action, daring, and competitiveness. In business, the masculinity dimension manifests as self-confidence, proactiveness, and leadership. Conversely, in feminine cultures, such as the Scandinavian countries, both men and women emphasize nurturing roles, interdependence among people, and caring for less fortunate people. Welfare systems are highly developed and education is subsidized.

THE FIFTH DIMENSION: LONG-TERM VERSUS SHORT-TERM ORIENTATION   The four dimensions of cultural orientation that Hofstede proposed have been widely accepted, but they do have limitations. First, the study is based on data collected around 1970. Much has changed since then, including successive phases of globalization, widespread exposure to transnational media, technological advances, and changes in the role of women in the workforce. The past few decades have seen much convergence in cultural values. Second, Hofstede's findings are based on the employees of a single company—IBM—in a single industry, making them difficult to generalize. Third, the data were collected using questionnaires, which are not effective for probing some of the deep issues that surround culture. Finally, Hofstede did not capture all potential dimensions of culture.

Partly in response to this last criticism, Hofstede added a fifth dimension to his framework: **long-term versus short-term orientation**.[10] This refers to the degree to which people and organizations defer gratification to achieve long-term success. That is, firms and people in cultures with a long-term orientation tend to take the long view to planning and living. They focus on years and decades. The long-term dimension is best illustrated by several Asian societies, including China, Japan, and Singapore. Values in such countries are partly based on the teachings of the Chinese philosopher Confucius (K'ung-Fu-tzu), who lived about 2,500 years ago. In addition to long-term orientation, Confucius advocated other values that are still the basis for much of Asian culture today. These include discipline, loyalty, hard work, regard for education, esteem for family, focus on group harmony, and control over one's desires. Scholars credit these values for the *East Asian miracle*, the remarkable economic growth and modernization of East Asian nations during the past several decades.[11] By contrast, the United States and most other Western countries emphasize a short-term orientation.

The Hofstede framework should be viewed as only a general guide, useful for a deeper understanding in cross-national interactions with business partners, customers, and value-chain members.

Subjective versus Objective Dimensions of Culture

National culture can be grouped into two broad dimensions: subjective and objective.

THE SUBJECTIVE DIMENSION   This dimension includes values and attitudes, manners and customs, deal versus relationship orientation, perceptions of time, perceptions of space, and religion.

Values represent a person's judgments about what is good or bad, acceptable or unacceptable, important or unimportant, and normal or abnormal.[12] Our values guide the development of our attitudes. *Attitudes* are similar to opinions but are often unconsciously held and may not have a rational basis. *Prejudices* are rigidly held attitudes, usually unfavorable and usually aimed at particular groups of people.[13] Typical values in North America, northern Europe, and Japan include hard work, punctuality, and the acquisition of wealth. People from such countries may misjudge those from developing economies who may not embrace such values.

Manners and *customs* are ways of behaving and conducting oneself in public and business situations, including eating habits, gift giving, and greetings. In much of the world, people greet by kissing each other on both cheeks. In Japan, bowing is the norm. Manners and customs are also manifested in the way men and women are treated. In Islamic cultures, women are highly protected. Some countries exhibit egalitarian, informal cultures, in which people are equal and work together cooperatively. In others, behavior is more formal, and influenced by status, hierarchy, and deference to power or elders.[14]

Cultures may have a deal or a relationship orientation. In *deal-oriented* cultures, managers focus on the task at hand and prefer getting down to business. They prefer to seal agreements with a legalistic contract and take an impersonal approach to settling disputes. Leading examples include Australia, northern Europe, and North America. In *relationship-oriented* cultures, managers put more value on affiliations with people. Emphasis is placed on building trust and rapport, and getting to know the other party. For the Chinese, Japanese, and many in Latin America, relationships are more important than the deal.[15] In China, the concept of *guanxi* (literally "connections" with family and between colleagues) is deeply rooted in ancient Confucian philosophy, which values social hierarchy and reciprocal obligations.

Cultures also vary regarding *perceptions of time*. Some societies are more oriented to the past, others to the present, and still others to the future. People in past-oriented cultures believe plans should be evaluated in terms of their fit with established traditions, customs, and wisdom. Innovation and change are justified in relation to their fit with past experience. Europeans are relatively past-oriented, favoring the conservation of traditions and historical precedents.

By contrast, young countries like Australia, Canada, and the United States are relatively focused on the present, with a **monochronic orientation** to time—a rigid perspective in which individuals emphasize schedules and time as a valuable resource not to be wasted. Punctuality is a virtue.

Some cultures have a **polychronic perspective** to time and favor doing many things at once. Managers put more value on relationships and spending time with people. They can change plans often and easily, and long delays are sometimes needed before taking action.

Cultures also differ in their perceptions of *physical space*. We have our own sense of personal space and feel uncomfortable if others violate it. For example, conversational distance is closer in Latin America than in northern Europe or the United States. Those who live in crowded Japan or Belgium have smaller personal space requirements than those in land-rich Russia or the United States. In Islamic countries, close proximity may be discouraged between a man and a woman who are not married.

Religion is one of the most important markers of culture. Religion is a system of common beliefs or attitudes concerning a being or a system of thought that people consider to be sacred, divine, or the highest truth. Religion also incorporates the moral codes, values, institutions, traditions, and rituals associated with this system. The major world religions, based on number of adherents, are Christianity (2 billion), Islam (1.5 billion), Hinduism (1 billion), Buddhism (1 billion), and Judaism (15 million).

Almost every culture is underpinned by religious beliefs, and most countries are home to several religions. Religion influences culture, and therefore business and consumer behavior, in various ways. For example, Protestantism emphasizes hard work, individual achievement, and a sense that people can control their environment. The Protestant work ethic provided some of the basis for the development of capitalism. In fundamentalist Muslim countries, Islam is the basis for government and legal systems as well as social and cultural order. People raised in Islamic cultures perceive God's will as the source of all outcomes. Islam's holy book, the *Qur'an*, prohibits drinking alcohol, gambling, usury, and immodest exposure.

OBJECTIVE DIMENSION   The *objective dimension* of culture includes material productions, such as the tools, architecture, and infrastructure unique to a society. *Material productions* are artifacts, objects, and technological systems that people construct to accomplish objectives, as well as to communicate and conduct exchanges within and between societies. The most important technology-based material productions are the infrastructures that supply energy, transportation, and communications. Creative expressions of culture include arts, folklore, music, dance, theater, and high cuisine. Food is among the most interesting cultural markers. In Japan, pizza is often topped with fish and seaweed. In France, it often comes with a variety of cheeses. In Mexico, people top their pizza with salsa.

Language

Language is another key attribute of culture. At present the world has nearly 7,000 active languages, including more than 2,000 each in Africa and Asia. But most languages have only a few thousand speakers.[16] Linguistic proficiency is useful in international business because it facilitates cross-cultural understanding. Learning one or more of the frequently spoken languages can greatly enhance an international business career.

Language has both verbal and nonverbal characteristics. Much language is unspoken and entails facial expressions and gestures.[17] In fact, most verbal messages are accompanied by nonverbal ones. In this and other ways, language is extremely subtle. National languages, dialects, and translation have a tendency to complicate straightforward communication. Ignorance can be embarrassing.

Business jargon unique to a culture can also impede communication. Examples of English jargon that puzzle non-native speakers include: "the bottom line," "wiggle room," "bang for the buck," "golden parachute," and "that dog won't hunt." Imagine the difficulty of translating such phrases!

OVERCOMING CROSS-CULTURAL RISK: MANAGERIAL GUIDELINES

Seasoned managers can achieve effective cross-cultural interaction by keeping an open mind, being inquisitive, and not rushing to conclusions about others' behaviors. Even experienced managers benefit from cultural training that emphasizes observational skills and human relations techniques. Let's review three guidelines managers can follow to prepare for successful cross-cultural encounters.

Guideline 1: Acquire factual and interpretive knowledge about the other culture, and try to speak the language.   Successful managers study the political and economic background of target countries—their history, current national affairs, and perceptions about other cultures—as well as their values, attitudes, and lifestyles. Sincere interest in the target culture helps establish trust and respect, laying the foundation for open and productive relationships. Even modest attempts to speak the local language are welcome. Higher levels of language proficiency pave the way for acquiring competitive advantages.

Guideline 2: Avoid cultural bias.   Problems arise when ethnocentric managers assume that foreigners think and behave just like the folks back home. People have a natural inclination to view their own culture as the norm; we call this the **self-reference criterion**—the tendency to view other cultures through our own lens. It is easy, but unwise, to be offended when a foreign counterpart does not appreciate our food, history, entertainment, or everyday traditions. In this way, cultural bias can be a significant barrier to successful interpersonal communication. Understanding the self-reference criterion is a critical first step to avoiding cultural bias and ethnocentric reactions.

What should you do when confronted with an awkward or uncomfortable situation in a cross-cultural interaction? **Critical incident analysis (CIA)** is a method that managers use to analyze awkward situations in cross-cultural encounters. CIA encourages a more effective approach to cultural differences by helping managers develop objectivity and empathy for other points of view. CIA involves the following steps:

- Identify the situations where you need to be culturally aware to interact effectively with people from another culture. These may include socializing, working in groups, negotiating, and reaching agreement.
- When confronted with seemingly strange behavior, discipline yourself to avoid making hasty judgments. Instead, try to view the situation or the problem in terms of the unfamiliar culture. Make observations and gather objective information from native citizens or secondary sources. In this way, you can isolate the self-reference criterion that led to your possibly inaccurate conclusion.
- Learn to make a variety of interpretations of others' behavior, to select the most likely one in the cultural context, and only then to formulate your own response. In this way, you can avoid the self-reference criterion and likely make a better decision.
- Learn from this process and continuously improve.

Guideline 3: Develop cross-cultural skills.   Each culture has its own ways of conducting business transactions, negotiations, and dispute resolution. In international business, therefore, you are exposed to high levels of ambiguity regarding concepts and relationships that can be understood in a variety of ways.[18] To be successful, you should make the required investment in your professional development and strive for cross-cultural proficiency, characterized by these four personality traits:

- ***Tolerance for ambiguity***—the ability to accept uncertainty and apparent lack of clarity in the thinking and actions of others.

- *Perceptiveness*—the ability to closely observe and appreciate subtle information in the speech and behavior of others.
- *Appreciation for personal relationships*—the ability to recognize the importance of interpersonal relationships, often much more important than achieving one-time goals or winning arguments.
- *Flexibility and adaptability*—the ability to be creative in devising innovative solutions, to be open-minded about outcomes, and to show grace under pressure.

Successful multinational firms seek to instill a geocentric cultural mind-set in their employees and use a geocentric staffing policy to hire the best people for each position, regardless of national origin. Over time, such firms develop a core group of managers who are comfortable in any cultural context.

ETHICS IN INTERNATIONAL BUSINESS

Ethics are moral principles and values that govern the behavior of people, firms, and governments, regarding right and wrong.[19] **Corruption** is the abuse of power to achieve illegitimate personal gain. More than 30 percent of senior business executives believe corruption is a major or severe concern in their activities worldwide.[20]

Ethics and appropriate behavior transcend all international business activities and should figure prominently in management decisions about financial performance and competitive advantage. However, corruption and bribes are commonplace in many countries and legal in some. Bribery frequently takes the form of *grease payments*, relatively small inducements intended to expedite decisions and transactions or otherwise gain favors.

Various organizations assess the level of corruption worldwide. The most well-known is Transparency International (www.transparency.org) and its Corruption Perceptions Index, which measures managers' perceptions of bribery, embezzlement, and other illicit behavior worldwide. Exhibit 4.2 lists a sample of countries and their perceived levels of corruption. Countries with the lowest scores have the least corruption, such as Canada and Denmark. Countries with substantial corruption include many nations in Africa and the former Soviet Union states.

Because standards vary around the world, ethics are a complex issue in international business. Simply obeying the law is usually insufficient to guard against violating fundamental standards of ethical behavior. The most advanced firms proactively emphasize not just ethical behavior, but also corporate social responsibility and sustainability. **Corporate social responsibility (CSR)** is the practice of operating a business in a manner that meets or exceeds the ethical, legal, and commercial expectations of all stakeholders, including customers, shareholders, employees, and the communities where the firm does business. **Sustainability** means meeting humanity's needs without harming future generations.

Global sourcing is one international activity that raises public debate about protecting the environment and ensuring human rights. For example, some companies operate factories abroad that pollute the air, water, or land, or sweatshops that employ workers, sometimes even children, in harsh conditions or for long hours at very low wages.[21] Some firms engage in deceptive marketing practices to induce people to buy their products or offer defective or harmful products or packaging. For example,

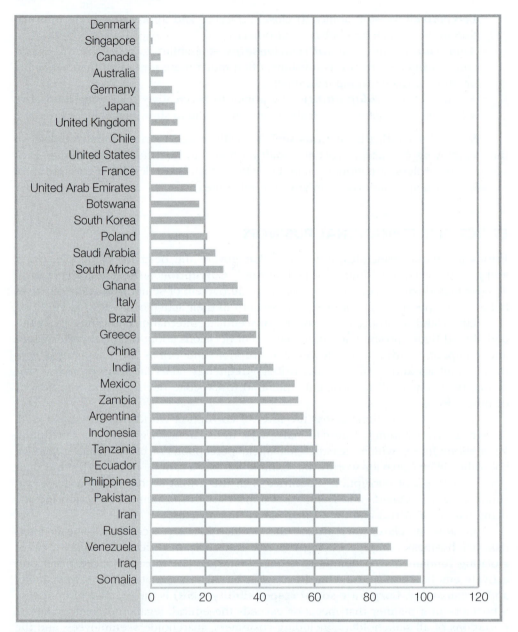

EXHIBIT 4.2 Corruption Perceptions Index.   *Sources: Global Integrity Report 2011*, at www.globalintegrity
.org; Maplecroft, *Political Risk Atlas 2011*, at http://maplecroft.com; Transparency International (2011), at www
.transparency.org; World Audit, Corruption Rank 2010, at www.worldaudit.org.

Note: Countries with the lowest scores have the lowest levels of corruption.

millions of electronic products, from cell phones to computers, are discarded every year, not because they are broken but because newer versions become available. Products that could be recycled instead end up in landfills.

Theft of intellectual property represents another ethical violation, one especially common in international business. **Intellectual property** refers to ideas or works created by individuals or firms and includes a variety of proprietary, intangible assets: discoveries and inventions; artistic, musical, and literary works; and words, phrases, symbols, and designs. In Russia, for example, where laws protecting intellectual property are limited and enforcement is weak, software and movies produced by such firms as Microsoft and Disney often fall prey to *counterfeiting*; the assets are reproduced without compensating those who originally created them, thereby eroding firms' competitive advantages and brand equity.

Trademarks, copyrights, and patents are examples of **intellectual property rights**, legal claims through which proprietary assets are protected from unauthorized use by other parties. *Trademarks* are distinctive signs and indicators that firms use to identify their products and services. *Copyrights* grant protections to the creators of art, music, books, software, movies, and TV shows. *Patents* confer the exclusive right to manufacture, use, and sell products or processes. Laws enacted in one country are enforceable only in that country and confer no protection abroad.[22]

The Value of Ethical Behavior

Behaving ethically is important for several reasons. First, it is simply the right thing to do. Second, it is often prescribed within laws and regulations. Violating laws and regulations has obvious legal consequences. Third, ethical behavior is demanded by customers, governments, and the news media. Finally, ethical behavior is good business, leading to enhanced corporate image and selling prospects. The firm with a reputation for high ethical standards gains advantages in partnering, hiring and motivating employees, and dealing with foreign governments. The major challenge is that ethical standards vary greatly around the world.

Variation in Ethical Standards among Countries

Appropriate behavior in one culture may be viewed as unethical behavior elsewhere.[23] In the United States, some CEOs receive compensation hundreds of times greater than that of their most junior employees, a practice widely considered unacceptable. Ethical standards also change over time. Although slavery is no longer tolerated, some multinational firms today tolerate working conditions that are akin to it.

Scholars and managers examine ethics from two different perspectives.[24] **Relativism** is the belief that ethical truths are not absolute but differ from group to group; according to this perspective, a good rule is, "When in Rome, do as the Romans do." Thus, a Japanese multinational firm adhering to the position that bribery is wrong might nevertheless pay bribes in countries where the practice is customary and culturally acceptable.

By contrast, **normativism** is a belief that ethical behavioral standards are universal, and firms and individuals should seek to uphold them consistently around the world. According to this view, managers of the Japanese multinational firm who believe bribery is wrong will enforce this standard everywhere in the world.

Most firms apply a combination of relativism and normativism abroad. However, this approach puts them at risk of violating norms that are increasingly universal. In countries with questionable ethical norms, it is usually best to maintain ethical standards *superior* to what is required by local laws and values. This strategy helps garner goodwill in the local market and averts potentially damaging publicity in the firm's other markets.

An Ethical Dilemma

Deciding what is right and wrong is not always clear. Ethical problems arise when requirements are ambiguous, inconsistent, or based on multiple legal or cultural norms. An *ethical dilemma* is a predicament with major conflicts among different interests and in which determining the most appropriate course is confounded by a set of solutions that are equally justifiable, and often equally imperfect. Possible actions may be mutually exclusive: choosing one automatically eliminates the other(s).[25]

Imagine you are a manager and visit a factory owned by an affiliate in Colombia, only to discover the use of child labor in the plant. You are told that without their children's income, families might go hungry and that the children will likely turn to other income sources, including prostitution or street crime. What should you do? Do you make a fuss about the immorality of child labor, or do you look the other way?

This example is typical of the type of ethical dilemmas that employees often encounter in international business. Managers embedded in host countries may be most exposed because they are caught between the ethical norms of their home country and those of the foreign country.

Linking Ethics, Corruption, and Responsible Behavior

In a world of ethical challenges, how should managers and companies respond? After complying with local law, management should ensure that company activities follow high ethical standards. As they expand abroad, most firms believe it is sufficient to comply with laws, regulations, and basic ethical standards. However, in addition, progressive MNEs now emphasize socially responsible behavior. Let's examine this notion in more detail.

CORPORATE SOCIAL RESPONSIBILITY

Adhering to principles of CSR implies a *proactive* approach to ethical behavior in which firms seek not only to maximize profits, but also to benefit society and the environment. Core CSR values include avoiding human rights abuses, upholding the right to join or form labor unions, eliminating child and compulsory labor, avoiding workplace discrimination, protecting the natural environment, guarding against corruption, and undertaking philanthropic efforts.[26] CSR is about business giving back to society.

Motorola (www.motorola.com) has delivered more than 16 million low-cost mobile phones to people in fifty developing countries. It developed a mobile phone system for disease management in Africa, through which field health workers file patient reports and check drug supplies. Cellular connectivity helps professionals in poor areas deal more effectively with disease outbreaks, medicine shortages, and health maintenance.[27]

Exhibit 4.3 summarizes additional CSR initiatives undertaken by firms worldwide.

Company	Industry	Sample Accomplishments
ABN AMRO (Netherlands)	Financial services	Finances various socially responsible projects, including biomass fuels and micro enterprises. Involved in carbon-emissions trading.
Dell (United States)	Computers	Accepts old computers from customers for recycling, free of charge.
GlaxoSmithKline (Britain)	Pharmaceuticals	Devotes substantial R&D to poor-country ailments, such as malaria and tuberculosis. Was first to offer AIDS medication at cost.
Marks & Spencer (Britain)	Retailing	Sources locally in order to cut fuel use and transportation costs. Provides good wages and benefits to retain staff.
Nokia (Finland)	Telecommunications	Makes telephones for low-income consumers. Has been a leader in environmental practices, such as phasing out toxic materials.
Norsk Hydro (Norway)	Oil and gas	Cut greenhouse gas emissions by 32 percent. Consistently measures the social and environmental impact of its projects.
Philips Electronics (Netherlands)	Consumer electronics	Top innovator of energy-saving appliances and lighting products, as well as medical devices for developing economies.
Scottish & Southern (Scotland)	Utilities	Proactively discloses the environmental risk, including air pollution and climate change, posed by its services.
Toyota (Japan)	Automobiles	The world leader in developing efficient gas-electric vehicles, such as the top-selling Prius.

EXHIBIT 4.3   Corporate Social Responsibility: A Sampling of MNE Accomplishments.   *Source:* Pete Engardio, "Beyond the Green Corporation," *Business Week*, January 29, 2007, pp. 50–64.

The Value of CSR

Like ethical behavior, CSR is simply the right thing to do. Second, it helps the firm recruit and retain loyal and high-quality employees. Third, strong CSR can help the firm differentiate itself in the marketplace and enhance its brand. Fourth, management can cut business costs through such CSR steps as reducing and recycling operational waste, and minimizing packaging and energy consumption. Finally, CSR helps the firm avoid increased taxation, regulation, and other legal actions by government authorities. In 2009, Denmark enacted a law that requires companies to undertake CSR activities and report on them in their financial reports.

Nongovernmental organizations (NGOs) are undertaking international CSR initiatives, often in conjunction with multinational firms. For example, *Médecins Sans Frontières* (Doctors Without Borders) and the Bangladesh Rural Advancement Committee work to reduce global poverty and frequently partner with private companies to provide vital products and services.[28]

The Role of Sustainability in International Operations

Sustainability is an ideal endorsed by economic development experts, environmentalists, human rights activists, and, increasingly, businesses. A sustainable business simultaneously pursues three types of interests:[29]

1. *Economic interests* refer to the firm's economic impact on the localities where it does business and on such local concerns as job creation, wages, tax flows, underserved communities, public works, and other areas where the firm can contribute positively to local economic interests.

2. *Social interests* refer to how well the firm performs relative to work conditions, including benefits and training and education opportunities, and diversity in hiring. It avoids using sweatshops, child labor, and other practices that harm workers.

3. *Environmental interests* describe the firm's contribution to reducing the effect of its value-chain activities on the natural environment. The sustainable firm minimizes pollutants, designs production lines to use water and energy efficiently, and constantly seeks ways to reduce and recycle waste. Many firms establish a green purchasing policy, through which they source inputs that support environmental interests.

Like CSR, sustainable practices pay off in various ways, such as by promoting a strong corporate reputation, the ability to hire and retain superior employees, cost savings from more efficient production, and better relations with partners and governments. Ethical, responsible, and sustainable practices are not just added costs but opportunities for improving society, the environment, and company performance.

Corporate Governance and Its Implications for Managers

The level of managers' commitment to appropriate behavior is critical to fostering ethics and CSR in international operations.[30] **Corporate governance** is the system of procedures and processes by which corporations are managed, directed, and controlled. It provides the means through which firms undertake ethical behaviors, CSR, and sustainability. Let's examine how.

Scholars have devised five standards that managers can use to examine ethical dilemmas.[31]

- According to the *utilitarian approach*, the best ethical action is the one that provides the most good or does the least harm to customers, employees, shareholders, the community, and the natural environment.
- In the *rights approach*, the decision maker chooses the action that best protects and respects everyone's moral rights to live life as they desire, to be free from harm, to pursue happiness, and so forth.
- The *fairness approach* suggests that employees should be treated equally and fairly, with a fair wage and a decent standard of living. Colleagues and customers should be treated as we would like to be treated.
- The *common good approach* suggests that actions should be based on the welfare of the entire community or nation. The basis for decision making should be respect and compassion for all, especially the vulnerable.

- The *virtue approach* argues that ethical actions should be consistent with truth, courage, compassion, generosity, tolerance, love, integrity, and prudence.

These five approaches occasionally conflict with each other, and not everyone agrees on which standard to use in all situations. Nevertheless, each standard is useful because it helps guide ethical behavior in almost any predicament. More often than not, the five lead to similar solutions.

How should you decide what constitutes ethical behavior? First, be alert to the ethical challenges that may confront the firm. Management should continually scan the business environment and potential partners for the possibility of ethical abuses. Areas that merit particular attention are labor conditions, partner firms, customer relations, accounting and other business practices, and the natural environment, as well as potential or existing value-chain activities including sourcing, production, marketing, and distribution.

The next step is to systematically explore the ethical aspects of each decision the firm may make about both current and potential activities. The firm should develop a cogent and practicable *code of ethics*, a formal statement that describes what management expects of employees in the face of ethical challenges.[32] In international business, the code should be designed to function like a moral compass for the firm's operations worldwide. Like a mission statement, it should guide employee behavior in all situations, so the firm avoids behaviors that compromise corporate ethical standards wherever it does business. The code is not a cure-all, but it can help employees deal with ethical dilemmas by prescribing or limiting specific activities.

To further clarify the process of scanning for and analyzing potential ethical concerns, we provide a framework for making ethical decisions below.

A FRAMEWORK FOR MAKING ETHICAL DECISIONS

Scholars suggest that managers follow a systematic approach to resolving ethical dilemmas. With practice, it can become second nature. Here is a four-step framework for arriving at ethical decisions:[33]

1. *Recognize an Ethical Problem:*   The first step is to acknowledge the presence of an ethical problem. Ask questions such as: Is there something wrong? Is an ethical dilemma present? Is there a situation that might harm personnel, customers, the community, or the nation? In international business, recognizing the issue can be tricky because subtleties of the situation may be outside your knowledge or experience. Often, it is best to rely on your instincts: If some action feels wrong, it probably is.

2. *Get the Facts:*   Determine the nature and dimensions of the situation. Have all the relevant persons and groups been consulted? What individuals or groups have a stake in the outcome? How much weight should be given to the interests of each? Do some parties have a greater stake because they are disadvantaged or have a special need?

3. *Evaluate Alternative Courses of Action:*   Identify potential courses of action and evaluate each. Initially, review any proposed action to ensure it is legal. If it violates host

(continued)

or home country laws or international treaties, it should be rejected. Next, review any proposed action to ensure it is acceptable according to company policy, the firm's code of conduct, and/or its code of ethics. If discrepancies are found, the action should be rejected. Finally, evaluate each proposed action to assess its consistency with accepted ethical standards, using the approaches described earlier:

- Utilitarian—Which action results in the most good and least harm?
- Rights—Which action respects the rights of everyone involved?
- Fairness—Which action treats people most fairly?
- Common good—Which action contributes most to the overall quality of life of the people affected?
- Virtue—Which action embodies the character strengths you value?

The goal is to arrive at the best decision or most appropriate course of action. It may be useful to enlist the aid of local colleagues familiar with the situation, to obtain insights and help generate options. Assess the consequences of each action from the perspective of all parties who will be affected by it. Test any decision by asking yourself whether you would feel comfortable explaining it to your mother, a colleague you respect, or a valued mentor. If you had to defend the decision on television, would you be comfortable doing so?

4. *Implement and Evaluate Your Decision:* Implement your decision. Then evaluate it to see how effective it was. How did it turn out? If you had to do it again, would you do anything differently?

Embracing CSR and Sustainability

In a world increasingly sensitive to social and environmental issues, forward-thinking managers undertake the following types of activities:

- Develop closer relations with foreign stakeholders to better understand their needs and jointly work toward solutions.
- Build internal and external capabilities to enhance the firm's contribution to the local community and global environment.
- Ensure diverse voices are heard by creating organizational structures that employ managers and workers from around the world.
- Develop global CSR standards and objectives that are communicated and implemented throughout the firm's operations worldwide.
- Train managers in global CSR principles and integrate these into managerial responsibilities.

Ethical behavior and CSR must become a key part of managers' day-to-day pursuits. Most executives agree that generating high returns for investors should be accompanied by a focus on providing good jobs, supporting social causes in local communities, and going beyond legal requirements to minimize pollution and other negative effects of business.

Summary

Culture is the learned, shared, and enduring orientations of a society, expressed in values, ideas, attitudes, behaviors, and other meaningful symbols and artifacts. **Cross-cultural risk** arises from a situation or event in which a cultural misunderstanding puts some human value at stake. **Ethnocentric orientation** refers to using one's own culture as the standard for judging other cultures. **Polycentric orientation** refers to a host country mind-set that gives the manager greater affinity to the country in which she or he conducts business. **Geocentric orientation** refers to a global mind-set with which the manager is able to understand a business or market without regard to country boundaries.

Culture can be interpreted through metaphors, distinctive traditions or institutions that serve as a guide or map for deciphering attitudes, values, and behavior. **Low-context cultures** rely on elaborated verbal explanations, putting much emphasis on spoken words. **High-context cultures** emphasize nonverbal communications and a holistic approach to communication that promotes harmonious relationships. Hofstede's typology of cultural dimensions consists of **individualism versus collectivism, power distance, uncertainty avoidance, masculinity versus femininity,** and **long-term versus short-term orientation.**

Managerial guidelines include the need to acquire factual and interpretive knowledge about the other culture, and to try to speak the language. Managers should avoid cultural bias and engage in **critical incident analysis** to avoid the **self-reference criterion.** Critical incident analysis requires being culturally aware, not making value judgments, and selecting the most likely interpretation of foreign behaviors. Experienced managers develop cross-cultural skills.

Ethics are the moral principles and values that govern the behavior of people, firms, and governments. Ethical standards vary around the world. **Relativism** is the belief that ethical truths are not absolute but differ from group to group. **Normativism** holds that ethical standards are universal, and firms and individuals should seek to uphold them consistently around the world. An *ethical dilemma* is a predicament with major conflicts among different interests. Maintaining **corporate social responsibility (CSR)** means operating a business in a manner that meets or exceeds the ethical, legal, commercial, and public expectations of stakeholders. **Sustainability** refers to meeting humanity's needs without harming future generations.

In addition to complying with laws, regulations, and basic ethical standards, prudent MNEs emphasize corporate social responsibility in their activities to motivate employees and develop superior strategy. Sustainable businesses simultaneously pursue three types of interests: economic, social, and environmental. They maximize the use of recycled materials and environmentally friendly energy. They provide health insurance and training and care for employees. They choose suppliers that follow high social and environmental standards.

Scholars have devised five standards to examine ethical dilemmas, based on utilitarianism, rights, fairness, common good, and virtue. Senior managers should develop a *code of ethics* that describes what the firm expects of its employees when facing ethical dilemmas. A four-step framework is recommended for making ethical decisions. First, recognize an ethical problem. Then, get the facts, evaluate alternative courses of action, and implement and evaluate the decision made.

Key Terms

acculturation *57*
corporate governance *70*
corporate social
   responsibility (CSR) *65*
corruption *65*
critical incident analysis
   (CIA) *64*
cross-cultural risk *55*
cultural metaphor *57*
culture *73*
ethics *65*
ethnocentric
   orientation *56*

geocentric
   orientation *56*
high-context
   cultures *59*
idiom *58*
individualism versus
   collectivism *60*
intellectual property
   rights *67*
intellectual property *67*
long-term versus short-term
   orientation *61*
low-context cultures *59*

masculinity versus
   femininity *61*
monochronic orientation *62*
normativism *67*
polycentric orientation *56*
polychronic perspective *62*
power distance *60*
relativism *67*
self-reference criterion *64*
socialization *57*
sustainability *65*
uncertainty avoidance *60*

Endnotes

1. V. Govindarajan and A. Gupta, *The Quest for Global Dominance* (San Francisco: Jossey-Bass/Wiley, 2001).

2. Robert Boyd and Peter Richerson, *Culture and Evolutionary Process* (Chicago: University of Chicago Press, 1985).

3. Harry C. Triandis, *Culture and Social Behavior* (New York: McGraw-Hill, 1994).

4. M. J. Herskovits, *Cultural Anthropology* (New York: Knopf, 1955).

5. Geert Hofstede, *Culture's Consequences* (Beverly Hills, CA: Sage, 1980).

6. Vern Terpstra and Kenneth David, *The Cultural Environment of International Business,* 3rd ed. (Cincinnati, OH: Southwestern, 1991).

7. Martin Gannon and Associates, *Understanding Global Cultures: Metaphorical Journeys through 17 Countries* (Thousand Oaks, CA: Sage, 1994).

8. Edward T. Hall, *Beyond Culture* (New York: Anchor, 1976).

9. Hofstede, 1980.

10. Hofstede, 1980.

11. Richard Priem, Leonard Love, and Margaret Shaffer, "Industrialization and Values Evolution: The Case of Hong Kong and Guangzhou, China," *Asia Pacific Journal of Management* 17, no. 3 (2000): 473–82.

12. F. Kluckhohn and F. Strodbeck, *Variations in Value Orientations* (Evanston, IL: Row Peterson, 1961).

13. Alice Eagly and Shelly Chaiken, *The Psychology of Attitudes* (New York: Harcourt Brace Jovanovich, 1993).

14. Joyce Osland, Silvio De Franco, and Asbjorn Osland, "Organizational Implications of Latin American Culture: Lessons for the Expatriate Manager," *Journal of Management Inquiry* 8, no. 2 (1999): 219–38.

15. Roger Axtell, *The DO's and TABOO's of International Trade* (New York: Wiley, 1994).

16. "Babel Runs Backwards," *Economist,* January 1, 2005.

17. Edward T. Hall, *The Silent Language* (Garden City, NY: Anchor, 1981).

18. Tomasz Lenartowicz and James P. Johnson, "A Cross-National Assessment of the Values of Latin America Managers: Contrasting Hues or Shades of Gray?" *Journal of International Business Studies* 34, no. 3 (2003): 266–81.

19. O. C. Ferrell and L. Gresham, "A Contingency Framework for Understanding Ethical Decision Making in Marketing," *Journal of Marketing* 49, no. 3 (1985): 87–96; Naresh Malhotra and G. Miller, "An Integrated Model for Ethical Decisions," *Journal of Business Ethics* 17, no.3 (1998): 263–280; D. McAlister,

O. C. Ferrell, and L. Ferrell, *Business and Society* (Boston: Houghton Mifflin, 2003).

20. Marco Celentani, Juan-Jose Ganuza, and Jose-Luis Peydros, "Combating Corruption in International Business Transactions," *Economica* 71, no. 283 (2004): 417–49; David Zussman, "Fighting Corruption Is a Global Concern," *Ottawa Citizen,* October 11, 2005, A15.

21. Tara Radin and Martin Calkins, "The Struggle against Sweatshops: Moving toward Responsible Global Business," *Journal of Business Ethics* 66 (2006): 261–68.

22. Transparency International (2009), Progress Report: OECD Anti-Bribery Convention 2009, www.transparency.org.

23. John Sullivan, *The Moral Compass of Companies: Business Ethics and Corporate Governance as Anti-Corruption Tools* (Washington, DC: International Finance Corporation, World Bank, 2009); Alan Muller and Ans Kolk, "Extrinsic and Intrinsic Drivers of Corporate Social Performance: Evidence from Foreign and Domestic Firms in Mexico," *Journal of Management Studies* 47, no.1 (2010): 1–26.

24. Ferrell and Gresham, 1985; McAlister, Ferrell, and Ferrell, 2003.

25. Larry Beer, *Business Ethics for the Global Business and the Global Manager: A Strategic Approach* (New York: Business Expert Press, 2010).

26. Alan Muller and Gail Whiteman, "Exploring the Geography of Corporate Philanthropic Disaster Response: A Study of Fortune Global 500 Firms," *Journal of Business Ethics* 8, no. 4 (2009): 589–603; UNCTAD, 2009; N. Isdell, "21st Century Capitalism," speech to Council on Foreign Relations, New York, 2009, http://fora.tv/2009/03/06/Neville_Isdell_21st_Century_Capitalism; K. Rehbein, S. Waddock, and S. Graves, "Understanding Shareholder Activism: Which Corporations are Targeted?" *Business and Society* 43, no. 3 (2004): 239–67.

27. Center for Corporate Citizenship, "In Good Company: Motorola," (Boston, MA: Boston College, Carroll School of Management, 2007), http://www.bcccc.net.

28. Beer, 2010; Philip Kotler and Nancy Lee, *Up and Out of Poverty: The Social Marketing Solution* (Upper Saddle River, NJ: Wharton School Publishing, 2009); Hildy Teegen, Jonathan Doh, and Sushil Vachani, "The Importance of Nongovernmental Organizations (NGOs) in Global Governance and Value Creation: An International Business Research Agenda," *Journal of International Business Studies* 35, no. 4(2004): 463–483.

29. Jo Johnson and Aline van Duyn, "Forced Child Labour Claims Hit Clothes Retailers," *Financial Times,* October 29, 2007, p. 3; Kaufmann, Reimann, Ehrgott, and Rauer, 2009; Nancy Landrum and Sandra Edwards, *Sustainable Business: An Executive's Primer* (New York: Business Expert Press, 2009).

30. Sheila Bonini, Lenny Lendonca, and Jeremy Oppenheim, Jeremy, "When Social Issues Become Strategic," *The McKinsey Quarterly*, no. 2, 2006, www.mckinseyquarterly.com; Muller and Kolk, 2010.

31. Ferrell and Gresham, 1985; T. Low, L. Ferrell, and P. Mansfield, "A Review of Empirical Studies Assessing Ethical Decision Making in Business," Journal of Business Ethics, 25, no. 3 (2000): 185-204; Malhotra and Miller, 1998; McAlister, Ferrell, and Ferrell, 2003.

32. Sullivan, 2009.

33. This framework appeared originally in *Issues in Ethics*, 1, no. 2, 1988. It was developed at the Markkula Center for Applied Ethics at Santa Clara University, California, USA. See also: Bonini, Lendonca, and Oppenheim, 2006; Erin Cavusgil "Merck and Vioxx: An Examination of an Ethical Decision-Making Model," *Journal of Business Ethics*, 76, no. 4 (2007): 451–61; Ferrell and Gresham, 1985; Low, Ferrell, and Mansfield, 2000; Malhotra and Miller, 1998; McAlister, Ferrell, and Ferrell, 2003; UNCTAD, *World Investment Report 2006* (New York: United Nations Conference on Trade and Development, 2006); Sullivan, 2009.

The International Business Environment

Political and Legal Systems in International Business

LEARNING OBJECTIVES
In this chapter, you will learn about:

1. The nature of country risk

2. Political systems

3. Legal systems

4. Types of country risk produced by political and legal systems

5. The nature of government intervention

6. Instruments of government intervention

7. How firms can respond to government intervention

THE NATURE OF COUNTRY RISK

Most of us expect a familiar business landscape when conducting business at home. But foreign markets frequently differ in terms of political and legal systems. Managers must be able to navigate difficult regulations and practices and avoid unethical or questionable conduct. At the same time, the political and legal context can present opportunities. Preferential subsidies, government incentives, and protection from competition reduce business costs and influence strategic decision-making. Many governments encourage domestic investment from foreign MNEs by offering tax holidays and cash incentives to employ local workers.

Country risk is exposure to potential loss or adverse effects on company operations and profitability caused by developments in a country's political and/or legal environments. Also referred to as *political risk,* it is one of the four major types of international business risks introduced in Chapter 1. While the immediate cause of country risk is a political or legal factor, underlying such factors may be economic, social, or technological developments. Dimensions of country risk in international business include the following:

- Harmful or unstable political systems
- Laws and regulations unfavorable to foreign firms
- Inadequate or underdeveloped legal system
- Bureaucracy and red tape
- Corruption and other ethical issues
- Government intervention, protectionism, and barriers to trade and investment
- Mismanagement or failure of the national economy

How Prevalent is Country Risk?

Exhibit 5.1 presents the level of country risk in various countries measured in terms of political stability, legal environment, economic indicators, and tax policy. Iraq is one of the riskiest countries in the wake of war and the emergence of a new political regime. Canada, Ireland, and Singapore are among the most politically stable countries.[1] Country risk tends to be lower in countries with a favorable legal climate and political stability and higher in countries with excessive regulatory burdens and political instability. Many of the riskiest locations are poor countries that would benefit enormously from direct investment and integration into the global economy. For the complete list of countries ranked by risk, visit the Risk Briefing site at the Economist Intelligence Unit viewswire.eiu.com.

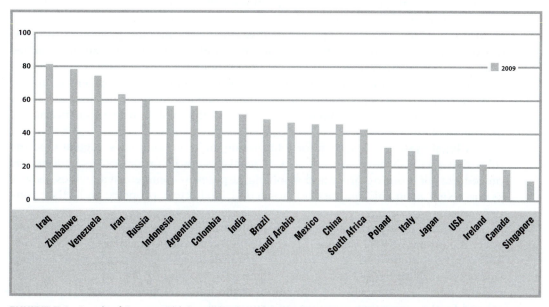

EXHIBIT 5.1   Levels of Country Risk in a Selection of Countries.   *Sources*: "Risk Briefing," Economist Intelligence Unit (2009), viewswire.eiu.com; Statistics section, United Nations, www.un.org; World Bank Development Indicators 2010, Washington DC: World Bank.

Country risk may affect all firms in a country equally or only a subset. Civil war in the former Yugoslavia in the 1990s tended to affect all firms. By contrast, the Russian government targeted only the Yukos Oil Company, with politically motivated persecution, despite the presence of several competitors in Russia such as ConocoPhillips and Royal Dutch Shell.[2]

A key source of risk facing nations in the advanced and developing economies alike is imbalances in the fiscal situation of national governments. Recently, fiscal imbalances in advanced economies have widened, mainly due to excessive government spending and exacerbated by the impact of the global financial crisis. In the long-term, a key fiscal challenge will be financing the unfunded liabilities of health care and pension programs. Weak financial systems are a source of risk in both advanced and emerging economies. Fragile states and geopolitical conflict are additional risks that threaten the stability of numerous countries and regions. Poverty and economic disparity provide an enabling environment for illicit trade, corruption, and organized crime. Fragility of Middle East states puts upward pressure on the price of fossil fuels and other commodities demanded by the advanced economies. Heightened risk in the Middle East, Africa, Russia, and even parts of southern Europe deters investment, threatens political stability, reduces sales prospects, increases capital costs, and generally increases business transaction costs.

Political and Legal Environments in International Business

A **political system** is a set of formal institutions that constitute a government. It includes legislative bodies, political parties, lobbying groups, and trade unions. *Constituents* are the people and organizations that support the political system and receive government resources.

The principal functions of a political system are to provide protection from external threats, establish stability based on laws, and govern the allocation of valued resources among the members of a society. A political system also defines how a society's groups interact with each other. Each country's political system is unique to its historical, economic, and cultural context. Political systems are also constantly evolving in response to constituent demands and the evolution of the national and international environment.

A **legal system** is a system for interpreting and enforcing laws, regulations, and rules that establish norms of conduct. A legal system incorporates institutions and procedures for ensuring order and resolving disputes in commercial activities, as well as for taxing economic output and protecting intellectual property and other company assets.

Political and legal systems are dynamic and interdependent—changes in one affect the other. Adverse developments in either system can give rise to country risk. These developments can result from the installation of a new government, shifting values or priorities in political parties, initiatives developed by special interest groups, and the creation of new laws or regulations. Exhibit 5.2 identifies the aspects of political and legal systems that contribute to country risk.

Country risk is *always* present, but its nature and intensity vary over time and between countries. In China, for example, the government is overhauling the legal

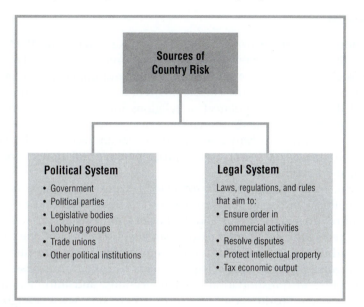

EXHIBIT 5.2   Sources of Country Risk.

system, making it increasingly more consistent with Western systems. Some new regulations have been poorly formulated or are confusing or contradictory. For example, at one point Beijing announced that foreign investments in China's Internet industry were illegal, but by that time Western firms had already invested millions in the Chinese dot-com sector. In disputes between local and foreign firms, governments are often inclined to protect local interests. Even when Western firms obtain favorable judgments in the courts, they may not be enforced. Let's delve into political and legal systems in greater detail.

POLITICAL SYSTEMS

Recent history has witnessed three major types of political systems: totalitarianism, socialism, and democracy. For example, Cuba, North Korea, and several countries in Africa are beset by elements of totalitarianism. Bolivia, China, India, Russia, and Venezuela are strongly characterized by socialism. Australia, Canada, Japan, the United States, and most European countries are largely democratic. However, these categories are not mutually exclusive. Most democracies also include some elements of socialism, and most former totalitarian regimes now embrace a mix of socialism and democracy. To control the recent global financial crisis, governments in Europe and the United States implemented relatively socialistic policies, such as nationalizing firms in the banking and automotive industries. China has applied relatively democratic approaches, such as land reforms and open markets, to stimulate commercial activity. Worldwide, political systems are evolving as governments experiment with ways to fight recession and avert financial crises.

Totalitarianism

Well-known totalitarian states from the past include Nazi Germany (1933–1945), Spain (1939–1975), China (1949–1980s), and the Soviet Union (1918–1991). A totalitarian government seeks to control not only all economic and political matters but also the attitudes, values, and beliefs of the citizenry. Often, the entire population is mobilized in support of the state and a political or religious ideology. Usually there is a state party led by a dictator, such as Kim Jong-il in North Korea. Party membership is mandatory for those seeking to advance within the social and economic hierarchy. Power is maintained by means of secret police, propaganda, regulation of free discussion and criticism, and terror tactics.[3]

Over time, many of the world's totalitarian states either have disappeared or shifted their political and economic systems toward democracy and capitalism. China initiated major reforms in the 1980s and the Soviet Union collapsed in 1991. The transition has not been easy, and former totalitarian governments continue to intervene in business via red tape that hinders the founding of new firms, bureaucratic accounting and tax regulations, inadequate legal systems to protect business interests, and weak infrastructure in transportation, communications, and information technology (for example, see the World Bank's *Doing Business* site, www.doingbusiness.org). Today, numerous states exhibit elements of totalitarianism, particularly in Africa, Asia, and the Middle East. Several are controlled by individuals with substantial dictatorial powers, such as Muammar al-Qaddafi in Libya, Hugo Chavez in Venezuela, and Robert Mugabe in Zimbabwe.

Socialism

Socialism's fundamental tenet is that capital and wealth should be vested in the state and used primarily as a means of production rather than for profit. The collective welfare of the people is believed to outweigh the welfare of the individual. Socialists argue that in a capitalist society, the pay of workers does not represent the full value of their labor, and thus government should control the basic means of production, distribution, and commercial activity.

Socialism has manifested itself in much of the world as *social democracy* and has been most successful in western Europe, where government frequently intervenes in the private sector and in business activities. Corporate income tax rates are often relatively high, as in France and Sweden. Even robust economies such as Germany's have experienced net outflows of FDI as businesses seek to escape extensive regulation.

Democracy

Democracy has become the prevailing political system in many of the world's advanced economies. It is characterized by two key features:

- *Private property rights.*   Refers to the ability to own property and assets and to increase one's asset base by accumulating private wealth. *Property* includes tangibles, such as land and buildings, as well as intangibles, such as stocks, contracts, patent rights, and intellectual assets. People are less likely to develop individual initiative and innovation if there is any uncertainty about whether they can control their property or profit from it.

• *Limited government.*   The government performs only essential functions that serve all citizens, such as conducting national defense, maintaining law and order and diplomatic relations, and constructing and maintaining infrastructure such as roads, schools, and public works. By allowing market forces to determine economic activity, the government ensures resources are allocated with maximal efficiency.[4]

Because people have differing levels of personal and financial resources, each performs with varying degrees of success, leading to social inequalities. Critics of pure democracy argue that when these inequalities become excessive, government should step in to correct them. In democracies such as Japan and Sweden, the rights and freedoms associated with democracy are construed in larger societal terms rather than on behalf of individuals.

Virtually all democracies include elements of socialism, such as government intervention in the affairs of firms when abuses or negative externalities occur. Many countries, including Australia, Canada, the United States, and the nations of Europe, are best described as having a *mixed* political system—characterized by a strong private sector *and* a strong public sector, with considerable government regulation and control.

Democracy's Link to Economic Freedom and Openness

Economic freedom, and usually higher living standards, flourishes when governments support the institutions necessary for that freedom, such as freely operating markets and rule of law. Exhibit 5.3 reveals that the more political freedom in a nation, the more economic freedom its citizens enjoy. Visit Freedom House (www.freedomhouse.org) to view the latest information about political and economic freedom around the world.

Democracy is closely associated with *openness*, or lack of regulation or barriers to the entry of firms in foreign markets. Absence of excessive regulations also benefits buyers by increasing the quantity, quality, and variety of products available. Increased efficiency and lower prices may follow. For example, since the 1980s the government of India has steadily lowered entry barriers in the Indian automobile market. Foreign automakers have steadily entered the market, greatly increasing the number of models available for sale, raising the quality of available cars, and lowering prices.[5]

The Relationship between Political Systems and Economic Systems

Generally speaking, totalitarianism is associated with command economies, socialism with mixed economies, and democracy with market economies. Let's review these economic systems.

COMMAND ECONOMY   Also known as a centrally planned economy, a command economy makes the state a dominant force in the production and distribution of goods and services. Central planners make resource allocation decisions, the state owns major sectors of the economy, and a sizable bureaucracy thrives. Central planning tends to be less efficient than market forces in synchronizing supply and demand. China and Russia still exhibit some characteristics of command economies. However, the system is gradually dying out in favor of mixed economies and market economies.

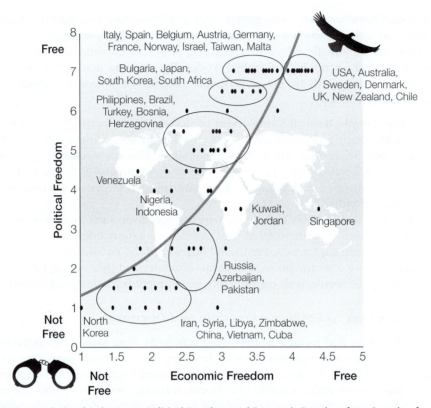

EXHIBIT 5.3   Relationship between Political Freedom and Economic Freedom for a Sample of Countries.   *Source: 2011 Index of Economic Freedom*, Heritage Foundation, www.heritage.org; Freedom House, 2010, www.freedomhouse.org; *World Bank Development Indicators 2010*, Washington DC: World Bank. .

MIXED ECONOMY   A mixed economy combines state intervention and market mechanisms for organizing production and distribution. Most industries are under private ownership, and entrepreneurs freely establish, own, and operate corporations. But the government controls functions such as pension programs, labor regulation, minimum wage levels, and environmental regulation and runs operations in key sectors such as transportation, telecommunications, and energy. In Germany, Japan, Norway, and Singapore, government often works closely with business and labor groups to determine industrial policy, regulate wage rates, and/or provide subsidies to support specific industries.

In the United States, combined government spending increased from about 3 percent of GDP in the 1930s to roughly 20 percent by the 1980s. During the same period in most other developed economies, average government spending as a percent of GDP rose from 8 percent to more than 40 percent. Governments in Europe, Japan, and North America imposed many new workplace regulations on private firms, especially after the most recent global financial crisis.[6]

MARKET ECONOMY   In a market economy, prices are determined by market forces—the interaction of supply and demand. Government intervention in the marketplace is limited, and economic decisions are left to individuals and firms. Market economies are closely associated with capitalism, in which the means of production are privately owned and operated. The task of the state is to establish a legal system that protects private property and contractual agreements. It may also intervene to address the inequalities that market economies sometimes produce.

LEGAL SYSTEMS

Legal systems provide a framework of rules and norms of conduct that mandate, limit, or permit specified relationships among people and organizations and provide punishments for those who violate these rules and norms. Legal systems are dynamic—they evolve over time to represent each nation's changing social values and changes in their social, political, economic, and technological environments.

In well-developed legal systems, such as in Australia, Canada, Japan, the United States, and most European countries, laws are widely known and understood. They are effective and legitimate because, generally, they are applied to all citizens equally, issued by means of formal procedures by recognized government authorities, and enforced systematically and fairly by police forces and formally organized judicial bodies. In these countries, a culture of law exists in which citizens consistently respect and follow the rule of law. **Rule of law** refers to a legal system in which rules are clear, publicly disclosed, fairly enforced, and widely respected by individuals, organizations, and the government. International business flourishes in societies where the rule of law prevails.

We can characterize nations as having one of four basic legal systems: common law, civil law, religious law, and mixed. For example, Australia, Canada, Ireland, New Zealand, the United Kingdom, and the United States are based primarily on common law. Civil law countries include Japan, Russia, South Korea, and much of Western Europe and Latin America. The Islamic countries of the Middle East and North Africa employ religious law systems. Bangladesh, India, Indonesia, Israel, Kenya, Malaysia, and the Philippines are characterized by mixed legal systems. Let's review these legal systems.

Common Law

Also known as case law, common law originated in England and spread to Australia, Canada, the United States, and former members of the British Commonwealth. It is based on tradition, previous cases, and legal precedents set by the nation's courts through interpretation of statutes, legislation, and past rulings. The national legislature in common-law countries (such as Parliament in Britain and Congress in the United States) holds ultimate power to pass or amend laws. Because common law is open to interpretation by courts, it is more flexible than other legal systems. Thus, judges in a common-law system have substantial power to interpret laws based on the unique circumstances of individual cases, including commercial disputes and other business situations.

Civil Law

Also known as code law, civil law is found in France, Germany, Italy, Japan, Turkey, and Latin America. Its origins go back to Roman law and the Napoleonic Code. Civil law is based on an all-inclusive system of laws that have been codified by a legislative

Legal Issues	Civil Law	Common Law
Ownership of intellectual property	Determined by registration.	Determined by prior use.
Enforcing agreements	Commercial agreements become enforceable only if properly notarized or registered.	Proof of agreement is sufficient for enforcing contracts.
Specificity of contracts	Contracts tend to be brief because many potential problems are already covered in the civil code.	Contracts tend to be very detailed, with all possible contingencies spelled out. Usually more costly to draft a contract.
Compliance with contracts	Noncompliance is extended to include unforeseeable human acts such as labor strikes and riots.	Acts of nature (floods, lightning, hurricanes, etc.) are the only justifiable excuses for noncompliance with the provisions of contracts.

EXHIBIT 5.4   Examples of Differences between Common Law and Civil Law.

body or some other supreme authority. It is divided into three separate codes: commercial, civil, and criminal.

A key difference between common and civil law is that common law is primarily judicial in origin and based on court decisions, whereas civil law is primarily legislative in origin and based on laws passed by national and local legislatures. Though they complement each other and many countries employ elements of both, the two systems pose various differences for international business; these are highlighted in Exhibit 5.4.

Religious Law

Religious law is strongly influenced by religious beliefs, ethical codes, and moral values viewed as mandated by a supreme being. The most important religious legal systems are based on Hindu law, Jewish law, and—the most widespread—Islamic law, which is found mainly in the Middle East and North Africa. Also known as the *sharia*, Islamic law is based on the Qur'an, the holy book of Muslims, and the teachings of the Prophet Mohammed. It spells out norms of behavior regarding politics, economics, banking, contracts, marriage, and many other social issues. Thus, Islamic law might be said to encompass all possible human relationships. Because it is seen as divinely ordained, it is relatively static and absolute and, unlike other legal systems, it evolves very little over time.

Mixed Systems

In most countries, legal systems evolve, adopting elements of one system or another that reflect their unique needs. Mixed systems consist of two or more legal systems operating together. For example, legal systems in South Africa and the Philippines mix elements of civil law and common law. Indonesia and most Middle East countries share elements of civil law and Islamic law.

TYPES OF COUNTRY RISK PRODUCED BY POLITICAL AND LEGAL SYSTEMS

How do political and legal systems create challenges for firms engaged in international business? Let's first examine the specific risks brought about by political systems.

Types of Country Risk Produced by Political Systems

GOVERNMENT TAKEOVER OF CORPORATE ASSETS   Governments seize corporate assets in two major ways: confiscation and expropriation. *Confiscation* is the seizure of corporate assets *without* compensation. *Expropriation* is seizure *with* compensation. The industry sectors most frequently targeted by such events are natural resources (for example, mining and petroleum), utilities, and manufacturing.

A third category of takeover, *nationalization*, describes government's seizing not a firm but an entire industry, with or without compensation. In 2006, for example, the government of Bolivia nationalized much of the oil and gas industry in that country.[7] Nationalization occurs in advanced economies as well. Following the recent global financial crisis, the federal government of the Netherlands nationalized part of the financial services company Fortis NV, and Britain nationalized the Royal Bank of Scotland.[8]

More common today is "creeping expropriation," a subtle form of country risk in which governments modify laws and regulations after foreign MNEs have made substantial local investments in property and plants.[9] Examples include abrupt termination of contracts and the creation of new laws that favor local firms. Such tactics occasionally force foreign MNEs to cede control of their operations to local interests.[10] For example, governments in Bolivia, Kazakhstan, Russia, and Venezuela have modified tax regimes to extract revenues from foreign coal, oil, and gas companies. Subtle or devious approaches to government takeover make country risk harder to predict.

EMBARGOES AND SANCTIONS   Governments may unilaterally resort to sanctions and embargoes in response to offensive activities of foreign countries or unresolved trade or policy disputes. A *sanction* is a type of trade penalty imposed on one or more countries by one or more other countries and typically takes the form of tariffs, trade barriers, import duties, and import or export quotas. Much evidence suggests that sanctions often do not achieve desired outcomes.

More serious is an *embargo,* an official ban on exports to or imports from a particular country, in order to isolate it and punish its government. The European Union has enacted embargoes against Belarus, Sudan, and China in certain areas, such as foreign travel, to protest human rights and weapon-trading violations.

BOYCOTTS AGAINST FIRMS OR NATIONS   Consumers and special interest groups occasionally target particular firms perceived to have harmed local interests. A *boycott* is a voluntary refusal to engage in commercial dealings with a nation or a company. It results in lost sales and increased costs for public relations activities needed to restore the firm's image. Disneyland Paris and McDonald's have been the targets of boycotts by French farmers, who believe these firms represent U.S. agricultural policies and globalization, which many French citizens despise.

WAR, INSURRECTION, AND VIOLENCE   The indirect effects of war, insurrection, and other forms of violence pose significant problems for business operations. For example, violent conflict among drug cartels and security services along the U.S.–Mexico border has led some firms and financiers to withdraw investments from Mexico because of perceived heightened risks and political instability. To minimize losses from violent acts, firms can purchase risk insurance.

TERRORISM   Terrorism is the threat or actual use of force or violence to attain a political goal through fear, coercion, or intimidation.[11] It is sometimes sponsored by national governments. Terrorism has escalated in much of the world, as exemplified by the 2001 attacks in the United States and the 2008 attacks in Mumbai, India.[12] Terrorism also can severely damage commercial infrastructure and disrupt the business activities of countless firms. It induces fear in consumers, who reduce their purchasing. Terrorism also affects financial markets. In the days following the 9/11/01 attacks, the value of the U.S. stock market dropped some 14 percent.[13]

Types of Country Risk Produced by Legal Systems

Country risk also arises due to peculiarities of national legal systems in both the host and the home country. In many countries, the legal system favors home country nationals. Particularly relevant to international business are *commercial law*, which specifically covers business transactions, and *private law*, which regulates relationships between persons and organizations, including contracts, and liabilities that may arise due to negligent behavior. Let's review specific sources of risk.

COUNTRY RISK ARISING FROM THE HOST COUNTRY LEGAL ENVIRONMENT   Governments in host countries can impose a variety of legal stipulations on foreign companies doing business there.

- *Foreign Investment Laws.*   These laws affect the type of entry strategy firms choose, as well as their operations and performance. Many nations impose restrictions on inward FDI. The United States restricts foreign investments that are seen to affect national security. In 2006, the U.S. Congress successfully opposed a pending deal granting operational control at several U.S. ports to Dubai Ports World, a firm based in the United Arab Emirates.
- *Controls on Operating Forms and Practices.*   These regulate how firms can conduct production, marketing, and distribution activities within countries' borders. For example, host countries may require companies to obtain permits to import or export. They may devise complex regulations that complicate transportation and logistical activities or limit the options for entry strategies.
- *Marketing and Distribution Laws.*   These determine which practices are allowed in advertising, promotion, and distribution. For example, Finland, France, and New Zealand prohibit cigarette advertising on television. Product safety and liability laws hold manufacturers and sellers responsible for damage, injury, or death caused by defective products.
- *Laws on Income Repatriation.*   These restrict MNEs' ability to transfer profits back to their home country. Such laws often discourage inward FDI and are common in countries experiencing shortage of hard currencies.

- *Environmental Laws.* These preserve natural resources; combat pollution and the abuse of air, earth, and water resources; and ensure health and safety. Nevertheless, governments attempt to balance environmental laws against the impact such regulations may have on employment, entrepreneurship, and economic development. For instance, environmental standards in Mexico are relatively loose, but the government is reluctant to strengthen them for fear that foreign MNEs will reduce their investments.

- *Contract Laws.* These attach rights, duties, and obligations to the contracting parties. Contracts are used in five main types of business transactions: (1) sale of goods or services, especially large sales; (2) distribution of the firm's products through foreign distributors; (3) licensing and franchising—that is, a contractual relationship that allows a firm to use another company's intellectual property, marketing tools, or other assets for a fee; (4) FDI, especially in collaboration with a foreign entity, in order to create and operate a foreign subsidiary; and (5) joint ventures and other types of cross-border collaborations.

- *Internet and e-Commerce Regulations.* These are the new frontier. Many consumer-privacy laws have yet to be enacted, and progress has been slow on methods to protect private data from criminal or competitive eyes. The recent adoption of e-signature laws should help protect online contracting. However, firms that undertake e-commerce in countries with weak laws face considerable risk.

- *Inadequate or Underdeveloped Legal Systems.* Just as laws and regulations can lead to country risk, an underdeveloped regulatory environment or poor enforcement of existing laws in both developed and developing countries can pose challenges for the firm. The most recent global financial crisis was precipitated, in part, by insufficient regulation in the financial and banking sectors of the United States, Europe, and other areas. Regulators seek to expand the reach of regulation, provide new means to increase transparency and information flows, and harmonize regulatory policies and legal frameworks across national borders.

COUNTRY RISK ARISING FROM THE HOME COUNTRY LEGAL ENVIRONMENT Home country legal systems are just as relevant. **Extraterritoriality** refers to the application of home country laws to persons or conduct outside national borders. In most cases, such laws are intended to prosecute individuals or firms located abroad for some type of wrongdoing. A French court ordered Yahoo! to bar access to Nazi-related items on its Web site in France, for instance, and to remove related messages and images from its sites accessible in the United States.[14] Businesses generally oppose extraterritoriality because it adds to the compliance and regulatory costs and causes considerable uncertainty.

- *The Foreign Corrupt Practices Act (FCPA).* The act passed by the U.S. government in 1977 and strengthened in 1998, makes it illegal for a firm to offer bribes to foreign parties for the purpose of securing or retaining business. The FCPA also requires firms with securities listed in the United States to meet U.S. accounting provisions.[15] One problem with the FCPA is that a "bribe" is not clearly defined. For example, the act draws a distinction between bribery and "facilitation payments"; the latter may be permissible if making such payments does not violate local laws.[16] Some U.S. managers argue the FCPA harms their interests because foreign competitors often are not constrained by such laws.

- *Antiboycott Regulations.*   These prevent companies from participating in restrictive trade practices or boycotts imposed by foreign countries if they discriminate against others on the basis of race, religion, gender, or national origin. Some Arab nations have long boycotted Israel and require any foreign company that wants to do business with them to also observe this boycott. Antiboycott regulations passed by the U.S. Congress in 1977 effectively prohibit U.S. firms from participating in the boycott of Israel when operating in these Arab nations.
- *Accounting and Reporting Laws.*   These differ greatly around the world. For example, when assigning value to stocks and other securities, most countries use the lower of cost or market value. However, Brazil encourages firms to adjust portfolio valuations in view of historically high inflation there. When valuing physical assets, Canada uses historical costs, but some Latin American countries use inflation-adjusted market value.
- *Transparency in Financial Reporting.*   This is the degree to which firms regularly reveal substantial information about their financial condition and accounting practices. In the United States, public firms are required to report financial results to stockholders and government authorities each quarter. In much of the world, however, financial statements may come out once a year or less often, and they often lack transparency.

Managing Country Risk

How should managers respond to country risk in a proactive manner? We next highlight five specific strategies managers can employ to manage country risk.

PROACTIVE ENVIRONMENTAL SCANNING   Anticipating country risk requires advance research. Initially, managers develop a comprehensive understanding of the political and legal environment in target countries. They then engage in *scanning* to assess potential risks and threats to the firm. One of the best sources of intelligence in the scanning process is employees working in the host country. They are knowledgeable about evolving events and can evaluate them in the context of local history, culture, and politics.

Once the firm has researched the political climate and contingencies of the target environment, it develops and implements strategies to facilitate effective management of relationships with policymakers and other helpful contacts in the host country. The firm then takes steps to minimize its exposure to country risks that threaten its performance.

STRICT ADHERENCE TO ETHICAL STANDARDS   Ethical behavior is important not only for its own sake but also because it helps insulate the firm from some country risks that less-conscientious firms encounter. Those companies that engage in questionable practices or operate outside the law naturally invite redress from the governments of the host countries where they do business.

ALLIANCES WITH QUALIFIED LOCAL PARTNERS   A practical approach to reducing country risk is to enter target markets in collaboration with a knowledgeable and reliable local partner. Qualified local partners are better informed about local conditions and better situated to establish stable relations with the local government. For instance, because of various challenges in China and Russia, Western firms often enter these countries by partnering with local firms that assist in navigating complex legal and political landscapes.

PROTECTION THROUGH LEGAL CONTRACTS   A legal contract spells out the rights and obligations of each party and is especially important when relationships go awry. Contract law varies widely from country to country, and firms must adhere to local standards. For example, a Canadian firm doing business in Belgium generally must comply with the laws of both Belgium and Canada, as well as with the evolving laws of the European Union, some of which may override Belgian law.

When international contractual disputes arise, firms generally employ one of three approaches for resolving them. *Conciliation,* the least adversarial method, is a formal process of negotiation through a conciliator, who meets separately with the involved parties in an attempt to resolve their differences. In *arbitration*, a neutral third party hears both sides of a case and decides in favor of one side, based on an objective assessment of the facts. Arbitration is often handled by supranational organizations, such as the International Chamber of Commerce in Paris or the Stockholm Chamber of Commerce. *Litigation* is the most adversarial approach and occurs when one party files a lawsuit against another in order to achieve desired ends. Litigation is most common in the United States; in most other countries, arbitration or conciliation are usually preferred.

THE NATURE OF GOVERNMENT INTERVENTION

Economists have long used trade theories to make the case that *free trade*, the unrestricted flow of products, services, and physical and intellectual capital across national borders, is good for the world. There is much empirical evidence to support free trade. One study examining more than 100 countries in the fifty years after 1945 found a strong association between market openness—that is, unimpeded free trade—and economic growth. Countries with an open economy enjoyed average annual per-capita GDP growth of 4.49 percent, while relatively closed countries—those with less free trade—grew at only 0.69 percent per year.[17] Other studies confirm that market liberalization and free trade are best for supporting economic growth and national living standards.[18]

In reality, however, there is no such thing as unimpeded free trade. Governments have long intervened in business and the international marketplace, imposing tariffs and quotas, restricting international investment, adding bureaucratic procedures and red tape, and limiting business and value-chain activities. Governments may provide subsidies and financial incentives intended to sustain domestic industries in ways that hamper the internationalization of foreign firms.

Government intervention is often motivated by **protectionism,** which refers to national economic policies designed to restrict free trade and protect domestic industries from foreign competition. Protectionism is typically manifested by tariffs, nontariff barriers such as quotas, and arbitrary administrative rules designed to discourage imports. A **tariff** (also known as a *duty*) is a tax imposed by a government on imported products, effectively increasing the final price of goods for the customer. A **nontariff trade barrier** is a government policy, regulation, or procedure that impedes trade through means other than explicit tariffs. Trade barriers are enforced as products pass through **customs,** the checkpoints at the ports of entry in each country where government officials inspect imported products and levy tariffs. An often-used form of nontariff trade barrier is a **quota,** a quantitative restriction placed on imports of a specific product over a specified period of time. Government intervention may also target FDI flows through *investment barriers* that restrict the operations of foreign firms.

Such intervention often leads to adverse *unintended consequences*—unfavorable outcomes of policies or laws. In a complex world, legislators and policymakers cannot foresee all possible outcomes. The problem of unintended consequences suggests that government intervention should be planned and implemented with great care.

Rationale for Government Intervention

Why does a government intervene in trade and investment activities? There are four main motives. First, tariffs and other forms of intervention can generate substantial revenue. Ghana and Sierra Leone generate more than 25 percent of their total government revenue from tariffs. Second, intervention can ensure the safety, security, and welfare of citizens by, for example, preventing the import of contaminated food. Third, intervention is a means for governments to pursue economic, political, or social objectives through policies that promote job growth and economic development. Fourth, intervention can help better serve the interests of the nation's firms and industries. Governments may devise regulations to stimulate development of homegrown industries.

Trade and investment barriers can be considered either defensive or offensive. Governments impose *defensive* barriers to safeguard industries, workers, and special interest groups and to promote national security. *Offensive* barriers support strategic or public policy objectives, such as increasing employment or generating tax revenues. Let's review these specific rationales for government intervention.

DEFENSIVE RATIONALE   Four major defensive motives are particularly relevant: protection of the nation's economy, protection of an infant industry, national security, and national culture and identity.

- *Protection of the National Economy.*   Proponents argue that firms in advanced economies cannot compete with those in developing countries that employ low-cost labor. Activists call for trade barriers to curtail the import of low-priced products, fearing that advanced-economy manufacturers will be undersold, wages will fall, and home country jobs will be lost. In response, critics counter that protectionism is at odds with the theory of comparative advantage, according to which nations should engage in *more* international trade, not less. Trade barriers interfere with country-specific specialization of labor. When countries specialize in the products they can produce best and then trade for the rest, they perform better in the long run, delivering superior living standards to their citizens. Critics also charge that blocking imports reduces the availability and increases the cost of products sold in the home market. Finally, protection can trigger retaliation, motivating foreign governments to impose their own trade barriers, reducing sales prospects for exporters.
- *Protection of an Infant Industry.*   In an emerging industry, companies are often small, inexperienced, and lack the latest technologies or know-how. Governments can impose temporary trade barriers on foreign imports to ensure

that young firms gain a large share of the domestic market. Government intervention allowed Japan and South Korea to become dominant players in the global automobile and consumer electronics industries. Once in place, however, such protection may be hard to remove.[19]

- *National Security.* Countries impose trade restrictions on products viewed as critical to national defense and security, such as military technology and computers that help maintain domestic production in security-related products. Countries may also impose **export controls**, measures intended to manage or prevent the export of certain products or trade with certain countries. The United States generally blocks exports of nuclear and military technology to countries it deems state sponsors of terrorism, such as Iran and Syria.

- *National Culture and Identity.* Should foreign entities, say the Japanese or the Saudis, be allowed to purchase national landmarks such as the Empire State building or the Rockefeller Center in New York? In most countries, certain occupations, industries, and public assets are seen as central to national culture and identity. Governments may impose trade barriers to restrict imports of products or services that may threaten assets considered to be part of the national heritage. France does not allow significant foreign ownership of its TV stations because of concerns about foreign influence on French culture.

OFFENSIVE RATIONALE   Offensive rationales for government intervention fall into two categories: national strategic priorities and increasing employment.

- *National Strategic Priorities.* Government intervention sometimes aims to encourage the development of industries that bolster the nation's economy. It is a *proactive* variation of the infant industry rationale and related to national industrial policy. Countries with many high-tech or high value-adding industries, such as information technology, pharmaceuticals, car manufacturing, or financial services, create better jobs and higher tax revenues than economies based on low value-adding industries, such as agriculture, textile manufacturing, or discount retailing.

- *Increasing Employment.* Insulating domestic firms from foreign competition stimulates national output, leading to more jobs in the protected industries. The effect is usually strongest in import-intensive industries that employ much labor. For example, the Chinese government has traditionally required foreign companies to enter its huge market through joint ventures with local Chinese firms. A joint venture between Shanghai Automotive Industry Corporation (SAIC) and Volkswagen created jobs in China.

INSTRUMENTS OF GOVERNMENT INTERVENTION

Principal instruments of trade intervention and the traditional forms of protectionism are tariffs and nontariff trade barriers. They constitute a serious impediment to cross-border business. The United Nations estimated that trade barriers alone cost developing countries more than $100 billion in lost trading opportunities with developed countries every year.[20] Exhibit 5.5 highlights the most common forms of government intervention and their effects. Let's describe the major barriers.

Intervention Type	Definition	Practical Effect on Customers, Firms, or Government	Contemporary Examples
Tariff	Tax imposed on imported products.	Increases cost to the importer, exporter, and usually the buyer of the product. Discourages imports of products. Generates government revenue.	Switzerland charges a tariff of 44% on agricultural product imports. Cote d'Ivoire charges a tariff on most finished products.
Quota	Quantitative restriction on imports of a product during a specified period of time.	Benefits early importers, giving them monopoly power and the ability to charge higher prices. Harms late importers, who may be unable to obtain desired products. Usually results in higher prices to the buyer.	Brazil has imposed a quota on the number of foreign films that can be imported for theatrical screening and home video distribution.
Local content requirements	Requirement that a manufacturer include a minimum percentage of added value that is derived from local sources.	Discourages imports of raw materials, parts, components, and supplies, thereby reducing sourcing options available to manufacturers. May result in higher costs and lower product quality for importers and buyers.	The Nigerian government requires that products and services used by foreign firms in the oil industry in Nigeria must contain over 50% Nigerian content.
Regulations and technical standards	Safety, health, or technical regulations; labeling requirements.	May delay or block the entry of imported products, and reduce the quantity of available products, resulting in higher costs to importers and buyers.	Saudi Arabia bans importation of firearms and used clothing. The European Union requires extensive testing on thousands of different imported chemicals.
Administrative and bureaucratic procedures	Complex procedures or requirements imposed on importers or foreign investors that hinder their trade or investment activities.	Slows the import of products or services. Hinders or delays firms' investment activities.	Russia imposes a series of inspections and bureaucratic procedures for the import of alcoholic beverages.
FDI and ownership restrictions	Rules that limit the ability of foreign firms to invest in certain industries or acquire local firms.	Reduces the amount of money that a foreigner can invest in a country, and/or the proportion of ownership that a foreigner can hold in an existing or new firm in the country. May require a foreign firm to invest in the country in order to do business there.	Switzerland requires foreign firms seeking to sell insurance there to do so by establishing a local subsidiary or branch office, via FDI. Brazil restricts foreign investment in its media industry and certain transportation industries.
Subsidy	Financing or other resources that a government grants to a firm or group of firms, intended to ensure their survival or success.	Increases the competitive advantage of the grantee, while diminishing the competitive advantages of those that do not receive the subsidy.	Turkey grants an export subsidy of up to 20% for local producers of wheat and sugar.
Countervailing duty	Increased duties imposed on products imported into a country to offset subsidies given to producers or exporters in the exporting country.	Reduces or eliminates the competitive advantages provided by subsidies.	India imposes countervailing duties on the import of numerous products.
Antidumping duty	Tax charged on an imported product whose price is below usual prices in the local market or below the cost of making the product	Reduces or eliminates the competitive advantage of imported products priced at abnormally low levels.	The United States has imposed antidumping duties on the import of low-cost steel, in order to support U.S.-based steel manufacturers.

EXHIBIT 5.5 Types of Effects of Government Intervention. *Source:* Adapted from the Office of the United States Trade Representative, retrieved from http://www.ustr.gov.

Tariffs

Some countries impose *export tariffs,* taxes on products exported by their own companies. The most common type of tariff, however, is the *import tariff*, a tax levied on imported products.

Import tariffs are usually *ad valorem*—that is, they are assessed as a percentage of the value of the imported product. Or a government may impose a *specific tariff*—a flat fee or fixed amount per unit of the imported product—based on weight, volume, or surface area, such as barrels of oil or square meters of fabric. A *revenue tariff* is intended to raise money for the government. A tariff on cigarette imports, for example, produces a steady flow of revenue. A *protective tariff* aims to protect domestic industries from foreign competition. A *prohibitive tariff* is one so high that no one can import the restricted item.

Import tariffs can generate substantial revenue for national governments. This helps explain why they are common in developing economies. Even in advanced economies, tariffs provide a significant source of revenue for the government. The European Union applies tariffs of up to 215 percent on meat, 116 percent on cereals, and 133 percent on sugar and confectionary products.[21] Significant tariffs and other trade barriers in the advanced economies hinder imports of agricultural goods from Africa, worsening already severe poverty in many African countries. Exhibit 5.6 provides a sample of import tariffs in selected countries.

Because high tariffs inhibit free trade and economic growth, governments have tended to reduce them over time. This was the primary goal of the General Agreement on Tariffs and Trade (GATT; now the WTO). Countries as diverse as Chile, Hungary, Turkey, and South Korea have liberalized their previously protected markets, lowering trade barriers and subjecting themselves to greater competition from abroad. In the early 1980s, average tariffs in the developing economies averaged about 30 percent. Today they are less than 8 percent. In the advanced economies as well, average tariffs averaged nearly 10 percent in the early 1980s, but have now declined to about 3 percent. Continued reductions represent a major driver of market globalization.

Country/Region	Average Import Tariff	
	Agricultural Products	Nonagricultural Products
Australia	2.8	5.6
Canada	10.8	2.9
China	16.0	9.1
European Union	11.8	2.4
India	41.9	5.5
Japan	10.1	1.3
Mexico	39.8	9.1
United States	5.3	2.0

EXHIBIT 5.6 Sampling of Import Tariffs. *Sources:* World Trade Organization statistics database, retrieved from http://stat.wto.org; United States Trade Representative reports, retrieved from http://www.ustr.org.

Nontariff Trade Barriers

Nontariff trade barriers are government policies or measures that restrict trade without imposing a direct tax or duty. They include quotas, import licenses, local content requirements, government regulations, and administrative or bureaucratic procedures. The use of nontariff barriers has grown substantially in recent decades. Governments sometimes prefer them because they are easier to conceal from the WTO and other organizations that monitor international trade.

Quotas restrict the physical volume or value of products that firms can import into a country. Governments can impose voluntary quotas, under which firms agree to limit exports of certain products. These are also known as *voluntary export restraints*, or *VERs*. For example, in 2005, import quotas in the European Union led to an impasse in which millions of Chinese-made garments piled up at ports and borders in Europe. The EU impounded the clothing because China had exceeded the voluntary import quotas it had negotiated with the EU. The action created hardship for European retailers, who had ordered their clothing stocks several months in advance.[22]

Governments occasionally require importing firms to obtain an **import license**, a formal permission to import, which restricts imports in a way that is similar to quotas. Do not confuse import licenses with licensing, which is a strategy for entering foreign markets in which one firm allows another the right to use its intellectual property in return for a fee. Governments sell import licenses to companies on a competitive basis or grant the licenses on a first-come, first-served basis. This tends to discriminate against smaller firms, which may lack the resources to purchase them.

Local content requirements force manufacturers to include a minimum of local value added—that is, production that takes place locally. Local content requirements are usually imposed in countries that are members of an economic bloc, such as the EU and NAFTA. The so-called *rules of origin requirement* specifies that a certain proportion of products and supplies, or of intermediate goods used in local manufacturing, must be produced within the bloc. For a car manufacturer, the tires or windshields it purchases from another firm are intermediate goods. When the firm does not meet this requirement, the products become subject to trade barriers that member governments usually impose on nonmember countries.

Government regulations and technical standards are another type of nontariff trade barrier. Examples include safety regulations for motor vehicles and electrical equipment, health regulations for hygienic food preparation, labeling requirements that indicate a product's country of origin, technical standards for computers, and bureaucratic procedures for customs clearance, including excessive red tape and slow approval processes.

Governments may impose *administrative or bureaucratic procedures* that hinder the activities of importers or foreign firms. Many countries in Africa and Latin America impose countless bureaucratic procedures that hinder commercial activities and business start-ups. By contrast, Australia, Britain, Canada, Ireland, New Zealand, and Singapore impose relatively few such procedures.[23]

Investment Barriers

Around the world, FDI and ownership restrictions are particularly common in such industries as broadcasting, utilities, air transportation, military technology, and financial services, as well as industries in which the government has major holdings, such as oil and key minerals. For example, the Canadian government restricts foreign ownership of local movie studios and TV networks to protect its home-grown film and TV industries from excessive foreign influence. FDI and ownership restrictions are particularly burdensome in the services sector because services usually cannot be exported and providers must establish a physical presence in target markets to conduct business there. Occasionally, governments impose investment barriers aimed at protecting home country industries and jobs.

Currency controls restrict the outflow of widely used currencies, such as the dollar, euro, and yen, and occasionally the inflow of foreign currencies. Controls can help conserve especially valuable currency or reduce the risk of capital flight. They are particularly common in developing economies. Some countries employ a system of dual official exchange rates, offering exporters a relatively favorable rate to encourage exports, while importers receive a relatively unfavorable rate to discourage imports.

Currency controls favor companies when they export their products from the host country but harm those that rely heavily on imported parts and components. Controls also restrict the ability of MNEs to *repatriate* their profits—that is, transfer revenues from profitable operations back to the home country.

Subsidies and Other Government Support Programs

Subsidies are monetary or other resources that a government grants to a firm or group of firms, intended either to encourage exports or simply to facilitate the production and marketing of products at reduced prices, to help ensure the companies prosper. Subsidies come in the form of outright cash disbursements, material inputs, services, tax breaks, the construction of infrastructure, and government contracts at inflated prices.

Critics argue that subsidies confer unfair advantages on recipients by reducing their cost of doing business. The WTO prohibits subsidies when it can be proven they hinder free trade. Subsidies, however, are hard to define. For example, when a government provides land, infrastructure, telecommunications systems, or utilities to the firms in a corporate park, this is technically a subsidy. Yet many view this type of support as an appropriate public function.

The U.S. government provides subsidies for more than two dozen commodities, including wheat, barley, cotton, milk, rice, peanuts, sugar, tobacco, and soybeans. In Europe, the Common Agricultural Policy (CAP) is a system of subsidies that represents about 40 percent of the EU's budget, amounting to tens of billions of euros annually. The U.S. and CAP subsidies have been criticized for promoting unfair competition and high prices because they encourage overproduction and therefore lower food prices at home, making agricultural imports from developing countries less competitive.

Governments sometimes retaliate against subsidies by imposing **countervailing duties**, tariffs on products imported into a country to offset subsidies given to producers or exporters in the exporting country. In this way, the duty serves to cancel out the effect of the subsidy by converting it into a direct income transfer by the exporting country to the rest of the world.

Subsidies may allow a manufacturer to practice **dumping**—that is, to charge an unusually low price for exported products, typically lower than that for domestic or third-country customers, or even lower than manufacturing cost.[24] While dumping is hard to prove because firms usually do not reveal data on their cost structures, it is against WTO rules because it amounts to unfair competition. A large MNE that charges very low prices could conceivably drive competitors out of a foreign market, achieving a monopoly, with the ability to raise prices later. Governments in the importing country often respond to dumping by imposing an **antidumping duty**—a tax imposed on products deemed to be dumped and thereby causing injury to producers of competing products in the importing country. The WTO allows this practice.[25] The duties are generally equal to the difference between the product's export price and their normal value.

Government subsidies are not always direct or overt. For example, governments may support home country businesses by funding R&D, granting tax exemptions, and offering business development services such as market information and trade missions. Most countries have agencies and ministries that provide such services to facilitate the international activities of their own firms. Governments also support domestic industries by adopting *procurement policies* that restrict purchases to home country suppliers.

Related to subsidies are governmental **investment incentives**, transfer payments or tax concessions made directly to individual foreign firms to entice them to invest in the country. Hong Kong's government put up most of the cash to build the Hong Kong Disney park (park.hongkongdisneyland.com). While the park and facilities cost about $1.81 billion, the government provided Disney an investment of $1.74 billion to develop the site.

Consequences of Government Intervention

We have seen that average tariffs have declined over time. At the same time world GDP, and especially world trade, have flourished. In the past two decades, just as trade barriers have fallen substantially, the volume of world trade has increased several hundred percent. In the same time period, world GDP has nearly tripled. Firms that participate actively in international trade and investment not only improve their performance but also contribute to reducing global poverty.[26]

One way of evaluating the effects of government intervention is to examine each nation's level of *economic freedom*, defined as the "absence of government coercion or constraint on the production, distribution, or consumption of goods and services beyond the extent necessary for citizens to protect and maintain liberty itself. In other words, people are free to work, produce, consume, and invest in the ways they feel are most productive."[27] The *Index of Economic Freedom* (www.heritage.org) measures economic freedom in 161 countries, based on criteria such as the level of trade barriers, rule of law, level of business regulation, and protection of intellectual property rights.[28] The index classifies virtually all the advanced economies as "free," all the emerging markets as either "free" or "mostly free," and all the developing economies as "mostly unfree" or "repressed," underscoring the close relationship between limited government intervention and economic freedom.

Economic freedom flourishes when government supports the institutions necessary for that freedom and provides an appropriate level of intervention and regulation. In 2010, for the first time, the United States fell into the second highest category, due to increased U.S. federal government intervention in the nation's economy following the recent global financial crisis.

Government intervention and trade barriers raise ethical concerns for developing economies. For example, United States import tariffs on clothing and shoes often exceed 20 percent. In 2008, duties on imported clothing alone produced $10 billion in revenue for the U.S. government. The tariffs hurt poor countries such as Bangladesh, Pakistan, India, and several nations in Africa, where clothing and shoe exporters are concentrated. The tariffs that confront such nations are often several times those faced by the richest countries.[29]

Government intervention can also offset harmful effects. For example, trade barriers can create or protect jobs. Subsidies can help counterbalance harmful consequences that disproportionately affect the poor, as when a government provides subsidies aimed at retraining unemployed workers.[30]

HOW FIRMS CAN RESPOND TO GOVERNMENT INTERVENTION

Although a manager's first inclination might be to avoid markets with high trade and investment barriers or excessive government intervention, this course is not usually practical. Depending on the industry and country, firms generally must cope with protectionism and other forms of intervention.

Strategies for Managers

We've seen that China, India, and numerous other countries in Africa, Asia, Latin America, and Eastern and Central Europe feature extensive trade barriers and government involvement. Yet many firms seek to target emerging markets and developing economies because of the huge long-term potential they offer.[31]

RESEARCH TO GATHER KNOWLEDGE AND INTELLIGENCE Experienced managers continually scan the business environment to identify the nature of government intervention and to plan market-entry strategies and host country operations. They review their return-on-investment criteria to account for the increased cost and risk of trade and investment barriers.

CHOOSE THE MOST APPROPRIATE ENTRY STRATEGIES Tariffs and most nontariff trade barriers apply to exporting, whereas investment barriers apply to FDI. Most firms choose exporting as their initial entry strategy. However, if high tariffs are present, managers should consider other strategies, such as FDI, licensing, and joint ventures that allow the firm to operate directly in the target market, avoiding import barriers.

However, even investment-based entry is affected by tariffs if it requires importing raw materials and parts to manufacture finished products in the host country. Tariffs often vary with the *form* of an imported product. Hence, companies may ship manufactured products "knocked-down" and assemble them in the target market. In countries with relatively high tariffs on imported personal computers, importers often bring in the parts and assemble the computers locally.

TAKE ADVANTAGE OF FOREIGN TRADE ZONES A **foreign trade zone (FTZ)** is an area within a country that receives imported goods for assembly or other processing and subsequent re-export.[32] Products brought into an FTZ are not subject to duties, taxes, or quotas until they, or the products made from them, enter into the non-FTZ commercial territory of the country where the FTZ is located. Firms use FTZs to assemble foreign dutiable materials and components into finished products, which are then re-exported. Alternatively, firms may use FTZs to manage inventory of parts, components, or finished products that the firm will eventually need at some other location. A successful experiment with FTZs is **maquiladoras**—export-assembly plants in northern Mexico that import materials and equipment on a tariff-free basis for assembly or manufacturing and then re-export the assembled products.

SEEK FAVORABLE CUSTOMS CLASSIFICATIONS FOR EXPORTED PRODUCTS One approach for reducing exposure to trade barriers is to have exported products classified in the appropriate harmonized product code to ensure the lowest tariff code. Or the manufacturer may be able to modify the exported product in a way that helps minimize trade barriers. By shifting manufacturing to rubber-soled shoes, Korean firms avoided a quota on non-rubber footwear to the United States and greatly increased their footwear exports.

TAKE ADVANTAGE OF INVESTMENT INCENTIVES AND OTHER GOVERNMENT SUPPORT PROGRAMS Obtaining economic development incentives such as reduced utility rates, employee training programs, tax holidays, and the construction of new infrastructure from host or home country governments is another strategy to reduce the cost of trade and investment barriers. Governments in Europe, Japan, and the United States increasingly provide incentives to companies that set up shop within their borders.

LOBBY FOR FREER TRADE AND INVESTMENT More nations are liberalizing markets to create jobs and increase tax revenues. The trend results partly from the efforts of firms to lobby domestic and foreign governments to lower their trade and investment barriers. The private sector lobbies federal authorities to undertake government-to-government trade negotiations, aimed at lowering barriers. Private firms bring complaints to world bodies, especially the WTO, to address unfair trading practices of key international markets.

Summary

International business is influenced by political and legal systems. **Country risk** reflects exposure to potential loss or to adverse effects on company operations and profitability caused by developments in national political and legal environments. A **political system** is a set of formal institutions that constitute a government. A **legal system** is a system for interpreting and enforcing laws. Adverse developments in political and legal systems increase country risk.

Democracy is characterized by private property rights and limited government. Socialism often occurs as *social democracy*. Today, most governments combine elements of socialism and democracy. Totalitarianism is associated with command economies, socialism with mixed economies, and democracy with market economies.

There are four major legal systems: common law, civil law, religious law, and mixed systems. The **rule of law** implies a legal system in which laws are clear, understood, respected, and fairly enforced. Governments impose constraints on corporate operating methods in areas such as production, marketing, and distribution. They may expropriate or confiscate the assets of foreign firms. Foreign investment laws include controls on operating forms and practices, regulations affecting marketing and distribution, restrictions on income repatriation, environmental laws, and Internet and e-commerce regulations. **Extraterritoriality** is the application of home country laws to conduct outside of national borders. Accounting and reporting laws vary around the world. **Transparency** is the degree to which firms reveal substantial and regular information about their financial condition and accounting practices.

Successful management of country risk requires developing an understanding of the political and legal context abroad. Despite the value of free trade, governments often intervene in international business. Protectionism refers to national economic policies designed to restrict free trade and protect domestic industries from foreign competition. Government intervention arises typically in the form of tariffs, nontariff trade barriers, and investment barriers. **Tariffs** are taxes on imported products, imposed mainly to collect government revenue and protect domestic industries from foreign competition. **Nontariff trade barriers** consist of policies that restrict trade without directly imposing a tax. An example of a nontariff trade barrier is a **quota**, a quantitative restriction on imports. Governments impose trade and investment barriers to achieve political, social, or economic objectives. Governments also provide **subsidies**, a form of payment or other material support. With **dumping**, a firm charges abnormally low prices abroad. Governments support homegrown firms by providing **investment incentives** and biased government procurement policies.

Firms should conduct research to understand the extent and nature of trade and investment barriers abroad. When trade barriers are substantial, FDI or joint ventures are often the most appropriate entry strategies. Where importing is essential, the firm can take advantage of **foreign trade zones**, areas where imports receive preferential tariff treatment. Government assistance in the form of subsidies and incentives helps reduce the impact of protectionism.

Key Terms

antidumping duty *98*
countervailing duties *97*
country risk *78*
currency controls *97*
customs *92*
dumping *97*
export controls *93*
extraterritoriality *89*

foreign trade zone
  (FTZ) *99*
import license *96*
investment incentives *98*
legal system *80*
maquiladoras *100*
nontariff trade
  barrier *91*

political system *80*
protectionism *91*
quota *92*
rule of law *85*
subsidies *97*
tariff *91*
transparency *101*

Endnotes

1. "Country Risk," *Economist*, February 26, 2005, p. 102.
2. "Getting Past Yukos," *Business Week*, September 13, 2004, p. 52.
3. Steven Soper, *Totalitarianism: A Conceptual Approach* (Lanham, MD: University Press of America, 1985); Carl J. Friedrich and Zbigniew Brzezinski, *Totalitarian Dictatorship and Autocracy*, 2nd ed. (Cambridge, MA: Harvard University Press, 1965).
4. Milton Friedman and Rose Friedman, *Free to Choose* (New York: Harcourt Brace Jovanovich, 1980).
5. Joseph Johnson and Gerald Tellis, "Drivers of Success for Market Entry into China and India," *Journal of Marketing* 72 (May 2008): 1–13.
6. Martin Schnitzer and James Nordyke, *Comparative Economic Systems* (Cincinnati, OH: Southwestern, 1983); Milton Friedman, "The Battle's Half Won," *Wall Street Journal*,

December 9, 2004, p. A16; Statistical Abstract of the United States, Economics and Statistics Administration (Washington, DC: U.S. Census Bureau, 2004).

7. J. Blas and C. Hoyos, "Oil Wrestling," *Financial Times,* May 5, 2006, p. 15.

8. Charles Forelle, "EU Investigates Breakup of Fortis," *Wall Street Journal,* April 9, 2009, p. C3; Patrick Jenkins and Kiran Stacey, "Bank 'Brainstorm' Marks Loan Drive," *Financial Times,* July 1, 2010, p. 2.

9. David Wernick and Sumit Kundu, "Terrorism, Political Risk and International Business: Conceptual Considerations," in *Proceedings: 2008 Annual Conference, Academy of International Business* (East Lansing, MI: Academy of International Business, 2008).

10. Jason Bush, "Russia's Raiders," *Business Week,* June 16, 2008, pp. 67–71.

11. Yonah Alexander, David Valton, and Paul Wilkinson, *Terrorism: Theory and Practice* (Boulder, CO: Westview, 1979).

12. M. Srivastava and N. Lakshman, "How Risky Is India?" *Business Week,* December 4, 2008, retrieved from http://www.businessweek.com.

13. Jonathan Laing, "Aftershock," *Barron's,* September 9, 2002, p. 23.

14. International Chamber of Commerce, "Policy Statement: Extraterritoriality and Business," July 13, 2006.

15. Kurt Stanberry, Barbara C. George, and Maria Ross, "Securities Fraud in the International Arena," *Business and Society* 30, no. 1 (1991): 27–36.

16. Randall Hess and Edgar Kossack, "Bribery as an Organizational Response to Conflicting Environmental Expectations," *Academy of Marketing Science* 9, no. 3 (1981): 206–26; Judith Scott, Debora Gilliard, and Richard Scott, "Eliminating Bribery as a Transnational Marketing Strategy," *International Journal of Commerce & Management* 12, no. 1 (2002): 1–17.

17. Jeffrey D. Sachs and Andrew Warner, "Economic Reform and the Process of Global Integration," *Brookings Papers on Economic Activity,* issue no. 1 (Washington, DC: Brookings Institute, 1995); Heritage Foundation, retrieved from www.heritage .org/research/features/index/.

18. David Dollar and Aart Kraay, "Trade, Growth, and Poverty," Policy Research Working Paper no. WPS 2615, June 2001, Washington DC: World Bank, Development Research Group; United Nations, *World Economic and Social Survey,* 2005, retrieved from http://www .un.org.

19. Stefanie Lenway, Kathleen Rehbein, and Laura Starks, "The Impact of Protectionism on Firm Wealth: The Experience of the Steel Industry," *Southern Economic Journal* 56, no. 4 (1990): 1079–93.

20. United Nations, 2009, retrieved from http:// www.un.org/reports/financing/profile.htm.

21. World Trade Organization, *Tariff Profile on the European Union,* 2009, retrieved from http://www.wto.org.; Dustin Smith, "The Truth about Industrial Country Tariffs," *Finance and Development* 39, no. 3 (2002); International Monetary Fund, retrieved from http://www.imf.org.

22. "Textiles: Knickers in a Twist," *Economist,* August 27, 2005, p. 50.

23. World Bank, *Doing Business: Benchmarking Business Regulations,* 2009, retrieved from http://www.doingbusiness.org.

24. World Trade Organization, Glossary, 2009, retrieved from http://www.wto.org.

25. *Ibid.*

26. "World Trade: Barriers to Entry," *Economist,* December 20, 2008, p. 121.

27. William Beach and Marc Miles, "Explaining the Factors of the Index of Economic Freedom," *2005 Index of Economic Freedom* (Washington, DC: Heritage Foundation), retrieved from http://www.heritage.org.

28. Heritage Foundation, *2010 Index of Economic Freedom* (Washington, DC: Heritage Foundation), retrieved from http:// www.heritage.org.

29. Smith (2002).

30. C. Giles, "Big Ideas Fail to Mop Up Europe's Current Mess," *Financial Times,* February 26, 2009, p. 2.

31. "In the Shadow of Prosperity," *Economist,* January 20, 2007, pp. 32–34.

32. Militiades Chacholidades, *International Economics* (New York: McGraw Hill, 1990); James Ingram, *International Economics* (New York: Wiley, 1983); William McDaniel and Edgar Kossack, "The Financial Benefits to Users of Foreign-Trade Zones," *Columbia Journal of World Business* 18, no. 3 (1983): 33–41.

CHAPTER

6

The International Monetary Environment and Financial Management in the Global Firm

LEARNING OBJECTIVES
In this chapter, you will learn about:

1. Exchange rates and currencies

2. How exchange rates are determined

3. The monetary and financial systems

4. Financial management in the global firm

5. Managing currency risk

6. Managing accounting and tax practices

EXCHANGE RATES AND CURRENCIES

International business transactions take place within the global monetary and financial systems. When people think of international trade, invariably they think of trade in products and services. However, the markets for foreign exchange and capital are much larger. Firms regularly trade the U.S. dollar, European euro, Japanese yen, and other leading currencies to meet their international business obligations.

More than 150 currencies are in use around the world. Cross-border transactions occur through an exchange of these currencies between buyers and sellers. A currency is a form of money and a unit of exchange. The **exchange rate**—the price of one currency expressed in terms of another—varies over time. It links different national currencies so that buyers and sellers can make international price and cost

	Currency per One U.S. Dollar	U.S. Dollars per Unit of Currency
Australian Dollar	1.057	0.946
Brazilian Real	1.607	0.622
British Pound	0.613	1.631
Canadian Dollar	0.987	1.013
Chinese Yuan	6.381	0.157
European Euro	0.693	1.443
Indian Rupee	46.125	0.022
Japanese Yen	76.630	0.013
Mexican Peso	12.479	0.080
New Zealand Dollar	1.199	0.834
Norwegian Kroner	5.395	0.185
Saudi Riyal	3.750	0.266
Singapore Dollar	1.203	0.831
South African Rand	7.192	0.139
South Korean Won	1077.205	0.001
Turkish Lira	1.752	0.571

EXHIBIT 6.1 Exchange Rates for the U.S. Dollar as of August 26, 2011. *Sources: Wall Street Journal*, http://www.wsj.com; Oanda Currency Converter, http://www.oanda.com; Everbank, http://www.everbank.com

comparisons. Exhibit 6.1 provides the exchange rates for the U.S. dollar and a sample of other currencies on one day. The values of these national currencies, and thus their exchange rates, fluctuate constantly. Fluctuations in exchange rates may have the following implications for managerial decisions and their outcomes: (1) the prices the firm charges can be quoted in the home country currency or in the currencies of its foreign customers; (2) the firm and its customers can use the exchange rate as it stands on the date of each transaction, or they can agree to use a specific exchange rate; and (3) because several months can pass between placement and delivery of an order, fluctuations in the exchange rate during that time can cost or earn the firm money.

Firms with international transactions face **currency risk**—the potential harm from unexpected changes in the price of one currency relative to another. If you buy from a supplier whose currency is appreciating against yours, you may need to pay a larger amount of your currency to complete the purchase. If you expect payment from a customer whose currency is depreciating against yours, you may receive a smaller amount of your currency if the sale price is expressed in the currency of the customer. Of course, if the foreign currency fluctuates in your favor, you may gain a windfall. Exporters and licensors also face risk because foreign buyers must either pay in a foreign currency or convert their currency into that of the vendor.

A *convertible currency* can be readily exchanged for other currencies. The most readily convertible ones are called *hard currencies*. These are strong, stable currencies—such as the U.S. dollar, Japanese yen, and European euro—that are universally accepted and the most used for international transactions. Nations prefer to hold hard currencies as reserves because of their strength and stability. A currency is *nonconvertible* when it is not acceptable for international transactions. Some governments may not allow their currency to be converted into a foreign currency to preserve their supply of hard currencies or to avoid the problem of capital flight. **Capital flight** is the rapid sell-off by residents or foreigners of their holdings in a nation's currency or other assets, usually in response to a domestic crisis that causes them to lose confidence in the country's economy. The Bank of Japan had to pump hundreds of billions of yen and other currencies into the struggling Japanese economy.

Domestic crises often result from country risk, such as adverse government policies. Crises can also result from natural causes outside a nation's control. For example, following the massive earthquake in Japan in 2011, the Japanese stock market tumbled. Tokyo Electric Power owned the disabled nuclear reactors in central Japan, and lost more than 50 percent of its share value on world stock markets. Major nuclear plant suppliers also saw steep share value declines.

Foreign exchange represents all forms of money that are traded internationally, including foreign currencies, bank deposits, checks, and electronic transfers. The **foreign exchange market** is the global marketplace for buying and selling national currencies. The market has no fixed location. Rather, trading occurs through continuous buying and selling among banks, currency traders, governments, and other exchange agents located worldwide.

Sometimes exchange rate fluctuations between the U.S. dollar, the euro, the yen, and other currencies are dramatic. In 2008, for example, the Indian rupee was trading at 40 rupees to the U.S. dollar. By mid-2010, the rate had fluctuated to 48 rupees. More rupees to the dollar means the rupee is worth less in terms of the dollar; hence the rupee had depreciated in value (from $0.025/rupee to $0.020833/rupee, which is a 16.67 percent decrease). Implications for international business with India were substantial. In the span of only 18 months, Indian firms perceived a significant upturn in their exports, as Indian products became less expensive in dollar terms. Meanwhile, as rupee-buying power for dollars decreased, U.S. firms experienced a decline in their exports to India.[1]

Fluctuating exchange rates affect both firms and consumers. Suppose today the euro/dollar exchange rate is €1 = $1; that is, for a European to buy one U.S. dollar, she or he must pay one euro. Next, suppose that during the coming year the exchange rate goes to €1.50 = $1. Now the dollar is much more expensive to European firms and consumers than before—it costs 50 percent more to acquire a dollar. Let's examine the effect of this change on Europeans.

Effect on European Firms

- European firms must pay more for inputs from the United States, such as raw materials, components, and support services they use to produce finished products and services.
- Higher input costs reduce profitability and may force firms to raise prices to final customers; these higher prices lower customer demand for goods and services.

- Because the euro has become less expensive for U.S. consumers, firms can increase their exports to the United States. Firms can even raise their export prices and remain competitive in the U.S. market.
- Increased exports to the United States generate higher revenues and higher profits.

Effect on European Consumers

- Because U.S. products and services now cost more, European consumers demand fewer of them.
- The cost of living rises for those Europeans who consume many dollar-denominated imports.
- Fewer European tourists can afford to visit the United States. Fewer European students study at U.S. universities.

Now, suppose the euro/dollar exchange rate goes to €0.50 =$1. The effects are essentially the opposite of those summarized above: European firms pay less for inputs from the United States, which means firms that use many such inputs can drop their prices on goods and services. Because U.S. products and services now cost less, consumers demand more of them. Given the potential volatility of exchange rates, managers must monitor exchange rates constantly and devise strategies to optimize firm performance.

HOW EXCHANGE RATES ARE DETERMINED

In a free market, the price of any currency—that is, its exchange rate—is determined by supply and demand. All else being equal, the greater the supply of a currency, the lower its price; the lower the supply of a currency, the higher its price. The greater the demand for a currency, the higher its price; and the lower the demand for a currency, the lower its price. Some of the main factors that influence the supply and demand for a currency are interest rates, inflation, market psychology, and government action.

Higher interest rates in a country can attract investment flows into the country, causing an increase in the demand for the country's currency, and hence, an appreciation of its value.

Inflation is an increase in the price of goods and services, so that money buys less than in preceding years. Inflation rates have reached very high levels in some countries. Argentina, Zimbabwe, and some other countries have had prolonged periods of *hyperinflation*—persistent annual double-digit and sometimes triple-digit rates of price increases. A practical effect of hyperinflation is the need, say, for a restaurant owner to change the menu every few days to list the most recent prices. In countries with high inflation, a currency's purchasing power is constantly falling and interest rates tend to be high because investors expect to be compensated for the inflation-induced decline in the value of their money. If inflation is running at 10 percent, for example, banks must pay *more* than 10 percent interest to attract customers to open savings accounts. Inflation occurs when the **central bank** increases the nation's supply of money faster than the real demand to hold money.

Exchange rates are often affected by *market psychology*—unpredictable behavior of investors. *Herding* is the tendency of investors to mimic each others' actions.

Momentum trading occurs when investors buy financial instruments whose prices have been rising and sell financial instruments whose prices have been falling. It is usually carried out using computers set up to do massive buying or selling when asset prices reach certain levels.

Because the pricing of currencies affects economic conditions and company performance, governments often act to influence the value of their own currencies. An undervalued national currency can result in a **trade surplus,** which arises when a nation's exports exceed its imports for a specific period of time, causing a net inflow of foreign exchange. By contrast, a **trade deficit** results when a nation's imports exceed its exports for a specific period of time, causing a net outflow of foreign exchange.

The *balance of trade* is the difference between the monetary value of a nation's exports and its imports over the course of a year. For example, if Germany exports cars to Kenya, money flows out of Kenya and into Germany, resulting in a surplus item in Germany's balance of trade and a deficit item in Kenya's balance of trade. Many economists believe a persistent trade deficit is harmful to the national economy. When a trade deficit becomes severe or persists for a long time, the nation's central bank may devalue its currency. **Devaluation** is usually accomplished by buying and selling currencies in the foreign exchange market. It aims to deter the nation's residents from importing from other countries, potentially reducing the trade deficit.[2]

At a broader level, governments must manage their **balance of payments,** the annual accounting of all economic transactions of a nation with all other nations. The balance of payments is a statement that shows the nation's flows, typically over a year, of trade, investment, and transfer payments with the rest of the world. The balance of payments represents the difference between the *total* amount of money coming into and going out of a country. Consider a Canadian MNE that builds a factory in China. In the process, money flows from Canada to China, generating a deficit item for Canada and a surplus item for China in their respective balance of payments. The balance of payments is affected by other transactions as well, as when citizens donate money to a foreign charity, when governments provide foreign aid, or when tourists spend money abroad.

The Contemporary Exchange Rate System

The Great Depression (1929–1939) and World War II (1939–1945) coincided with a collapse of the international trading system and relationships among nations. In 1944, the governments of forty-four countries signed the Bretton Woods Agreement, which pegged the value of the U.S. dollar to an established value of gold and compelled the U.S. government to buy and sell unlimited amounts of gold in order to maintain this fixed rate. All the other Bretton Woods signatory countries agreed to establish a par value of their currencies in terms of the U.S. dollar and to maintain this pegged value through central bank intervention. In this way, the Bretton Woods system kept exchange rates of major currencies fixed at a prescribed level relative to the U.S. dollar and, therefore, to each other. However, in 1971, unfavorable economic conditions led to the demise of the Bretton Woods agreement. The link between the U.S. dollar and gold was suspended and the promise to exchange gold for U.S. dollars was withdrawn.

Bretton Woods left a legacy of principles and institutions that remain today. First is the concept of international monetary cooperation, especially among the central banks of leading nations. Second, Bretton Woods established the notion of fixing exchange rates within an international regime to minimize currency risk. Third, it created the **International Monetary Fund** (**IMF**; www.imf.org) and the **World Bank** (www.worldbank.org). The IMF is an international agency that attempts to stabilize currencies by monitoring the foreign exchange systems of member countries and lending money to developing economies. The World Bank is an international agency that provides loans and technical assistance to low and middle-income countries, with the goal of reducing poverty. Finally, Bretton Woods established the importance of currency convertibility, in which countries agree not to impose restrictions on currency trading and to avoid discriminatory currency arrangements.

Today most major currencies are traded freely, with their value floating according to the forces of supply and demand. The price of gold fluctuates freely on world markets and governments use the exchange rate system that best suits their needs. Countries are no longer compelled to maintain specific pegged values for their currency. Instead, they generally emphasize policies that support the stability of their currency relative to others. The exchange rate system today consists of two main types of foreign exchange management: the floating system and the fixed system.

Most advanced economies use the *floating exchange rate system*, in which the government refrains from systematic intervention, and the nation's currency floats independently, its value determined by market forces. In this way, exchange rates for major world currencies—including the Canadian dollar, British pound, euro, U.S. dollar, and Japanese yen—are determined by supply and demand on world exchange markets. Their values fluctuate constantly. By contrast, the *pegged exchange rate system* (sometimes called the *fixed exchange rate system)* is similar to the system used under the Bretton Woods agreement. The value of a currency is set relative to the value of another (or to the value of a basket of currencies) at a specified rate. The pegged system is used mainly by developing economies and emerging markets. China pegs its currency to the value of a basket of currencies. Belize pegs its currency to the U.S. dollar. To maintain the peg, the governments of such countries intervene in currency markets to buy and sell dollars and other currencies.

THE MONETARY AND FINANCIAL SYSTEMS

Firms want to get paid for the goods they sell abroad. Portfolio investors seek to invest in stocks and other liquid assets around the world. The resulting monetary flows take the form of various currencies traded among nations. Accordingly, the **international monetary system** consists of the institutional frameworks, rules, and procedures that govern how national currencies are exchanged for one another. By providing a framework for the monetary and foreign exchange activities of firms and governments worldwide, the system facilitates international trade and investment. To function well, national governments and international agencies have focused on creating a system that inspires confidence and ensures liquidity in monetary and financial holdings.

The **global financial system** consists of the collective financial institutions that facilitate and regulate flows of investment and capital funds worldwide. Key players in the system include finance ministries, national stock exchanges, commercial banks, central banks, the *Bank for International Settlements*, the *World Bank*, and the

International Monetary Fund. Thus, the system incorporates the national and international banking systems, the international bond market, the collective of national stock markets, and the market for bank deposits denominated in foreign currencies.

Money flowing abroad as portfolio investments is a relatively new trend. The volume of these flows is enormous. In 2008, for example, foreigners held about 18 percent of total outstanding U.S. long-term securities.[3] In developing economies, inward investment increases foreign exchange reserves, reduces the cost of capital, and stimulates local development of financial markets. The growing integration of financial and monetary activity worldwide has resulted from several factors, including the loosening of monetary and financial regulations worldwide; expansion of new technologies, payment systems, and the Internet in global financial activities; increased global and regional interdependence of financial markets; and the growing role of single-currency systems, such as the euro.

A variety of national, international, private, and government players make up the international monetary system and the global financial system. Exhibit 6.2 highlights the major players and the relationships among them. These players operate at the levels of the firm, the nation, and the world.

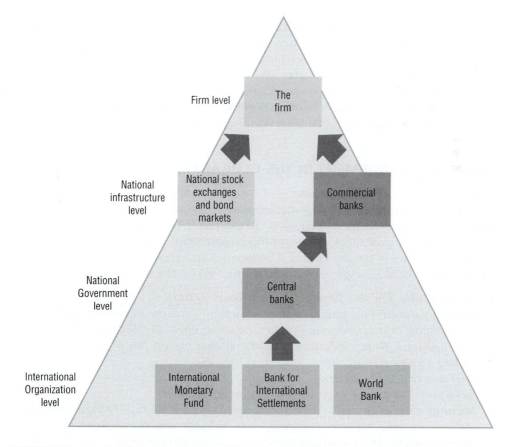

EXHIBIT 6.2 Key Participants and Relationships in the Global Monetary and Financial Systems.

Based in Basel, Switzerland, the Bank for International Settlements (www.bis .org) is an international organization that fosters cooperation among central banks and other governmental agencies. It provides banking services to central banks and assists them in devising sound monetary policy.[4] Headquartered in Washington, DC, the International Monetary Fund (IMF) provides the framework of and determines the code of behavior for the international monetary system. The agency promotes international monetary cooperation, exchange rate stability, and orderly exchange arrangements and encourages countries to adopt sound economic policies.[5]

The IMF plays an important role in addressing financial and monetary crises faced by nations around the world. Typical crises fall into three major categories. A *currency crisis* results when the value of a nation's currency depreciates sharply or when its central bank must expend substantial reserves to defend the value of its currency, thereby pushing up interest rates. A *banking crisis* results when domestic and foreign investors lose confidence in a nation's banking system, leading to widespread withdrawals of funds from banks and other financial institutions. A *foreign debt crisis* arises when a national government borrows an excessive amount of money, either from banks or from the sale of government bonds. Despite its efforts at assisting countries, the IMF has been criticized because its prescriptions often require nations to undertake painful reforms.

The World Bank (www.worldbank.org) aims to reduce world poverty and is active in development projects to bring water, electricity, and other infrastructure to poor countries. Headquartered in Washington, DC, the bank is a specialized agency of the United Nations, with more than 100 offices worldwide. Its subagencies oversee various international development activities, such as loaning funds to the world's poorest countries, promoting economic development, and providing guarantees to foreign investors to encourage FDI to developing countries.

FINANCIAL MANAGEMENT IN THE GLOBAL FIRM

International financial management is the acquisition and use of funds for cross-border trade, investment, R&D, manufacturing, marketing, outsourcing, and other commercial activities. Financial managers access funds from investors, foreign bond markets, local stock exchanges, foreign banks, venture capital firms, and intracorporate financing—wherever in the world capital is cheapest. In a typical multinational firm, the international financial manager must be competent in five financial management tasks:

1. *Raise funds for the firm's international activities.*   Obtain financing for funding value-adding activities and investment projects. Financing might come from selling stocks, borrowing money, or using internally generated funds.
2. *Manage cash flow.*   Administer funds passing in and out of the firm's value-adding activities.
3. *Perform capital budgeting.*   Assess the financial attractiveness of major investment projects, such as expansion into a foreign market.
4. *Manage currency risk.*   Oversee transactions in various foreign currencies and manage risk exposure resulting from exchange rate fluctuations.
5. *Manage accounting and tax practices.*   Learn to operate in a global environment with diverse accounting practices and international tax regimes.

The relevance of these tasks increases as the firm expands the scale of its international operations and must dedicate more attention to efficient cross-border acquisition and use of funds. Yet, it is precisely this scale of global operations that gives the firm strategic flexibility thanks to increased opportunities to tap capital at lower cost, minimize tax obligations, achieve efficient scale of financial operations, and gain bargaining power with lenders. Let's delve more deeply into the tasks summarized above.

Raising Funds for the Firm's International Activities

Companies can obtain financing in the **global money market**, the collective financial markets where firms and governments raise *short-term* financing. Alternatively, companies may obtain financing from the **global capital market**, the collective financial markets where firms and governments raise *intermediate and long-term* financing. Since funding for most projects comes from instruments whose maturity period is over one year, we refer to all such funding as *capital*. By participating in the global capital market, investors access a wide range of investment opportunities, and corporations can obtain funds from a large pool of sources at competitive cost.[6]

The global capital market is concentrated in major *financial centers*: New York, London, and Tokyo. Major secondary centers include Frankfurt, Hong Kong, Paris, San Francisco, Singapore, Sydney, and Zurich. At these locations, firms access the major suppliers of capital through banks, stock exchanges, and venture capitalists. Global capital markets have grown rapidly over time due to government deregulation, innovation in information and communication technologies, increased competitive pressures, and *securitization* of financial instruments—conversion of illiquid financial instruments, such as bank loans, into tradable securities, such as bonds.

The three primary sources of funds are equity financing, debt financing, and intracorporate financing. In **equity financing**, the firm obtains capital by selling stock, giving shareholders a percentage of ownership in the firm and, often, a stream of dividend payments. The firm can also retain earnings—that is, reinvest profit rather than pay it out as dividends to investors. The main advantage of equity financing is the firm obtains capital without debt. Internationally, many companies obtain equity financing in the **global equity market**—stock exchanges worldwide where investors and firms meet to buy and sell shares of stock. The world's largest stock exchanges by total value of share trading are the NASDAQ OMX and the New York Stock Exchange Euronext, both based in the United States. They are followed by the Shanghai Stock Exchange, the Tokyo Stock Exchange, and the London Stock Exchange. Foreign exchanges provide new opportunities for lucrative investing and help investors diversify their holdings.

Debt financing comes from either of two sources: loans from banks and other financial intermediaries or the sale of corporate bonds to individuals or institutions. Using debt financing can add value to the firm because some governments allow firms to deduct interest payments from their taxes. To minimize the possibility of bankruptcy and maintain a good credit rating, most MNEs keep the debt proportion of their capital structure below a threshold they can service even in adverse conditions. However, not all countries view substantial debt as risky. The average debt ratio in Germany, Italy, Japan, and numerous developing economies typically exceeds 50 percent.

Borrowing internationally is complicated by differences in national banking regulations, inadequate banking infrastructure, shortage of loanable funds, macroeconomic difficulties, and fluctuating currency values.[7] Another source of loan-able funds is money deposited in banks outside its country of origin. Although its role has declined in favor of the euro, the U.S. dollar accounts for the largest proportion of these funds.[8] **Eurodollars** are U.S. dollars held in banks outside the United States, including foreign branches of U.S. banks. Thus, a U.S. dollar-denominated bank deposit in Barclays Bank in London or Citibank in Tokyo is a Eurodollar deposit. More broadly, any currency deposited in a bank outside its origin country is called **Eurocurrency**. The Eurocurrency market is attractive to firms because these funds usually are not subject to the government regulations of their home country banking systems, such as reserve requirements.

A major source of debt financing is **bonds**, debt instruments that enable the issuer (borrower) to raise capital by promising to repay the principal along with interest on a specified date (maturity). Along with firms, governments, states, and other institutions also sell bonds. Investors purchase bonds and redeem them at face value in the future. The **global bond market** is the international marketplace in which bonds are bought and sold, primarily through bond brokers. **Foreign bonds** are sold outside the bond issuer's country in the currency of the country where issued. When Mexico's Cemex sells dollar-denominated bonds in the United States, it is issuing foreign bonds. **Eurobonds** are sold outside the bond issuer's home country but denominated in its own currency. When Toyota sells yen-denominated bonds in Canada, it is issuing Eurobonds.

Funding for international operations also can be obtained from within the firm's network of subsidiaries and affiliates. At times, when some units of an MNE are cash-rich and others are cash-poor, they can lend each other money. **Intracorporate financing** is funds from sources inside the firm (both headquarters and subsidiaries) in the form of equity, loans, and trade credits. Trade credit arises in the firm when a supplier unit grants a buyer unit the option to pay at a later date. Firms often prefer intersubsidiary loans because of tax benefits, the opportunity to minimize bank transaction costs, the ability to avoid diluting ownership, and because intracorporate loans have little effect on the parent's balance sheet since the funds are simply transferred from one area of the firm to another.

Managing Cash Flow

As part of working capital management, firms manage all current accounts, such as cash, accounts receivable, inventory, and accounts payable. Cash comes from various sources, especially sales revenue. An important goal of working capital management is ensuring cash is available when and where needed. Cash flow needs arise from everyday activities, such as buying raw materials, compensating workers, and making interest and tax payments. To optimize global operations, international finance managers devise strategies for transferring funds among the firm's operations worldwide. For companies with extensive international operations, the network of funds transfers can be vast. Roughly *one-third* of world trade consists of intracorporate buying and selling.

Financial managers employ various methods for transferring funds within the MNE. Funds must be moved efficiently, minimizing transaction costs and tax liabilities while maximizing returns. Within its network, an MNE can transfer funds through trade credit, dividend remittances, royalty payments, fronting loans, transfer pricing, and multilateral netting. Here is how each works:

- Through *trade credit*, a subsidiary can defer payment for goods and services received from the parent firm. The 30-day credit is the U.S. norm, while 90-day credit is typical in Europe, with longer terms elsewhere.
- *Dividend remittances* are common for transferring funds from foreign subsidiaries to the parent but vary depending on tax levels and currency risks. Some host governments levy high taxes on dividend payments or limit how much MNEs can remit.
- *Royalty payments* are compensation paid to owners of intellectual property. Assuming the subsidiary has licensed technology, trademarks, or other assets from the parent or other subsidiaries, royalties can be an efficient way to transfer funds and are tax deductible in many countries. A parent MNE can collect royalties from its own subsidiaries as a way of generating funds.
- In a **fronting loan**, the parent deposits a large sum in a foreign bank, which transfers it to a subsidiary as a loan. Fronting allows the parent to circumvent restrictions that foreign governments impose on direct intracorporate loans. While some countries restrict the amount of funds MNEs can transfer abroad, such restrictions usually do not apply to repayment of bank loans.
- *Transfer pricing* (also known as *intracorporate pricing*) is the means by which subsidiaries and affiliates charge each other as they exchange goods and services. For example, the Toyota car factory in Britain might purchase parts from the Toyota engine plant in Canada. Firms can use transfer pricing to shift profits from high-tax to low-tax countries, optimizing internal cash flows.
- **Multilateral netting** is the strategic reduction of cash transfers within the MNE family through the elimination of offsetting cash flows involving three or more subsidiaries that hold accounts payable or accounts receivable with another subsidiary. MNEs with numerous subsidiaries usually establish a netting center, a central exchange, that headquarters supervises. A typical MNE will pool funds in a regional or global *centralized depository*, and then direct these funds to needy subsidiaries or invest them to generate income.

    Let's give an example. Suppose a firm's Japanese subsidiary owes the Spanish subsidiary $8 million and the Spanish subsidiary owes the Japanese subsidiary $5 million. While the firm could cancel these debts in separate transactions, a better solution has the Japanese subsidiary pay the Spanish subsidiary $3 million. Transferring an amount considerably lower than either of the two original amounts greatly reduces transactions costs such as fees and delays in funds transfers.

Capital Budgeting

How do firms decide whether to launch a major exporting effort, acquire a distribution center, build a new factory, or refurbish industrial equipment? The purpose of *capital budgeting* is to help managers decide which international projects provide the best financial return. Managers typically employ net present value (NPV) analysis to evaluate domestic and international capital investment projects. NPV is the difference between the present value of a project's incremental cash flows and its initial investment requirement.[9] International capital budgeting is relatively complex because project cash flows are usually in a foreign currency, subject to country risk and differing tax rules, and governments may limit the international transfer of funds.

There are two approaches for addressing such international challenges. First, management may estimate the incremental after-tax operating cash flows in the subsidiary's local currency and *then* discount them at the project's cost of capital, or required rate of return, appropriate for its risk characteristics. If the NPV is positive, the project is expected to earn its required return and add value to the subsidiary. This approach takes the *project's perspective* in capital budgeting, and managers can use it as a first screening method. The second approach, called the *parent's perspective*, estimates future cash flows from the project in the *functional currency* of the parent—that is, the currency of the primary economic environment in which it operates. Thus, U.S.-based firms' functional currency is the U.S. dollar; for Japan-based firms it is the yen. This conversion forecasts *spot exchange rates*, or forward rates, and calculates their present value using a discount rate in line with the required return on projects of similar risk. Managers then compute the NPV in the parent's functional currency by subtracting the initial investment cash flow from the present value of the project cash flows. To be acceptable the project must add value to the parent firm, producing a positive NPV from the parent's perspective.

MANAGING CURRENCY RISK

Shifting currency values are among the biggest day-to-day challenges facing international firms. Foreign direct investors face currency risk because they receive payments and incur obligations in foreign currencies. Managers of foreign investment portfolios also face currency risk. A Japanese stock might gain 15 percent in value, but if the yen falls 15 percent, the stock gain is zero. Firms face currency risk when cash flows and the value of assets and liabilities shift due to changes in foreign exchange rates. Exporters and licensors face currency risk from unexpected exchange rate fluctuations as foreign buyers typically pay in their own currency.

Currency fluctuations result in three types of exposure for the firm: transaction exposure, translation exposure, and economic exposure.[10] **Transaction exposure** is currency risk that companies face when outstanding accounts receivable or payable are denominated in foreign currencies. Resulting gains or losses affect the firm's value directly by affecting its cash flows and profit. **Translation exposure** results when an MNE translates financial statements denominated in a foreign currency into the functional currency of the parent firm, as part of consolidating international financial results, that is, combining and integrating the financial results of foreign subsidiaries into the parent's financial records. **Economic exposure** (also known as *operating exposure*) results from exchange rate fluctuations that affect the pricing of products and inputs, and the value of foreign investments. Exchange rate fluctuations help or hurt sales by making the firm's products relatively more or less expensive for foreign buyers.

Foreign Exchange Trading

A relatively small number of currencies facilitate cross-border trade and investment. Nearly two-thirds of official foreign reserves are in U.S. dollars, one-quarter are in euros, and less than 5 percent are in British pounds, Japanese yen, and other currencies.[11] In 2010, the daily volume of global trading in foreign exchange amounted to some $3.2 trillion, which was more than 100 times the daily value of global trade in products and services.[12]

Large banks maintain reserves of major currencies and work with foreign *correspondent banks* to facilitate currency buying and selling. Currency transactions between banks occur in the *interbank market.* Currencies are also bought and sold through specialized brokers, especially active in major financial centers such as London, New York, and Sydney. Trading is also done online at sites such as www .forex.com and www.everbank.com. The foreign exchange market uses specialized terminology to describe the functions that currency dealers perform. The **spot rate** is the exchange rate applied when the current exchange rate is used for immediate receipt of a currency. The rate applies to transactions between banks for delivery within two business days, or immediate delivery for over-the-counter transactions involving nonbank customers—for example, when you buy currencies at airport kiosks.

The **forward rate** is the exchange rate applicable to the collection or delivery of foreign currencies at some future date. Dealers in the forward exchange market promise to receive or deliver foreign exchange at a specified time in the future, but at a rate determined at the time of the transaction. The function of the forward market is to provide protection against currency risk. Dealers quote currency exchange rates in two ways. The **direct quote**, also known as the *normal quote,* is the number of units of domestic currency needed to acquire one unit of foreign currency. For example, on September 1, 2011, it cost $1.44 to acquire one euro (€1). The **indirect quote** is the number of units of foreign currency obtained for one unit of domestic currency. For example, on September 1, 2011, it cost €0.69 to acquire $1.00. Foreign exchange dealers always quote a *bid* (buy) rate and an *offer* (sell) rate at which they will buy or sell any particular currency. The difference between the bid and offer rates—*the spread*—is the margin on which the dealer earns a profit.

Hedging, Speculation, and Arbitrage

The three main types of currency traders are hedgers, speculators, and arbitragers. **Hedgers**, typically MNEs and other international trade or investment firms, seek to minimize their risk of exchange rate fluctuations, often by entering into forward contracts or similar financial instruments. They are not necessarily interested in profiting from currency trading. **Speculators** are currency traders who seek profits by investing in currencies with the expectation their value will rise in the future and then sell them later at the higher value. The speculator can also bet on a currency's downturn by taking a *short position* in that currency. When investors take a short position, they sell a currency that they previously borrowed from a third party (usually a broker) with the intention of re-buying the identical currency at a later date to return to the lender. In so doing, the short seller hopes to profit from a decline in the value of the currency between the sale and the repurchase, as the seller will pay less to buy the currency than the seller received on selling it. **Arbitragers** are currency traders who buy and sell the same currency in two or more foreign-exchange markets to profit from differences in the currency's exchange rate. But unlike the speculator who bets on the future price of a currency, the arbitrager attempts to profit from a current disequilibrium in world currency markets based on known prices.

Losses due to exchange rate risk are common in international business, and arise from macroeconomic events, political risk, and other such phenomena. Firms with extensive international operations develop sophisticated capabilities to forecast exchange rates that combine in-house forecasting with reports provided by major banks and professional forecasters.

If a firm insists on quoting prices and getting paid in its own currency, the burden is on foreign buyers to monitor and manage foreign exchange. Even small exporters learn to operate in foreign currencies to remain competitive. The most common method for managing exposure is **hedging**, using financial instruments and other measures to lock in guaranteed foreign exchange positions. If the hedge is perfect, the firm is protected against the risk of adverse changes in the price of a currency. Banks offer forward contracts, options, and swap agreements to facilitate hedging and charge fees and interest payments on amounts borrowed to carry out the transactions. The firm must balance these costs against expected benefits.

Hedging Instruments

MNEs seek to minimize losses from international operations by employing various financial instruments. The four most common hedging instruments are forward contracts, futures contracts, currency options, and currency swaps. A **forward contract** is an agreement to exchange two currencies at a specified exchange rate on a set future date. No money changes hands until the delivery date of the contract. Banks quote forward prices in the same way as spot prices—with bid and ask prices at which they will buy or sell currencies. The bank's bid–ask spread is a cost for its customers. Forward contracts are especially appropriate for hedging transaction exposure.

Like a forward contract, a **futures contract** represents an agreement to buy or sell a currency in exchange for another at a specified price on a specified date. Unlike forward contracts, futures contracts are standardized to enable trading in organized exchanges, such as the Chicago Mercantile Exchange. While the terms of forward contracts are negotiated between a bank and its customer, futures contracts have standardized maturity periods and amounts. Futures contracts are especially useful for hedging transaction exposure.

A **currency option** differs from forward and futures contracts in that it gives the purchaser the right, but not the obligation, to buy a certain amount of foreign currency at a set exchange rate within a specified amount of time. The seller of the option must sell the currency at the buyer's discretion, at the price originally set. Currency options typically are traded on organized exchanges, such as the London Stock Exchange (www.londonstockexchange.com) and the Philadelphia Stock Exchange (PHLX; www .nasdaqtrader.com), and only for the major currencies.[13]

There are two types of options. A *call option* is the right, but not the obligation, to buy a currency at a specified price within a specific period (called an *American option*) or on a specific date (called a *European option*). A *put option* is the right to sell the currency at a specified price. Each option is for a specific amount of currency. In a **currency swap,** two parties agree to exchange a given amount of one currency for another and, after a specified period of time, give back the original amounts. Thus, a swap is a simultaneous spot and forward transaction. When the agreement is activated, the parties exchange principal at the current spot rate. Usually each party must pay interest on the principal as well.

Emerging Markets, Developing Economies, and Advanced Economies

LEARNING OBJECTIVES
In this chapter, you will learn about:

1. Advanced economies, developing economies, and emerging markets

2. What makes emerging markets attractive for international business

3. Assessing the true potential of emerging markets

4. Risks and challenges of emerging markets

5. Strategies for doing business in emerging markets

ADVANCED ECONOMIES, DEVELOPING ECONOMIES, AND EMERGING MARKETS

Advanced economies are postindustrial countries characterized by high per-capita income, highly competitive industries, and well-developed commercial infrastructures. They are the world's richest nations and include Australia, Canada, Japan, New Zealand, the United States, and most European countries. **Developing economies** are low-income countries characterized by limited industrialization and stagnant economies. They make up the largest group of countries. They are found throughout Africa, most of south Asia, and much of Latin America, among other regions. Bangladesh, Nicaragua, and Zaire are examples. Emerging market economies or **emerging markets** are former developing economies that have achieved substantial industrialization, modernization, and rapid economic growth since the 1980s.

Currently, more than two dozen countries are considered emerging markets and are found mainly in Asia, Latin America, and Eastern Europe. The largest are Brazil, Russia, India, and China (sometimes abbreviated as "BRIC").

One way to visualize the three groups of countries is to examine a map of the world at night, available at various locations online. By reviewing such a map, you will see the advanced economies are the most visible areas because they have the highest levels of industrialization. You will also see evidence of significant economic activity in the emerging market countries and very low levels across large stretches of Africa, central Asia, eastern Russia, and major parts of Latin America. Little or no light indicates very limited industrial activity.

Exhibit 7.1 provides an overview of the key differences among the three groups of countries.

Advanced Economies

Advanced economies have largely evolved from manufacturing into service-based economies. Home to only 14 percent of the world's population, they account for about one-half of world GDP, more than one-half of world trade in products, and three-quarters of world trade in services. Advanced economies have democratic, multiparty systems of government and economic systems usually based on capitalism.

Dimension	Advanced Economies	Developing Economies	Emerging Markets
Representative countries	Canada, France, Japan, United Kingdom, United States	Angola, Bolivia, Nigeria, Bangladesh	Brazil, China, India, Indonesia, Turkey
Approximate number of countries	30	150	27
Population (% of world)	14%	24%	62%
Approximate average per-capita income (U.S. dollars; PPP basis)	$33,750	$4,968	$13,620
Approximate share of world GDP (PPP basis)	48%	9%	43%
Population (millions)	896	1,971	3,912
Telephone lines per 1,000 people (fixed and mobile)	1,369	355	724
Personal computers per 1,000 people	1,473	355	810
Internet users per 1,000 people	726	148	400

EXHIBIT 7.1 Key Differences among the Three Major Country Groups. *Sources:* World Bank at http://www.worldbank.org; International Monetary Fund at http://www.imf.org.

They wield tremendous purchasing power, with few restrictions on international trade and investment, and host the world's largest MNEs.

Developing Economies

Consumers in developing economies have low discretionary incomes; approximately 17 percent live on less than $1 per day; around 40 percent live on less than $2 per day.[1] Despite poor economic conditions, developing countries tend to be highly developed in historical and cultural terms but are hindered by high infant mortality, malnutrition, short life expectancy, illiteracy, and poor education systems. Fewer than half of children finish primary school in most African countries.[2]

Governments in developing economies often carry debt that approaches or exceeds their annual gross domestic product. Much of Africa's poverty is the result of government policies that discourage entrepreneurship, trade, and investment. For example, starting a new business in Africa's sub-Saharan countries requires an average of 11 different approvals and takes 62 days to complete (compared to six approvals and 17 days in the advanced economies).[3] As Exhibit 7.2 illustrates, there are substantial differences in critical trade conditions across the three country groups.

Emerging Market Economies

Rapidly transforming emerging markets are found in East and South Asia, Eastern Europe, Southern Africa, Latin America, and the Middle East. Perhaps their most distinguishing characteristics are rapidly improving living standards and a growing middle class with rising economic aspirations. As a result, their attractiveness as destinations for exports, FDI, and sourcing has been on the rise.

Because their economies have progressed to a fairly high level, one can argue that Hong Kong, Israel, Singapore, South Korea, and Taiwan have developed beyond the emerging market stage. Several emerging markets will join the group of wealthy

Trade Condition	Advanced Economies	Developing Economies	Emerging Markets
Industry	Highly developed	Poor	Rapidly improving
Competition	Substantial	Limited	Moderate but increasing
Trade barriers	Minimal	Moderate to high	Rapidly liberalizing
Trade volume	High	Low	High
Inward FDI	High	Low	Moderate to high

EXHIBIT 7.2 Trade Conditions with Major Country Groups. *Sources:* International Monetary Fund at http://www.imf.org, World Bank, 2010 at http://www.worldbank.org, and Central Intelligence Agency, CIA World Factbook 2009 at http://www.cia.gov/cia/publications/factbook.

nations in the not too distant future. Recently, Bulgaria and Romania received a boost when they became members of the European Union and adopted stable monetary and trade policies. They leverage their low-cost labor to attract investment from Western Europe, thereby boosting their economies.

Similarly, some countries currently classified as developing economies have the potential to become emerging markets in the near future. These frontier economies include the European countries of Estonia, Latvia, Lithuania, Slovakia; the Latin American countries of Costa Rica, Panama, and Uruguay; and Kazakhstan, Nigeria, and the United Arab Emirates.

Finally, economic prosperity often varies *within* emerging markets. In these countries, there are usually two parallel economies: those in urban areas and those in rural areas. Urban areas tend to have more developed economic infrastructure and consumers with greater discretionary income in comparison to rural areas.

Certain emerging markets that have evolved from centrally planned economies to liberalized markets—specifically China, Russia, and several countries in Eastern Europe—are called **transition economies**. These countries were once socialist states but have been largely transformed into capitalism-based systems, partly via a process of **privatization**—the transfer of state-owned industries to private concerns. Privatization and the promotion of new, privately owned businesses have allowed the transition economies to attract substantial direct investment from abroad. They hold much potential.[4]

Exhibit 7.3 contrasts the national characteristics of emerging markets with the other two country groups. Exhibit 7.4 shows that emerging markets account for more than 40 percent of world GDP. Similarly, they represent more than 30 percent of exports and receive more than 20 percent of FDI.

In the mid-2000s, the emerging markets collectively enjoyed an average annual GDP growth rate of around 7 percent, a remarkable feat. While the economies of most emerging markets were disrupted by the recent global recession and financial crisis, their average growth rates have remained strongly positive. As Exhibit 7.5 shows, emerging markets have been growing much faster than the advanced economies.

The presence of low-cost labor, knowledge workers, government support, low-cost capital, and powerful, highly networked conglomerates have helped make these countries formidable challengers in the global marketplace. **New global challengers** are top firms from emerging markets that are fast becoming key contenders in world markets. For example, Orascom Telecom (www.orascomtelecom.com) is an Egyptian mobile telecommunications provider that has leveraged managerial skills, superior technology, and rapid growth to become an industry leader in Africa and the Middle East.[5]

Each year, *Forbes* magazine catalogs the top 2,000 global firms. Its analysis revealed that between 2004 and 2008 a total of 117 MNEs entered the list from such emerging markets as China, India, Brazil, and Russia. Meanwhile, in the same period, 233 firms from the United States, Japan, and Britain *fell off* the Forbes list. In 1990, only 19 companies from low-income countries were among the *Fortune* Global 500 listing of the world's largest MNEs. By 2010, China alone had 54 companies in the Global 500. These statistics reveal how new global challengers are displacing traditional MNEs from the advanced economies and becoming key competitors in world markets. Managers need to devise innovative strategies to compete with them effectively.[6]

Characteristic	Advanced Economies	Developing Economies	Emerging Markets
Median age of citizens	40 years	26 years	34 years
Major sector focus	Services, branded products	Agriculture, commodities	Manufacturing, some services
Education level	High	Low	Medium
Economic and political freedom	Free or mostly free	Mostly repressed	Moderately free or mostly not free
Economic/political system	Capitalist	Authoritarian, socialist, or communist	Rapidly transitioning to capitalism
Regulatory environment	Minimal regulations	Highly regulated, burdensome	Achieved much economic liberalization
Country risk	Low	Moderate to high	Variable
Intellectual property protection	Strong	Weak	Moderate and improving
Infrastructure	Well-developed	Inadequate	Moderate but improving

EXHIBIT 7.3   National Characteristics of Major Country Groups.   *Sources:* International Monetary Fund at http://www.imf.org; World Bank at http://www.worldbank.org; and Central Intelligence Agency; *CIA World Factbook 2010* at http://www.cia.gov/cia/publications/factbook.

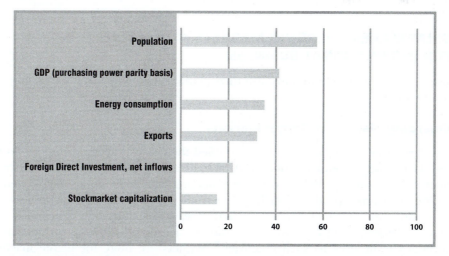

EXHIBIT 7.4   Why They Matter: Emerging Markets as a Percent of World Total.   *Sources: "The New Titans,"* Economist, September 14, 2006, survey section; International Monetary Fund at http://www.imf.org; Central Intelligence Agency, *CIA World Factbook* 2008, at http://www.cia.gov/cia/publications/factbook; World Bank at http://www.worldbank.org.

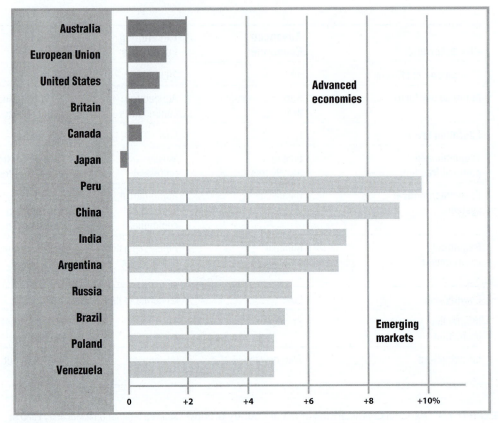

EXHIBIT 7.5 GDP Growth Rates in Advanced Economies and Emerging Markets. *Source:* International Monetary Fund (2009), World Economic Outlook Database, at http://www.imf.org.

WHAT MAKES EMERGING MARKETS ATTRACTIVE FOR INTERNATIONAL BUSINESS

Emerging markets are attractive as target markets, manufacturing bases, and sourcing destinations.

Emerging Markets as Target Markets

The largest emerging markets have doubled their share of world imports in the past few years and account for one-third of total merchandise exports from the United States. The growing middle class in emerging markets implies rising demand for various consumer products, such as electronics and automobiles, and services such as health care.[7] Even during the global recession, technology firms such as Cisco, Hewlett-Packard, and Intel were generating a large and growing proportion of their revenues from sales to such countries.[8] Markets are huge for textile machinery in India, for agricultural equipment in China, and for oil and gas exploration technology in Russia.

Emerging Markets as Manufacturing Bases

Firms from Japan, Europe, the United States, and other advanced economies have invested vast sums to develop manufacturing facilities in emerging markets. These markets are home to low-wage, high-quality labor for manufacturing and assembly operations. In addition, some emerging markets have large reserves of raw materials and natural resources. Mexico and China are important production platforms for manufacturing cars and consumer electronics. South Africa is a key source for industrial diamonds. Brazil is a center for mining bauxite, the main ingredient in aluminum. Thailand has become an important manufacturing location for Japanese MNEs such as Sony and Sharp. Motorola, Intel, and Philips manufacture semiconductors in Malaysia and Taiwan.

Emerging Markets as Sourcing Destinations

In recent years, companies sought ways of transferring or delegating noncore tasks or operations from in-house groups to specialized contractors. This business trend is known as **outsourcing**—the procurement of selected value-adding activities, including production of intermediate goods or finished products, from independent suppliers or company-owned subsidiaries. When sourcing relies on foreign suppliers or production bases, it is known as **global sourcing** or *offshoring*. Emerging markets have served as excellent platforms for sourcing. We dedicate Chapter 13 to global sourcing topics.

ASSESSING THE TRUE POTENTIAL OF EMERGING MARKETS

Unique country conditions such as limited data, unreliable information, or the high cost of carrying out market research can make it challenging for Western firms to estimate the true market potential of emerging markets. Often firms may need to improvise.[9] To overcome these challenges, in the early stages of market research, managers examine three important statistics to estimate market potential: per-capita income, size of the middle class, and market potential indicators.

Per-Capita Income as an Indicator of Market Potential

Managers often start by examining aggregate country data, such as gross national income (GNI) or per-capita GDP, expressed in terms of a reference currency such as the U.S. dollar. The second column in Exhibit 7.6 provides per-capita GDP for a sample of emerging markets and the United States, for comparison purposes. For example, in 2009 China's per-capita GDP converted at market exchange rates was $3,180, while that of the United States was $47,025.

However, per-capita GDP converted at market exchange rates overlooks the substantial price differences between advanced economies and emerging markets. Economists therefore estimate real buying power by calculating GDP statistics based on *purchasing power parity* (PPP). PPP implies that per-capita GDP figures have been adjusted for price differences between two countries. The PPP concept suggests that, in the long run, exchange rates should move toward levels that would equalize the prices of an identical basket of goods and services in any two countries. Adjusted per-capita GDP more accurately

Country	Per-Capita GDP, Converted Using Market Exchange Rates (US$)	Per-Capita GDP, Converted Using PPP Exchange Rates (US$)
Argentina	$ 8,522	$14,354
Brazil	8,676	10,298
Bulgaria	6,849	12,372
China	3,180	5,943
Hungary	16,343	19,829
South Korea	19,637	26,340
Mexico	10,747	14,581
Russia	12,579	16,161
Turkey	11,468	13,447
United States	47,025	47,025

EXHIBIT 7.6   Difference in Per Capita GDP, in Conventional and Purchasing Power Parity (PPP) Terms, 2009.   *Source:* International Monetary Fund, World Economic Outlook Database, 2009, at http://www.imf.org.

represents the amount of products consumers can buy in a given country, using *their own currency* and consistent with *their own standard of living.*

Now examine per-capita GDP, adjusted for purchasing power parity, for the same sample of countries in the third column in Exhibit 7.6. Note that a more accurate estimate of China's per-capita GDP is $5,943—nearly double the per-capita GDP at market exchange rates.

We should note four cautions here. First, official data do not account for the existence of a potentially large *informal economy,* where economic transactions occur that are not officially recorded in a nation's GDP. Second, the great majority of the population is on the low end of the income scale in emerging markets and developing economies, so median income provides a more accurate depiction of purchasing power than mean or average. Third, *household* income is substantially larger than per-capita income because of multiple wage earners within individual households. Finally, governments in these countries may underreport national income so they can qualify for low-interest loans and grants from international aid agencies and development banks.

Middle Class as an Indicator of Market Potential

Middle-class households—those with increasing discretionary incomes—make up the largest proportion of households in advanced economies. In emerging markets, the size and growth rate of the middle class indicate the extent of a promising, dynamic economy. Exhibit 7.7 provides data for a sample of emerging markets with relatively sizable middle-class populations.[10] India and Indonesia rank at the very top, given their large populations, although per-capita GDP in these countries is rather modest

Country	Middle-Class Population (millions)	Percent of Income Held by Middle Class	Per-Capita GDP, (PPP, U.S.$)
Brazil	65	35%	$10,456
China	587	45	6,546
India	534	49	2,932
Indonesia	105	48	4,149
Mexico	42	41	13,542
Russia	67	47	15,039
South Korea	26	55	25,403
Thailand	28	45	7,998
Turkey	32	45	12,339

EXHIBIT 7.7   Size of Middle-Class Population for a Sample of Emerging Markets, 2009.
Sources: International Monetary Fund at http://www.imf.org, World Bank at http://www.worldbank.org, and globalEDGE™ at http://globalEDGE.msu.edu.

compared to South Korea, China, Russia, and Mexico. However, the percentage of income held by the middle class in India and Indonesia is relatively high, at 49 and 48 percent respectively, compared to Brazil at just 35 percent. In the coming two decades, the proportion of middle-class households in emerging markets will become much bigger, acquiring enormous spending power.[11]

RISKS AND CHALLENGES OF EMERGING MARKETS

Emerging markets exhibit certain risks that affect their viability for international business. Let's review the most common, and the most harmful, of these risks.

- *Political Instability.*   The absence of reliable or consistent governance from recognized government authorities adds to business costs, increases risks, and reduces managers' ability to forecast business conditions.
- *Weak Intellectual Property Protection.*   Even when they exist, laws that safeguard intellectual property rights may not be enforced, or the judicial process may be painfully slow. Counterfeiting and weak patent laws often discourage investment by foreign firms.
- *Bureaucracy, Red Tape, and Lack of Transparency.*   Burdensome administrative rules and excessive requirements for licenses, approvals, and paperwork all delay business activities. Bribery, kickbacks, and extortion, especially in the public sector, cause difficulty for managers. In *Transparency International's* ranking of the most corrupt countries (www.transparency.org), emerging markets such as Russia, Venezuela, and the Philippines are among those with substantial corruption.[12]
- *Poor Physical Infrastructure.*   In emerging markets, high-quality roads, sewers, and electrical utilities are often sorely lacking. Industrial cities like

Bangalore and Pune in India regularly experience power outages that can last 24 hours or more.[13] A subsidiary of Tata Chemicals, part of India's giant Tata conglomerate, had to build its own road and railway infrastructure in Africa to support the firm's operations there.[14]

• ***Partner Availability and Qualifications.*** To access local market knowledge, establish supplier and distributor networks, and develop key government contacts, foreign firms should seek alliances with well-qualified local companies in countries characterized by inadequate legal and political frameworks.

• ***Dominance of Family Conglomerates.*** A **family conglomerate (FC)** is a large, highly diversified company that is privately owned. FCs control much economic activity and employment in emerging markets like South Korea, where they are called *chaebols;* in India, where they are called *business houses;* and in Latin America, where they are called *grupos*. Exhibit 7.8 illustrates some of the world's leading FCs.

Economic disparity is an important challenge that besets both emerging markets and developing economies. It is akin to poverty and refers to differences in income and living standards that occur between people, both within and between countries. Economic disparity is closely related to corruption and fragile states. It influences the likelihood of disease, food shortages, terrorism, illicit trade, and migration (such as illegal immigration into the United States). In much of the world, people cannot access clean water, proper nutrition, health care, education, clothing, and shelter.

Economic disparity implies the absence of a basic capacity to participate effectively in society. It often implies living in marginal or fragile environments, without access to the well-developed social infrastructure common in the advanced economies. Limited ability to participate in economic development worsens peoples' living conditions. An excellent approach for addressing economic disparity is to increase international trade and investment with the affected countries. Nations that participate actively in the global economy bring higher living standards to their citizens. In this way, the appearance of increasingly affluent emerging market economies is an important global trend.

STRATEGIES FOR DOING BUSINESS IN EMERGING MARKETS

Traditional business strategies that work well in the advanced economies are often inappropriate for the unique circumstances in emerging markets. In such countries, foreign firms must devise creative ways to ensure success.[15] Here are three strategies firms employ to succeed in emerging markets.

Customize Offerings to Unique Emerging Market Needs

Successful firms develop a deep understanding of distinctive characteristics of buyers, local suppliers, and distribution channels in emerging markets. They build good relationships with the communities in which they operate, partly to better understand local conditions and partly to earn customer respect and loyalty. The ability to customize offerings and devise innovative business models depends largely on the firm's *flexibility* and entrepreneurial orientation. Where suppliers and distribution channels are lacking, Western firms develop their own infrastructure to obtain vital raw materials and components or move finished goods to local buyers.[16]

Family Conglomerate	Home Country	Primary Sectors	Distinction
ALFA	Mexico	Petrochemicals, machinery, foods, electronics, telecommunications	One of the world's largest producers of engine blocks and petrochemicals
Astra	Indonesia	Motor vehicles, financial services, heavy equipment, agribusiness, information technology	Largest distributor of automobiles and motorcycles in Indonesia
Ayala	Philippines	Real estate, financial services, utilities, telecommunications, electronics	The oldest and largest conglomerate in the Philippines
Hyundai	South Korea	Automobiles, shipbuilding	A truly global car company, selling Sonatas, Elantras, and other models in nearly 200 countries
Reliance Industries	India	Petroleum products, retailing, chemicals, textiles, solar energy systems	Named by *Forbes* as one of the "World's 100 Most Respected Companies"
Russian Standard	Russia	Alcoholic beverages, banking, life insurance	The leading premium producer of vodka in Russia
Sabanci Holding	Turkey	Cars, cement, energy, retailing, insurance, telecom, tires, plastic, hotels, paper, tobacco	Controls about seventy companies, which include Turkey's largest bank, Akbank
Tatung	Taiwan	Computers, liquid crystal display televisions, network devices, media players, home appliances	OEM manufacturer for HP, Acer, and Dell. World's largest producer of flat panels for the TV industry
Votorantim Group	Brazil	Finance, energy, agribusiness, mining, steel, paper	One of the largest industrial conglomerates in Latin America

EXHIBIT 7.8   A Sample of Leading Family Conglomerates.

Partner with Family Conglomerates

By collaborating with a family conglomerate, the foreign firm can: (1) reduce the risks, time, and capital requirements of entering the market; (2) develop helpful relationships with governments and other key local players; (3) target market opportunities more rapidly and effectively; (4) overcome infrastructure-related hurdles; and (5) leverage FC resources and local contacts.

There are many examples of successful FC partnering. Ford partnered with Kia to introduce the Sable line of cars in South Korea and benefited from Kia's strong distribution and after-service network. Digital Equipment Corporation (DEC) designated Tatung, a Taiwanese FC, as the main distributor of its workstations and client-server products in Taiwan. DEC benefited from Tatung's local experience and distribution network. In Turkey, Sabanci entered a joint venture with Danone, the French yogurt producer and owner of the Evian brand of bottled water. Danone brought ample technical knowledge in packaging and bottling and a reputation for healthy and environmentally friendly products, but it lacked information about the local market. As the Turkish market leader, Sabanci knew the market, retailers, and distributors. The collaboration helped make Danone the most popular bottled water in the first year.

Target Governments in Emerging Markets

Governments and state enterprises in such areas as utilities, railways, airlines, banking, and manufacturing buy enormous quantities of products (such as computers, furniture, office supplies, motor vehicles) and services (such as architectural, legal, and consulting services). Public sector buyers regularly announce **tenders**—formal offers to purchase certain products or services. A tender is also known as a *request for proposals* (RFPs). Vendors submit bids to the government to fill the stated needs.

Summary

Advanced economies are post-industrial countries characterized by high per-capita income, highly competitive industries, and well-developed commercial infrastructure. They are mainly post-industrial societies of Western Europe, Japan, the United States, Canada, Australia, and New Zealand. The **developing economies** are low-income countries that have not yet industrialized. Due to low buying power and limited resources, their global participation is limited. The **emerging markets** are former developing economies on their way to becoming advanced economies. Located mainly in Asia, Eastern Europe, and Latin America, emerging markets are liberalizing trade and investment policies, privatizing industries, and forming economic blocs. Brazil, Russia, India, and China are leading exemplars. Emerging markets are promising export markets for products and services. They are ideal bases for manufacturing and global sourcing activities.

However, emerging markets pose various risks, including political instability, inadequate legal and institutional frameworks, lack of transparency, and inadequate intellectual property protection. Family conglomerates are large, diversified, family-owned businesses that dominate many emerging markets and represent formidable rivals and attractive choices for partnerships.

Firms should adapt strategies and tactics to suit unique, local conditions. Some firms succeed by partnering with family conglomerates. Governments are often major buyers, but require specific strategies. Successful advanced-economy firms conduct research and acquire capabilities specific to target markets.

Key Terms

advanced economies *123*
developing economies *123*
emerging markets *123*
family conglomerate (FC) *132*

global sourcing *129*
new global challengers *126*
outsourcing *129*
privatization *126*

tenders *134*
transition economies *126*

Endnotes

1. World Bank, *World Bank Development Indicators* (Washington, DC: World Bank, 2009).
2. *Ibid.*
3. World Bank, *Doing Business: Benchmarking Business Regulations,* 2009, retrieved from http://www.doingbusiness.org.
4. Jack Behrman and Dennis Rondinelli, "The Transition to Market-Oriented Economies in Central and Eastern Europe," *European Business Journal* 12 (2000): 87–99.
5. M. Bartiromo, "Power Player Naguib Sawiris," *Business Week,* December 8, 2008, p. 23; Profile of Orascom at http://www.hoovers.com; Stanley Reed, "This Mobile Upstart Really Gets Around," *Business Week,* July 31, 2006, p. 49.
6. "Creative Destruction," *Forbes,* April 21, 2008, p. 170; "Fortune Global 500" for 2008, *Fortune,* retrieved from http://money.cnn.com/magazines/fortune/global500.
7. "Two Billion More Bourgeois: The Middle Class in Emerging Markets," *Economist,* February 14, 2009, p. 18.
8. L. Lee, "Thank Heaven for Emerging Markets," *Business Week,* January 7, 2008, pp. 62–63.
9. S. Tamer Cavusgil and Lyn S. Amine, "Demand Estimation in a Developing Country Environment: Difficulties, Techniques, and Examples," *Journal of the Market Research Society* 28 (1986): 43–65.
10. The "percent of income held by middle class" refers to percentile distribution of income in a nation. In particular, it represents the proportion of national income earned by the middle 60 percentile of the population when the top 20 percentile (the wealthiest) and the bottom 20 percentile (the poorest) are excluded. For example, the middle class— 60 percent of the population sandwiched between the wealthiest and the poorest— in Brazil accounted for only 35 percent of national income, suggesting a relatively unequal distribution of national income.
11. Surjit Bhalla, *Second among Equals: The Middle Class Kingdoms of India and China,* (Washington, DC: Peterson Institute for International Economics, Washington, forthcoming); "Burgeoning Bourgeoisie: A Special Report on the New Middle Classes in Emerging Markets," *Economist,* February 14, 2009, special section.
12. Transparency International, *Corruption Perceptions Index 2009,* retrieved from http://www.transparency.org.
13. "Creaking, Groaning: Infrastructure Is India's Biggest Handicap," *Economist,* December 13, 2008, pp. 11–13.
14. M. Valente and A. Crane, "Private, but Public," *Wall Street Journal,* March 23, 2009, p. R6.
15. A. Bhattacharya and D. Michael, "How Local Companies Keep Multinationals at Bay," *Harvard Business Review,* March 2008, pp. 85–95.
16. Ted London and Stuart Hart, "Reinventing Strategies for Emerging Markets: Beyond the Transnational Model," *Journal of International Business Studies* 35 (2004): 350–63; Valente & Crane (2009).

PART

3

International Business Strategy and Implementation

Strategy and Organization in the International Firm

LEARNING OBJECTIVES
In this chapter, you will learn about:

1. Strategy in international business

2. Building the global firm

3. The integration-responsiveness framework

4. Strategies based on the integration-responsiveness framework

5. Organizational structure

6. Organizational structures for international operations

Organizing the firm on a global scale is challenging. It requires skillfully configuring activities across diverse settings, integrating and coordinating these activities, and implementing common processes to ensure the activities are performed optimally. In addition, the firm must simultaneously respond to the specific needs and conditions that characterize the individual locations where it does business. In this chapter, we discuss the roles of strategy and organization and the various company attributes that support them in building the successful international firm.

STRATEGY IN INTERNATIONAL BUSINESS

Strategy is a planned set of actions that managers employ to make best use of the firm's resources and core competences to gain competitive advantage. When developing strategies, managers start by examining the firm's specific strengths and weaknesses. They then analyze the particular opportunities and challenges that confront the firm. Once they understand the firm's strengths, weaknesses, opportunities, and challenges, they decide which customers to target, what product lines to offer, how best to contend with competitors, and how generally to configure and coordinate the firm's activities around the world.

International strategy is strategy carried out in two or more countries. Managers in experienced MNEs develop international strategies to help the firm allocate scarce resources and configure value-adding activities on a worldwide scale, participate in major markets, implement valuable partnerships abroad, and engage in competitive moves in response to foreign rivals.[1]

Managers devise strategies that develop and ensure the firm's competitive advantages. A widely accepted prescription for building sustainable, competitive advantage in international business is that of Bartlett and Ghoshal.[2] These scholars argued the firm should strive to develop "global-scale efficiency in its existing activities; multinational flexibility to manage diverse country-specific risks and opportunities; and learn from international exposure and exploit that learning on a worldwide basis."[3] Accordingly, firms aspiring to become globally competitive must seek simultaneously three strategic objectives—efficiency, flexibility, and learning.[4] Let's review each objective.

EFFICIENCY   *The firm must build efficient international value chains.* Efficiency means lowering the cost of the firm's operations and activities on a global scale. MNEs with multiple value chains must pay special attention to how they organize their R&D, manufacturing, product sourcing, marketing, and customer service activities.

FLEXIBILITY   *The firm must develop worldwide flexibility to accommodate diverse country-specific risks and opportunities.* Managers may opt for contractual relationships with independent suppliers and distributors in one country, while engaging in direct investment in another. They may adapt their marketing, pricing, and human resource practices to suit unique country conditions. The firm structures its operations to ensure it can respond to specific customer needs in individual markets, especially those critical to company performance.[5]

LEARNING   *The firm must create the ability to learn from operating in international environments and exploit this learning on a worldwide basis.* By operating in various countries, the MNE can acquire new technical and managerial know-how, new product ideas, improved R&D capabilities, partnering skills, and survival capabilities in unfamiliar environments. The firm's partners or subsidiaries capture and disseminate this learning throughout their corporate network.

International business success is determined in the end by the degree to which the firm achieves efficiency, flexibility, and learning. But it is often difficult to excel in all three simultaneously. One firm may be highly efficient, while another may excel at flexibility and a third at learning. Many Japanese firms achieved international success by developing highly efficient and centralized manufacturing systems. Numerous European firms succeeded internationally by being locally responsive, despite sometimes failing to achieve substantial efficiency or technological leadership. Many U.S.-based MNEs have struggled to adapt their activities to the cultural and political diversity of national environments and instead have proven adept at achieving efficiency via economies of scale. During the recent global financial crisis, efficiency and flexibility became particularly important to the success of multinational firms.[6]

BUILDING THE GLOBAL FIRM

Exhibit 8.1 illustrates the requisite dimensions of the successful international firm. Truly global firms are characterized by visionary leadership, strong organizational culture, and superior organizational processes, as well as strategies that optimize international operations and appropriate organizational structures.[7] We examine these key dimensions next.

Visionary Leadership

Visionary leadership is a quality of senior management that provides superior strategic guidance for managing efficiency, flexibility, and learning.[8] It is vital in firms with complex international operations.

How do leaders differ from managers? The main difference is that managers are relatively focused on directing the firm's day-to-day operations. By contrast, leaders are visionary and hold a long-term perspective on the challenges and opportunities that confront the firm. They are exceptionally skilled at motivating people and at setting the tone for how the firm will pursue its goals and objectives.

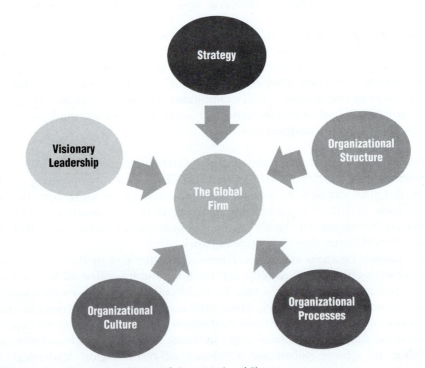

EXHIBIT 8.1 Key Dimensions of Successful International Firms.

Visionary leaders are characterized by four major traits:

- ***International mind-set and cosmopolitan values.*** Visionary leadership requires managers to acquire an international mind-set—an openness to and awareness of diversity across cultures.[9] Those who lack this mind-set are likely to fail.
- ***Willingness to commit resources.*** Visionary leaders commit to international ventures and unswervingly believe the firm will eventually succeed. Commitment drives them to develop the financial, human, and other resources their firms need to achieve their international goals.
- ***Strategic vision.*** Visionary leaders articulate a *strategic vision*—what the firm wants to be in the future and how it will get there. This vision is a central rallying point for all plans, employees, and employee actions.[10]
- ***Willingness to invest in human assets.*** Visionary *leaders must nur*ture the most critical asset of any organization—human capital. In global firms, senior leaders adopt such human resource practices as hiring foreign nationals, promoting multicountry careers, and providing cross-cultural and language training to develop international supermanagers.[11]

Organizational Culture

Organizational culture is the pattern of shared values, behavioral norms, systems, policies, and procedures that employees learn and adopt. It spells out the desired way for employees to perceive, think, and behave in relation to new problems and opportunities facing the firm.[12]

A *global* organizational culture plays a key role in the development and execution of corporate global strategy. Companies that proactively build a global organizational culture: [13]

- Value and promote a global perspective in all major initiatives
- Value global competence and cross-cultural skills among their employees
- Adopt a single corporate language for business communications
- Promote interdependency between headquarters and subsidiaries
- Subscribe to globally accepted ethical standards

Firms aspiring to become truly global seek to maintain strong ethical standards in all the markets where they do business. Ultimately, management should cultivate a culture that welcomes social responsibility and is deliberate about fulfilling its role.

Visionary leadership with organizational culture needs to be supplemented with processes that define how managers will carry out day-to-day activities to achieve company goals. Let's examine these processes next.

Organizational Processes

Organizational processes are the managerial routines, behaviors, and mechanisms that allow the firm to function as intended. Typical processes include mechanisms for collecting strategic information, ensuring quality control in manufacturing, and maintaining efficient payment systems for international sales. For instance, General Electric digitizes all key documents and uses intranets and the Internet to automate many value-chain activities and reduce operating costs.

Managers achieve global coordination and integration not just by subscribing to a particular organizational design, but also by implementing common integrating processes or *globalizing mechanisms* that allow for meaningful cross-fertilization and knowledge. Globalizing mechanisms include *global teams* and *global information systems.*

A **global team** is an internationally distributed group of employees charged with a specific problem-solving or best-practice mandate that affects the entire organization.[14] Team members are drawn from geographically diverse units of the MNE and may interact via in-person meetings, corporate intranets, and video conferencing.

Tasks of global teams vary. *Strategic global teams* identify or implement initiatives that enhance the long-term direction of the firm in its global industry. *Operational global teams* focus on the efficient and effective operation of the business across the whole network.[15] The most successful teams are flexible, responsive, and innovative. To develop global strategies, the team should include culturally diverse managers whose business activities span the globe. Culturally diverse teams have three valuable roles: (1) to create a global view inside the firm while remaining in touch with local realities; (2) to generate creative ideas and make fully informed decisions about the firm's global operations; and (3) to ensure team decisions are implemented throughout the firm's global operations.

Top managers' desire to create a globally coordinated company is motivated by the need for world-scale efficiency and minimal redundancy. In the past, geographic distance and cross-cultural differences were impediments. *Global information systems*—global IT infrastructure and tools such as intranets, the Internet, and electronic data interchange—ensure that distant parts of the global network share knowledge and learn from each other.

Next let's distinguish between multidomestic and global industries and introduce the global integration–local responsiveness framework.

The Distinction between Multidomestic and Global Industries

Companies in industries such as processed food, beverages, consumer products, fashion, retailing, and publishing have long approached international business by catering to the specific needs and tastes of each of the countries where they do business. For example, the British publisher Bloomsbury has translated its Harry Potter series into at least 65 local languages to adapt to every one of the roughly 200 countries where the books are sold. Industries in which the firm must adapt its offerings to suit the culture, laws, income level, and other specific characteristics of each country, are known as **multidomestic industries**. Accordingly, a multidomestic industry is one in which competition takes place on a *country-by-country* basis.

By contrast, in industries such as aerospace, automobiles, metals, computers, chemicals, and industrial equipment, firms generally approach international business by catering to the needs and tastes of customers on a regional or global scale. For example, Dupont sells essentially the same chemicals around the world. Industries such as this, in which competition takes place on a *regional or worldwide* basis, are known as **global industries**. Most global industries are characterized by a handful of major players that compete head-on in multiple markets.

THE INTEGRATION-RESPONSIVENESS FRAMEWORK

Global integration is the *coordination* of the firm's value-chain activities across multiple countries to achieve worldwide efficiency, synergy, and cross-fertilization in order to take advantage of similarities between countries. Firms that emphasize global integration make and sell products and services that are relatively standardized—that is, uniform or with minimal adaptation—to capitalize on converging customer needs and tastes worldwide. Such firms compete on a *regional or worldwide* basis. They seek to minimize operating costs by centralizing value-chain activities and emphasizing economies of scale.[16]

In contrast to global integration, many companies seek to respond to specific conditions in individual countries. Accordingly, **local responsiveness** refers to managing the firm's value-chain activities and addressing diverse opportunities and risks on a *country-by-country* basis. It emphasizes meeting the specific needs of customers in individual markets.

When they operate internationally, firms try to strike the right balance between the objectives of global integration and local responsiveness. The *integration-responsiveness (IR) framework* (Exhibit 8.2) illustrates the pressures firms face in attempting to achieve these often-conflicting objectives.[17] The framework was developed to help managers better understand the trade-offs common in international business.

The primary goal of firms that emphasize global integration is to maximize the efficiency of their value-chain activities on a worldwide scale. Designing variations

EXHIBIT 8.2   Integration-Responsiveness Framework: Competing Pressures on the Internationalizing Firm.

of the same product for individual markets is costly, and globally integrated firms minimize it. They also promote learning and cross-fertilization of knowledge within their global network in order to enhance innovation and gain competitive advantages. Firms that emphasize global integration are typically found in *global industries.*

In contrast, companies that emphasize local responsiveness adjust the firm's practices to suit distinctive needs and conditions in each country. They adapt to local customer requirements, language, culture, regulation, the competitive environment, and the local distribution structure. They are typically found in *multidomestic* industries.

Pressures for Global Integration

Let's examine the specific factors that compel companies to globally integrate their activities.[18] These include the need to:

- *Seek cost reduction through scale economies.* Some industries profit from concentrating their manufacturing in a few key locations, where firms can take advantage of economies of scale in production. Concentrating production also makes it easier to control the quality, speed, and cost of manufacturing.
- *Capitalize on converging consumer trends and universal needs.* Making and selling products that are standardized, like electronic components, is more cost effective than adapting products for each market. Standardization has become possible as buyer needs and tastes have become more similar worldwide.
- *Provide uniform service to global customers.* Services are easiest to standardize when firms can centralize their creation and delivery. MNEs with operations in numerous countries particularly value service inputs that are consistent worldwide.
- *Conduct global sourcing of raw materials, components, energy, and labor.* Sourcing inputs from large-scale, centralized suppliers allows firms to obtain economies of scale, more consistent quality, lower costs, and generally more efficient operations.
- *Monitor and respond to global competitors.* For MNEs with extensive operations, competing on a global basis is usually more effective than competing only locally. Thus, it is generally best to formulate strategies that challenge competitors on an integrated, global basis.
- *Take advantage of media that reaches buyers in multiple markets.* The availability of cost-effective, global media—such as TV, magazines, and the Internet—makes it possible for firms to design advertising and other promotional activities that target multiple countries simultaneously.

Pressures for Local Responsiveness

On the other hand, there are other pressures that compel companies to be locally responsive in individual countries. These include:

- *Leverage natural endowments available to the firm.* Each country has distinctive resources such as raw materials and skilled knowledge workers that provide foreign firms with competitive advantages.
- *Cater to local customer needs.* Particularly in multidomestic industries, buyer needs vary from country to country. The internationalizing firm must adapt its products to meet diverse cross-national needs.

- ***Accommodate differences in distribution channels.***   Channels can vary from market to market and may increase the need for local responsiveness. Foreign firms that ordinarily distribute their goods via large stores must adapt their approach when doing business in Latin America where small stores are the norm.
- ***Respond to local competition.***   Foreign firms are disadvantaged in markets that have numerous local competitors. To outdo local rivals, successful MNEs must devise offerings that best meet local demand.
- ***Adjust to cultural differences.***   Where cultural differences are important, such as in sales of food and clothing, the firm must adapt its products and marketing activities accordingly.
- ***Meet host government requirements and regulations.***   To protect local firms, governments sometimes impose trade barriers or other restrictions, which the MNE can counter by establishing local operations to attain the status of a local firm.

STRATEGIES BASED ON THE INTEGRATION-RESPONSIVENESS FRAMEWORK

The integration-responsiveness framework is associated with four distinct strategies, summarized in Exhibit 8.3. Internationalizing firms pursue one or a combination of these strategies.

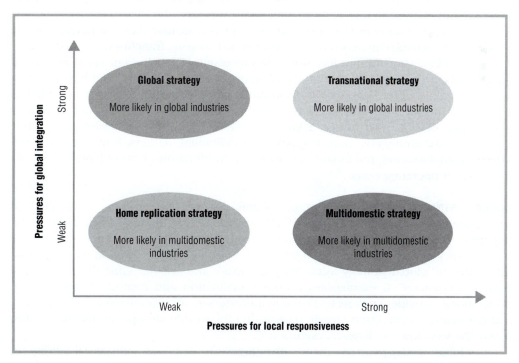

EXHIBIT 8.3   Four Distinct Strategies Emerging from the Integration-Responsiveness Framework.

HOME REPLICATION STRATEGY   Using **home replication strategy**, the firm designs products with domestic customers in mind and pursues international business in order to extend product life cycles and replicate home-market success. Management expects little useful knowledge to flow from its foreign operations.[19] Firms that make and sell commodities (such as raw materials and basic parts) sometimes use this strategy because such products often do not require a sophisticated internationalization approach. The strategy can also succeed when the firm targets only markets that are similar to the home market.

Home replication strategy is typically employed by the smaller firm that contracts with an intermediary in each of several foreign markets to import and distribute its products and generally does not adapt them for foreign customers. Because the firm relies heavily on these intermediaries, it maintains little control over how its products are marketed abroad and gains few competitive advantages there. Thus, home replication is usually a temporary approach rather than a long-term strategy.

MULTIDOMESTIC STRATEGY   A second, more advanced approach is **multidomestic strategy** (sometimes called *multilocal strategy*), in which the firm develops subsidiaries or affiliates in each of numerous foreign markets, letting them operate independently and pursue local responsiveness with little incentive to share knowledge and experience with managers in other countries. Products and services are carefully adapted to suit the unique needs of each country.[20]

The multidomestic approach has several advantages. If the foreign subsidiary includes a factory, locally produced products can be better adapted to the local market. There is minimal pressure on headquarters staff because local operations are managed by individual managers in each country. Firms with limited international experience find multidomestic strategy an easy option, because they can delegate many tasks to their country managers (or to foreign distributors, franchisees, or licensees).

Multidomestic strategy has some disadvantages. Each foreign subsidiary manager tends to develop a local strategic plan, organizational culture, and business processes that can differ substantially from those of headquarters. Because subsidiaries have little incentive to share knowledge and experience, the firm may suffer reduced economies of scale and forego a knowledge-based competitive advantage.[21] While multidomestic strategy is more responsive to individual markets, it may lead to inefficient manufacturing, redundant operations, a proliferation of overadapted products, and higher operating costs.[22]

GLOBAL STRATEGY   The disadvantages of multidomestic strategy may eventually lead management to abandon it in favor of a third approach—**global strategy**. Here, headquarters seeks substantial control over its country operations in order to minimize redundancy and achieve maximum efficiency, learning, and integration worldwide. In the extreme, global strategy asks, "Why not make and sell the same thing, the same way, everywhere?" It emphasizes central coordination and control of international operations. Activities such as R&D and manufacturing are centralized at headquarters, where managers are often largely responsible for worldwide operations and tend to view the world as one large marketplace.[23]

Global strategy offers many advantages. It provides substantial ability to respond to worldwide opportunities. It increases opportunities for cross-national learning and cross-fertilization of the firm's knowledge among all its subsidiaries. It creates economies of scale, which result in lower operational costs. Global strategy can also improve the quality of products and processes, primarily by simplifying manufacturing and other processes. High-quality products give rise to global brand recognition, increased consumer preference, and efficient international marketing programs.

Many factors make it easier to pursue global strategy, including converging buyer characteristics worldwide, growing acceptance of global brands, increased diffusion of uniform technology (especially in industrial markets), the spread of international collaborative ventures, and the integrating effects of globalization and advanced communications technologies.

Like other approaches, global strategy has limitations. It is challenging for management to closely coordinate the activities of widely dispersed international operations. The firm must maintain ongoing communications between headquarters and its subsidiaries, as well as among the subsidiaries. When carried to an extreme, global strategy results in a loss of responsiveness and flexibility in local markets.

TRANSNATIONAL STRATEGY A final alternative is **transnational strategy**, a coordinated approach to internationalization in which the firm strives to be relatively responsive to local needs while retaining sufficient central control of operations to ensure efficiency and learning. Transnational strategy combines the major advantages of multidomestic and global strategies while minimizing their disadvantages.[24] It is a flexible approach: *Standardize where feasible; adapt where appropriate.* To implement transnational strategy, the firm should:

- Exploit scale economies by sourcing from a reduced set of global suppliers and concentrate manufacturing in relatively few locations where competitive advantages can be maximized.
- Organize production, marketing, and other value-chain activities on a global scale.
- Optimize local responsiveness and flexibility.
- Facilitate global learning and knowledge transfer.
- Coordinate global *competitive moves*—that is, rather than following a country-by-country approach, deal with competitors on a global, integrated basis.[25]

Given the difficulty of balancing central control and local responsiveness, most MNEs find it difficult to implement transnational strategy. In the long run, almost all need to include some elements of localized decision making, because each country has relatively unique characteristics.

ORGANIZATIONAL STRUCTURE

While a strategy is the blueprint for action, a firm needs a structure with people, resources, and processes to implement it—an organizational structure. **Organizational structure** describes the reporting relationships inside the firm, the "boxes and lines" that specify the links between people, functions, and processes that allow the firm to implement its vision and strategies and carry out its operations. In the large, experienced MNE, these linkages are extensive and include the firm's subsidiaries and affiliates. How much decision-making responsibility should the firm retain at headquarters and how much should it delegate to foreign subsidiaries and affiliates? This is the choice between *centralization* and *decentralization*. Let's examine these options in more detail.

Centralized or Decentralized Structure?

A *centralized approach* gives headquarters considerable authority and control over the firm's activities worldwide. A *decentralized approach* means substantial autonomy and decision-making authority are delegated to the firm's subsidiaries around the world. In every company, management tends to devise a structure consistent with its vision and strategies. Thus, MNEs that emphasize global integration tend to have a centralized structure and those that emphasize local responsiveness generally are decentralized.

Whether headquarters or the subsidiary will make decisions about the firm's value-chain activities depends on the firm's products, the size of its markets, the nature of competitor operations, and the size and strategic importance of each foreign venture. Generally, the larger the financial outlay or the riskier the anticipated result, the more headquarters will contribute to decision making. For example, decisions about developing new products or building factories abroad tend to be centralized to headquarters. Decisions that affect two or more countries are best left to headquarters managers who have a regional or global perspective.[26] Decisions about local products that will be sold in only one country, however, are typically the joint responsibility of corporate and country-level managers, with the latter taking the lead role. Decisions on day-to-day human resource issues in individual subsidiaries are usually left to local managers.

Generally, it is neither beneficial nor feasible for the firm to centralize all its operations. Companies must strike the right balance between centralization and local autonomy.[27] The phrase, "Think globally, act locally," oversimplifies the true complexities of today's global competition; "Think globally *and* locally, *and act appropriately*" better describes the reality faced by MNEs today.[28]

Highly centralized, top-down decision making ignores subsidiary managers' intimate knowledge of host countries. Highly decentralized, bottom-up decision making by autonomous subsidiary managers ignores the big-picture knowledge of headquarters managers and fails to integrate strategies across countries and regions. Ultimately, most decisions are subject to headquarters' approval. Headquarters' management should promote positive, open-minded, collaborative relationships with country managers. Specifically, they should:

- Encourage local managers to identify with broad, corporate objectives.
- Visit subsidiaries periodically to instill corporate values and priorities.
- Rotate employees within the corporate network to promote development of a global perspective.
- Encourage country managers to interact and share experiences with each other through regional and global meetings.
- Provide incentives and penalties to promote compliance with headquarters' goals.

ORGANIZATIONAL STRUCTURES FOR INTERNATIONAL OPERATIONS

As a general rule, structure follows strategy. That is, we can think of organizational structure as a *tool* that facilitates the implementation of strategy and ultimately the firm's strategic vision.[29] Organizational structures also tend to evolve over time: As the firm's involvement in international business increases, it adopts increasingly complex organizational structures. Exhibit 8.4 describes the advantages and disadvantages of each structure. Let's explore the major types of organizational structures in detail.

Structure	Advantages	Disadvantages
Export Department A unit within the firm charged with managing the firm's export operations	• Export activities unified under one department • Efficiencies in selling, distribution, and shipping • Small resource commitment	• Focus on the domestic market • Minimal learning about foreign markets • Minimal control of international operations. Potential to rely excessively on foreign intermediaries
International Division All international activities are centralized within one division in the firm, separate from domestic units	• Greater focus on internationalization • Concentration and development of international expertise • Increased commitment to, and coordination and management of, international operations	• Potential for fierce competition between domestic and international units for company resources • Limited knowledge sharing among the foreign units and with headquarters • R&D and future-oriented planning activities are separate for foreign operations and headquarters • Possibility that corporate management may favor domestic over international operations because most will have advanced through the domestic organization
Geographic Area Structure Management and control are decentralized to individual geographic regions, whose managers are responsible for operations within their region	• Greater responsiveness to customer needs and wants in each regional/local market • Better balance between global integration and local adaptation • Improved communications and coordination among the subsidiaries within each geographic region	• Geographic area managers' lack of global orientation for developing and managing products • Limited communications, coordination, and knowledge sharing with other geographic units and with headquarters • Limited economies of scale among the far-flung geographic regional units
Product Structure Management of international operations is organized by major product line	• Development of expertise with specific products, on a global basis • Individual product lines are coordinated and managed globally • Scale economies and sharing of product knowledge among units worldwide	• Duplication of corporate support functions for each product division • Possibility that headquarters may favor subsidiaries offering fastest returns • Potential for excessive focus on products and too little on developments in the firm's markets

(continued)

EXHIBIT 8.4   Advantages and Disadvantages of International Organizational Structures.

Structure	Advantages	Disadvantages
Functional Structure Management of international operations is organized by functional activity	• Small central staff that provides strong central control and coordination • United, focused global strategy with a high degree of functional expertise	• Headquarters may lack expertise in coordinating functions in diverse geographic locations • Coordination becomes unwieldy when the firm has numerous product lines • May not respond well to specific customer needs in individual markets
Global Matrix Structure Blends product, geographic area, and functional structures to leverage the benefits of global strategy and local responsiveness	• Leverages the benefits of global strategy while responding to local needs • Aims to combine the best elements of the geographic area, product, and functional structures • Emphasizes interorganizational learning and knowledge sharing among the firm's units worldwide	• Dual reporting chain of command with risk of employees receiving contradictory instructions from multiple managers • Can result in conflicts • Difficulties managing many subsidiaries or products, or operations in many foreign markets

EXHIBIT 8.4   *(continued)*

Export Department

For manufacturing firms, exporting is usually the first foreign market entry strategy. It rarely requires much organizational structure until export sales reach a critical point. Initially, the firm will channel exports through an outside intermediary, such as a foreign distributor. When export sales reach a substantial proportion of total sales, the firm will usually establish a separate **export department** charged with managing export operations. The approach is most closely associated with home replication strategy. Exhibit 8.5 illustrates the export department structure.

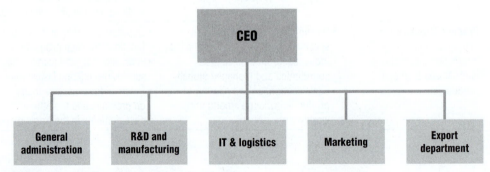

EXHIBIT 8.5   The Export Department Structure.

International Division Structure

Over time, as the firm undertakes more advanced activities abroad such as licensing and small-scale FDI, management will typically create an **international division structure**, making a separate unit within the firm dedicated to managing its international operations and shifting resources to sharpen this focus. Exhibit 8.6 illustrates this structure.[30] Typically, a vice president of international operations is appointed who reports directly to the corporate CEO. Division managers oversee the development and maintenance of relationships with foreign suppliers, distributors, and other value-chain partners. In the early stages, the structure is most closely associated with home replication strategy. Eventually management may advance toward multidomestic or global strategies.

The international division structure offers several advantages. It centralizes management and coordination of international operations. It is staffed with international experts who focus on developing new business opportunities abroad and offering assistance and training for foreign operations. Its creation signals that management is committed to international operations.

Initially, however, this structure can lead to a domestic versus international power struggle over, for example, control of financial and human resources. There is likely to be little sharing of knowledge between the foreign units and domestic operations or among the foreign units themselves. Thus, many companies eventually evolve out of the international division structure.[31]

Geographic Area Structure (Decentralized Structure)

To reap the benefits of economies of scale and scope—that is, high-volume manufacturing and more efficient use of marketing and other strategic resources over a wider range of products and markets—more advanced organizational structures emphasize

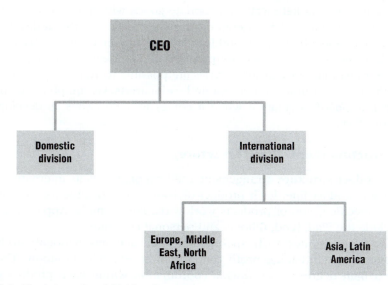

EXHIBIT 8.6   The International Division Structure.

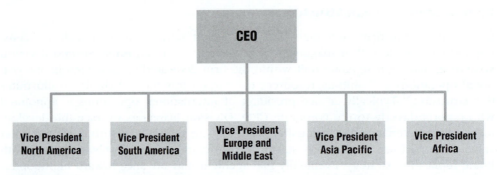

EXHIBIT 8.7   The Geographic Area Structure.

a decentralized structure, typically organized around geographic areas, or a central-ized structure, organized around product or functional lines.

Geographic area structure is an organizational arrangement in which manage-ment and control are highly decentralized to the level of individual geographic re-gions, where local managers are responsible for operations within their own regions. Exhibit 8.7 illustrates this type of organizational design. Firms that organize their operations geographically tend to market products that are relatively standardized across entire regions or groupings of countries. The structure is decentralized because headquarters management delegates operations for each locality to the respective regional managers. The structure is typically associated with multidomestic strategy.

Firms that use the geographic area approach are often in mature industries with narrow product lines, such as the pharmaceutical, food, automotive, cosmetics, and beverage industries. For example, Nestlé organizes itself into a South America divi-sion, a North America division, an Asia division, and so forth. All areas work in unison toward a common global strategic vision. Assets, including capital, are distributed to ensure optimal return on corporate goals, not area goals. Geographic area units usu-ally manufacture and market locally appropriate goods within their own areas.

The main advantage of the geographic area structure is the ability to strike a balance between global integration and local adaptation on a regional basis. The area managers have the authority to modify products and strategy. Improved communica-tions and coordination between subsidiaries are possible within each region but often lacking with other area units and corporate headquarters. Geographic area managers typically lack a *global* orientation when it comes to such issues as developing and managing products.[32]

Product Structure (Centralized Structure)

Under the **product structure** arrangement, the firm organizes its international opera-tions by major product line. Each product division is responsible for producing and marketing a specific group of products worldwide. For example, Apple's product cat-egories include the iPad, iPod, iPhone, and personal computers.

Exhibit 8.8 illustrates such an organization. Each international product divi-sion operates as a stand-alone profit center with substantial autonomy. The goal is to achieve a high degree of worldwide coordination within each product category. Increased coordination facilitates economies of scale and sharing of technology

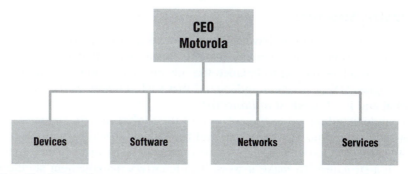

EXHIBIT 8.8   The Product Structure.

and product knowledge among the firm's operations worldwide. Thus, the product division structure is highly centralized and typically associated with global strategy.

The advantage of the product division structure is that all support functions, such as R&D, marketing, and manufacturing, are focused on the product. Such an approach increases the ease with which products can be tailored for individual markets. However, the product division structure may lead to duplication of corporate support functions for each product division and a tendency for managers to focus their efforts on subsidiaries with the greatest potential for quick returns.[33]

Functional Structure (Centralized Structure)

In the **functional structure**, management of the firm's international operations is organized by functional activities, such as production and marketing. Exhibit 8.9 illustrates such an arrangement. For example, oil companies tend to organize their worldwide operations along two major functional lines—*production* and *marketing* of petroleum products. The advantages of functional division are a small central staff, which provides strong centralized control and coordination, and a united, focused global strategy with a high degree of functional expertise. However, the functional approach may falter if headquarters lacks expertise in coordinating manufacturing, marketing, and other functions in diverse geographic locations. In addition, when the firm deals with numerous product lines, coordination can become unwieldy.[34]

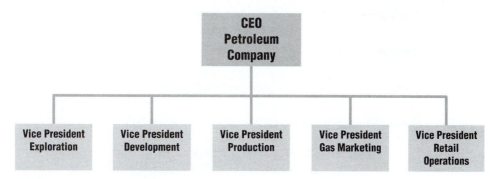

EXHIBIT 8.9   The Functional Structure.

Global Matrix Structure

In recent decades, conditions have evolved toward a more globally oriented world economy. At the same time, in many markets, customers often prefer local brands. Firms find themselves having to balance the advantages of both global and multidomestic strategies. MNE managers understand that such tendencies require them to address global and local needs *simultaneously.*

This understanding led to the creation of the **global matrix structure**, a combination of the geographic area, product, and functional structures that seeks to leverage the benefits of global strategy *and* responsiveness to local needs. Exhibit 8.10 shows such a structure. To make it work, headquarters management should simultaneously: (1) coordinate and control international operations; (2) respond to needs in individual countries; and (3) maximize interorganizational learning and knowledge sharing among the firm's units worldwide.[35]

The global matrix structure is closely associated with transnational strategy. Managerial responsibility for each product is shared by each product unit and the particular geographic areas of the firm. Thus, firms develop a dual reporting system in which, for example, an employee in a foreign subsidiary reports to two managers—the local subsidiary general manager and the corporate product division manager. The manager working in this structure shares decision making with other managers, wherever they may be, to achieve best practice for the firm's operations worldwide.

Like the other organizational structures, the global matrix structure has shortcomings. The chain of command from superiors to subordinates can become muddled. Employees may receive contradictory instructions from multiple managers who may be located far apart and come from different cultural and business backgrounds.

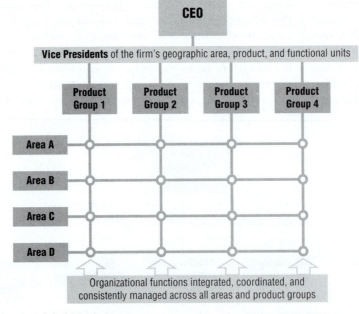

EXHIBIT 8.10   The Global Matrix Structure.

The matrix structure can waste managerial time and result in conflicts and organizational chaos. Potential limitations tend to emerge as the firm's international operations become more complex over time. For this reason, many firms that experimented with the global matrix structure eventually returned to simpler organizational arrangements.[36]

Summary

Strategy is a planned set of actions that managers employ to make best use of the firm's resources and core competences, to gain competitive advantage. The globally competitive firm seeks simultaneously three strategic objectives—efficiency, flexibility, and learning. Managers who exhibit **visionary leadership** possess an international mind-set, cosmopolitan values, and a globally strategic vision. Leading international firms value global competence, cross-cultural and language skills, and promote interdependency between headquarters and company subsidiaries. International organizational processes include **global teams** and global information systems.

The integration-responsiveness (IR) framework describes how internationalizing firms simultaneously seek global integration and local responsiveness. **Local responsiveness** refers to managing the firm's value-chain activities, and addressing diverse opportunities and risks, on a country-by-country basis. **Global integration** describes efforts to coordinate the firm's value-chain activities cross-nationally to achieve worldwide efficiency, synergy, and cross-fertilization to take maximum advantage of similarities across countries.

The IR framework presents four alternative strategies. Using **home replication strategy**, products are designed with domestic consumers in mind, and the firm is essentially a domestic company, with some foreign activities. **Multidomestic strategy** is a more committed approach, in which managers treat individual markets separately but on a stand-alone basis, with little cross-national integration of company efforts. **Global strategy** aims to integrate the firm's major objectives, policies, and activities into a cohesive whole, targeted primarily to the global marketplace. Top management performs sourcing, resource allocation, market participation, and competitive moves on a global scale. Using **transnational strategy**, the firm strives to be both more responsive to local needs and globally efficient by emphasizing global learning and knowledge transfer.

Organizational structure consists of the reporting relationships in the firm between people, functions, and processes that facilitate carrying out international operations. It determines the degree of *centralization* and *decentralization* in decision making and value-chain activities in the firm's operations worldwide. The **export department** is the simplest organizational structure, in which a unit within the firm manages all export operations. Slightly more advanced is the **international division structure**, in which all international activities are centralized within one organizational unit, separate from the firm's domestic units. The **geographic area structure** features control and decision making that are decentralized to the level of individual geographic regions. Using the **product structure**, decision making and management of international operations are centralized and organized by major product line. The **functional structure** organizes decision making by functional activity, such as production and marketing. The **global matrix structure** blends the geographic area, product, and functional structures in an attempt to leverage the benefits of a purely global strategy and maximize global organizational learning while keeping the firm responsive to local needs.

Key Terms

export department *150*
functional structure *153*
geographic area
    structure *152*
global industries *142*
global integration *143*
global matrix structure *154*
global strategy *146*

global team *142*
home replication
    strategy *146*
international division
    structure *151*
local responsiveness *143*
multidomestic industries *142*
multidomestic strategy *146*

organizational culture *141*
organizational
    processes *141*
organizational structure *147*
product structure *152*
strategy *138*
transnational strategy *147*
visionary leadership *140*

Endnotes

1. S. Tamer Cavusgil, Sengun Yeniyurt, and Janell Townsend, "The Framework of a Global Company: A Conceptualization and Preliminary Validation," *Industrial Marketing Management* 33 (2004): 711–16; G. T. Hult, S. Deligonul, and S. Tamer Cavusgil, "The Hexagon of Market-Based Globalization: An Empirical Approach Towards Delineating the Extent of Globalization in Companies," in *New Perspectives in International Business Thought,* A. Lewin, ed. (London: Palgrave, 2006); George Yip, *Total Global Strategy II* (Upper Saddle River, NJ: Prentice Hall, 2003).

2. Christopher A. Bartlett and Sumantra Ghoshal, *Managing Across Borders: The Transnational Solution* (Boston, MA: Harvard Business School Press, 1989).

3. Christopher A. Bartlett and Sumantra Ghoshal, *Transnational Management: Text, Cases, and Readings in Cross-Border Management,* 3rd ed. (Boston, MA: Irwin/ McGraw-Hill, 2000), p. 273.

4. *Ibid.*

5. Bruce Kogut, "Designing Global Strategies: Profiting from Operational Flexibility," *Strategic Management Journal* 27 (1985): 27–38.

6. L. Bryan and D. Farrell, "Leading through Uncertainty," *The McKinsey Quarterly*, December 2008, retrieved from http://www. mckinseyquarterly.com.

7. Cavusgil, Yeniyurt, and Townsend (2004); Hult, Deligonul, and Cavusgil (2006); Yip (2003).

8. Hult, Deligonul, and Cavusgil (2006); Ben L. Kedia and Akuro Mukherji, "Global Managers: Developing a Mindset for Global Competitiveness," *Journal of World Business* 34 (1999): 230–51; Robert Waterman, Tom Peters, and J. R. Philips, "Structure Is Not Organization," *Business Horizons* 23, no. 3 (1980): 14–26.

9. Stephen Rhinesmith, *A Manager's Guide to Globalization* (Homewood, IL: Business One Irwin, 1998).

10. Gary Hamel and C. K. Prahalad, "Strategic Intent," *Harvard Business Review, (*May–June 1989), pp. 63–76.

11. Cavusgil, Yeniyurt, and Townsend (2004).

12. Joel Nicholson and Yim-Yu Wong (2001), "Culturally Based Differences in Work Beliefs," *Management Research News* 24, no. 5 (2001): 1-10; Edgar H. Schein,

Organizational Culture and Leadership, 2nd ed. (San Francisco: Jossey-Bass, 1997).

13. Cavusgil, Yeniyurt, and Townsend (2004); Rhinesmith (1998); George S. Yip, Johny K. Johansson, and J. Roos, "Effects of Nationality on Global Strategy," *Management International Review* 37 (1997): 365–85.

14. Martha L. Maznevski and Nicholas A. Athanassiou, "Guest Editors' Introduction to the Focused Issue: A New Direction for Global Teams Research," *Management International Review* 46 (2006): 631–46.

15. Terence Brake, *Managing Globally* (New York: Dorling Kindersley, 2002).

16. Bartlett and Ghoshal (1989); Gary Hamel and C. K. Prahalad, "Do You Really Have a Global Strategy?" *Harvard Business Review* 63 (July–August 1985): 139–49.; T. Hout, Michael Porter, and E. Rudden, "How Global Companies Win Out," *Harvard Business Review* 60 (September–October 1982): 98–105; Theodore Levitt, "The Globalization of Markets," *Harvard Business Review* 61 (May–June 1983): 92–102; Robert T. Moran and John R. Riesenberger, *The Global Challenge* (London: McGraw-Hill, 1994); Kenichi Ohmae, "Planning for a Global Harvest," *Harvard Business Review* 67 (July–August 1989): 136–45.

17. Bartlett and Ghoshal (1989); Timothy M. Devinney, David F. Midgley, and Sunil Venaik, "The Optimal Performance and the Global Firm: Formalizing and Extending the Integration-Responsiveness Framework," *Organization Science* 11 (2000): 674–95; Yves L. Doz, Christopher Bartlett, and C. K. Prahalad, "Global Competitive Pressures and Host Country Demands: Managing Tensions in MNCs," *California Management Review* 23 (1981): 63–74; Yadong Luo, "Determinants of Local Responsiveness: Perspectives from Foreign Subsidiaries in an Emerging Market," *Journal of Management* 26 (2001): 451–77; C. K. Prahalad, *The Strategic Process in a Multinational Corporation,* unpublished doctoral dissertation (Graduate School of Business Administration, Harvard University, Cambridge, MA, 1975).

18. Bartlett and Ghoshal (1989); Moran and Riesenberger (1994).

19. Bartlett and Ghoshal (2000).

20. Bartlett and Ghoshal (2000); G. Ghislanzoni, R. Penttinen, and D. Turnbull, "The Multilocal Challenge: Managing Cross-Border Functions," *The McKinsey Quarterly*, 2008, retrieved from http://www.mckinseyquarterly.com.

21. Moran and Riesenberger (1994).

22. Bartlett and Ghoshal (2000).

23. Bartlett and Ghoshal (1989); Hamel and Prahalad (1985); Hout, Porter, and Rudden (1982); Levitt (1983); Moran and Riesenberger (1994); Ohmae (1989).

24. Bartlett and Ghoshal (2000).

25. Shaoming Zou and S. Tamer Cavusgil, "The GMS: A Broad Conceptualization of Global Marketing Strategy and Its Effect on Firm Performance," *Journal of Marketing* 58 (January 2002): 1–21; Yip (2003).

26. Pankaj Ghemawat, "Regional Strategies for Global Leadership," *Harvard Business Review* 83 (December 2005): 98–106.

27. Moran and Riesenberger (1994); Franklin Root, *Entry Strategies for International Markets* (San Francisco: Jossey-Bass, 1998).

28. Moran and Riesenberger (1994).

29. Alfred D. Chandler, *Strategy and Structure* (Cambridge, MA: MIT Press, 1962).

30. Moran and Riesenberger (1994).

31. *Ibid.*

32. *Ibid.*

33. *Ibid.*

34. *Ibid.*

35. Bartlett and Ghoshal (1989); Moran and Riesenberger (1994); G. T. Hult, Deligonul, and Cavusgil (2006).

36. Moran and Riesenberger (1994).

Global Market Opportunity Assessment

LEARNING OBJECTIVES
In this chapter, you will learn about:

1. Assessing global market opportunities

2. Analyzing organizational readiness to internationalize

3. Assessing the suitability of products and services for foreign markets

4. Screening countries to identify target markets

5. Assessing industry market potential

6. Choosing foreign business partners

7. Estimating company sales potential

ASSESSING GLOBAL MARKET OPPORTUNITIES

Managers' choices determine the future of the firm. Making good choices depends on having objective evidence and hard data about what products and services to offer and where to offer them. The more managers know about an opportunity, the better equipped they will be to exploit it. This is particularly true in international business, which usually entails greater uncertainty and unknowns than domestic business.[1] To skillfully navigate international markets, managers require substantial information on potential threats and opportunities and how to conduct business abroad.[2] Managers devise strategies as part of planned actions to optimize the firm's competitive advantages. Planning involves estimating, forecasting, and problem solving and therefore requires substantial information inputs.

Central to a firm's research is identifying and defining the best business opportunities in the global marketplace. A **global market opportunity** is a favorable combination of circumstances, locations, and timing that offers prospects for exporting, investing, sourcing, or partnering in foreign markets. In such locations, the firm may perceive opportunities to sell its products and services; establish factories or other production facilities to produce its offerings cheaper or more competently; procure raw materials, components, or services of lower cost or superior quality; or enter beneficial collaborations with foreign partners. Global market opportunities can enhance

Task	Objective	Procedure
1. Analyze organizational readiness to internationalize	To provide an objective assessment of the company's preparedness to engage in international business activity.	• Examine company strengths and weaknesses, relative to international business, by evaluating the availability in the firm of key factors, such as: — appropriate financial and tangible resources — relevant skills and competencies — commitment by senior management to international expansion • Take action to eliminate deficiencies in the firm that hinder achieving company goals.
2. Assess the suitability of the firm's products and services for foreign markets	To conduct a systematic assessment of the suitability of the firm's products and services for international customers; to evaluate the degree of fit between the product or service and foreign customer needs.	• For each possible target market, identify those factors that may hinder market potential. Determine how the product or service may need to be adapted for each market. Specifically, for each potential market, assess the firm's products and services with regard to such factors as: — foreign customer characteristics and preferences — relevant laws and regulations — requirements of channel intermediaries — characteristics of competitors' offerings
3. Screen countries to identify target markets	To reduce the number of countries that warrant in-depth investigation as potential target markets to a manageable few.	• Identify the five or six country markets that hold the best potential for the firm by assessing each candidate country market with regard to such criteria as: — size and growth rate — market intensity (customers' buying power) — consumption capacity (size and growth rate of the middle class) — receptivity to imports — infrastructure for doing business — degree of economic freedom — country risk
4. Assess industry market potential	To estimate the most likely share of industry sales within each target country; to investigate and evaluate any potential barriers to market entry.	• Develop three- to five-year forecast of industry sales for each target market. Specifically, assess industry market potential in each market by examining such criteria as: — market size and growth rate — relevant trends in the industry — degree of competitive intensity — tariff and nontariff trade barriers — relevant standards and regulations — availability and sophistication of local distribution intermediaries — specific customer requirements and preferences — industry-specific market potential indicators — industry-specific market entry barriers

(continued)

EXHIBIT 9.1   Key Tasks in Global Market Opportunity Assessment.

5. Choose foreign business partners	To decide on the type of foreign business partner, clarify ideal partner qualifications, and determine appropriate market entry strategy.	• Determine what value-adding activities must be performed by foreign business partners. • Based on needed value-adding activities, determine the most desirable attributes in foreign business partners. • Assess and select foreign business partners. That is, evaluate each potential business partner based on criteria such as: — specific industry expertise — commitment to the international venture — access to local distribution channels — financial strength — technical expertise — quality of staff — appropriate facilities and infrastructure
6. Estimate company sales potential	To estimate the most likely share of industry sales the company can achieve, over a period of time, for each target market.	• Develop three- to five-year forecast of company sales in each target market. Estimate the potential to sell the firm's product or service, based on criteria such as: — capabilities of partners — access to distribution — competitive intensity — pricing and financing — market penetration timetable of the firm — risk tolerance of senior managers • Determine the factors that will influence company sales potential

EXHIBIT 9.1   (*continued*)

company performance, often far beyond what the firm can normally achieve in its home market. For example, John Deere & Company saw an opportunity to sell small tractors to India's 300 million small farmers. After conducting extensive research, the firm developed four small tractor models for the new market and is now doing considerable business there.[3]

In this chapter we discuss six key tasks that managers should perform to define and pursue global market opportunities. Exhibit 9.1 illustrates the objectives, outcomes, and selection criteria associated with each task. Such a formal process is especially appropriate for pursuing marketing or collaborative venture opportunities abroad. The six tasks are:

1. Analyze organizational readiness to internationalize.
2. Assess the suitability of the firm's products and services for foreign markets.
3. Screen countries to identify attractive target markets.
4. Assess the industry market potential, or the market demand, for the product(s) or service(s) in selected target markets.
5. Choose qualified business partners, such as distributors or suppliers.
6. Estimate company sales potential for each target market.

In performing this systematic process, the manager will need to employ objective *selection criteria* by which to make choices, as listed in the final column of Exhibit 9.1. Let's examine each task in detail.

TASK ONE: ANALYZING ORGANIZATIONAL READINESS TO INTERNATIONALIZE

Before undertaking an international venture, whether launching a product abroad or sourcing from a foreign supplier, the firm should conduct a formal assessment of its readiness to internationalize. An evaluation of organizational capabilities is useful for both firms new to international business and those with considerable experience. Such a self-audit is similar to a SWOT analysis—that is, an evaluation of the firm's strengths, weaknesses, opportunities, and threats.

When assessing the firm's readiness to internationalize, managers peer into their organization to determine the degree to which it has the motivation, resources, and skills necessary to successfully engage in international business. They measure the firm's degree of international experience; the goals and objectives it envisions for internationalization; the quantity and quality of skills, capabilities, and resources available for internationalization; and the actual and potential support provided by the firm's network of relationships. If one or more key resources are lacking, management must acquire or develop them *before* allowing the contemplated venture to go forward. Organizational culture plays an important role, because key employees should possess the motivation and commitment to expand the firm's activities into foreign markets.

Managers also examine conditions in the *external* business environment by studying opportunities and threats in the markets where the firm seeks to do business. They research the specific needs and preferences of buyers, as well as the nature of competing products and the risks inherent in foreign markets.

Consider Home Instead, Inc. (www.homeinstead.com), a small U.S. firm that provides services for the elderly who choose to live independently at home but require companionship, assistance with meal preparation, and help with shopping and housekeeping. Following an assessment of its readiness to internationalize, management perceived substantial international opportunities, particularly in Japan, but also recognized deficiencies in certain key capabilities. The firm hired Yoshino Nakajima, who is fluent in Japanese and an expert on the Japanese market, to be vice president for international development. She launched the franchise in Japan, which captured substantial market share. Next, management tapped into the global network of trade specialists at the United States Commercial Service, a government agency that provided leads and contacts in countries identified as the best target markets. Such research helped Home Instead expand into numerous markets, including various countries in Europe.[4]

A formal analysis of organizational readiness to internationalize requires managers to address the following questions:

- ***What do we hope to gain from international business?*** Objectives might include increasing sales or profits, following key customers who locate abroad, challenging competitors in their home markets, or pursuing a global strategy of establishing production and marketing operations at various locations worldwide.

- ***Is international expansion consistent with other firm goals, now or in the future?*** The firm should evaluate and manage internationalization in the context of its mission and business plan to ensure it represents the best use of company resources.

- *What demands will internationalization place on firm resources, such as management, human resources, and finance, as well as production and marketing capacity?*   How will the firm meet such demands? Management must ensure the firm has enough production and marketing capacity to serve foreign markets. It is frustrating to channel members and management when insufficient capacity hampers fulfilling customer orders from abroad. Achieving company plans requires having the appropriate personnel on board.
- *What is the basis of the firm's competitive advantage?*   Companies seek competitive advantages by doing things better than their competitors. Competitive advantage can be based on strong R&D, superior input goods, cost-effective or innovative manufacturing capacity, skillful marketing, highly effective distribution channels, or other capabilities.

Diagnostic tools help managers audit the firm's readiness to internationalize. One of the best known is CORE (COmpany Readiness to Export, available at globalEDGE.msu.edu). Widely adopted by companies, consultants, and the U.S. Department of Commerce, CORE emphasizes the factors that contribute to successful exporting. It is also an ideal tutorial for self-learning and training. CORE asks managers questions about their organizational resources, skills, and motivation to arrive at an objective assessment of the firm's readiness to successfully engage in exporting. It generates assessments of both organizational and product readiness to identify the useful assets managers have and the additional ones they need to make internationalization succeed. The assessment emphasizes exporting, since it is the typical entry mode for most newly internationalizing firms.

Assessing organizational readiness to internationalize is an ongoing process. Managers need to continuously verify the firm's ability to modify its products to suit conditions, needs, and tastes in foreign markets. In marketing its denim jeans, for example, Levi Strauss (www.levi.com) assessed its ability to adapt its products for various markets. In evaluating entry into Islamic countries, Levi discovered that women are reluctant to wear tight-fitting attire, so the firm made a line of loose-fitting jeans. When Levi entered Japan, management assessed the firm's ability to make its famous blue jeans tighter and slimmer, to fit the smaller physique of many Japanese. When targeting consumers in hot climates, Levi evaluated its ability to produce shorts and thinner denim in bright colors.[5]

TASK TWO: ASSESSING THE SUITABILITY OF PRODUCTS AND SERVICES FOR FOREIGN MARKETS

Once management has confirmed the firm's readiness to internationalize, it next determines the suitability of its products and services for foreign markets. Most companies produce a portfolio of offerings, some or all of which may hold the potential for generating international sales.

Factors Contributing to Product Suitability for International Markets

The products or services with the best international prospects tend to have the following four characteristics:

1. ***Sell well in the domestic market.*** Offerings received well at home are likely to succeed abroad, especially where similar needs and conditions exist.
2. ***Cater to universal needs.*** For example, buyers worldwide demand personal-care products, medical devices, and banking services. International sales may be promising if the product or service is unique or has important features that are appealing to foreign customers and are hard for foreign firms to duplicate.
3. ***Address a need not well served.*** Potential may exist in countries where the product or service does not currently exist, or where demand is just starting to emerge.
4. ***Address a new or emergent need abroad.*** Demand for some products and services can suddenly emerge after a disaster or emergent trend. For example, an earthquake may create a need for easy-to-build housing. Growing affluence in emerging markets is spurring demand for restaurants and hospitality services.

Key Issues to Resolve in Measuring Product Potential

When assessing the market potential of a product or service, managers should seek answers to the following questions:

- ***Who initiates purchasing?*** Homemakers are usually the chief decision makers for household products. Professional buyers make purchases on behalf of firms.
- ***Who uses the product or service?*** Children consume various products, but their parents may be the actual buyers. Employees consume products their company purchases.
- ***Why do people buy the product or service?*** What specific needs does it fulfill? Such needs vary worldwide. For example, in advanced economies portable generators are used for recreational purposes. In developing economies, they are used for everyday heating and lighting.
- ***Where do people purchase the product or service?*** In the advanced economies, for example, many products are sold via the Internet. In other countries, sales are handled through traditional retail stores.
- ***What economic, cultural, geographic, and other factors in the target market may limit sales?*** Countries vary substantially in terms of buyer income levels, preferences, location, and other factors that can inhibit or facilitate purchasing behavior.

One of the simplest ways to determine if a product or service will sell abroad is to ask intermediaries in the target market about likely local demand. Another is to attend an industry trade fair in the market and interview prospective customers or distributors there. Since trade fairs often draw participants from entire regions, such as Asia or Europe, this approach is efficient for learning about the market potential of several countries at once.

TASK THREE: SCREENING COUNTRIES TO IDENTIFY TARGET MARKETS

Screening to identify the best countries is an essential task, especially in the early stages of internationalization. For most firms, it is also the most time-consuming part of opportunity assessment. Failure to choose the right countries not only results in financial loss, it also incurs opportunity costs, tying up resources the firm might have used more profitably elsewhere. Exporting, foreign direct investment, and sourcing each require a different set of screening criteria. Let's see why.

Screening Countries for Exporting

Exporters first examine such criteria as population, income, demographic characteristics, government stability, and nature of the general business environment in individual countries. Statistics that span several years help determine which markets are growing and which are shrinking. Many exporters buy reports from professional market research firms that provide assessments of and key statistics for particular markets. National governments also provide much useful information, typically free of charge. In the United States, for example, the Department of Commerce (www.export.gov) conducts and publishes numerous market surveys, such as *The Water Supply and Wastewater Treatment Market in China*; *Automotive Parts and Equipment Industry Guide in France*; and *Country Commercial Guide for Brazil*.

Some firms target countries that are *psychically* near—that is, countries similar to the home country in language, culture, legal environment, and other factors. Such countries fit management's comfort zone. Australian firms often choose Britain, New Zealand, or the United States as their first target markets abroad. As managerial experience, knowledge, and confidence grow, firms expand into more complex and culturally distant markets, such as China or Japan. Other firms are more venturesome and target nontraditional, higher-risk countries.

The information necessary for country screening varies by product type or industry. For example, in marketing consumer electronics, the researcher emphasizes countries with large populations having adequate discretionary income and ample electric power. For farming equipment, the best targets are countries with substantial agricultural land and large numbers of farmers. Health insurance companies target countries with many hospitals and doctors.

Often, the firm may target a region or group of countries rather than individual countries. This approach is more cost effective, particularly in markets with similar characteristics. The European Union comprises 27 countries that are relatively similar in income levels, regulations, and infrastructure. When entering Europe, rather than planning separate efforts in individual countries, firms often devise a pan-European strategy that considers many EU member countries simultaneously.

In other cases, the firm may target *gateway countries*, or regional hubs, that serve as entry points to nearby or affiliated markets. For example, Hong Kong is an important gateway to China, Turkey is a good platform for the central Asian republics, and Panama is a friendly entry to Latin America. Firms base their operations in a gateway country to serve the larger adjacent region.

SCREENING METHODOLOGY FOR POTENTIAL COUNTRY MARKETS   It is expensive and impractical to target all of the more than 200 countries worldwide. Management must choose markets that offer the best prospects. There are two basic methods for doing this: (1) gradual elimination and (2) indexing and ranking.

   Gradual Elimination.   Using *gradual elimination*, the researcher starts with a large number of prospective target countries and gradually narrows the choices by examining increasingly specific information. As indicated in Exhibit 9.1, the researcher aims to reduce to a manageable five or six the number of countries that warrant in-depth investigation as potential target markets. Because research is expensive, it is essential to eliminate unattractive markets quickly.

   In the early stages, the researcher first obtains general information on macro-level indicators such as population, income, and economic growth before delving into specific information. Broad screening data are readily available from sources such as globalEDGE™ (globalEDGE.msu.edu). The researcher then employs more specific indicators, such as import statistics, to narrow the choices. Import statistics help reveal the size of the market, the presence of competitors, and the market's viability for accepting new sales. The level of the country's exports also should be investigated, because some countries, such as Panama and Singapore, function as major transit points for international shipments and may not be actual product users. By analyzing research data and gradually narrowing the choices, the researcher identifies the most promising markets for further exploration.

   Indexing and Ranking.   The second important method for choosing promising foreign markets is *indexing and ranking*. Here, the researcher assigns scores to countries for their overall market attractiveness. For each country, the researcher first identifies a comprehensive set of market-potential indicators—such as population, income level, and political stability—and then assigns weights to each one to establish its relative importance. The more important an indicator, the greater its weight. The researcher uses the resulting weighted scores to rank the countries.

ASSESSING THE EXPORT POTENTIAL OF EMERGING MARKETS   The indexing and ranking method is illustrated by the Market Potential Index for Emerging Markets, featured at globalEDGE™ (globalEDGE.msu.edu).[6] The index ranks countries on a collection of variables for emerging markets. From it, a manager would conclude that China, Hong Kong, and Singapore are attractive markets. China has steadily risen in the index in recent years, as have Hungary, Poland, and the Czech Republic. The data are also helpful for decisions on entry via FDI and for sourcing.

   The weights that managers give to various ranking criteria can be adjusted up or down to fit the unique characteristics of any industry. For example, in evaluating market size, food industry firms may attach more weight to market size, while firms exporting telecommunications equipment give weight to national infrastructure and country risk. The researcher can add variables or countries to refine the tool for greater precision.

   The size and growth rate of the middle class are often critical indicators of promising targets. The *middle class* is measured by the share of national income available to middle-income households. It is often the best prospect in emerging markets because the upper class is relatively small and the poorest segment has little disposable income. Exhibit 9.2 shows how the middle class as a percentage of world population

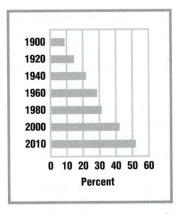

EXHIBIT 9.2   Middle Class Population in All Countries as a Percent of Total World Population.
Source: "Burgeoning Bourgeoisie," by Surjit Bhalla © *The Economist,* London (February 12, 2009); "The Emerging Middle Class In Developing Countries," by Homi Kharas, OECD Development Centre, Working Paper No. 285 (January 2010); "The New Global Middle Class: Potentially Profitable—but Also Unpredictable," *Knowledge@Wharton* (July 09, 2008).

has consistently increased over time, thanks to rising affluence in emerging markets and developing economies.[7]

In recent years, indices such as the Market Potential Index have revealed some interesting patterns. For example, Russia has a large market size but scores poorly in economic freedom. It also ranks low in market intensity and market receptivity. This implies there are always *trade-offs* in selecting target countries. No single country is attractive on all dimensions. Along with desirable features, the researcher also must contend with less desirable ones. For example, both Singapore and Hong Kong are favorable in terms of commercial infrastructure, but they are city-states with small populations.

Country attractiveness is not static; it evolves due to events or country-specific developments. For example, the introduction of modern banking systems and legal infrastructure is increasing Russia's attractiveness as an export market. The accession of Bulgaria and Romania into the European Union will improve the economic prospects of these countries. Chile has achieved substantial progress in economic reforms and higher living standards, while economic stagnation has reduced Argentina's attractiveness.

Once a collection of attractive countries has been identified, the researcher should do more detailed analyses, eventually focusing on specific industry factors. For medical equipment, for example, the researcher should gather additional data on health care expenditures and the number of physicians and hospital beds per capita. Financial services firms require specific data on commercial risk, interest rates, and density of banks. Depending on the industry, researchers may also apply different weights to each market-potential indicator. Population size is relatively less important for a firm that markets yachts than for one that sells footwear.

Country Screening for Foreign Direct Investment

Because acquiring major productive assets such as land, plant, and equipment for FDI is costly and because FDI investments are usually undertaken for the long term, choosing the right market is critical, and different variables apply than for exporting. For example, compared to exporting, the availability of skilled labor and managerial talent in a country is relatively more important for FDI ventures. When seeking the best locations for FDI, researchers typically consider the following variables:

- Long-term prospects for growth and substantial returns
- Cost of doing business, based on the price and availability of commercial infrastructure, tax rates, wages, and worker productivity levels
- Country risk, including regulatory, financial, political, and cultural barriers, and the effectiveness of intellectual property laws
- Competitive environment and intensity of competition from other firms
- Government incentives such as tax holidays, subsidized training, grants, or low-interest loans

The researcher can access numerous sources of information for screening countries for FDI, such as the United Nations Conference on Trade and Development (UNCTAD; www.unctad.org). Another is the consulting firm A.T. Kearney, which prepares the *Foreign Direct Investment Confidence Index* (www.atkearney.com) that tracks how political, economic, and regulatory changes affect the FDI intentions and preferences of the world's top 1,000 firms. Seven of the top 10 FDI destinations in the Kearney Index are emerging markets: China, India, Hong Kong, Brazil, Singapore, United Arab Emirates, and Russia. Investors prefer China because of its huge size, fast-growing consumer market, and position as an excellent, low-cost manufacturing site. China also enjoys favorable government incentives and a stable macroeconomic climate. However, executives see India as the world's leader for business process and outsourcing IT services. India has a well-educated workforce, strong managerial talent, established rule of law, and transparent transactions and rules.

Among the advanced economies, the Kearney Index reveals that investors have the highest FDI confidence in the United Kingdom, Germany, and the United States. Advanced economies engage in substantial cross-investments in each other's markets. For example, Europe and the United States are each other's most important partners for FDI. Their transatlantic economy represents more than $2.5 trillion in total foreign affiliate sales and mutually supports nearly a quarter of the world's entire foreign affiliate workforce employed by MNEs abroad.

Country Screening for Sourcing

Global sourcing and offshoring describe the practice of procuring finished products, intermediate goods, and services from suppliers located abroad. When seeking foreign sources of supply, managers examine such factors as cost and quality of inputs, stability of exchange rates, reliability of suppliers, and the presence of a workforce with superior technical skills.

Firms source services from abroad to achieve various types of advantages. A.T. Kearney prepares the *Global Services Location Index* (www.atkearney.com), which compares the factors that make countries attractive as potential locations for offshoring service activities such as IT, business processes, and call centers. The index evaluates countries using three major dimensions:

- ***Financial attractiveness.*** Accounts for compensation costs (average wages), infrastructure costs (for electricity and telecom systems), and tax and regulatory costs (tax burden, corruption, and fluctuating exchange rates).

- *People skills and availability.*   Account for suppliers' experience and skills, labor-force availability, education and language proficiency, and employee-attrition rates.
- *Business environment.*   Assesses economic and political aspects of the country, commercial infrastructure, cultural adaptability, and security of intellectual property.

In the service sector, numerous emerging market countries—for example, India, China, and Malaysia—have become popular sourcing destinations. In addition to low labor costs, managers also cite productivity level, technical skills, and customer service skills as important factors. India and China (and to a lesser extent, Brazil and Mexico) are characterized by superior people skills.

TASK FOUR: ASSESSING INDUSTRY MARKET POTENTIAL

The methods for screening countries discussed so far provide insights into individual markets and reduce the complexity of choosing appropriate foreign locations. Once the number of potential countries has been reduced to a manageable few, the next step is to conduct an in-depth analysis of each. In earlier stages, the researcher examined macro-level indicators. Now, because market potential is industry-specific, the researcher narrows the focus to examine industry-level indicators.

Industry market potential is an estimate of the likely sales for all firms in a particular industry over a specific period. It is different from *company sales potential*, the share of industry sales the focal firm itself can expect to achieve during a given year. Most firms forecast both industry market potential and company sales potential at least three years into the future.

Estimating industry market potential enables the researcher to refine the analysis and identify the most attractive countries for the firm's product or service, as well as gain industry-specific insights and understand how the firm needs to adapt its product and marketing approaches.

To estimate industry market potential, managers obtain data and insights on the following variables for each country:

- Size and growth rate of the market and trends in the specific industry
- Tariff and nontariff trade barriers to market entry
- Standards and regulations that affect the industry
- Availability and sophistication of distribution for the firm's offerings in the market
- Unique customer requirements and preferences
- Industry-specific market potential indicators

In addition to generic determinants of demand, each industry sector—from airplanes to zippers—has its own *industry-specific potential indicators* or *distinctive drivers of demand*. Marketers of cameras, for example, examine climate-related factors such as the average number of sunny days in a typical year, given that most pictures are taken outdoors. A manufacturer of electric generators might examine the rate of industrialization and dependence on hydroelectricity. A marketer of cooling equipment will consider the number of institutional buyers, such as restaurants and hotels. These are all industry-specific market potential indicators.

The researcher also evaluates factors that affect marketing and use of the product, such as consumer characteristics, culture, distribution channels, and business practices. Because intellectual property rights and enforcement vary around the world, it is important to protect the firm's critical assets by looking into regulations, trademark rules, and product liability. The researcher should also investigate subsidy and incentive programs from home and foreign governments that reduce the cost of foreign market entry.

Practical Methods for Managers to Assess Industry Market Potential

Managers use various methods to estimate industry market potential:

- *Simple trend analysis.* This method quantifies the total likely amount of industry market potential by examining aggregate production for the industry as a whole, adding imports from abroad and deducting exports. Trend analysis provides a rough estimate of the size of current industry sales in the country.
- *Monitoring key industry-specific indicators.* The manager examines unique industry drivers of market demand by collecting data from various sources. For example, Caterpillar, a manufacturer of earth-moving equipment, examines the volume of announced construction projects, number of issued building permits, growth rate of households, infrastructure development, and other pertinent leading indicators as a way of anticipating countrywide sales of its construction equipment.
- *Monitoring key competitors.* Here, the manager investigates the degree of major competitor activity in the countries of interest. If Caterpillar is considering Mexico, its managers investigate the presence there of Cat's top competitor, the Japanese firm Komatsu, and gather competitive intelligence to anticipate Komatsu's likely future moves in Mexico.
- *Following key customers around the world.* Automotive suppliers anticipate future sales potential by monitoring the international expansion of their customers, such as Honda or Mercedes-Benz.
- *Tapping into supplier networks.* Many suppliers serve multiple clients and can be a major source of information about competitors. Firms gain valuable leads by asking current suppliers about the activities of competitors, as long as the questions are ethical and don't expose competitors' trade secrets and other proprietary information.
- *Attending international trade fairs.* By attending a trade fair in the target country, a manager can learn a great deal about market characteristics that help indicate industry sales potential. Trade fairs are also helpful for identifying potential distributors and other business partners.

Data Sources for Estimating Industry Market Potential

For each target country, the manager seeks data that directly or indirectly report levels of industry sales and production, as well as the intensity of exports and imports for the product of interest. Exhibit 9.3 summarizes sites useful for estimating industry market potential, as well as accessing various statistics for conducting market opportunity assessment and other international business research.

Managers must be creative in finding and consulting resources that shed light on the task at hand. Data and resources in international research are rarely complete or

Site	Address	Description
globalEDGE	globalEDGE.msu.edu	Data, information, search engines, and diagnostic tools on a full range of international business topics
Export.gov	www.export.gov	Country commercial guides and other U.S. government resources to support international sales and marketing
UK Trade and Investment	www.uktradeinvest.gov.uk	United Kingdom data and resources to support international business
Industry Canada	www.ic.gc.ca	Canada data and resources to support international business
United Nations Commission on Trade and Development (UNCTAD)	www.unctad.org	Country fact sheets and statistics for analysis of international trade, FDI, and economic trends
World Trade Organization (WTO)	www.wto.org	Statistics on tariffs, government intervention, and economic conditions worldwide
World Bank	www.worldbank.org	National and international statistics, financial and technical information, sectoral data, trends in the world economy
World Bank Doing Business	www.doingbusiness.org	Reports on doing business in various countries
International Monetary Fund (IMF)	www.imf.org	Data and statistics on countries, and economic and financial indicators
A.T. Kearney	www.atkearney.com	Various indices, including the Foreign Direct Investment Confidence Index

EXHIBIT 9.3 A Sampling of Sites for Conducting International Business Research.

precise. For example, Teltone Corporation sought to enter Mexico with its inexpensive brand of cellular telephones and needed to estimate industrywide demand. It consulted numerous sources, including reports by the International Telecommunications Union (in Geneva, Switzerland) and several United Nations publications. Teltone researched the size of the Mexican upper class and its average income, the nature of support infrastructure for cellular systems in Mexico, and the density of retail stores handling cell phones. From the National Telecommunications Trade Association, they ascertained the number of competitors active in Mexico and their approximate sales volumes. Using these sources, Teltone estimated the market size for telephones in Mexico.

TASK FIVE: CHOOSING FOREIGN BUSINESS PARTNERS

Success abroad typically depends on having the right partners, including distribution-channel intermediaries, facilitators, suppliers, joint venture partners, licensees, or franchisees. Once the firm has selected a target market, it must identify the types of partners it needs, negotiate terms, and support and monitor partner conduct.

Exporters tend to collaborate with foreign market intermediaries such as distributors and agents. Firms that choose to sell their intellectual property, such as know-how, trademarks, and copyrights, tend to work through foreign licensees. **Licensing** partners are independent businesses that apply intellectual property to produce products in their own country. Under **franchising**, the foreign partner is a franchisee, an independent business that acquires rights and skills from the focal firm to conduct operations in its own market (such as in the fast-food or car-rental industries). The focal firm also can internationalize by initiating an **international collaborative venture**, a business activity undertaken jointly with other firms. These collaborations may be project-based or require equity investments. Other types of international partnerships include global sourcing, contract manufacturing, and supplier partnerships. We describe these in greater detail in later chapters.

Criteria for Choosing a Partner

The focal firm should identify the ideal qualifications of potential foreign partners. The firm should seek a good fit in terms of both strategy (common goals and objectives) and resources (complementary core competencies and value-chain activities). It is helpful to anticipate the potential degree of synergy with the prospective partner for the intermediate term, three to six years into the future.

Brunswick Corporation (www.brunswick.com), a leading manufacturer of recreational goods such as boats and bowling equipment, looks for the following when screening for potential foreign distributors:

- Financial soundness and resourcefulness, to ensure the venture receives the appropriate level of support initially and in the long run
- Competent and professional management, with qualified technical and sales staff
- Solid knowledge of the industry, with access to distribution channels and end users in the marketplace
- Reputation in the marketplace and good connections with local government (political clout is often helpful, especially in emerging markets)
- Commitment, loyalty, and willingness to invest in the venture and grow it over time.

Firms also seek partners with complementary expertise. For example, while the focal firm may bring engineering and manufacturing expertise to the partnership, the local distributor may bring knowledge of local customers and distribution channels. Desirable characteristics are not always available in prospective partners, especially if the firm enters a market late. The firm must be ready and able to strengthen the partner's capabilities by transferring appropriate managerial skills, technical know-how, and other resources.

Searching for Prospective Partners

The process of screening and evaluating business partners can be overwhelming. Commercial banks, consulting firms, and trade journals, as well as country and regional business directories such as *Kompass* and *Dun & Bradstreet,* are helpful in developing a list of partner candidates. National governments offer inexpensive services that assist firms in finding partners in specific foreign markets. The knowledge portal globalEDGE™ (globaledge.msu.edu) provides additional resources, including diagnostic tools, to help managers make systematic choices among partner candidates.

Onsite visits and research from independent sources and trade fairs are very helpful in the early stages of assessing a partner. Companies also find it useful to ask prospective partners to prepare a formal business plan before entering into an agreement. The quality and sophistication of such a plan provides insights into the capabilities of the prospective partner and serves as a test of the partner's commitment.

TASK SIX: ESTIMATING COMPANY SALES POTENTIAL

Once management has identified several promising country markets, verified industry market potential, and assessed the availability of qualified business partners, the next step is to determine company sales potential in each country. **Company sales potential** is an estimate of the share of annual industry sales the firm expects to generate in a particular target market. Arriving at it is often more challenging than earlier tasks, because the researcher typically needs to obtain highly refined information from the market and make some fundamental assumptions to project the firm's revenues and expenses three to five years into the future. These estimates are never precise and require much judgment and creative thinking.

For example, research suggests that fewer than 10 percent of people in Vietnam have a banking relationship. But demand for banking is growing rapidly, by as much as 25 percent annually. It is highest among Vietnamese 21–29 year olds who are less wary of banking and more open to foreign banks than their elders. Vietnam's economy is growing rapidly, with rising household income, and few competitors in the marketplace.[8]

Determinants of Company Sales Potential

In estimating company sales potential, managers collect and review various research findings and assess the following:

- *Intensity of the competitive environment.* Local or third-country competitors are likely to intensify their own marketing efforts when confronted by new entrants. Their actions are often unpredictable and not easily observed.
- *Pricing and financing of sales.* The degree to which pricing and financing are attractive to both customers and channel members is critical to initial entry and ultimate success.
- *Financial resources.* Sufficient capital is a prerequisite for any project. International ventures often require substantial financial outlays.
- *Human resources.* Management must ensure it has personnel with sufficient capabilities in language, culture, and other areas to do business in target markets.
- *Partner capabilities.* The competencies and resources of foreign partners, including channel intermediaries and facilitators, influence how quickly the firm can enter and generate sales in the target market.

- *Access to distribution channels.*   The ability to establish and make best use of channel intermediaries and distribution infrastructure in the target market determines sales.
- *Market penetration timetable.*   A key decision is whether managers opt for gradual or rapid market entry. Gradual entry gives the firm time to develop and leverage resources and strategies but may cede market share to competitors. Rapid entry can ensure first-mover advantages but also tax the firm's resources and capabilities.
- *Risk tolerance of senior managers.*   Venture performance depends on the level of resources top management is willing to commit, which in turn depends on management's tolerance for risk.
- *Special links, contacts, and capabilities of the firm.*   The extent of the focal firm's network in the market—its existing relationships with customers, channel members, and suppliers—can strongly affect venture success.
- *Reputation.*   The firm can succeed faster in the market if target customers are already familiar with its brand name and reputation.

Such a comprehensive assessment should lead to general estimates of potential sales, which managers can compare to actual sales of incumbent firms in the market, when such data are available. Thus, the process of estimating company sales is more like starting from multiple angles, then converging on an ultimate estimate that relies heavily on judgment.

Exhibit 9.4 provides a framework for estimating company sales. Managers combine information about customers, intermediaries, and competition and see whether the result points to a reasonable estimate. Managers may make multiple estimates based on best-case, worst-case, and most-likely case scenarios. They will usually make assumptions about the degree of firm effort, price aggressiveness, possible competitive reactions, degree of intermediary effort, and so on. The firm's sales prospects also hinge on factors both controllable by management (such as prices charged to intermediaries and customers) and uncontrollable (such as intensity of competition). Ultimately, the process of estimating company sales potential is more art than science.

Practical Approaches to Estimating Company Sales Potential

When estimating company sales potential, management should begin with the factors in Exhibit 9.4. In addition, experienced managers find the following activities very helpful:

- *Survey of end users and intermediaries.*   The firm can survey a sample of customers and distributors to estimate the level of potential sales.
- *Trade audits.*   Managers may visit retail outlets and question channel members to assess relative price levels of competitors' offerings and perceptions of competitor strength. In this approach, managers estimate market potential through the eyes of intermediaries (distributors) responsible for handling the product in the market. The trade audit also can indicate opportunities for new modes of distribution, identify types of alternative outlets, and provide insights into company standing relative to competitors.

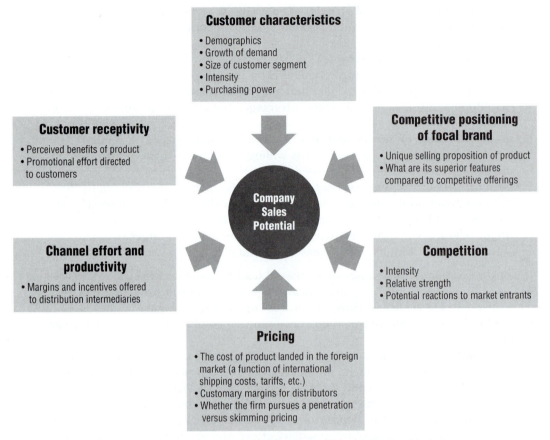

Customer characteristics

- Demographics
- Growth of demand
- Size of customer segment
- Intensity
- Purchasing power

Customer receptivity

- Perceived benefits of product
- Promotional effort directed to customers

Competitive positioning of focal brand

- Unique selling proposition of product
- What are its superior features compared to competitive offerings

Company Sales Potential

Channel effort and productivity

- Margins and incentives offered to distribution intermediaries

Competition

- Intensity
- Relative strength
- Potential reactions to market entrants

Pricing

- The cost of product landed in the foreign market (a function of international shipping costs, tariffs, etc.)
- Customary margins for distributors
- Whether the firm pursues a penetration versus skimming pricing

EXHIBIT 9.4 A Framework for Estimating Company Sales Potential in the Foreign Market.

- *Competitor assessment.* The firm may benchmark itself against principal competitors in the market and estimate the level of sales it can attract away from them. If key competitors are large and powerful, competing head-on could prove costly. Even in countries dominated by large firms, however, research may reveal untapped or underserved market segments that can be attractive, particularly for smaller firms with modest sales goals.
- *Estimates from local partners.* Collaborators such as distributors, franchisees, or licensees already experienced in the market are often best positioned to develop estimates of market share and sales potential.
- *Limited marketing efforts to test the waters.* Some companies may choose to undertake limited entry in the market, a sort of "test market" to gauge long-term sales potential or improve understanding of the market. From these early results, it is possible to forecast longer-term sales.

OTHER TECHNIQUES In developing economies and emerging markets, where information sources are especially limited, two other techniques are useful for estimating company sales potential. These are *analogy* and *proxy indicators*.

- *Analogy.* Using this method, the researcher draws on known statistics from one country to gain insights into the same phenomenon for another, similar country. For example, if the researcher knows the total consumption of citrus drinks in India, then—assuming citrus drink consumption patterns do not vary much in neighboring Pakistan—a rough estimate of Pakistan's consumption can be made, adjusting, of course, for the difference in population. If a firm knows X number of bottles of antibiotics are sold in a country with Y number of physicians per 1,000 people, it can assume the same ratio (of bottles per 1,000 physicians) will apply in a similar country.

- *Proxy indicators.* Here, the researcher uses known information from a particular phenomenon or consumption category to infer sales potential for a given product, especially if the two are complementary. A proxy indicator of demand for professional hand tools might be the level of construction activity in the country; for a particular piece of surgical equipment, it might be the total number of surgeries performed.

ASSESSING THE MARKET Research for a major market entry via FDI should be especially comprehensive. For example, when Britain's huge retailer Tesco assessed its entry into the United States, researchers investigated every detail of the country's in-store offerings and grocery buyer behavior. The firm set up a mock store in Los Angeles and invited groups of 250 customers in, to watch how they shopped and ask for feedback. The researchers moved into sixty California families' homes for two weeks, sifting through their cupboards and refrigerators, shopping and cooking with them, and keeping diaries of their every movement, from how they got their kids to school to what they did at night. The research paid off, making Tesco the world's most successful international food retailer, outpacing Walmart.[9]

In Conclusion

The decision to internationalize is never easy. Some firms are attracted to foreign markets by the promise of revenues and profits, others by the prospect of increasing production efficiency. Still others internationalize to beat back competitive pressures or keep pace with rivals. Whatever the rationale, when companies fail in international ventures, it is often because they neglect to conduct a systematic and comprehensive assessment of global market opportunities.

Although we've presented the six tasks of global market opportunity assessment in a sequence, firms do not necessarily pursue them that way. Indeed, they often pursue two or more simultaneously. The process is dynamic because market conditions change, partner performance fluctuates, and competitive intensity may increase. These events require managers to constantly evaluate their decisions and commitments, remaining open to course changes as circumstances dictate.

Some choices managers make are interrelated. For example, the choice of business partner is a function of the country. The type of distributor to use varies from market to market—for example, between the Netherlands and Nigeria. The degree of country risk may imply a need for a politically well-connected business partner. In nontraditional markets, such as Vietnam, the firm may need a partner that can serve as both distributor and cultural adviser.

Seasoned executives contend that even the most attractive country cannot compensate for a poor partner. While the quantity and quality of market information about individual countries have increased substantially, firms often struggle to identify qualified and interested business partners, especially in emerging markets. The most qualified partners are likely to be already subscribed and representing other foreign firms. This necessitates recruiting second- or even third-best candidates and then committing adequate resources to ensure their success.

Summary

A **global market opportunity** is a favorable combination of circumstances, locations, or timing that offer prospects for exporting, investing, sourcing, or partnering in foreign markets. The firm may perceive opportunities to sell, establish factories, obtain inputs of lower cost or superior quality, or enter collaborative arrangements with foreign partners that support the focal firm's goals. Such opportunities help improve company performance. Managers seek the most relevant information to make the most of international opportunities. There are six key tasks that managers perform in defining and pursuing global market opportunities.

First, management considers the firm's readiness to internationalize by assessing the strengths and weaknesses for doing international business. Management assesses the external business environment through formal research on the firm's opportunities and threats. The firm must develop resources it lacks.

Products and services that are good candidates for selling abroad sell well in the domestic market, cater to universal needs, address a need not well served in the target market, or address a new or emergent need abroad. Choosing the right country(s) is critical. The best markets for sales are large and fast-growing.

Once a firm reduces the number of potential country targets to five or six, it next conducts in-depth analyses of each. **Industry market potential** is an estimate of the likely sales for all firms in the particular industry for a specific period.

International business partners include distribution channel intermediaries, facilitators, suppliers, joint venture partners, licensees, and franchisees. Some partners undertake **licensing**, **franchising**, and **international collaborative ventures**. Management in the focal firm must decide the types of partners it needs.

Company sales potential is the share of annual industry sales the firm can realistically achieve in the target country. Estimating it requires obtaining highly refined market data, and information on issues such as partner capabilities, access to distribution channels, the competitive environment, timetable for market entry, and the firm's capabilities.

Key Terms

Endnotes

1. Jeen-Su Lim, Thomas Sharkey, and Ken Kim, "Competitive Environmental Scanning and Export Involvement: An Initial Inquiry," International Marketing Review 13 (1996): 65–80.

2. L. Bryan and D. Farrell, "Leading through Uncertainty," *The McKinsey Quarterly*, December 2008, retrieved from http://www.mckinseyquarterly.com.

3. Jenny Mero, "John Deere's Farm Team," *Fortune*, April 14, 2008, pp. 119–26.

4. F. Cunningham, "Commerce Department Helps Franchisors Go Global," *Franchising World*, December 2005, pp. 63–67.

5. D. Vrontis and P. Vronti, "Levis Strauss: An International Marketing Investigation," *Journal of Fashion Marketing and Management* 8 (2004): 389–98.

6. S. Tamer Cavusgil, "Measuring the Potential of Emerging Markets: An Indexing Approach," *Business Horizons* 40 (January–February 1997): 87–91; GlobalEDGE™, "Market Potential Index for Emerging Markets–2009," retrieved from http://globaledge.msu.edu/resourcedesk/mpi.

7. "Burgeoning Bourgeoisie: A Special Report on the New Middle Classes in Emerging Markets," *Economist*, February 14, 2009, special section.

8. N. Andrade, J. Lottner, and C. Roland, "How Young Consumers Could Shape Vietnam's Banks," The McKinsey Quarterly, March 2008, retrieved from http://www.mckinseyquarterly.com.

9. C. Miller and P. Olson, "Tesco's Landing," *Forbes*, June 4, 2007, pp. 116–18.

CHAPTER 10

Exporting and Countertrade

LEARNING OBJECTIVES
In this chapter, you will learn about:

1. An overview of foreign market entry strategies

2. Internationalization of the firm

3. Exporting as a foreign market entry strategy

4. Managing export-import transactions

5. Export-import financing

6. Identifying and working with foreign intermediaries

7. Countertrade: a popular approach for emerging markets and developing economies

AN OVERVIEW OF FOREIGN MARKET ENTRY STRATEGIES

The choice of foreign market entry strategy is one of the key decisions management makes in international business. Let's review the various approaches:

1. **Trade of products and services** refers to primarily *home-based* international exchange activities, such as *global sourcing, exporting,* and *countertrade.* **Global sourcing**, also known as *importing, global procurement,* or *global purchasing*, is the strategy of buying products and services from foreign sources and bringing them into the home country or a third country. While sourcing and **importing** represent an inbound flow, exporting represents *outbound* international business. Thus, **exporting** is the strategy of producing products

or services in one country (often the producer's home country) and selling and distributing them to customers located in other countries. Global sourcing and exporting operations are usually based in and managed from the home country. **Countertrade** refers to an international business transaction in which full or partial payments are made in kind rather than cash. That is, instead of receiving money, the firm receives other products or commodities as payment for exported products.

2. **Equity or ownership-based international business activities** typically are *foreign direct investment (FDI)* and equity-based *collaborative ventures.* In contrast to home-based international operations, here the firm establishes a presence in the foreign market by investing capital in and securing ownership of a factory, subsidiary, or other facility there. Collaborative ventures include joint ventures in which the firm makes similar equity investments abroad, but in partnership with another company.

3. **Contractual relationships** usually take the form of *licensing* and *franchising*, in which the firm allows a foreign partner to use its intellectual property in return for royalties or other compensation. Firms such as McDonalds, Dunkin' Donuts, and Century 21 Real Estate use franchising to serve customers abroad.

Each foreign market entry strategy has advantages and disadvantages, and each places specific demands on the firm's managerial and financial resources. Exporting, licensing, and franchising require a relatively low level of managerial commitment and dedicated resources. By contrast, FDI and equity-based collaborative ventures necessitate a high level of commitment and resources.

When undertaking foreign market entry, the focal firm must consider numerous factors, including:

- Its *goals* and *objectives*, such as desired profitability, market share, or competitive positioning
- The degree of *control* the firm wants to maintain over the decisions, operations, and strategic assets involved in the venture
- The specific financial, organizational, and technological *resources* and *capabilities* available to the firm (for example, capital, managers, technology)
- The degree of *risk* that management is willing to tolerate in each proposed foreign venture, relative to the firm's goals
- The *characteristics of the product or service* to be offered
- *Conditions in the target country*, such as legal, cultural, and economic circumstances and the nature of business infrastructure such as distribution and transportation systems
- The nature and extent of *competition* from existing rivals and from firms that may enter the market later
- The availability and capabilities of *partners* in the market
- The *value-adding activities* the firm is willing to perform itself in the market and the activities that it will leave to partners
- The long-term *strategic importance* of the market

While all these factors are relevant, perhaps none is more critical than the degree of control the firm wants to maintain over the venture. *Control* is the ability

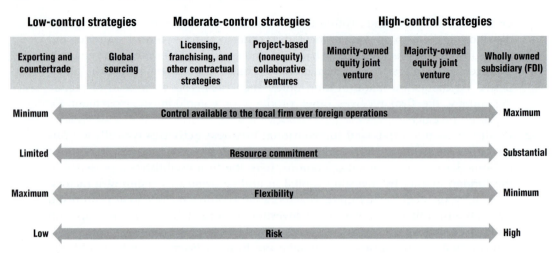

EXHIBIT 10.1   A Classification of Foreign Market Entry Strategies Based on Degree of Control Afforded by the Focal Firms.

to influence the decisions, operations, and strategic resources involved in the foreign venture. Exhibit 10.1 illustrates another useful way to organize foreign market entry strategies based on the degree of control each strategy affords the focal firm over foreign operations.

- *Low-control strategies* are exporting, countertrade, and global sourcing. They provide the least control over foreign operations because the focal firm delegates considerable responsibility to foreign partners, such as distributors or suppliers.
- *Moderate-control strategies* are contractual relationships such as licensing and franchising and project-based collaborative ventures.
- *High-control strategies* are equity joint ventures and FDI. The focal firm attains maximum control by establishing a physical presence in the foreign market.

The particular arrangement of entry strategies in Exhibit 10.1 also highlights trade-offs that the focal firm makes when entering foreign markets. First, high-control strategies require substantial *resource commitments* by the focal firm. Second, because the firm becomes anchored or physically tied to the foreign market for the long term, it has less *flexibility* to reconfigure its operations there as conditions in the country evolve over time. Third, longer-term involvement in the market also implies considerable *risk* due to uncertainty in the political and customer environments. Especially important are political risk, cultural risk, and currency risk.

In addition to control, the specific characteristics of the product or service, such as fragility, perishability, and ratio of value to weight, can strongly influence the choice of internationalization strategy. For example, products with a low value/weight ratio (such as tires and beverages) are expensive to ship long distances, suggesting the firm should internationalize through a strategy other than exporting. Similarly, fragile or perishable goods (such as glass and fresh fruit) are expensive or impractical to ship long distances because they require special handling or refrigeration. Complex products (such as copy machines and computers) require significant technical support and after-sales service, which can necessitate a substantial presence in the foreign market.

INTERNATIONALIZATION OF THE FIRM

In this chapter, we explore home-based international trade activities: exporting, importing, and countertrade. Exporting is the typical foreign market entry strategy for most firms, and thus deserves much attention. First, however, let's consider the nature and characteristics of firm internationalization.

Diverse Motives for Pursuing Internationalization

When selecting an entry mode, management must identify the firm's underlying motivation for venturing abroad.[1] Some motivations are *reactive* and others *proactive*. For example, following major customers abroad is a reactive move. When large automakers such as Ford or Toyota set up manufacturing in foreign countries, their suppliers, such as Denso and Lear, are compelled to follow them. In contrast, seeking high-growth markets abroad or preempting a competitor in its home market are proactive moves. Some companies are pulled into international markets because of the unique appeal of their products. MNEs such as HP, Nestlé, and IKEA may venture abroad to enhance various competitive advantages, learn from foreign rivals, or acquire new product ideas.

The motives of companies that launch exporting, licensing, or franchising ventures are usually straightforward. They typically seek to maximize returns from investments they have made in products, services, and know-how by seeking a larger customer base in foreign markets. When firms such as Boston Scientific (medical instruments) and Subway (fast food) internationalize, they are essentially exploiting their competitive assets in a broader geographic space. In contrast, FDI and collaborative ventures are riskier and usually flow from more complex motivations. The Swedish appliance maker Electrolux (www.electrolux.com) has built assembly operations in diverse markets such as Hungary, Mexico, and Thailand. Home appliances represent a complex global industry in which profit margins are tight and competition is intense. By undertaking product development, manufacturing, supply-chain coordination, and workforce management in relatively risky markets, Electrolux has assumed formidable challenges.[2]

Characteristics of Firm Internationalization

We can identify certain patterns and characteristics associated with international expansion:[3]

1. ***Push and pull factors serve as initial triggers.***   Typically, a combination of internal and external triggers is responsible for initial international expansion. *Push factors* include unfavorable trends in the domestic market that compel firms to explore opportunities beyond national borders, such as declining demand, growing competition at home, and arrival at the mature phase in a product's life cycle. *Pull factors* are favorable conditions in foreign markets that make international expansion attractive, such as the potential for faster growth and higher profits, foreign government incentives, or increased opportunities to learn from competitors.

2. ***Initial international expansion can be accidental or unplanned.***   DLP, Inc., a manufacturer of medical devices for open-heart surgery, made its first major sale

to foreign customers that its managers met at a trade fair. Without any deliberate planning, DLP got started in international business right from its founding.

3. *Risk and return must be balanced.* Because of their higher costs and greater complexity, international ventures often take much time to become profitable. Risk-averse managers prefer entering safe markets using conservative entry strategies. They usually target markets with a culture and language similar to the home country. For example, a risk-averse Australian firm would prefer Britain over Saudi Arabia.

4. *Internationalization is an ongoing learning experience.* Internationalization exposes managers to new ideas and valuable lessons they can apply to the home market and to other foreign markets.[4] For example, while developing fuel-efficient automobiles for the United States, General Motors (GM) leveraged ideas it had acquired in Europe, where it had been marketing smaller cars for some time.

5. *Firms may evolve through stages of internationalization.* Most firms internationalize in stages, employing relatively simple and low-risk strategies early on and progressing to more complex strategies as they gain experience and knowledge. Exhibit 10.2 illustrates the typical firm's internationalization stages and the justifications for each. With growing experience and competence, the firm will target increasingly complex markets, using more challenging entry strategies such as FDI and collaborative ventures.

Stages of internationalization	Critical management activity or orientation	How the firm behaves
Domestic market focus	Exploit home market opportunities	Firm operates only in its home market due to limited resources or lack of motivation
Preinternationalization stage	Research and evaluate the feasibility of undertaking international business activity	*Typical triggers from outside the firm:* • The firm receives unsolicited orders from foreign customers. • The firm is contacted by change agents (such as distributors), who want to represent it abroad. *Typical triggers from inside the firm:* • Managers seek to increase the firm's profits or other advantages. • Managers are proactive about international expansion.
Experimental involvement	Initiate limited international business activity, typically through exporting	• Managers consider foreign market opportunities attractive.
Active involvement	Explore international expansion, including entry strategies other than exporting	• Managers' accumulated experience reinforces expectations about the benefits of international business. • Managers commit further resources to international expansion. • Managers dedicate more resources to expand into new foreign markets.
Committed involvement	Allocate resources based on international opportunities	• The firm performs well in various international ventures. • The firm overcomes barriers to doing international business.

EXHIBIT 10.2 Typical Stages in Firm Internationalization. *Sources:* S. Tamer Cavusgil (1980) "On the Internationalization Process of Firms," *European Research* 8 vol. 6 (1980): 273–281; S. Tamer Cavusgil (1984) "Differences Among Exporting Firms Based on Their Degree of Internationalization," *Journal of Business Research* 12 (2): 195–208; Michael Czinkota (1982) *Export Development Strategies: US Promotion Policies,* New York: Praeger Publishers; Jan Johanson and Finn Wiedersheim-Paul (1975) "The Internationalization of the Firm," *Journal of Management Studies* 12 (3): 305–322.

While firms generally follow the pattern described in Exhibit 10.2, *born global* firms reach a stage of active engagement in international business within the first few years of their founding.

EXPORTING AS A FOREIGN MARKET ENTRY STRATEGY

Because it entails limited risk, expense, and knowledge of foreign markets and transactions, exporting is what most companies prefer as their primary foreign market entry strategy. Typically, the focal firm retains its manufacturing activities in its home market but conducts marketing, distribution, and customer service activities in the export market, either itself or through an independent distributor or agent.

Exporting and the Global Economy

Exporting is the entry strategy responsible for the massive inflows and outflows that constitute global trade and generates substantial foreign exchange earnings for nations. Japan has benefited from export earnings for years. China has become the leading exporter in various sectors, providing enormous revenues to its economy. Smaller economies such as Belgium and Finland use the foreign exchange they receive from exporting to pay for their sizable imports of foreign goods.

When government agencies cite statistics on trade deficits, trade surpluses, and the volume of merchandise trade for individual countries, these data generally refer to firms' collective exporting and importing activities. For example, the United States is the primary export market for Canadian goods and accounts for some three-quarters of Canada's exports yearly. The two-way trade between Canada and the United States represents the largest bilateral trade relationship in the world. China recently surpassed Europe, Japan, and the United States to become the world's top exporter of information technology (IT) products.

Exporting: A Popular Entry Strategy

Beyond initial entry, most firms, large and small, use exporting as part of their internationalization portfolio. Some of the largest exporters in the United States include aircraft manufacturers Boeing and Lockheed Martin. Large manufacturing firms typically account for the largest overall value of exports and make up about three-quarters of the total value of U.S. exports. However, the vast majority of exporting firms—more than 90 percent in most countries—are SMEs with fewer than 500 employees.

As an entry strategy, exporting is very flexible. The exporter can enter and withdraw from markets fairly easily, with minimal risk and expense. Experienced international firms usually export in combination with other strategies, such as joint ventures and FDI. Toyota has used FDI to build factories in key locations in Asia, Europe, and North America from which it exports cars to neighboring countries and regions.

Exhibit 10.3 shows the degree to which various U.S. manufacturing industries, and firms within those industries, depend on international sales. The data represent international sales from both the headquarters country and the firm's foreign subsidiaries. The exhibit suggests that firms in industries such as computers, chemicals, and medical equipment are more dependent on international sales than firms in electrical equipment, publishing, and autos. What are the common features of the most

Industry	Average International Sales in the Industry (as percentage of total sales)	Example of a Leading Firm in the Industry	Example Firm's International Sales (as percentage of total sales)
Computers and other electronic products	60%	Fairchild Semiconductor International Inc.	92%
Chemicals	44	OM Group Inc.	84
Medical instruments and equipment	42	Bio-Rad Laboratories Inc.	66
Motor vehicle parts	42	TRW Automotive Holdings Corp.	70
Communications equipment	40	3Com Corp.	90
Pharmaceuticals	37	Merck and Co.	70
Aerospace and defense	36	Boeing Corp.	39
Food	32	Chiquita Brands International Inc.	41
Plastics	32	Tupperware Corp.	73
Apparel	31	Nike Inc.	66
Beverages	30	Coca-Cola Co.	75
Electrical equipment and appliances	28	Exide Technologies	61
Publishing and printing (including software)	27	Oracle Corp.	56
Motor vehicles	26	Paccar Inc.	68

EXHIBIT 10.3   International Sales Intensity of Various United States-Based Industries.   *Sources:* Industry Week, http://www.industryweek.com, Industry Week 500; Hoovers corporate profiles at http://www.hoovers.com

geographically diversified industries? Many are high value-adding, high-technology industries strongly affected by globalization.

Services Sector Exports

In most advanced economies, services are the largest component of economic activity. Hollywood film studios earn billions by exporting their movies and videos. Construction firms send their employees abroad to work on major construction projects. Accountants and engineers often provide their services via the Internet, by telephone and mail, and by visiting customers directly in their home countries. The U.S. firm PMI Mortgage Insurance Co. exports mortgage insurance packages to various foreign markets in Asia and Europe.[5]

Most services are delivered to foreign customers either through local representatives or agents or in conjunction with other entry strategies such as FDI, franchising, or licensing. The Internet provides the means to export some types of services, from airline tickets to architectural services, helping make the services sector one of the fastest-growing areas of exports in international business.[6]

However, many *pure* services cannot be exported because they cannot be transported. You cannot box up a haircut and ship it overseas. Most retailing firms, such as Carrefour and Marks & Spencer, offer their services by establishing retail stores in their target markets—that is, they internationalize via FDI because retailing requires direct contact with customers. Many service firms can export *some* of what they produce but rely on other entry strategies to provide other offerings abroad.

Services are a critical component in the production and marketing of most types of tangible products. In this way, services often play a key role in the promotion and maintenance of product exports. For example, few people would buy a car if there were no repair services available to maintain it. Thus, firms that export cars must provide a means for the vehicles to be repaired in the recipient countries. They establish customer service facilities in target markets through FDI or they contract with local shops to provide such services.

Advantages of Exporting

Exporting is a beneficial growth strategy. Exhibit 10.4 illustrates the advantages for the firm. The low-cost, low-risk nature of exporting, combined with the exporter's ability to leverage foreign partners, makes it especially suitable for SMEs. In the $1 billion U.S. wine export industry, for instance, small California wineries sell nearly 20 percent of their total output abroad. They also face the challenge at home of imports from cost-effective wine-producing countries such as Chile and South Africa.[7]

Limitations of Exporting

As an entry strategy, exporting also has some drawbacks. First, since there is no need for the firm to establish a physical presence in the foreign market (in contrast to FDI),

- Increase overall sales volume, improve market share, and generate profit margins that are often more favorable than in the domestic market
- Increase economies of scale, reducing per-unit cost of manufacturing
- Diversify customer base, reducing dependence on home markets
- Stabilize fluctuations in sales associated with economic cycles or seasonality of demand
- Minimize the cost of foreign market entry; the firm can use exporting to test new markets before committing greater resources through FDI.
- Minimize risk and maximize flexibility, compared to other entry strategies
- Leverage the capabilities and skills of foreign distributors and other business partners located abroad

EXHIBIT 10.4 Advantages of Exporting.

exporting offers management fewer opportunities to learn about customers, competitors, and other aspects of the market. The firm may thus fail to optimally perceive opportunities and threats. It may miss some knowledge it needs for long-term success in the market.

Second, exporting requires the firm to acquire new capabilities and dedicate organizational resources to properly conduct complex export transactions, putting a strain on its resources. Exporters must acquire proficiency in international sales contracts and transactions, new financing methods, and logistics and documentation.

Third, compared to other entry strategies, exporting is much more sensitive to tariff and other trade barriers, as well as fluctuations in exchange rates. Exporters run the risk of being priced out of foreign markets if shifting exchange rates make their products too costly to foreign buyers. For example, the U.S. dollar gained 25 percent against the euro and the pound in 2008–2009. This slowed U.S. exports to Europe and the United Kingdom, harming firms that rely heavily on exporting for generating international sales.

A Systematic Approach to Exporting

Experienced managers use a systematic approach to successful exporting by assessing potential markets, organizing the firm to undertake exporting, acquiring appropriate skills and competencies, and implementing export operations. Exhibit 10.5 highlights the steps in this process. Let's examine each.

STEP ONE: ASSESS GLOBAL MARKET OPPORTUNITY As a first step, management assesses the various global market opportunities available to the firm. It analyzes the readiness of the firm and its products to carry out exporting, screens for the most attractive export markets, identifies qualified distributors and other foreign business partners, and estimates industry market potential and company sales potential.

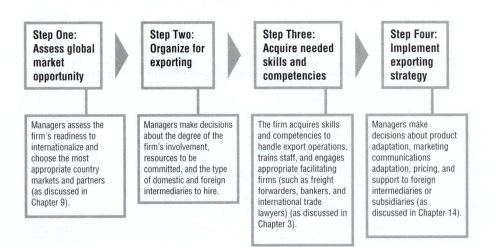

EXHIBIT 10.5 A Systematic Approach to Exporting.   *Source:* Reprinted by permission of American Marketing Association. All rights reserved.

STEP TWO: ORGANIZE FOR EXPORTING   Next, managers ask what types of managerial, financial, and productive resources the firm should commit to exporting. What timetable should the firm follow for achieving export goals and objectives? To what degree should the firm rely on domestic and foreign intermediaries to implement exporting?

Exhibit 10.6 illustrates alternative organizational arrangements in exporting. **Indirect exporting** is accomplished by contracting with intermediaries in the firm's home market who assume responsibility for finding foreign buyers, shipping products, and getting paid. The main advantage of indirect exporting for most companies is it provides a relatively inexpensive way to penetrate foreign markets without the complexities and risks of more direct exporting.

In contrast, **direct exporting** is typically achieved by contracting with intermediaries located in the foreign market. The foreign intermediaries serve as an extension of the exporter, negotiating on behalf of the exporter and assuming such responsibilities as local supply-chain management, pricing, and customer service. The exporter retains greater control over the export process but also must dedicate substantial time and resources to developing and managing export operations.

Another exporting arrangement occurs when the firm sets up a sales office or a **company-owned subsidiary** in the foreign market to handle marketing, physical

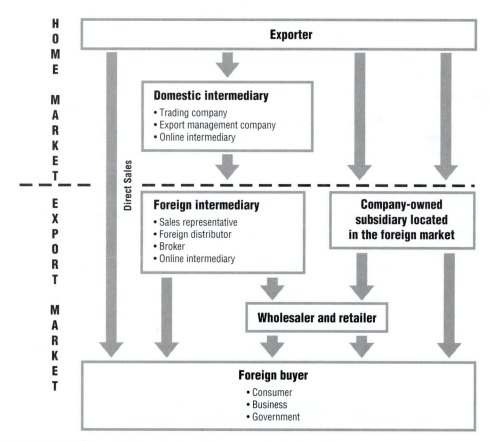

EXHIBIT 10.6   Alternative Organizational Arrangements for Exporting.

distribution, promotion, and customer service activities. Management may pursue this route if the foreign market is likely to generate a high volume of sales or has substantial strategic importance. At the extreme, the firm may establish distribution centers and warehouses or a full-function marketing subsidiary staffed with a local sales force.

STEP THREE: ACQUIRE NEEDED SKILLS AND COMPETENCIES   Export transactions require specialized skills and competencies in areas such as product development, distribution, logistics, finance, contract law, and currency management. Managers may also need to acquire foreign language skills and the ability to interact with customers from diverse cultures. Fortunately, numerous facilitators, such as those described in Chapter 3, are available to assist firms that lack specific competencies.

STEP FOUR: EXPORT MANAGEMENT   In the final stage, the firm implements and manages its exporting strategy, often requiring management to refine approaches to suit market conditions. *Product adaptation* means modifying a product to make it fit the needs and tastes of the buyers in the target market. *Marketing communications adaptation* refers to modifying advertising, selling style, public relations, and promotional activities to suit individual markets. *Price competitiveness* keeps foreign pricing in line with that of competitors. SMEs often compete not by charging low prices, but by emphasizing the nonprice benefits of their products such as quality, reliability, and brand leadership. *Distribution strategy* often hinges on developing strong and mutually beneficial relations with foreign intermediaries.[8]

Importing

The counterpart of exporting is **importing**, in which the firm chooses to buy products and services from foreign sources and bring them into the home market. The sourcing may be from independent suppliers abroad or from company-owned subsidiaries or affiliates.

Manufacturing firms often import raw materials and parts used for assembling finished products. Many retailers secure a substantial portion of their merchandise from foreign suppliers. In the United States, retailers such as Walmart, Home Depot, Best Buy, and Target are among the largest importers. By itself, Walmart accounts for about 10 percent of U.S. imports from China, over $20 billion per year.

The fundamentals of exporting, payments, and financing also apply to importing. Exporting and importing collectively refer to *international trade*, and is characterized by numerous interesting patterns. For example, as single countries, Canada and the United States are each others' top trading partners. China and the U.S. are the most important trading partners of the European Union. China's merchandise exports to the United States are massive. Most international trade occurs among the advanced economies and increasingly between the advanced economies and emerging markets.

MANAGING EXPORT-IMPORT TRANSACTIONS

When comparing domestic and international business transactions, key differences arise in documentation and shipping.

Documentation

Documentation consists of the official forms and other paperwork required in export transactions for shipping and customs procedures. The exporter usually first issues a *quotation* or *pro forma invoice* upon request by potential customers. It informs them about the price and description of the exporter's product or service. The *commercial invoice* is the actual demand for payment issued by the exporter when a sale is made.

Firms usually ship exported goods abroad by ocean transport, although air transport is also used. The *bill of lading* is the basic contract between exporter and shipper. It authorizes a shipping company to transport the goods to the buyer's destination and also serves as the importer's receipt and proof of title for purchase of the goods. The shipper's *export declaration* lists the contact information of the exporter and the buyer (or importer), as well as a full description of the products being shipped. Government authorities use the export declaration to ascertain the content of shipments, control exports, and compile statistics on the goods entering and leaving the country. The *certificate of origin* is the "birth certificate" of the goods being shipped and indicates the country where they originate. Exporters usually purchase an *insurance certificate* to protect the exported goods against damage, loss, pilferage (theft), and, in some cases, delay.

The exporter typically entrusts the preparation of documents to an international freight forwarder who assists with tactical and procedural aspects of exporting such as logistics, packing, labeling, and clearing customs.

Another important document is the *license*, a permission to export. National governments sometimes require exporters to obtain a license for reasons of national security and foreign policy. In addition, some governments impose sanctions on trade with certain countries as part of their foreign policy. Lastly, governments may forbid the export of certain types of essential goods, such as petroleum products, if they are in short supply in the home country.

Shipping and Incoterms

In the past, disputes sometimes arose over who should pay the cost of freight and insurance in international transactions: the seller (that is, the exporter) or the foreign buyer. To eliminate such disputes, a system of universal standard terms of sale and delivery, known as **Incoterms** (short for International Commerce Terms), was developed by the International Chamber of Commerce (www.iccwbo.org). Commonly used in international sales contracts, Incoterms specify how the buyer and the seller share the cost of freight and insurance, and at which point the buyer takes title to the goods. Exhibit 10.7 illustrates the implications of the three most commonly used Incoterms.

Payment Methods in Exporting and Importing

Receiving payment is often complicated in international business. Foreign currencies may be unstable or governments may be reluctant to allow funds to leave the country. Local laws and enforcement mechanisms may favor local companies in payment disputes with foreign firms. Some customers in developing economies may lack payment mechanisms such as credit cards and checking accounts. In advanced economies and many emerging markets, firms often extend credit to buyers or structure payment on

Incoterms	Definition	Key Points	Arrangement of Shipping
EXW Ex works (named place)	Delivery takes place at the seller's premises or another named place (i.e., works, factory, or warehouse).	EXW represents minimal obligation for the seller; the buyer bears all costs and risks involved in claiming the goods from the seller's premises.	Buyer arranges shipping.
FOB Free on board (named port of shipment)	Delivery takes place when the goods pass the ship's rail at the named port of shipment.	The buyer bears all the costs and risks of loss or damage upon delivery. The seller clears the goods for export.	Buyer arranges shipping.
CIF Cost, insurance and freight (named port of destination)	Delivery takes place when the goods pass the ship's rail in the port of shipment.	The seller pays for freight and insurance to transport the goods to the named port of destination. At that point, responsibility for the goods is transferred from the seller to the buyer.	Seller arranges shipping and insurance.

EXHIBIT 10.7 Incoterms: Examples of How Transport Obligations, Costs, and Risks Are Shared between the Buyer and the Seller. *Source:* International Chamber of Commerce, http://www.iccwbo.org/incoterms; J. Sherlock and J. Reuvid (2008), *The Handbook of International Trade,* London: GMB Publishing; K. Shakespeare, (2011), *Trade for Good,* Cornwall, UK: Ecademy Press.

open account. In trading with some developing economies, however, exporters evaluate new customers carefully and may decline a request for credit if the risk is too great.

There are several methods for getting paid in international business. Listed roughly in order from most to least secure, they are: *cash in advance, letter of credit, open account,* and *countertrade.* Countertrade is also a distinct form of foreign market entry that we discuss later in this chapter. We explain each of the other three payment methods next.

CASH IN ADVANCE When the exporter receives cash in advance, payment is collected before the goods are shipped to the customer. The main advantage is that the exporter need not worry about collection problems and can access the funds almost immediately upon concluding the sale. From the buyer's standpoint, however, cash in advance is risky and may cause cash flow problems. The buyer may hesitate for fear the exporter will not follow through with shipment, particularly if the buyer does not know the exporter well. For these reasons, cash in advance is unpopular with buyers and tends to discourage sales. Exporters who insist on it may lose out to competitors who offer more flexible payment terms.

LETTER OF CREDIT   Because it protects the interests of both seller and buyer, the letter of credit has become the most popular method for getting paid in export transactions. Essentially, a **letter of credit** is a contract between the banks of the buyer and seller that ensures payment from the buyer to the seller upon receipt of an export shipment. The system works because virtually all banks have established relationships with correspondent banks around the world. Once established, an *irrevocable letter of credit* cannot be canceled without agreement of both buyer and seller. The selling firm will be paid as long as it fulfills its part of the agreement.

The letter of credit also specifies the documents that the exporter is required to present, such as a bill of lading, commercial invoice, and certificate of insurance. Before making a payment, the buyer's bank first verifies that all documents meet the requirements the buyer and seller agreed to in the letter of credit. In the typical cycle of an international sale through letter of credit,

1. An exporter signs a contract for sale of goods to a foreign buyer, the importer.
2. The importer asks its bank (the importer's bank) to open a letter of credit in favor of the exporter, the beneficiary of the credit.
3. The importer's bank notifies the exporter's bank that a letter of credit has been issued.
4. The exporter's bank confirms the validity of the letter of credit.
5. The exporter prepares and ships the products to the importer as specified in the letter of credit.
6. The exporter presents the shipment documents to its bank, the exporter's bank, which examines them to ensure they fully comply with the terms of the letter of credit. The documents typically include an invoice, bill of lading, and insurance certificate, as specified in the letter of credit.
7. The exporter's bank sends the documents to the importer's bank, which similarly examines them to ensure they comply fully with the letter of credit.
8. Upon confirmation that everything is in order, the importer's bank makes full payment for the goods to the exporter, via the exporter's bank.
9. The importer makes full payment to its bank within the time period granted, which, in many countries, can extend to several months.

A related payment method is the *draft*. Similar to a check, the draft is a financial instrument that instructs a bank to pay a precise amount of a specific currency to the bearer on demand or at a future date. For both letters of credit and drafts, the buyer must make payment upon presentation of documents that convey title to the purchased goods and confirm that specific steps have been taken to prepare the goods and their shipment to the buyer. The exporter can sell any drafts and letters of credit in its possession, to avoid having to wait weeks or months to be paid for its exports.

OPEN ACCOUNT   When the exporter uses an *open account*, the buyer pays the exporter at some future time following receipt of the goods, in much the same way a retail customer pays a department store on account for products he or she has purchased. Because of the risk involved, exporters use this approach only with customers of long standing or excellent credit, or with a subsidiary owned by the exporter. The exporter simply bills the customer, who is expected to pay under agreed terms at some future time. However, in international transactions, an open account is risky, and the firm should structure such payment methods with care.

EXPORT-IMPORT FINANCING

The ability to offer attractive payment terms is often necessary to generate sales. Four key factors determine the cost of financing for export sales:

1. ***Creditworthiness of the exporter.*** Firms with little collateral or minimal international experience, or large export orders that exceed their manufacturing capacity, may encounter difficulty in obtaining financing from banks and other lenders at reasonable interest rates, or they may not receive financing at all.
2. ***Creditworthiness of the importer.*** An export sales transaction often hinges on the ability of the buyer to obtain sufficient funds to purchase the goods. Some buyers, particularly from developing economies or countries with currency controls, may be unable to secure financing through letters of credit.
3. ***Riskiness of the sale.*** Riskiness is a function of the value and marketability of the good being sold, the extent of uncertainty surrounding the sale, the degree of political and economic stability in the buyer's country, and the likelihood the loan will be repaid.
4. ***Timing of the sale.*** Influences the cost of financing. In international trade, the exporter usually wants to be paid as soon as possible, while the buyer prefers to delay payment, especially until it has received or resold the goods. A common challenge arises when the firm receives an unusually large order from a foreign buyer and needs to draw on substantial working capital to fill it. This is particularly burdensome for resource-constrained SMEs.

Ultimately, the cost of financing affects the pricing and profitability of a sale as well as the payment terms the exporter can offer. Fortunately, there are various sources for financing international sales, which we discuss next.

Commercial Banks

The same commercial banks that finance domestic activities can often finance export sales. A logical first step for the exporter is to approach the local commercial bank with which it already does business, or a commercial bank with an international department that is familiar with exporting and may also provide international banking services such as letters of credit. Another option is to have the bank make a loan directly to the foreign buyer to finance the sale.

Factoring, Forfaiting, and Confirming

Factoring is the discounting of a foreign account receivable by transferring title of the sold item and its account receivable to a *factoring house* (an organization that specializes in purchasing accounts receivable) for cash at a discount from the face value. *Forfaiting* is the selling, at a discount, of long-term accounts receivable of the seller or promissory notes of the foreign buyer. Numerous forfaiting houses specialize in this practice. *Confirming* is a financial service in which an independent company confirms an export order in the seller's country and makes payment for the goods in that country's currency.

Distribution Channel Intermediaries

In addition to acting as export representatives, many intermediaries such as trading and export management companies provide short-term financing or simply purchase exported goods directly from the manufacturer, eliminating the need for financing and any risks associated with the export transaction.

Buyers and Suppliers

Foreign buyers of expensive products often make down payments that reduce the need for financing from other sources. In addition, buyers may make incremental payments as the seller completes production of the goods or project. Some industries use letters of credit that allow for progress payments upon inspection by the buyer's agent or receipt of a statement by the exporter that a certain percentage of the product has been completed.

Intracorporate Financing

Large multinational enterprises with foreign subsidiaries have many more options for financing exports. The MNE may allow its subsidiary to retain a higher than usual level of its own profits in order to finance export sales. The parent firm may provide loans, equity investments, and trade credit (such as extensions on accounts payable) as funding for the international selling activities of its subsidiaries. The parent can also guarantee loans obtained from foreign banks by its subsidiaries. Finally, large MNEs can often access equity financing by selling corporate bonds or shares in stock markets.

Government Assistance Programs

Numerous government agencies offer programs to assist exporters with their financing needs. Some provide loans or grants to the exporter, while others offer guarantee programs that require the participation of a bank or other approved lender. Under such arrangements, the government pledges to repay a loan made by a commercial bank in the event the importer is unable to repay.

In the United States, the *Export-Import Bank* (Ex-Im Bank; www.exim.gov) is a government agency that issues credit insurance to protect firms against default on exports sold under short-term credit. The U.S. Small Business Administration (www .sba.gov) helps small exporters obtain trade financing. Canada's Export Development Corporation (www.edc.ca), India's Export Credit & Guarantee Corporation (www .ecgc.in), and Argentina's Compania Argentina de Seguros de Credito (www.casce .com.ar) provide services similar to those of the Ex-Im Bank.

Multilateral Development Banks

Multilateral development banks (MDBs) are international financial institutions owned by multiple governments within world regions or other groups. Their individual and collective objective is to promote economic and social progress in their member countries, many of which are developing countries. MDBs include the African Development Bank (www.afdb.org), the Asian Development Bank (www.adb.org), the European Bank for Reconstruction and Development (www.ebrd.com), the Inter-American Development Bank (www.iadb.org), and the World Bank Group (www.worldbank.org). These institutions fulfill their missions by providing loans, technical cooperation, grants, capital investment, and other types of assistance to governments and agencies in the member countries.

IDENTIFYING AND WORKING WITH FOREIGN INTERMEDIARIES

Success in exporting usually depends on establishing strong relationships with distributors, sales representatives, and other foreign market intermediaries. Trade fairs are a good way to meet potential intermediaries, become familiar with key players in the industry, and pick the brains of other, more experienced exporters. In other cases, for finding suitable foreign intermediaries, exporters may consult the following sources:

- Country and regional business directories, such as *Kompass, Japanese Trade Directory, Kellysearch*, and *Dun & Bradstreet*, as well as foreign *Yellow Pages* (often available online).
- Trade associations that support specific industries, such as the National Furniture Manufacturers Association or the National Association of Automotive Parts Manufacturers.
- Government departments, ministries, and agencies charged with assisting economic and trade development, such as Austrade in Australia (www.austrade.gov.au), Export Development Canada (www.edc.ca), and the International Trade Administration of the U.S. Department of Commerce (www.trade.gov).
- Commercial attachés in embassies and consulates abroad.
- Branch offices of certain foreign government agencies located in the exporter's country, such as JETRO, the Japan External Trade Organization (www.jetro.org).

Often, the best way to identify and qualify intermediaries is to visit the target market. Managers can also inspect the facilities as well as gauge the capabilities, technical staff, and sales capabilities of prospective intermediaries. Once they have narrowed the choices to one or two, experienced exporters can request a prospective intermediary to prepare a business plan for the proposed venture. The plan's quality and sophistication provide a basis for judging the candidate's true capabilities.

Working with Foreign Intermediaries

In exporting, the most typical intermediary is the foreign-based independent distributor. The exporter substantially relies on the distributor for capabilities regarding marketing, physical distribution, and customer service activities in the export market. Experienced firms go to great lengths to build *relational assets*—that is, high-quality, enduring business and social relationships with key intermediaries and facilitators abroad that provide enduring competitive advantages.

Firms develop these relationships in various ways. The best approach is to sincerely respond to intermediary needs and build solidarity by being reliable, building trust, and demonstrating solid commitment.[9] To create a positive working relationship, the exporter should develop a good understanding of the intermediary's objectives and work in earnest to address them. In general, foreign intermediaries expect exporters to provide:

- Good, reliable products for which there is a ready market
- Products that provide significant profits
- Opportunities to handle other product lines
- Support for marketing communications, advertising, and product warranties
- A payment method that does not unduly burden the intermediary
- Training for intermediary staff and the opportunity to visit the exporter's facilities (at the exporter's expense) to gain first-hand knowledge of the exporter's operations
- Help establishing after-sales service facilities, including training of local technical representatives and the means to replace defective parts, as well as a ready supply of spare parts, to maintain or repair the products

The exporter in turn has expectations that its intermediaries should meet. Exhibit 10.8 summarizes the selection criteria that experienced exporters use to qualify prospective intermediaries.

When Intermediary Relations Go Bad

Despite good intentions, disputes can arise between the exporter and its intermediaries about such issues as:

- Compensation arrangements (for example, the intermediary may want to be compensated even if not directly responsible for a sale in its territory)
- Pricing practices
- Advertising and promotion practices, and the extent of advertising support
- After-sales service
- Return policies
- Adequate inventory levels
- Incentives for promoting new products
- Adapting the product for local customers

In anticipation of disagreements, exporters generally establish a contract-based, legal relationship with the partner. A typical contract clarifies the tasks and responsibilities of both parties, specifies the duration of the relationship, defines the intermediary's sales territory, and explains the dispute resolution and termination processes if, for instance, the intermediary falls short of performance requirements such as sales targets. Some firms require candidate intermediaries to undergo a probationary period during which they evaluate performance and can terminate the relationship if it is not optimal.

Exporters should ascertain the legal requirements for termination of a contract in advance and specify the intermediary's rights for compensation. In many countries,

Intermediary Dimension	Evaluation Criteria
Organizational Strengths	• Ability to finance sales and growth in the market • Ability to provide financing to customers • Management team quality • Reputation with customers • Connections with influential people or government agencies in the market
Product-related Factors	• Knowledge about the exporter's product • Quality and superiority of all product lines handled by the intermediary • Ability to ensure security for patents and other intellectual property rights • Extent to which intermediary handles competing product lines
Marketing Capabilities	• Experience with the product line and target customers • Extent of geographic coverage provided in the target market • Quality and quantity of sales force • Ability to formulate and implement marketing plans
Managerial Commitment	• Percent of intermediary's business consisting of a single supplier • Willingness to maintain inventory sufficient to fully serve the market • Commitment to achieving exporter's sales targets

EXHIBIT 10.8   Criteria for Evaluating Export Intermediaries.   *Sources: Business International*, "How to Evaluate Foreign Distributors," pp. 145–149 (May 10, 1985); S. Tamer Cavusgil, Poh-Lin Yeoh and Michel Mitri (1995), "Selecting Foreign Distributors: An Expert Systems Approach," *Industrial Marketing Management*, 24 (4), pp. 297–304; International Trade Administration (2011), *Basic Guide to Exporting: The Official Government Resource for Small and Medium-Sized Businesses*, Washington DC: International Trade Administration; Root, Franklin (1998), *Entry Strategies for International Markets*, Hoboken, NJ: Jossey-Bass, 1983.

commercial regulations favor local intermediaries and may require the exporter to indemnify—that is, compensate—the intermediary even if there is just cause for termination. In some countries, legal contracts may prove insufficient to protect the exporter's interests.

Just as in their domestic operations, exporters occasionally encounter problems with buyers or intermediaries who default on payment. As a rule, problems with bad debt are easier to avoid than to correct after they occur. Before entering an agreement, the exporter should perform a check on the credit and other background of potential intermediaries and large-scale buyers. In terms of payment mechanisms, cash in advance or letter of credit are usually best. The exporter also can buy specialized insurance covering commercial credit risks for international transactions.

If a buyer or intermediary does default, the exporter's best recourse is to negotiate with patience, understanding, and flexibility. If negotiations fail and the cost of termination is substantial, the exporter may need to seek assistance from its bank or attorney. At the extreme, it may pursue litigation, arbitration, or other legal means for enforcing payment on a sale.

COUNTERTRADE: A POPULAR APPROACH FOR EMERGING MARKETS AND DEVELOPING ECONOMIES

In emerging markets and developing economies, conventional means of receiving payment are often costly, underdeveloped, or nonexistent. Thus, the firm may need to resort to countertrade, a form of barter, in which goods and services are traded for other goods and services. Consider Caterpillar, which exported earth-moving equipment to Venezuela in exchange for 350,000 tons of iron ore received from the Venezuelan government. Also called two-way or reciprocal trade, countertrade operates on the principle, "I'll buy your products if you'll buy mine."

In countertrade deals, typically the products that developing countries offer are commodities (for example, agricultural grains, minerals, or manufactured goods with limited international sales potential). The firm that receives such goods must find a way to sell them in order to get paid. Countertrade transactions are generally more complicated than conventional cash-for-goods trade. Multiple transactions may take years to complete.

Magnitude and Drivers of Countertrade

Many MNEs have pursued nontraditional trade deals since the 1960s, not only with developing economies that lack hard currencies but also in industrialized nations. While the exact extent of countertrade is unknown, some observers estimate it accounts for as much as one-third of all world trade. Countertrade deals are common in large-scale government procurement projects. For example, countertrade has been mandatory in Australian federal government foreign purchases of more than 2.5 million Australian dollars. In South Korea, countertrade is mandated for government telecommunications and defense procurement exceeding $1 million.

Countertrade occurs in response to two primary factors. First is the chronic shortage of hard currency common to developing economies. Second is the lack of international marketing prowess among developing-economy firms. Countertrade enables such firms to generate hard currency and access markets that might otherwise be inaccessible to them.

Types of Countertrade

There are four main types of countertrade: barter, compensation deals, counterpurchase, and buy-back agreements.

- **Barter**—the oldest form of trade—is exercised even in domestic trade in straightforward, one-shot deals. It requires a single contract, has a short time span, and is less complicated than other forms, requiring little managerial commitment or additional resources.
- **Compensation deals** include payment in both goods and cash. For example, a company may sell its equipment to the government of Brazil and receive half the payment in hard currency and the other half in merchandise.
- **Counterpurchase,** also known as a back-to-back transaction or offset agreement, requires two distinct contracts. In the first, the seller agrees to a set price for goods and receives cash from the buyer. However, this first deal is contingent on a second contract wherein the seller also agrees to purchase goods from the

buyer (or produce and assemble a certain proportion of goods in the buyer's country) for the same cash amount as the first transaction or a set percentage of it. If the two exchanges are not of equal value, the difference can be paid in cash. Counterpurchase is common in the defense industry, where a government purchasing military hardware might require a defense contractor to purchase some local products or contribute to local employment.

• In a product **buy-back agreement,** the seller agrees to supply technology or equipment to construct a facility, and receives payment in the form of goods produced by the facility. For example, the seller might design and construct a factory in the buyer's country to manufacture tractors. The seller is compensated by receiving finished tractors from the factory it built, which it then sells in world markets. Product buy-back agreements may require several years to complete and therefore entail substantial risk.

Risks of Countertrade

Firms can encounter five problems in countertrade.

1. The goods the customer offers may be inferior in quality, with limited sales potential in international markets.
2. It is often difficult to put a market value on goods that the customer offers, because they are typically commodities or low-quality manufactured products. In addition, the buyer may not have the opportunity to inspect the goods or analyze their marketability.
3. Each party to the transaction will tend to pad its prices, anticipating that its counterpart will do the same. The seller may then experience difficulty reselling the commodities it receives as payment. In a typical scenario, General Electric (GE) will place the products it receives as payment in countertrade (furniture, tomato paste) with a broker who sells them in world markets for a commission. Consequently, GE will build the cost of disposing of the goods into the price it quotes to the buyer. The buyer, anticipating that GE will quote a price on the high end, will pass the extra cost on to its customers. Thus, the resulting transaction between GE and the buyer is inefficient.
4. Countertrade is usually complex, cumbersome, and time-consuming. Deals are often difficult to bring to fruition.
5. Government rules can make countertrade highly bureaucratic and often prove frustrating for the exporting firm.

Why Consider Countertrade?

Although most firms avoid countertrade, there are five reasons to consider it.

1. The alternative may be no trade at all, as in the case of mandated countertrade.
2. Countertrade can help the firm get a foothold in new markets, leading to new customer relationships. For example, in the mining industry, certain types of minerals are available only in developing economies. Mining rights may be available only to firms willing to countertrade.

CHAPTER

11

Foreign Direct Investment and Collaborative Ventures

LEARNING OBJECTIVES
In this chapter, you will learn about:

1. International investment and collaboration

2. Motives for FDI and collaborative ventures

3. Characteristics of foreign direct investment

4. Types of foreign direct investment

5. International collaborative ventures

6. Managing collaborative ventures

7. The experience of retailers in foreign markets

INTERNATIONAL INVESTMENT AND COLLABORATION

The cross-border spread of capital and ownership is one of the most remarkable facets of globalization. **Foreign direct investment (FDI)** is an internationalization strategy in which the firm establishes a physical presence abroad through direct ownership of productive assets such as capital, technology, labor, land, plant, and equipment.

An **international collaborative venture** is a cross-border business partnership in which collaborating firms pool their resources and share costs and risks of a new venture. Here the focal firm partners with one or more companies to pursue a joint project or other business venture. International collaborative ventures are also sometimes called *international partnerships* or *international strategic alliances*.

A **joint venture** is a form of collaboration between two or more firms to create a new, jointly owned enterprise, typically by investing money. The venture may endure for many years, and each partner may attain minority, equal, or majority ownership. For example, by undertaking numerous FDI and collaborative ventures in the 2000s, SABMiller has become the world's third-largest beer brewer, with operations in more than 60 countries.[1] FDI and international collaborative ventures are primary entry strategies that focal firms use to expand abroad.

Trends in FDI and Collaborative Ventures

FDI is the most advanced and complex foreign market entry strategy. It entails establishing manufacturing plants, marketing subsidiaries, or other facilities in target countries. However, FDI is relatively risky because establishing a physical presence abroad necessitates investing substantial resources.

In a typical year, there are over 200 cross-border acquisitions valued at more than $1 billion.[2] The top three recipient countries were Britain, Canada, and the United States. Recent examples of typical cross-border investments include the following:

- Global cargo firm FedEx acquired the Indian logistics company AFL.
- The Dutch manufacturer AkzoNobel spent $338 million to build a chemical factory in China.
- The Indian firm Tata Advanced Systems formed a joint venture with Lockheed Martin to manufacture aircraft components.
- Yildiz, a Turkish holding company that owns the confectionary company Ulker, acquired chocolatier Godiva from Campbell Soup Company. Campbell Soup had earlier acquired Godiva from a Belgium-based firm.

Such examples help illustrate several trends in the contemporary global economy. First, companies from both advanced economies and emerging markets are active in FDI. Second, destination or recipient countries for such investments include both advanced economies and emerging markets. Third, companies employ multiple strategies to enter foreign markets as investors, including acquisitions and collaborative ventures. Fourth, companies from all types of industries, including retailing and services, are active in FDI and collaborative ventures.

MOTIVES FOR FDI AND COLLABORATIVE VENTURES

The ultimate goal of FDI and international collaborative ventures is to enhance company competitiveness in the global marketplace. As summarized in Exhibit 11.1, managers employ FDI for three types of complex reasons: market-seeking motives, resource or asset-seeking motives, and efficiency-seeking motives.[3] In any one venture, several motives may apply. Let's examine them in greater detail.

Market-Seeking Motives

Managers may seek new market opportunities as a result of either unfavorable developments in their home market (that is, they may be pushed into international

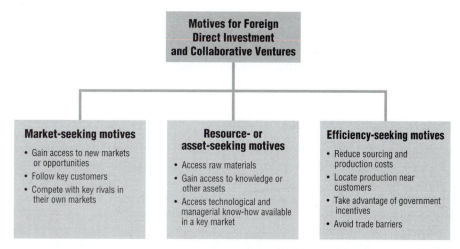

EXHIBIT 11.1   Firm Motives for Foreign Direct Investment and Collaborative Ventures.

markets) or the existence of attractive opportunities abroad (they may be pulled into international markets). There are three primary market-seeking motivations:

1. ***Gain access to new markets or opportunities.***   The presence of a substantial market motivates many firms to produce offerings at or near customer locations. Local production improves customer service and reduces the cost of transporting goods to buyer locations.

2. ***Follow key customers.***   Companies often follow their key customers abroad to generate sales or preempt other vendors. This is especially true of firms that generate much of their sales from large-scale industrial customers. Establishing local operations positions the firm to better serve customer needs.

3. ***Compete with key rivals in their own markets.***   Some MNEs may choose to confront current or potential competitors directly, in competitors' home markets. The strategic purpose is to weaken competitors by forcing them to expend resources to defend their markets.

Resource or Asset-Seeking Motives

Firms frequently want to acquire production factors that are more abundant or less costly in a foreign market. Or they may seek complementary resources and capabilities of partner companies headquartered abroad. Specifically, FDI or collaborative ventures may be motivated by the firm's desire to attain:

   1. ***Raw materials needed in extractive and agricultural industries.*** Firms in the mining, oil, and crop-growing industries have little choice but to go where the raw materials are located. In the wine industry, companies establish wineries in countries suited for growing grapes, such as France and Chile.

   2. ***Knowledge or other assets.***[4]   FDI provides the foreign firm better access to local market knowledge, customers, and distribution systems, and better control over local operations. By collaborating in R&D, manufacturing, and marketing, the focal firm can benefit from the partner's know-how.

3. *Technological and managerial know-how.* [5] Companies often benefit by establishing themselves in industrial clusters abroad, such as the robotics industry in Japan, chemicals in Germany, fashion in Italy, or software in the United States. Many firms enter collaborative ventures abroad as a prelude to operating wholly owned FDI.

Efficiency-Seeking Motives

In expanding abroad, many firms seek to create economies of scale and economies of scope—that is, they attempt to reduce business costs by employing corporate resources (factories, R&D facilities, etc.) across a relatively large number of products and markets. Typically, MNEs concentrate production in only a few locations to maximize efficiencies in manufacturing. [6] Firms typically disseminate their best practices in production and other activities to all their foreign subsidiaries to augment operational efficiencies worldwide. Many develop global brands to increase the efficiency of marketing activities. There are four major efficiency-seeking motives:

1. ***Reduce sourcing and production costs by accessing inexpensive labor and other cheap inputs to the production process.*** [7] This motive accounts for the massive investment by foreign firms in factories and service-producing facilities in China, Mexico, Eastern Europe, and India.
2. ***Locate production near customers.*** Firms may choose to locate operations in markets characterized by rapid change or where customers have exacting needs, in order to ensure optimal responsiveness.
3. ***Take advantage of government incentives.*** [8] Governments frequently offer subsidies and tax concessions to foreign firms to encourage them to invest locally, as a means of generating jobs, capital, and transfer of know-how to locals.
4. ***Avoid trade barriers.*** Entry via FDI helps companies avoid tariffs and other trade barriers, which usually apply only to exporting. By establishing a physical presence inside a country or an economic bloc, the foreign firm obtains the same advantages as local companies. Partnering with a local firm also helps overcome regulations or trade barriers and satisfy local content rules. Note, however, this motive has lost importance because trade barriers have declined in many countries.

CHARACTERISTICS OF FOREIGN DIRECT INVESTMENT

Internationalizing through FDI enables the firm to maintain a physical presence in key markets, secure direct access to customers and partners, and perform value-chain activities locally. FDI is an equity or ownership form of foreign market entry. It is the entry strategy most associated with large MNEs—such as Ford, Unilever, and Bombardier—that have extensive physical presences around the world. As they venture abroad, firms that specialize in products usually establish manufacturing plants. Firms that offer services, such as banks, cruise lines, and restaurant chains, usually establish agency relationships and retail facilities.

FDI should not be confused with **international portfolio investment**, which refers to passive ownership of foreign securities such as stocks and bonds for the purpose of generating financial returns. International portfolio investment is a form of international investment, but it is not FDI, which seeks ownership control of a business abroad and represents a long-term commitment. The United Nations uses the benchmark of at least 10 percent ownership in the enterprise to differentiate FDI from portfolio investment. However, this percentage is misleading because control is not usually achieved unless the investor owns at least 50 percent of a foreign venture.

Key Features of Foreign Direct Investment

FDI has several key features, which we consider next.

- *FDI represents substantial resource commitment.*   As the ultimate internationalization strategy, it is far more taxing on the firm's resources and capabilities than any other approach. For example, the U.S. firm General Electric owns more than $400 billion in factories, subsidiaries, and other operations outside the United States.[9]
- *FDI implies local presence and operations.*   Some firms concentrate their operations in one or a handful of locations; other firms disperse their FDI among numerous countries. Often, MNEs' networks of operations become so extensive that the nationality of individual firms is not always clear. For example, although based in Switzerland, Nestlé generates more than 90 percent of its sales from abroad.
- *Firms invest in countries that provide specific comparative advantages.*   Managers choose particular countries in which to invest, based on the advantages these locations offer. Thus, firms tend to perform R&D activities in those countries with leading-edge knowledge and experience for their industry, source from countries where suppliers provide the best-value products, build production facilities at locations that provide the best ratio of productivity to labor costs, and establish marketing subsidiaries in countries with the greatest sales potential.
- *FDI entails substantial risk and uncertainty.*   Compared to other entry strategies, establishing a permanent, fixed presence in a foreign country makes the firm vulnerable to country risk and intervention by local government on issues such as wages, hiring practices, and product pricing. Direct investors also must contend with inflation, recessions, and other local economic conditions.
- *Direct investors must deal more intensively with language and cultural variables in the host market.*   MNEs with high-profile, conspicuous operations are especially vulnerable to close public scrutiny of their actions. To minimize potential problems, managers often favor investing in countries that are culturally and linguistically familiar. When setting up shop in continental Europe, for example, U.S. firms frequently choose the Netherlands because English is widely spoken there.[10]

These features of FDI pose formidable challenges for the firm.

Corporate Social Responsibility and FDI

Multinational firms increasingly strive to behave in *socially responsible* ways in host countries. Many invest in local communities and apply global standards of fair treatment for workers. Unilever (www.unilever.com), the giant Dutch-British producer of consumer products, operates a free community laundry in a São Paulo slum, provides financing to assist tomato growers to convert to environmentally friendly irrigation, and recycles 17 million pounds of waste annually at one of its toothpaste factories. In Bangladesh, where there are relatively few doctors, Unilever funds a hospital that offers free medical care to the needy. In Ghana, the company teaches palm oil producers to reuse plant waste while providing drinkable water to deprived communities. In India, Unilever provides small loans to help women in remote villages start small-scale enterprises. In all the countries where it operates, Unilever discloses how much carbon dioxide and hazardous waste it produces.[11]

Many other MNEs are responding to such global agendas as *sustainability,* or meeting humanity's needs without harming future generations. For example, Nokia is a leader in phasing out toxic materials. GlaxoSmithKline and Merck offer AIDS drugs at cost in numerous impoverished countries. Suncor Energy helps Native Americans deal with social and ecological issues in Canada's far north.

Most Active Firms in FDI

Exhibit 11.2 provides a sample of leading MNEs engaged in FDI. General Electric, Vodafone, and other firms in the exhibit are listed based on the volume of factories, subsidiaries, and other assets they own in foreign countries, ranked by asset value. For example, U.K.-based Vodafone is a mobile phone supplier with sales offices in cities around the world. The most internationally active MNEs are in the automotive, oil, and telecommunications industries.

Rank	Company	Home Country	Industry	Assets (billions of U.S. dollars) Foreign	Total	Sales (billions of U.S. dollars) Foreign	Total	Approximate Number of Subsidiaries and Affiliates Foreign	Total
1	General Electric	United States	Electrical & electronic equipment	$400	$798	$98	$183	787	1,157
2	Vodafone	United Kingdom	Telecommunications	205	223	52	60	70	198
3	Royal Dutch Shell	Netherlands & United Kingdom	Petroleum	222	282	262	458	328	814
4	BP	United Kingdom	Petroleum	187	228	284	366	445	611
5	Exxon Mobil	United States	Petroleum	161	228	322	460	237	314
6	Toyota Motor	Japan	Motor vehicles	183	320	144	226	129	341
7	Total	France	Petroleum	141	165	190	250	410	576
8	Electricité de France	France	Electricity, gas & water	129	279	42	90	204	264
9	Ford Motor	United States	Motor vehicles	103	223	76	129	130	216
10	E.ON	Germany	Electricity, gas & water	141	219	50	121	303	596

EXHIBIT 11.2   World's Most International Nonfinancial MNEs, Based on Volume of Foreign Assets.   *Source:* UNCTAD, World Investment Report 2009 (New York: United Nations, 2009, p. 225, "Annex table A.1.9. The World's Top 100 non-financial TNCs, ranked by foreign assets, 2007a"), accessed June 4, 2010 at http://unctad.org/en/docs/wir2009_en.pdf.

Service Firms and FDI

Companies in the services sector, such as retailing, construction, and personal care, must offer their services where they are consumed. This requires establishing either a permanent presence through FDI (as in retailing) or a temporary relocation of the service company personnel (as in the construction industry).[12] Management consulting is a service usually embodied in experts who interact directly with clients to dispense advice. Many support services, such as advertising, insurance, accounting, legal work, and overnight package delivery, are also best provided at the customer's location. FDI is vital for internationalizing services.[13]

Exhibit 11.3 portrays the world's most international financial institutions and the breadth of their operations abroad. The firms are ranked based on the number of foreign subsidiaries and affiliates and the number of countries where the MNEs do business. For example, Citigroup has representative offices in 75 countries.

Leading Destinations for FDI

Advanced economies long have been popular destinations for FDI because of their strong GDP per capita, GDP growth rate, density of knowledge workers, and superior business infrastructure, such as telephone systems and energy sources.[14] In recent years, however, emerging markets are also gaining appeal as FDI destinations. According to A. T. Kearney's Global Location Index, the top destinations for foreign

Company	Home Country	Number of Subsidiaries and Affiliates		Number of Host Countries
		Foreign	Total	
Citigroup, Inc.	United States	723	1,020	75
Allianz SE	Germany	612	823	52
ABN AMRO	Netherlands	703	945	48
Generali	Italy	342	396	41
HSBC	United Kingdom	683	1,048	54
Société Générale	Italy	345	526	53
Zurich Financial Services	Switzerland	383	393	34
UBS	Switzerland	432	465	35
Unicredito Italiano	Italy	1,052	1,111	34
Axa	France	464	575	39

EXHIBIT 11.3   World's Most International Financial MNEs, Based on Breadth of Worldwide Operations.   *Source:* UNCTAD, World Investment Report 2009 (New York: United Nations, 2009, p. 225, "Annex table A.1.12. The top 50 financial TNCs ranked by Geographical Spread Index (GSI), 2008"), http://unctad.org/en/docs/wir2009_en.pdf.

investment today are China and India (www.atkearney.com). China is popular because of its size, rapid growth rate, and low labor costs. India is popular because of its managerial talent, well-educated workforce, and relatively fewer cultural barriers.[15] China and India are also attractive for strategic reasons: They have much long-term potential as target markets and new sources of competitive advantage.

Factors to Consider in Choosing FDI Locations

Exhibit 11.4 lists the criteria firms use to evaluate countries as potential targets for FDI projects. In the Czech Republic, for example, giant Chinese electronics manufacturer Sichuan Changhong (www.changhong.com) built a $30 million factory that can produce one million flat-screen televisions per year. Several of the criteria in Exhibit 11.4 attract such firms to Eastern Europe. First, wages there are relatively low: Engineers in Slovakia earn half what Western engineers make and assembly line workers earn one-quarter. Second, East European governments offer incentives, from financing to low taxes, as in Slovakia where all taxes are a simple 19 percent. Third, local manufacturing allows firms to avoid trade barriers. Sichuan Changhong's presence in the Czech Republic helps it avoid tariffs imposed by the European Union on imports from China. Fourth, companies prefer Eastern Europe because of its physical proximity to the huge EU market.[16]

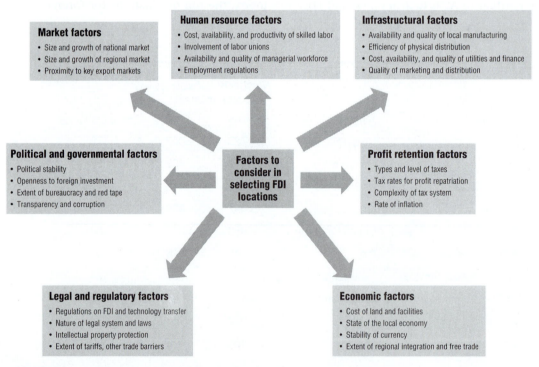

EXHIBIT 11.4   Factors to Consider in Selecting Foreign Direct Investment Locations.   *Source:* John Dunning (1993) *Multinational Enterprises and the Global Economy*, Reading, MA: Addison-Wesley; Hwychang Moon (1988) *Firm-Specific Determinants of Foreign Direct Investment in Some Selective Industries*, Seattle: University of Washington; P. O'Sullivan (1985) "Determinants and Impact of Private Foreign Direct Investment in Host Countries," *Management International Review*, 25 (4): 28-35; Franklin R. Root (1998) *Entry Strategies for International Markets*, Hoboken, NJ: Jossey-Bass.

TYPES OF FOREIGN DIRECT INVESTMENT

We can classify FDI activities by form (greenfield versus mergers and acquisitions), nature of ownership (wholly owned versus joint venture), and level of integration (horizontal versus vertical).

Greenfield Investment versus Mergers and Acquisitions

Greenfield investment occurs when a firm invests to build a new manufacturing, marketing, or administrative facility, as opposed to acquiring existing facilities. As the name *greenfield* implies, the investing firm typically buys an empty plot of land and builds a production plant, marketing subsidiary, or other facility there for its own use.

An **acquisition** is the purchase of an existing company or facility. For example, the Chinese personal computer manufacturer Lenovo acquired IBM's PC business, which now accounts for some two-thirds of its annual revenue and helped it rapidly become a global player.[17]

Compared to greenfield FDI, firms often prefer acquisition because it confers ownership of existing assets such as plant, equipment, and human resources, as well as access to existing suppliers and customers. Acquisition also provides an immediate stream of revenue and accelerates the MNE's return on investment. However, host country governments usually want MNEs to undertake greenfield FDI, and offer incentives to encourage it, because it creates new jobs and production capacity, facilitates technology and know-how transfer to locals, and improves linkages to the global marketplace.

A **merger** is a special type of acquisition in which two companies join to form a new, larger firm. Mergers are more common between companies of similar size because they are capable of integrating their operations on a relatively equal basis. The merger between Lucent Technologies in the United States and Alcatel in France created the world's largest firm in the global telecommunications equipment industry (Alcatel-Lucent). Like joint ventures, mergers can generate many positive outcomes, including interpartner learning and resource sharing, increased economies of scale, cost savings from elimination of duplicative activities, a broader range of products and services for sale, and greater market power. Cross-border mergers address many challenges related to national differences in culture and competition policy. However, success requires substantial advance research, planning, and commitment.

The Nature of Ownership in FDI

By taking either full or partial ownership in a venture, foreign direct investors also choose their degree of control over decisions about product development, expansion, and profit distribution. Partial ownership is known as **equity participation**.

Wholly owned direct investment is FDI in which the investor assumes 100 percent ownership of the business and secures complete managerial control over its operations. Many foreign automotive firms have established fully owned manufacturing plants in the United States to serve this large market from within. For example, Toyota has numerous plants at locations around the United States. By contrast, an **equity joint venture** creates a separate firm through the investment or pooling of assets by two or more parent firms that gain joint ownership of the new legal entity.[18] A partner in a joint venture may hold majority, equal (50–50), or minority ownership. Minority ownership provides little control over the operation.

Many firms find joint ventures attractive because collaborating with a local partner increases the foreign entrant's ability to navigate the local market. Collaborative ventures also benefit small and medium-sized enterprises by providing them with needed capital and other assets.

In the event 100 percent foreign ownership in local enterprises is forbidden by the local government (a type of protectionism aimed at safeguarding local industries), a joint venture with a local partner may be the only entry strategy available to the focal firm. However, governments are relaxing such regulations in most industries, and they are now relatively receptive to FDI.

Vertical versus Horizontal Integration

A third way of classifying FDI is by whether integration takes place vertically or horizontally. **Vertical integration** is an arrangement whereby the firm owns, or seeks to own, multiple stages of a value chain for producing, selling, and delivering a product or service. Vertical FDI takes two forms. In *forward* vertical integration, the firm develops the capacity to sell its outputs by investing in downstream value-chain facilities—that is, in marketing and selling operations. Forward vertical integration is less common than *backward* vertical integration, in which the firm acquires the capacity abroad to provide inputs for its foreign or domestic production processes by investing in upstream facilities, typically factories, assembly plants, or refining operations. Firms can carry out both backward and forward vertical integration. In various countries, for example, Honda owns both suppliers of car parts and dealerships that sell cars.

Horizontal integration is an arrangement whereby the firm owns, or seeks to own, the activities performed in a single stage of its value chain. Microsoft's primary business is developing computer software. In addition to producing operating systems, word processing, and spreadsheet software, it has also developed subsidiaries that make other types of software, such as a Montreal-based firm that produces software for creating movie animations. As this example suggests, companies invest abroad in their own industry to expand their capacity and activities. A firm may acquire another firm engaged in an identical value-chain activity to achieve economies of scale, expand its product line, increase its profitability, or, in some cases, eliminate a competitor.

INTERNATIONAL COLLABORATIVE VENTURES

Collaborative ventures, sometimes called *international partnerships* or *international strategic alliances*, are essentially partnerships between two or more firms.[19] They help companies overcome together the often substantial risks and costs involved in achieving international projects that might exceed the capabilities of any one firm operating alone. Groups of firms sometimes form partnerships to undertake large-scale projects such as developing new technologies or building power plants. Advantages like these help explain why the volume of such partnerships has grown substantially in the past few decades.[20]

While collaboration can take place at similar or different levels of the value chain, it is typically focused on R&D, manufacturing, or marketing. International collaborative ventures have been on the rise to realize joint R&D in knowledge-intensive, high-technology sectors such as robotics, semiconductors, pharmaceuticals, and commercial aircraft.

There are two basic types of collaborative ventures: equity joint ventures and project-based, nonequity ventures. *Equity joint ventures* are traditional collaborations of a type that has existed for decades. In recent years, however, there has been a proliferation of newer *project-based collaborations.*

Equity Joint Ventures

Joint ventures are usually formed when no one party possesses all the assets needed to exploit an available opportunity. In a typical international deal, the foreign partner contributes capital, technology, management expertise, training, or some type of product. The local partner contributes the use of its factory or other facilities, knowledge of the local language and culture, market navigation know-how, useful connections to the host country government, or lower-cost production factors such as labor or raw materials.

Project-Based Nonequity Ventures

Increasingly common in cross-border business, the **project-based nonequity venture** is a collaboration in which the partners create a project with a relatively narrow scope and a well-defined timetable, without creating a new legal entity. Combining staff, resources, and capabilities, the partners collaborate on new technologies or products until the venture bears fruit or they no longer consider collaboration valuable. Such partnering reduces the enormous fixed costs of R&D, especially in technology and knowledge-intensive industries, and helps firms catch up with rivals.

Differences between Equity and Project-Based Nonequity Ventures

Project-based collaborations differ from traditional equity joint ventures in four important ways. First, no new legal entity is created. Partners carry on their activity within the guidelines of a contract. Second, parent companies do not necessarily seek ownership of an ongoing enterprise. Instead, they contribute their knowledge, expertise, staff, and monetary resources to derive knowledge or other benefits. Third, collaboration tends to have a well-defined timetable and end date; partners go their separate ways once they have accomplished their objectives or have no further reason for continuation. Fourth, collaboration is narrower in scope than in equity joint venturing, typically emphasizing a single project, such as development, manufacturing, marketing, or distribution of a new product.

Exhibit 11.5 highlights advantages and disadvantages of the two types of international collaborative ventures.

Consortium

A **consortium** is a project-based, usually nonequity venture initiated by multiple partners to fulfill a large-scale project. It is typically formed by a contract, which delineates the rights and obligations of each member and allocates work to the members on the same basis as profits. Consortia are popular for innovation in industries such as commercial aircraft, computers, pharmaceuticals, and telecommunications, where the costs of developing and marketing a new product often reach hundreds of millions of dollars and require sweeping expertise. For example, Boeing, Fuji, Kawasaki, and Mitsubishi joined forces to design and manufacture major components of the Boeing 767 aircraft.

	Advantages	Disadvantages
Equity joint ventures	• Afford greater control over future directions • Facilitate transfer of knowledge between the partners • Common goals drive the joint venture	• Complex management structure • Coordination between the partners may be a concern • Difficult to terminate • Greater exposure to political risk
Project-based nonequity ventures	• Easy to set up • Simple management structure; can be adjusted easily • Takes advantage of partners' respective strengths • Can respond quickly to changing technology and market conditions • Easy to terminate	• Knowledge transfer may be less straightforward between the partners • No equity commitment; thus, puts greater emphasis on trust, good communications, and developing relationships • Conflicts may be harder to resolve • Division of costs and benefits may strain relationship

EXHIBIT 11.5 Advantages and Disadvantages of International Collaborative Ventures.

Often, several firms pool their resources to bid on a major project, such as building a power plant or a high-tech manufacturing facility. Each brings a unique specialty to the project but would be unable to win the bid on its own. No formal legal entity is created; each firm retains its individual identity, and if one party withdraws, the consortium can continue with the remaining participants. iNavSat is a consortium formed among several European firms to develop and manage Europe's global satellite navigation system.

Cross-Licensing Agreements

A **cross-licensing agreement** is a type of a project-based nonequity venture whose partners each agree to access licensed intellectual property developed by the other on preferential terms. For example, Microsoft entered such an agreement with Japan's JVC to share patented knowledge on software and other products. Two firms also might enter a cross-distribution agreement, in which each partner has the right to distribute products or services produced by the other on preferential terms. For instance, the Star Alliance is an agreement among some 25 airlines—including Air Canada, United, Lufthansa, SAS, Singapore Airlines, and Air New Zealand—to market each others' airline flights (www.staralliance.com).

MANAGING COLLABORATIVE VENTURES

In FDI and exporting, the focal firm emphasizes competing skillfully against rival companies. In collaborative ventures, however, it must cooperate with one or more other firms that, in different circumstances or other countries, may actually be its competitors. This requires managers to acquire skills in developing and consummating partnerships with other firms around the world.[21] Let's review the key managerial tasks in successful collaboration.

Understand Potential Risks in Collaboration

Firms that collaborate have decided the potential benefits of partnering outweigh potential risks. In analyzing a possible collaboration, management should ask:

- As a firm, are we likely to grow dependent on our partner?
- By partnering, will we stifle growth and innovation in our own organization?
- Will we share our competencies excessively, to the point where corporate interests are threatened? How can we safeguard our core competencies?
- Will we be exposed to significant commercial, political, cultural, or currency risks?
- Will we close off certain growth opportunities by participating in this venture?
- Will managing the venture place an excessive burden on our corporate resources, such as managerial, financial, or technological resources?

The potential partner may be a current or potential competitor, is likely to have its own agenda, and will probably gain important competitive advantages from the relationship.[22] Management must protect its hard-won capabilities and other organizational assets to preserve its bargaining power and ability to compete. Harmony is not necessarily the most important goal, and accepting some conflict and tension between the partners may be preferable to surrendering core skills. In collaborations with partners in China, known for weak intellectual property rights, Intel has been careful not to share too much of its proprietary technology.[23]

Pursue a Systematic Process for Partnering

The initial decision in internationalization is to choose the most appropriate target market, because the market determines the characteristics needed in a business partner. If the firm is planning to enter an emerging market, for example, it may want a partner with political clout or connections. Exhibit 11.6 outlines the process for identifying and working with a suitable business partner.[24]

When managers first contemplate internationalization via FDI, they usually think in terms of a wholly owned operation. Many are accustomed to retaining the control and sole access to profits that come with 100 percent ownership. The nature of the industry or product may also make partnering less desirable. But management should consider collaboration an option. Typically the firm enters a collaborative venture when it discovers a weak or missing link in its value chain and chooses a partner that can remedy the deficiency.

Ensure Success with Collaborative Ventures

About half of all collaborative ventures fail within the first five years of operation because of unresolved disagreements, confusion about venture goals, and other problems. In addition to facing complex business issues, managers must contend with differences in culture and language, as well as differences in political, legal, and economic systems. Collaborative ventures in developing economies have an even higher failure rate than those in advanced economies.[25]

French food giant Danone (www.danone.com) terminated its joint venture with a local Chinese partner in 2009 after years of contentious relations. Danone had formed the partnership in 1996, when the Chinese government often required such

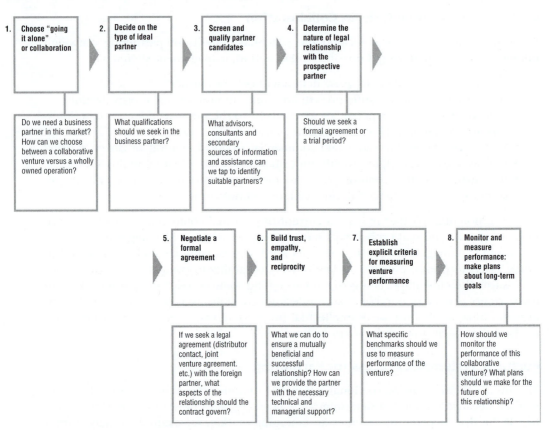

EXHIBIT 11.6   A Systematic Process to International Business Partnering.

ventures from foreign firms.[26] In later years, however, the Chinese partner established a mirror business that sold the same products the joint venture was marketing. The partner claimed that contract terms were unfair and accused Danone of trying to gain control of its other businesses.

Experience suggests several guidelines managers should follow for enhancing success:

- *Be tolerant of cultural differences.*   The partners may never arrive at a common set of values and organizational routines, especially if they're from very distinct cultures—say, Norway and Nigeria. But establishing compatibility is important despite cultural differences.
- *Pursue common goals.*   Japanese firms tend to value market share over profitability, while U.S. firms value profitability over market share. Because different strategies are required to maximize each of these performance goals, a joint venture between Japanese and U.S. firms may fail. To overcome such challenges, partners need to regularly interact and communicate at three levels of the organization: senior management, operational management, and the workforce.
- *Give due attention to planning and management of the venture.*   Without agreement on questions of management, decision making, and control, each

partner may seek to control all the venture's operations, which can strain the managerial, financial, and technological resources of both. When one of the partners is clearly the driver or the leader in the relationship, there is less likelihood of a stalemate or prolonged negotiations.

- *Safeguard core competencies.* Collaboration takes place between current or potential competitors that must walk a fine line between cooperation and competition. Volkswagen and General Motors succeeded in China by partnering with the Chinese firm, Shanghai Automotive Industry Corporation (SAIC; www .saicmotor.com). The Western firms transferred much technology and know-how to their Chinese partner. Having learned much from them, SAIC is now poised to become a significant player in the global automobile industry and even a competitor to its earlier partners.[27]
- *Adjust to shifting environmental circumstances.* When environmental conditions change, the rationale for a collaborative venture may weaken or disappear. An industry or economic downturn may shift priorities in one or both firms. Cost overruns can make the venture untenable. New government policies or regulations can increase costs or eliminate anticipated benefits. Managers should maintain flexibility to adjust to changing conditions.

THE EXPERIENCE OF RETAILERS IN FOREIGN MARKETS

Retailers represent a special case of international service firms that internationalize substantially through FDI and collaborative ventures. Retailing takes various forms and includes department stores (Marks & Spencer, Macy's), specialty retailers (Body Shop, Gap), supermarkets (Sainsbury, Safeway), convenience stores (7-Eleven, Tom Thumb), discount stores (Zellers, Target), and big-box stores (Home Depot, IKEA).

The major drivers of retailer internationalization have been saturation of home country markets, deregulation of international investment, and opportunities to benefit from lower costs abroad. Most emerging markets exhibit pent-up demand, fast economic growth, a growing middle class, and increasingly sophisticated consumers attracted by a wide selection of merchandise at low prices.

Retailers usually choose between FDI and franchising as a foreign market entry strategy. The larger, more experienced firms, such as Carrefour, Royal Ahold, and Walmart, tend to internationalize via FDI; that is, they typically own their stores and maintain direct control over operations and proprietary assets. Smaller and less internationally experienced firms such as Banana Republic tend to rely on networks of independent franchisees. In franchising, the retailer adopts a business system from, and pays an ongoing fee to, a franchise operator. Other firms may employ a dual strategy—using FDI in some markets and franchising in others. While franchising facilitates rapid internationalization, it affords the firm less control over its foreign operations.

Many retailers have floundered in foreign markets. When the French department store Galleries Lafayette opened in New York City, it could not compete with the city's numerous posh competitors. In its home market in Britain, Marks & Spencer succeeds with store layouts that blend food and clothing offerings in relatively small spaces, a formula that translated poorly in Canada and the United States. IKEA experienced problems in Japan, where consumers value high-quality furnishings, not the low-cost products that IKEA offers.

Challenges of International Retailing

Retailing depends for much of its success on the store environment and the shopping experience and is strongly affected by factors in each national environment. Four barriers stand in the way of successfully transplanting home market success to international markets.

First, *culture and language* are significant obstacles. Compared to most businesses, retailers are close to customers. They must respond to local market requirements by customizing their product and service portfolio, adapting store hours, modifying store size and layout, training local workers, and meeting labor union demands.

Second, consumers tend to develop strong *loyalty to indigenous retailers.* As Galleries Lafayette in New York and Walmart in Germany discovered, local consumers are usually more faithful to local, homegrown firms.

Third, managers must address *legal and regulatory barriers* that can be idiosyncratic. Japan's Large-Scale Store Law required foreign discount retailers to get permission from existing small retailers before setting up shop. Although it has been relaxed in recent years, the law presented a major obstacle to the entry of stores such as Toys "R" Us.[28]

Fourth, when entering a new market, retailers must develop *local sources* for thousands of products, including some that local suppliers may be unwilling or unable to provide. Some retailers end up importing many of their offerings, which requires establishing complex and costly international supply chains.

International Retailing Success Factors

The most successful retailers pursue a systematic approach to international expansion. First, advanced research and planning are essential. A thorough understanding of the target market, combined with a sophisticated business plan, allows the firm to anticipate potential problems and prepare for success. In the run-up to launching stores in China, for example, management at French retailer Carrefour spent twelve years building up its business in Taiwan, where it developed a deep understanding of Chinese culture. Carrefour became China's biggest foreign retailer, rapidly developing a network of hypermarkets in 25 cities.[29]

Second, international retailers need to establish efficient logistics and purchasing networks in each market where they operate to maintain adequate inventory and minimize cost. Scale economies in procurement are especially critical.

Third, international retailers should assume an entrepreneurial, creative approach to foreign markets. Starting from one London location in 1975, founder Richard Branson expanded Virgin Megastore to numerous markets throughout Europe, North America, and Asia. The stores were big and well lighted and stocked music albums in a logical order. Consequently, sales turnover was much faster than that of smaller music retailers.

Fourth, retailers must be willing to adjust their business models to suit local preferences for selection, price, marketing, and store design. Home Depot in Mexico offers payment plans for small budgets and promotes the do-it-yourself mind-set in a country where most cannot afford to hire professional builders.[30]

Summary

Foreign direct investment (FDI) is an internationalization strategy in which the firm establishes a physical presence abroad through ownership of productive assets such as capital, technology, labor, land, plant, and equipment. An **international collaborative venture** is a cross-border business alliance where partnering firms pool their resources and share costs and risks of the venture. A **joint venture** is a form of collaboration between two or more firms that leads to minority, equal, or majority ownership.

Firms employ FDI for various reasons, including *market-seeking motives*, to enter new markets and gain new customers; *resource/asset-seeking motives*, to acquire production factors abroad that may be cheaper or more abundant; and *efficiency-seeking motives*, to enhance the efficiency of the firm's value-adding activities. Motivations for international collaborative ventures include the ability to gain access to new markets, opportunities, or knowledge; to undertake international activities too costly or risky for one firm alone; to reduce costs; to meet government requirements; and to prevent or reduce competition.

FDI is the most advanced, risky and complex entry strategy and requires establishing manufacturing plants, marketing subsidiaries, or other facilities abroad. FDI is most commonly used by MNEs—large firms with extensive international operations. Services are typically location-bound, requiring the firm to establish a foreign presence, usually via FDI.

FDI can be **wholly owned direct investment**, in which the firm owns 100 percent of foreign operations, or an **equity joint venture** with one or more partners. Firms may engage in **greenfield investment** by building a facility from scratch or by acquiring an existing facility from another firm through **acquisition**. With **vertical integration**, the firm seeks to own multiple stages of its value chain. With **horizontal integration**, the firm seeks to own activities involved in a single stage of its value chain. A **merger** is a special type of acquisition in which two companies join together to form a new, larger firm.

Joint ventures (JVs) are normally formed when no one party possesses all the assets needed to exploit an opportunity. The **project-based**, **nonequity venture** emphasizes a contractual relationship between the partners and is formed to pursue certain goals or meet an important business need while the partners remain independent. A **consortium** is a project-based, nonequity venture initiated by multiple firms to undertake a large-scale activity that is beyond the capabilities of the individual members.

Collaboration requires much research and analysis up-front, as well as strong negotiation skills to allocate planning responsibility for and day-to-day control over management, production, finance, and marketing. At least half of all collaborative ventures fail prematurely. Firms should choose their partners carefully and follow a systematic process for managing ventures. Retailing requires intensive customer interaction and is particularly susceptible to culture and income level differences, strong loyalty to local retailers, and legal and regulatory barriers.

Key Terms

acquisition *209*

consortium *211*

cross-licensing
agreement *212*

equity joint venture *209*

equity participation *209*

foreign direct investment
(FDI) *201*
greenfield
investment *209*
horizontal
integration *210*

international collaborative
venture *201*
international portfolio
investment *204*
joint venture *202*
merger *209*

project-based nonequity
venture *211*
vertical
integration *210*
wholly owned direct
investment *209*

Endnotes

1. B. Bhavna, "The Beer Market in India," *Just—Drinks,* March 2007, pp. 65–87; company profile of SABMiller at http://www.hoovers.com.
2. UNCTAD, *World Investment Report* (New York: United Nations, 2009).
3. John Dunning, *International Production and the Multinational Enterprise* (London: Allen and Unwin, 1981).
4. Lilach Nachum and Srilata Zaheer, "The Persistence of Distance? The Impact of Technology on MNE Motivations for Foreign Investment," *Strategic Management Journal,* 26 (2005): 747–67.
5. Wilbur Chung and Juan Alcacer, "Knowledge Seeking and Location Choice of Foreign Direct Investment in the United States," *Management Science* 48 (2002): 1534–42.
6. Lilach Nachum and Cliff Wymbs, "Product Differentiation, External Economies and MNE Location Choices: M&As in Global Cities," *Journal of International Business Studies* 36 (2005): 415–23.
7. Nachum and Zaheer (2005).
8. Barbara Katz and Joel Owen, "Should Governments Compete for Foreign Direct Investment?" *Journal of Economic Behavior & Organization* 59 (2006): 230–38.
9. "Biggest Transnational Companies," *Economist,* October 3, 2009, p. 121.
10. Thomas C. Head and P. Sorensen, "Attracting Foreign Direct Investment: The Potential Role of National Culture," *The Journal of American Academy of Business* 6 (2005): 305–309.
11. "Beyond the Green Corporation," *Business Week,* January 29, 2007, pp. 50–64.
12. M. K. Erramilli and C. P. Rao, "Service Firms' International Entry-Mode Choice: A Modified Transaction-Cost Analysis Approach," *Journal of Marketing* 57 (July 1993): 19–38; J. Li and S. Guisinger, "The Globalization of Service Multinationals in the 'Triad' Regions: Japan, Western Europe, and North America," *Journal of International Business Studies* 23 (1992): 675–96; United Nations, *The Transnationalization of Service Industries* (New York: Transnational Corporations and Management Division, Department of Economic and Social Development, 1993).
13. Rajshekhar Javalgi, David A. Griffith, and D. Steven White, "An Empirical Examination of Factors Influencing the Internationalization of Service Firms," *Journal of Services Marketing* 17 (2003): 185–201.
14. UNCTAD, *World Investment Report* (New York: United Nations, 2006).
15. A. T. Kearney, *FDI Confidence Index* (Alexandria, VA: Global Business Policy Council, 2004).
16. John Tagliabue, "Would Stalin Drive a Peugeot?" *New York Times,* November 25, 2006, pp. B1, B9; David Rocks, "Made in China—Er, Veliko Turnovo," *Business Week,* January 8, 2007, p. 43.
17. UNCTAD (2006).
18. In this book, we adopt the customary definition of joint venture, where it is assumed to carry equity interest by the parent firms that founded it. That is, a joint venture is always an equity venture. Nevertheless, in the popular literature the term *equity venture* is incorrectly used to refer to all types of collaborative ventures, including

project-based collaborations. Therefore, we will use the term *equity joint venture* rather than simply *joint venture* to avoid miscommunication.

19. Farok Contractor and Peter Lorange, *Cooperative Strategies and Alliances* (Oxford, England: Elsevier Science, 2002); Janell Townsend, "Understanding Alliances: A Review of International Aspects in Strategic Marketing," *Marketing Intelligence & Planning* 21 (2003): 143–58.

20. Donald Fites, "Make Your Dealers Your Partners," *Harvard Business Review* 74 (1996): 84–91; Masaaki Kotabe, Hildy Teegen, Preet Aulakh, Maria Cecilia Coutinho de Arruda, Roberto Santillan-Salgado, and Walter Greene, "Strategic Alliances in Emerging Latin America: A View from Brazilian, Chilean, and Mexican Companies," *Journal of World Business* 35 (2000): 114–32.

21. Contractor and Lorange (2002); Gary Hamel, "Competition for Competence and Inter-Partner Learning within International Strategic Alliances," *Strategic Management Journal,* Special Issue: Global Strategy 12 (Summer 1991): 83–103; Gary Hamel, Yves Doz, and C. K. Prahalad, "Collaborate with Your Competitors—and Win," *Harvard Business Review* 67 (January–February 1989): 133–39; S. Tamer Cavusgil, "International Partnering: A Systematic Framework for Collaborating with Foreign Business Partners," *Journal of*

International Marketing 6 (1998): 91–107; Destan Kandemir, Attila Yaprak, and S. Tamer Cavusgil, "Alliance Orientation: Conceptualization, Measurement and Impact on Market Performance," *Journal of the Academy of Marketing Science* 34 (2006): 324–40.

22. *Ibid.*

23. Fred Vogelstein, "How Intel Got Inside," *Fortune,* October 4, 2004, pp. 127–36; Bruce Heimana and Jack Nickerson, "Empirical Evidence Regarding the Tension Between Knowledge Sharing and Knowledge Expropriation in Collaborations," *Managerial and Decision Economics* 25 (2004): 401–20.

24. S. Tamer Cavusgil, "International Partnering: A Systematic Framework for Collaborating with Foreign Business Partners," *Journal of International Marketing* 6 (1998): 91–107.

25. Cavusgil (1998); Kandemir, Yaprak, and Cavusgil (2006).

26. James Areddy, "Danone Pulls Out of Disputed China Venture," *Wall Street Journal*, October 1, 2009, p. B1.

27. "Asian Alliances: New Ties for VW, GM and Peugeot Citroen," *Economist,* December 12, 2009, p. 72.

28. Amy Kazmin, "Ikea Axes Push After India Refuses to Alter Law," *Financial Times*, June 12, 2009, p. 16.

29. Clay Chandler, "The Great Wal-Mart of China," *Fortune,* July 25, 2005, pp. 104–16.

30. Andrew Ward, "Home Depot in Mexico," *Financial Times,* April 6, 2006, p. 8.

Licensing, Franchising, and Other Contractual Strategies

LEARNING OBJECTIVES
In this chapter, you will learn about:

1. Contractual entry strategies

2. Licensing as an entry strategy

3. Advantages and disadvantages of licensing

4. Franchising as an entry strategy

5. Advantages and disadvantages of franchising

6. Other contractual entry strategies

7. Guidelines for protecting intellectual property

In this chapter, we address various types of cross-border contractual relationships, including licensing and franchising. **Contractual entry strategies in international business** are cross-border exchanges in which the relationship between the focal firm and its foreign partner is governed by an explicit contract. **Intellectual property** describes ideas or works created by individuals or firms, including discoveries and inventions; artistic, musical, and literary works; and words, phrases, symbols, and designs. Intellectual property is safeguarded through **intellectual property rights**, the legal claim through which proprietary assets are protected from unauthorized use by other parties.[1]

CONTRACTUAL ENTRY STRATEGIES

Two common types of contractual entry strategies are *licensing* and *franchising*. **Licensing** is an arrangement in which the owner of intellectual property grants another firm the right to use that property for a specified period of time in exchange for *royalties* or other compensation. A **royalty** is a fee paid periodically to compensate a licensor for the temporary use of its intellectual property, often based on a percentage of gross sales generated from the use of the licensed asset. As an entry strategy, licensing requires neither substantial capital investment (FDI) nor involvement of the licensor in the foreign market. It is a relatively inexpensive way for the firm to gain a presence in the market.

    Franchising is an advanced form of licensing in which one firm allows another the right to use an entire business system in exchange for fees, royalties, or other forms of compensation.

    Contractual relationships are fairly common in international business and allow companies to routinely transfer their knowledge assets to foreign partners. Professional service firms such as those in architecture, engineering, advertising, and consulting extend their international reach through contracts with foreign partners. Similarly, retailing, fast food, car rental, television programming, and animation firms rely on licensing and franchising agreements. 7-Eleven (www.7-eleven.com) runs the world's largest chain of convenience stores, with about 42,000 locations in eighteen countries. While the parent firm in Japan owns most of them, several thousand in China, Mexico, South Korea, Thailand, and numerous other countries are operated by entrepreneurs through franchising arrangements.

Unique Aspects of Contractual Relationships

Cross-border contractual relationships share several common characteristics.

- ***They are governed by a contract that provides the focal firm a moderate level of control over the foreign partner.***   A formal agreement specifies the rights and obligations of both partners. *Control* refers to the ability of the focal firm to influence the decisions, operations, and strategic resources of the foreign venture and ensure the partner undertakes assigned activities and procedures. The focal firm maintains ownership and jurisdiction over its intellectual property and may influence the partner's decisions, operations, and strategic resources. However, contractual agreements do not afford the same level of control as foreign direct investment, since they require the focal firm to rely on independent businesses abroad.
- ***They typically include the exchange of intangibles (intellectual property) and services.***   Intangibles that firms exchange include various intellectual property, technical assistance, and know-how. Firms may also exchange products or equipment to support the foreign partner.
- ***Firms can pursue them independently or in conjunction with other foreign market entry strategies.***   In responding to international opportunities, firms may employ contractual agreements alone, or they may combine them with FDI and exporting.[2] The use of such agreements is context specific; that is,

the firm may pursue a contractual relationship with certain customers, countries, or products, but not others.

- ***They provide dynamic, flexible choice.*** Some focal firms use contractual agreements to make initial entry in foreign markets. Then, as conditions evolve, they switch to another, often more advanced entry strategy. When McDonald's and Coca-Cola occasionally acquire some of their franchisees and bottlers, they switch from a contractual approach to an ownership-based entry strategy.
- ***They often reduce local perceptions of the focal firm as a foreign enterprise.*** A contractual relationship with a local firm allows the focal firm to blend into the local market, attracting less attention and less of the criticism sometimes directed at firms that enter through more visible entry strategies such as FDI.
- ***They generate a consistent level of earnings from foreign operations.*** In comparison to FDI, contractual relationships are less susceptible to volatility and risk, bringing both parties a more predictable stream of revenue.[3]

Types of Intellectual Property

A *patent* provides an inventor the right to prevent others from using or selling an invention for a fixed period—typically, up to twenty years.[4] It is granted to those who invent or discover a new and useful process, device, manufactured product, or an improvement on these. A *trademark* is a distinctive design, symbol, logo, word, or series of words placed on a product label. It identifies a product or service as coming from a common source and having a certain level of quality. Examples include Honda's H-shaped symbol, Louis Vuitton's 'LV' logo, and Nike's swoosh mark. A *service mark* serves the same purpose for identifying services. A *copyright* protects original works of authorship, giving the creator the exclusive right to reproduce the work, display and perform it publicly, and authorize others to perform these activities. Copyrights cover music, art, literature, films, and computer software.

An *industrial design* describes the appearance or features of a product. The design is intended to improve the product's aesthetics and usability as well as increase its production efficiency, performance, or marketability. The Apple iPod is a well-known industrial design. A *trade secret* is confidential know-how or information that has commercial value.[5] Trade secrets include production methods, business plans, and customer lists. The formula to produce Coca-Cola is a trade secret. A *geographical indication* is a name or sign that denotes a specific geographical location or origin, such as a region or country, and intended to signify superior quality or reputation. Examples include "Champagne," "Florida Oranges," and "Darjeeling Tea."

Intellectual property rights (IPRs) are the legal claims that protect the proprietary assets of firms and individuals from unauthorized use by other parties. They derive from patents, trademarks, copyrights, and other protections associated with intellectual property and provide inventors with a monopoly advantage for a specific time period, so they can exploit their inventions in the marketplace free of direct competition. The availability and enforcement of these rights vary from country to country.

LICENSING AS AN ENTRY STRATEGY

A licensing agreement specifies the nature of the relationship between the owner of intellectual property, the *licensor,* and the user of the property, the *licensee.* High-technology firms routinely license their patents and know-how to foreign companies.

Warner licenses images from the Harry Potter books and movies to companies worldwide. Disney (disney.go.com) licenses its trademark names and logos to manufacturers of apparel, toys, and watches, who can adapt materials, colors, and other design elements to suit local tastes.

Upon signing a licensing contract, the licensee pays the licensor a fixed amount up front *and* an ongoing royalty, typically 2 to 5 percent of gross sales generated from using the licensed asset.[6] The fixed amount covers the licensor's initial costs of transferring the licensed asset to the licensee, including consultation, training in how to use the asset, engineering, or adaptation. Certain types of licensable assets, such as copyrights and trademarks, may have lower transfer costs. The royalty percentage may escalate with increasing sales.

A typical licensing contract runs five to seven years and is renewable. Once the relationship has been established and the licensee fully understands its role, the licensor usually has no direct involvement in the market and provides no ongoing managerial guidance. Most firms enter into *exclusive agreements*, in which the licensee is not permitted to share the licensed asset with any other company within a prescribed territory. In addition to operating in its domestic market, the licensee also may be permitted to export to other countries.

If the licensor is an MNE, it may enter a licensing arrangement with its own wholly or partly owned foreign affiliate. In this case, licensing is an efficient way to compensate the foreign affiliate, especially when it is a separate legal entity, and transfer intellectual property to it within a formal legal framework.

The national origin of some popular brands might surprise you. Switzerland-based Nestlé sells its KitKat brand of chocolate bars in the United States under license through Hershey Foods. Planters and Sunkist are brands owned by U.S. companies and sold in Britain and Singapore through licensing agreements with local companies. Evian bottled water is owned by the French company Danone and distributed in the United States under license by Coca-Cola. Indeed, a review of annual reports from 120 of the largest multinational food companies revealed that at least half engage in some form of international product licensing.[7]

There are two major types of licensing agreements: (1) trademark and copyright licensing and (2) know-how licensing. Let's review each.

Trademark and Copyright Licensing

Trademark licensing grants a firm permission to use another firm's proprietary names, characters, or logos for a specified time period in exchange for a royalty. Organizations and individuals with name-brand appeal benefit from trademark licensing, such as Coca-Cola, Harley-Davidson, Perry Ellis, Disney, LeBron James, and even your favorite university. A famous trademark like Harry Potter can generate millions of dollars with little effort. U.S. companies derive trademark-licensing revenues well in excess of $100 billion annually.

In the United States and a number of other countries, firms acquire rights to trademarks through first use and continuous usage. In other countries, however, rights to trademarks are acquired through registration with government authorities. When a firm registers its trademark, it formally notifies government authorities that it owns the trademark and is entitled to intellectual property protection.

In many countries, a *copyright* gives the owner the exclusive right to reproduce the work, prepare derivative works, distribute copies, or perform or display the work publicly. Original works include art, music, and literature, as well as computer software. The term of protection varies by country, but the creator's life plus fifty years is typical. Because many countries offer little or no copyright protection, it is wise to investigate local copyright laws before publishing a work abroad.[8]

Know-How Licensing

Gaining access to technology is an important rationale for licensing. A **know-how agreement** is a contract in which the focal firm provides technological or management knowledge about how to design, manufacture, or deliver a product or a service to a licensee in exchange for a royalty. The royalty may be a lump sum, a *running royalty* based on the volume of products produced from the know-how, or a combination of both.

In some industries, such as pharmaceuticals and semiconductors, inventions and other intellectual property are acquired in reciprocal licensing arrangements between firms in the same or similar industries. Known as *cross-licensing*, the practice is common in industries with rapid technological advances that often build on each other. Technology licensing from competitors reduces the cost of innovation by avoiding duplication of research, while reducing the risk of excluding any one firm from access to new developments.

AT&T (www.att.com) once held most of the key patents in the semiconductor industry. As more firms entered the industry and the pace of research and development (R&D) quickened, AT&T risked being surpassed by competitors in Europe, Japan, and the United States, where thousands of semiconductor patents were being awarded. In such a complex network of patents, few firms would have succeeded without obtaining licenses from competitors. AT&T, Intel, Siemens, and numerous other competitors began licensing their patents to each other, creating synergies that greatly accelerated innovation in semiconductors.

Pharmaceutical firms frequently cross-license technologies to each other, exchanging scientific knowledge about producing specific products, as well as the right to distribute them in certain geographic regions.[9] In other industries, firms may license technology and know-how from competitors to compensate for insufficient knowledge, fill gaps in their product line-ups, enter new businesses, or save time and money.

The World's Top Licensing Firms

Exhibit 12.1 lists the world's leading licensing firms by annual revenues. All but one (Sanrio) are based in the United States. The greatest amount of licensing occurs in the apparel, games, and toy industries. In 2009, Disney acquired Marvel Entertainment for $4 billion, greatly expanding Disney's inventory of licensed assets. Licensing sales have benefited immensely from the emergence of large-scale retailers, such as Walmart and Carrefour, and Internet-based selling.

Rank	Firm Name	Annual Licensing Revenues (U.S. $ billions)	Typical Deals
1	Disney Consumer Products	$28.6	Toy and apparel licensing for Disney movies such as *Little Mermaid* and *Hannah Montana*, and characters such as Winnie the Pooh and Mickey Mouse
2	ICONIX	12.0	Apparel licensing for such brands as OP, Starter, and Danskin
3	Phillips-Van Heusen	8.7	Apparel and accessories licensing for such brands as Arrow, Izod, and Van Heusen
4	Mattel	7.0	Toy manufacturer and licensor of iconic toy and game brands such as Barbie, Hot Wheels, and UNO
5	Warner Bros. Consumer Products	6.0	Toy and apparel licensing from movies such as *Batman*, *Scooby-Doo*, and *Harry Potter*
6	Marvel Entertainment	5.6	Toy, game, and apparel licensing for Marvel comic characters such as *Iron Man* and *X-Men*
7	Nickelodeon Consumer Products	5.5	Toy and apparel licensing for TV programs such as *SpongeBob SquarePants* and *Dora the Explorer*
8	Sanrio (Japan)	5.0	Toys and apparel tied to the *Hello Kitty* character
9	Major League Baseball	5.0	Baseball-related video games, apparel, toys
10	The Collegiate Licensing Company	4.3	Licensed merchandise for universities and collegiate sports teams

EXHIBIT 12.1   Annual reports of the individual companies; Company profiles at www.hoovers.com; International Licensing Industry Merchandisers' Association, at www.licensing.org; License! Global (2011), "Top 100 Global Licensors," May, pp.19–41.

ADVANTAGES AND DISADVANTAGES OF LICENSING

Exhibit 12.2 summarizes the advantages and disadvantages of licensing from the perspective of the licensor. Let's highlight some key points.

Advantages of Licensing

Licensing requires neither substantial capital investment nor direct involvement of the licensor in the foreign market. Unlike other entry strategies, the licensor need not establish a physical presence in the market or maintain inventory there. Simultaneously, the licensee benefits by gaining access to a key technology at a much lower cost and

Advantages	Disadvantages
• Does not require capital investment or presence of the licensor in the foreign market • Ability to generate royalty income from existing intellectual property • Appropriate for entering markets that pose substantial country risk • Useful when trade barriers reduce the viability of exporting or when governments restrict ownership of local operations by foreign firms • Useful for testing a foreign market prior to entry via FDI • Useful as a strategy to preemptively enter a market before rivals	• Revenues are usually more modest than with other entry strategies • Difficult to maintain control over how the licensed asset is used • Risk of losing control of important intellectual property, or dissipating it to competitors • The licensee may infringe the licensor's intellectual property and become a competitor • Does not guarantee a basis for future expansion in the market • Not ideal for products, services, or knowledge that are highly complex • Dispute resolution is complex and may not produce satisfactory results

EXHIBIT 12.2   Advantages and Disadvantages of Licensing to the Licensor.

in less time than if it had developed the technology itself.[10] Licensing makes entry possible in countries that restrict foreign ownership in security-sensitive industries, such as defense and energy. Licensing also facilitates entry in markets that are difficult to enter because of trade barriers, tariffs, and bureaucratic requirements, which usually apply only to exporting or FDI. Licensing can be used as a low-cost strategy to test the viability of foreign markets. By establishing a relationship with a local licensee, the foreign firm can learn about the target market and devise the best future strategy for establishing a more durable presence there. Licensing also can help the firm develop its brand name in a target market and preempt the later entry of competitors.

Disadvantages of Licensing

From the licensor's standpoint, licensing is a relatively passive entry strategy. Profits tend to be lower than those from exporting or FDI, and licensing does not guarantee a basis for future expansion. To earn royalties, the licensor must rely on the licensee's production quality as well as sales and marketing prowess. To avoid such problems, experienced firms require foreign licensees to meet minimum quality and performance standards. For example, Budweiser beer is made and distributed in Japan through a licensing arrangement with Kirin (www.kirin.co.jp/english). Kirin is one of Japan's most reputable brewers and produces the beer according to Budweiser's strict standards.

If the licensee is very successful, the licensor may regret not entering the market through a more lucrative entry strategy. Televisa (www.televisa.com), a media and television conglomerate based in Mexico, opted for a licensing arrangement with California-based Univision to enter the U.S. market. Despite more than 40 million native Spanish speakers in the United States, Televisa receives only 9 percent of Univision's Spanish market advertising revenue.

Because licensing requires sharing intellectual property with other firms, the risk of creating a future competitor is substantial.[11] The rival may exploit the licensor's intellectual property by entering third countries or creating products based on knowledge gained in the relationship. Japan's Sony (www.sony.net) originally licensed transistor technology from U.S. inventor Bell Laboratories to make hearing aids. But instead Sony used the technology to create battery-powered transistor radios and soon grew to dominate the market worldwide.[12]

FRANCHISING AS AN ENTRY STRATEGY

Franchising is an advanced form of licensing in which the focal firm, the *franchisor*, allows an entrepreneur, the *franchisee*, the right to use an entire business system in exchange for compensation. As with licensing, an explicit contract defines the terms of the relationship. McDonald's, Subway, Hertz, and FedEx are well-established international franchisors. Others that use franchising to expand abroad include Benetton, Body Shop, Yves Rocher, and Marks & Spencer. Franchising is common in international retailing.

The most typical franchising arrangement is *business format franchising* (sometimes called *system franchising*).[13] In a typical agreement, the franchisor transfers to the franchisee a total business method, including production and marketing methods, sales systems, procedures, and management know-how, as well as usage rights for its name, products, patents, and trademarks.[14] The franchisor also provides the franchisee with training, ongoing support, incentive programs, and the right to participate in cooperative marketing programs.

In return, the franchisee pays some type of compensation to the franchisor, usually a royalty representing a percentage of the franchisee's revenues. The franchisee may be required to purchase certain equipment and supplies from the franchisor to ensure standardized products and consistent quality. Burger King and Subway require franchisees to buy food preparation equipment from specified suppliers.

While licensing relationships are often short-lived, franchising parties typically establish an ongoing relationship that may last many years. Franchising is also more comprehensive than licensing; the franchisor tightly controls the business system to ensure consistent standards and quality, and guarantee the customer a uniform retail experience. Completely standardized business activities, however, are difficult to replicate across diverse markets. In crowded Japan, for example, KFC and McDonalds reduce property costs by building multistoried restaurants. The challenge is to strike the right balance, adapting the format to respond to local markets without affecting overall image and service.[15]

Some focal firms may choose to work with a single, coordinating franchisee in a particular country or region. In this **master franchise** arrangement, an independent company is licensed to establish, develop, and manage the entire franchising network in its market. The master franchisee has the right to subfranchise to other independent businesses and thus assume the role of the local franchisor. It therefore gains an exclusive, large, predefined territory (often an entire country), and substantial economies of scale based on operating numerous sales outlets simultaneously. McDonald's is organized this way in Japan. From the focal firm's perspective, the arrangement is the least capital- and time-intensive although it sacrifices considerable control over its foreign market operations. Master franchisees gain access to a proven retailing and marketing concept. They develop relations with corporate headquarters and other franchisees, obtaining support, know-how, and the latest innovations in the field. Master franchising accounts for as much as 80 percent of international franchising deals.[16]

Who Are the Top Global Franchisors?

Franchising is a global phenomenon and accounts for a large proportion of international trade in services, especially fast-food outlets, professional business services, home improvement, and various types of retailers.[17] Exhibit 12.3 profiles several other leading global franchisors.[18]

The United States dominates international franchising. U.S. franchisors and their franchisees account for roughly $1 trillion in annual U.S. retail sales—an astonishing 40 percent of total U.S. retail sales. Approximately one in every twelve retail establishments in the United States is a franchised business.[19] The United Kingdom is home to numerous home-grown franchisors, such as Eden Delicious and Perfect Pizza. Annual franchised sales of fast food in Britain are said to account for 30 percent of all food eaten outside the home.

Franchisor	Type of Business	International Profile	Major Markets
Subway	Submarine sandwiches and salads	32,239 shops in 90 countries	Canada, Australia, UK, New Zealand, Germany
McDonald's	Fast-food restaurants	32,000 restaurants in 120 countries	Canada, France, UK, Australia, China
7-Eleven	Convenience stores	35,141 stores in 15 countries	Japan, Thailand, Mexico, United States
Dunkin' Donuts	Coffee and donuts	8,924 restaurants in 30 countries	China, Japan, Taiwan
Jani-King	Commercial cleaning	13,046 franchisees in 18 countries	Canada, Australia, Brazil, France, Malaysia
Kumon Math & Reading Centers	Supplemental education	26,311 franchises in 40 countries	Canada, Japan, United States
Pizza Hut	Pizza, pasta, chicken wings	13,500 outlets in 98 countries	China, Brazil, Canada, Japan
Curves	Women's fitness and weight-loss	10,000 centers in 60 countries	Brazil, France, Mexico, Australia, Ireland, UK
UPS Store/Mail Boxes Etc.	Postal, business, and communications services	6,000 locations in 40 countries	Canada, Germany, China, India
WSI Internet	Internet services	1,700 franchises in 87 countries	Canada, UK

EXHIBIT 12.3   Leading International Franchisors.   *Sources:* Entrepreneur.com; Hoovers.com; company Web sites and reports.

The ability to exchange information instantaneously through the Internet enhances the franchisor's ability to control international operations and saves time and money. Some franchisees use electronic point-of-sale equipment that links their sales and inventory data to the franchisor's central warehouse and distribution network.

ADVANTAGES AND DISADVANTAGES OF FRANCHISING

In an ideal relationship, franchisor and franchisee complement each other. The franchisor possesses economies of scale, extensive intellectual property, and know-how about its industry, while the franchisee has entrepreneurial drive, and substantial knowledge about the local market and how to run a business there. A large pool of well-chosen franchisees greatly enhances the speed and quality of the franchisor's performance abroad.[20]

The Franchisor Perspective

Exhibit 12.4 highlights the advantages and disadvantages of franchising to the franchisor. Firms prefer franchising when they lack the capital or international experience to get established abroad through FDI, or when exporting or basic licensing is ineffective as an internationalization strategy. Foreign markets often provide greater profitability than the home market. For example, the Beijing KFC store has generated more sales than any other KFC outlet worldwide partly due to the novelty and popularity of the offering and lack of direct competition. Governments in host countries often encourage franchising by foreign entrants because most of the profits and investment remain in the local economy.

For the franchisor, franchising is a quick, low-risk, low-cost entry strategy. The franchisor can generate profit on a relatively large scale with only incremental investments in capital, staff, production, and distribution.

Advantages	Disadvantages
• Entry into numerous foreign markets can be accomplished quickly and cost effectively • No need to invest substantial capital • Established brand name encourages early and ongoing sales potential abroad • The firm can leverage franchisees' knowledge to efficiently navigate and develop local markets	• Maintaining control over franchisee may be difficult • Conflicts with franchisee are likely, including legal disputes • Preserving franchisor's image in the foreign market may be challenging • Requires monitoring and evaluating performance of franchisees, and providing ongoing assistance • Franchisees may take advantage of acquired knowledge and become competitors in the future

EXHIBIT 12.4 Advantages and Disadvantages of Franchising to the Franchisor.

The major disadvantages include the need to maintain control over potentially thousands of outlets worldwide and the risk of creating competitors. Franchisees may also jeopardize the franchisor's image by not upholding its standards. Dunkin' Donuts experienced problems in Russia when it discovered some franchisees selling vodka along with donuts.

When the franchisor depends heavily on a foreign partner as master franchisee, it is critical to cultivate friendly, durable relationships. However, even experienced franchisors sometimes encounter major challenges. In 2010, nearly thirty years after opening its first outlet in Japan, restaurant chain Wendy's could not reach a new agreement with its Japanese master franchisee, Zensho Company, and chose to close its seventy-one restaurants there to the disappointment of many customers.[21]

Another major challenge is to become familiar with foreign laws and regulations. The European Union has strict laws that favor the franchisee, sometimes hampering the franchisor's ability to control its operations. Local laws and foreign exchange fluctuations can affect the payment of royalties.

Franchising emphasizes standardized products and marketing, but this does not imply 100 percent uniformity. Local franchisees exercise some latitude in tailoring offerings to local needs and tastes. In China, Starbucks offers a Green Tea Cream Frappuccino, TCBY sells sesame-flavored frozen yogurt, and Mrs. Fields markets mango muffins.[22]

The Franchisee Perspective

Exhibit 12.5 shows the advantages and disadvantages of franchising to the franchisee. Franchising is especially beneficial to SMEs, many of which lack substantial resources and strong managerial skills. The big advantage is the ability to launch a business using a tested business model, greatly increasing the small firm's chances for success.[23]

Managerial Guidelines for Licensing and Franchising

Licensing and franchising are complex and require skillful research, planning, and execution. The focal firm must conduct advance research on the host country's laws on

Advantages	Disadvantages
• Gain a well-known, recognizable brand name • Acquire training and know-how; receive ongoing support from the franchisor • Operate an independent business • Increase likelihood of business success • Become part of an established international network	• Initial investment or royalty payments may be substantial • Franchisee is required to purchase supplies, equipment, and products from the franchisor only • The franchisor holds much power, including superior bargaining power • Franchisor's outlets may proliferate in the region, creating competition for the franchisee • Franchisor may impose inappropriate technical or managerial systems on the franchisee

EXHIBIT 12.5 Advantages and Disadvantages of Franchising to the Franchisee.

intellectual property, repatriation of royalties, and contracting with local partners. Key challenges include establishing whose national law takes precedence for interpreting and enforcing the contract, deciding whether to grant an exclusive or nonexclusive arrangement, and determining the geographic scope of territory to be granted to the foreign partner.

As with other entry strategies, the most critical success factor is often finding the right partner abroad, one who is unlikely to become a competitor in the future. Qualified franchisees tend to have entrepreneurial drive, access to capital and prime real estate, a successful business track record, good relationships with local and national government agencies, strong links to other firms (including facilitators), motivated employees, and a willingness to accept oversight and follow company procedures. In emerging markets such as China and Russia, partnering with a state-owned enterprise may be necessary to gain access to key resources and navigate legal and political environments.

Developing capable partners in local supply chains is also a prerequisite. In developing economies and emerging markets, host country suppliers may be inadequate. In Turkey, Little Caesars pizza franchisees found it difficult to locate dairy companies that could produce the cheese varieties they required. In Russia and Thailand, McDonald's had to develop its own potato supply lines to ensure the quality of its French fries.

OTHER CONTRACTUAL ENTRY STRATEGIES

Several other types of contractual agreements in international business cover building major construction projects, manufacturing products under contract, providing management and marketing services, or leasing major assets. Global sourcing is a specific form of international contracting. Here, we discuss turnkey contracting, build-operate-transfer arrangements, management contracts, and leasing.

Turnkey Contracting

Turnkey contracting is an arrangement in which the focal firm or a consortium of firms plans, finances, organizes, manages, and implements all phases of a project abroad and then hands it over to a foreign customer after training local workers. Contractors are typically firms in construction, engineering, design, and architectural services. In a typical turnkey project, a contractor builds a major facility (such as a nuclear power plant or a subway system), puts it into operation, and then transfers control to the project sponsor, often a national government. The contractor may provide follow-up services such as testing and operational support.

Among the most popular turnkey projects are extensions and upgrades to transportation systems, such as bridges, roadways, and railways, and the construction of airports, harbors, refineries, and hospitals. Financed largely from public budgets, most projects are in Asia and Western Europe, where demand is driven by intensifying urbanization and worsening congestion. In Abu Dhabi, a collection of companies received a multibillion dollar contract to build an integrated processing plant for natural gas. The team included JGC of Japan, Tecnimont of Italy, and Hyundai Engineering & Construction (HDEC; http://en.hdec.kr) of South Korea. HDEC has built industrial, infrastructure, commercial, and multifamily residential projects in about fifty countries.[24]

Build-Operate-Transfer Arrangements (BOT)

Under a **build-operate-transfer (BOT)** arrangement, a firm or consortium of firms contracts to build a major facility abroad, such as a dam or water treatment plant, operates it for a specified period, and then transfers ownership to the project sponsor, typically the host country government or public utility. This is a variation of turnkey contracting in which, instead of turning over the completed facility to the project sponsor, the builder first operates it for a number of years.

While the consortium operates the facility, it can charge user fees, tolls, and rentals to recover its investment and generate profits. Or the host country government can pay the BOT partner for services provided by the facility, such as water from a treatment plant, at a price that covers its construction and operating costs and provides a reasonable return.

Governments often grant BOT concessions to get needed infrastructure built cost effectively. Typical projects include sewage treatment plants, highways, airports, mass transit systems, and telecommunications networks. In Vietnam, rapid growth in industry and tourism has greatly increased demand for electric power. The Vietnamese government commissioned the construction of the 720 megawatt Phu My 3 power plant, the country's first privately owned major energy facility, as a BOT project by Siemens Power Generation (Germany). It is owned by a consortium that includes BP (Britain) and Kyushu Electric Power (Japan).[25]

Management Contracts

Under a **management contract**, a contractor supplies managerial know-how to operate a hotel, hospital, airport, or other facility in exchange for compensation. The client organization receives assistance in managing local operations, while the management company generates revenues without having to make a capital outlay. Much of Disney's income from its theme parks in France and Japan comes from providing management services for the parks, which are largely owned by other interests. Spain's BAA Limited manages the retailing and catering operations of various airports in Europe and the United States. Both the Marriott and Four Seasons corporations run luxury hotels worldwide through management contracts without owning the properties.

Management contracts can help foreign governments with infrastructure projects when the country lacks local people with the skills to run them. Occasionally the offering of a management contract is the critical element in winning a bid for other types of entry strategies, such as BOT deals and turnkey operations. A key disadvantage of management contracts is they require the training of foreign firms that may become future competitors.[26]

Leasing

Under international leasing, a focal firm, the lessor, rents out machinery or equipment to foreign corporate or government clients, the lessees, often for several years at a time. The lessor retains ownership of the property throughout the lease period and receives regular payments from the lessee. From the perspective of the lessee, leasing helps reduce the costs of using needed machinery and equipment. A major advantage for the lessor is the ability to gain quick access to target markets, while putting assets to use earning profits. Leasing can be more profitable in international than in domestic markets because of tax regulations.[27] International leasing benefits developing economies that may lack the financial resources to purchase needed equipment. One of the top leasing firms is Japan's ORIX (www.orix.co.jp), which leases everything from computers and measuring equipment to aircraft and ships. The firm operates 1,500 offices worldwide and generated $12 billion in revenues in 2011.

The Special Case of Internationalization by Professional Service Firms

Professional services include accounting, advertising, market research, consulting, engineering, legal counsel, and IT services. Firms in these industries have rapidly internationalized over the past three decades. Some simply follow their key clients abroad. The Internet has greatly aided the international spread of some business process services such as software engineering, increasingly centralized in cost-effective locations such as India and Eastern Europe.

What international market-entry strategies do professional service firms encounter three unique challenges when going international. First, professional qualifications that allow firms to practice law, dentistry, medicine, or accounting in the home country are rarely recognized by other countries. If you are licensed as a certified public accountant in the United States and want to practice accounting in Argentina, you must earn local certification in Argentina. Second, professionals who work abroad for long periods generally must obtain employment visas in the countries where they are employed. Third, professional services often require intensive interaction with the local public, which necessitates having language and cultural skills.[28]

What international market-entry strategies do professional service firms prefer? Typically, they use a mix of direct investment and contractual strategies. An advertising agency such as Publicis Groupe, based in France, will maintain a network of company-owned branches around the world while simultaneously entering contractual relationships with independent local firms. Focal firms in professional services are likely to serve their major markets with direct investment and operate company-owned offices there. In small markets, however, they will enter contractual relationships with independent partner firms in the same line of business, typically known as *agents*, *affiliates*, or *representatives*. Focal firms with limited international experience often prefer to employ foreign partners that can provide international business know-how.

GUIDELINES FOR PROTECTING INTELLECTUAL PROPERTY

Working with independent partners through contractual arrangements provides the focal firm with only moderate control. Ultimately, the best way to ensure successful outcomes is to develop close and trusting relationships with foreign partners by providing strong technical and managerial support.

Infringement of intellectual property, which amounts to piracy, is the unauthorized use, publication, or reproduction of products and services protected by a patent, copyright, trademark, or other intellectual property right. The total value of counterfeit and pirated products crossing borders and traded online worldwide exceeds $600 billion annually.[29] Counterfeiting is common in such industrial products as clothing, accessories, medicines, medical devices, appliances, and car parts. Counterfeiters even have faked entire motor vehicles![30]

Don't assume counterfeiting is confined to lower-income countries. In one week in 2009, investigators closed thirty-one stores in New York City for selling counterfeit designer goods.[31] The Internet has also added a new dimension to international counterfeiting. In Russia, Web sites sell popular music downloads for as little as 5 cents each, or less than $1 for an entire CD.[32]

Advanced economies have taken the lead in signing treaties that support international protection of intellectual property, including the Paris Convention for the Protection of Industrial Property, the Berne Convention for the Protection of Literary and Artistic Works, and the Rome Convention for the Protection of Performers and Broadcasting Organizations. The World Intellectual Property Organization (WIPO; www .wipo.int)—an agency of the United Nations—administers these multilateral agreements.

Recently, the World Trade Organization (WTO; www.wto.org) created the Agreement on Trade Related Aspects of Intellectual Property Rights (TRIPS), a comprehensive international treaty that specifies remedies, dispute-resolution procedures, and enforcements to protect intellectual property. Exceptions are allowed that benefit developing economies, such as the ability to access patent medication for ailments such as AIDS.

Experienced firms devise sophisticated strategies to reduce the likelihood of intellectual property violations and help avoid their adverse effects. Let's elaborate on key strategies:

- Understand local intellectual property laws and enforcement procedures.
- Register patents, trademarks, trade secrets, and copyrights with the government in each country where the firm intends to do business, and in countries where counterfeiting is prevalent.
- Require that intellectual property is used as intended and improvements on the asset are shared with the licensor.[33]
- Pursue criminal prosecution or litigation against those who infringe on protected assets.[34]
- Monitor franchisee, distribution, and marketing channels for any asset infringements and for potential leaks of vital information and assets.[35]
- Require that franchisees, suppliers, and distributors report infringements of intellectual property rights.
- Use password-based security systems, surveillance, and firewalls to limit access to intellectual property.
- Include noncompete clauses in employee contracts for all positions to prevent employees from serving competitors up to three years after quitting the firm.[36]
- Use biotech tags, electronic signatures, or holograms to deter counterfeiting.
- Continuously update technologies and products, helping ensure counterfeiters cannot keep pace with new designs and innovations.
- Lobby national governments and international organizations for stronger intellectual property laws and more vigilant enforcement.

Summary

Contractual entry strategies in international business grant foreign partners permission to use the focal firm's **intellectual property** in exchange for a continuous stream of payments. Intellectual property rights are the legal claims through which the proprietary assets of firms and individuals are protected from unauthorized use by other parties. **Licensing** grants a firm the right to use another firm's intellectual property for a specified time period in exchange for royalties or other compensation. **Franchising** allows one firm the right to use another's entire business system in exchange for fees, royalties, or other forms of compensation. A **royalty** is a fee paid to the licensor at regular intervals to compensate for use of intellectual property.

Licensing's main advantage to the licensor is it does not require substantial capital investment or physical presence in the foreign market. The licensor can avoid political risk, government regulations, and other risks associated with FDI. But licensing generates lower profits and limits the firm's ability to control its intellectual property, and one-time licensees can become competitors.

Franchisors employ widely identifiable trademarks and attempt to guarantee the customer a consistent retail experience and product quality. A **master franchise** gives a franchisee the right to develop franchised outlets to serve a country or a region. Franchising is common in international retailing but difficult to replicate across diverse markets.

Franchising allows franchisees to gain access to well-known, well-established brand names and business systems, allowing them to launch successful businesses with minimal risk. The franchisor can rapidly internationalize by leveraging the drive and knowledge of local franchisees but risks disseminating its intellectual property to unauthorized parties.

Under **build–operate–transfer (BOT)** arrangements, the firm contracts to build a major facility that it operates for a period and then transfers to the host country government or other public entity. In **turnkey contracting** one or several firms plan, finance, organize, and manage all phases of a project which, once completed, they hand over to a host country customer. **Management contracts** occur when a company contracts with another to supply management know-how in the operation of a facility, such as a hotel.

Managers should safeguard their proprietary assets by registering patents, trademarks, and other assets in each country, and minimize operations in major counterfeiting countries and those with weak intellectual property laws.

Key Terms

Endnotes

1. International Centre for Trade and Sustainable Development (ICTSD), *Property Rights: Implications for Development Policy, Policy Discussion Paper,* Intellectual Property Rights & Sustainable Development Series (Geneva, Switzerland: ICTSD and New York: UNCTAD, 2003).

2. Farok J. Contractor, "Strategic Perspectives for International Licensing Managers: The Complementary Roles of Licensing, Investment and Trade in Global Operations," Working Paper no. 99.002 (Rutgers, NJ: Rutgers University, 1999).

3. *Ibid.*

4. ICTSD (2003).

5. Kay Millonzi and William Passannante, "Beware of the Pirates: How to Protect Intellectual Property," *Risk Management* 43 (1996): 39–42.

6. D. E. Welch and L. S. Welch, "In the Internationalization Process and Networks: A Strategic Management Perspective," *Journal of International Marketing* 4 (1996): 11–28.

7. Dennis Henderson, Ian Sheldon, and Kathleen Thomas, "International Licensing of Foods and Beverages Makes Markets Truly Global," *FoodReview* (September 1994): 7–12.

8. Graham Pomphrey, "Pooh at 80," *License Europe!* April 1, 2006, retrieved from http://www.licensemag.com/licensemag.

9. Piero Telesio, *Technology Licensing and Multinational Enterprises* (New York: Praeger, 1979).

10. *Ibid.*

11. Telesio (1979).

12. Akio Morita, Edwin Reingold, and Mitsuko Shimomura, *Made in Japan: Akio Morita and Sony* (New York: EP Dutton, 1986).

13. F. Burton and A. Cross, "International Franchising: Market versus Hierarchy," in *Internationalisation Strategies,* eds. G. Chryssochoidis, C. Millar, and J. Clegg, (New York: St. Martin's Press, 2001), pp. 135–52.

14. L. S. Welch, "Internationalization by Australian Franchisors," *Asia Pacific Journal of Management* 7 (1990): 101–21.

15. K. Fladmoe-Lindquist, "International Franchising," in *Globalization of Services,* eds. Y. Aharoni and L. Nachum (London: Routledge, 2000), pp. 197–216.

16. *Ibid.*; C. Steinberg, "A Guide to Franchise Strategies," *World Trade* 7 (1994): 66–70.

17. John Stanworth and Brian Smith, *The Barclays Guide to Franchising for the Small Business* (Oxford, UK: Basil Blackwell, 1991).

18. Carlye Adler, "How China Eats a Sandwich," *Fortune Small Business*, March 2005, pp. 72–76.

19. David Kaufmann, "The Big Bang: How Franchising Became an Economic Powerhouse the World Over—Franchise 500®," *Entrepreneur,* January 2004, retrieved from http://www.entrepreneur.com.

20. Barry Quinn and Anne Marie Doherty, "Power and Control in International Retail Franchising," *International Marketing Review* 17 (2000): 354–63.

21. Adler (2005), pp. F210B–D.

22. "Wendy's Shuts Doors in Japan," *The New York Times*, January 2, 2010, p. B3.

23. Stanworth (1991).

24. "Public Funds and Turnkey Contracts Fuel Growing Global Subway Work," *ENR,* October 25, 2004, p. 32; "Abu Dhabi Awards $9 Billion in Gas Project Contracts," *Oil & Gas Journal,* July 27, 2009, 32–33.

25. Robert Peltier, "Phu My 3 Power Plant, Ho Chi Minh City, Vietnam," *Power,* August 2004, p. 42.

26. Farok Contractor and Sumit Kundu, "Modal Choice in a World of Alliances: Analyzing Organizational Forms in the International Hotel Sector," *Journal of International Business Studies* 29 (1998): 325–56; V. Panvisavas and J. S. Taylor, "The Use of Management Contracts by International Hotel Firms in Thailand," *International Journal of Contemporary Hospitality Management* 18 (2006): 231–40.

27. David A. Ricks and Saeed Samiee-Esfahani, "Leasing: It May Be Right Abroad Even When It Is Not at Home," *Journal of International Business Studies* 5 (1974): 87–90.

28. Lloyd Downey, "Marketing Services: How TPOs Can Help," *International Trade Forum* 4 (2005): 7–8; Geoffrey Jones and Alexis Lefort, "McKinsey and the Globalization of Consultancy," Harvard Business School case study 9–806–035 (Cambridge, MA: Harvard Business School, 2006).

29. International Chamber of Commerce, "OECD Study a Vital Step to Understanding the Global Scope of Counterfeiting," 2007, retrieved from http://www.iccwbo.org.

30. Murray Hiebert, "Chinese Counterfeiters Turn Out Fake Car Parts," *Wall Street Journal,* March 3, 2004, p. A14; Joon Muller, "Stolen Cars," *Forbes,* February 16, 2004, p. 58.

31. Jane O'Donnell, "Raids Crack Down on Counterfeit Goods," *USA Today,* December 18, 2009, retrieved from http://www.usatoday.com

32. Vauhini Vara (2005), "Russian Sites Sell Song Downloads For Pennies, But Are They Legal?" *Wall Street Journal,* January 25, 2005, p. 59; Jack Goldsmith and Tim Wu, *Who Controls the Internet: Illusions of a Borderless World* (Oxford, England: Oxford University Press, 2006).

33. A. Dayal-Gulati and Angela Lee, *Kellogg on China: Strategies for Success* (Evanston, IL: Northwestern University Press, 2004).

34. Millonzi and Passannante (1996).

35. Dietz, Shao-Tin Lin, and Yang (2005).

36. *Ibid.*

Global Sourcing

LEARNING OBJECTIVES
In this chapter, you will learn about:

1. Outsourcing, global sourcing, and offshoring

2. Benefits of global sourcing

3. Risks of global sourcing

4. Strategies for minimizing the risks of global sourcing

5. Implementing global sourcing through supply-chain management

6. Global sourcing and corporate social responsibility

Global sourcing has changed the way companies do business in all kinds of industries. Focal firms shop the world for inputs and finished products to meet efficiency and strategic objectives and to remain competitive. Many of the products sold by general retailers such as Best Buy and Marks & Spencer are sourced from low-cost suppliers in emerging markets. Steinway procures parts and components from a dozen foreign countries to produce its grand pianos. HP provides much of its technical support to customers from call centers in India.

In many cases, firms move entire sections of their value chains abroad, such as R&D, manufacturing, or technical support. In the sports apparel industry, firms such as Nike and Reebok subcontract nearly all their athletic shoe production to lower-cost manufacturers abroad. Today, Nike and Reebok function primarily as brand owners and marketers, not as manufacturers.

The total worldwide sourcing market for product manufacturing and services exceeds $300 billion. The total *potential* market is estimated to be nearly $1 trillion. The IT industry alone in India now employs more than two million people. Worldwide, the most frequently outsourced business processes include logistics and procurement, sales and marketing, and customer service, followed by finance and accounting.[1] Global sourcing by the private sector now accounts for more than half of all imports by major countries.[2]

OUTSOURCING, GLOBAL SOURCING, AND OFFSHORING

Outsourcing refers to the procurement of selected value-adding activities, including production of intermediate goods or finished products, from external independent suppliers. Firms outsource because they generally are not superior at performing *all* value-chain activities. Each company finds it more cost effective to outsource *some* activities that it might otherwise perform itself. **Business process outsourcing (BPO)** occurs when firms procure, from an external supplier, such services as accounting, payroll, human resource functions, travel services, IT services, customer service, and/or technical support.[3] Firms contract with third-party service providers to reduce the cost of performing service tasks that are not part of the firm's core competencies or not critical to maintaining its competitive position in the marketplace. BPO can be divided into two categories: *back-office activities*, which include internal, upstream business functions such as payroll and billing, and *front-office activities*, which include downstream, customer-related services such as marketing and technical support.

In undertaking outsourcing, managers face two key decisions: (1) which, if any, value-chain activities should be outsourced, and (2) where in the world should these activities be performed? Let's consider these choices.

Decision 1: Outsource or Not?

Managers must decide between *internalization* and *externalization*—whether each value-adding activity should be conducted in house or by an external, independent supplier. In business, this is traditionally known as the *make or buy* decision: "Should we make a product or perform a value-chain activity ourselves, or should we source it from an outside contractor?"

Firms usually internalize those value-chain activities they consider part of their *core competencies,* those that require the use of proprietary knowledge and trade secrets they want to control. For example, Canon uses its core competencies in precision mechanics, fine optics, and microelectronics to produce some of the world's best cameras, printers, and copiers. It usually performs R&D and product design itself to reduce the risk of divulging proprietary knowledge to competitors and to generate continuous improvement in these competencies. By contrast, firms will usually source from *external* suppliers when they can obtain noncore products or services at lower cost or from suppliers specialized in providing them.

Decision 2: Where in the World Should Value-Adding Activities Be Located?

A second key decision firms face is whether to keep each value-adding activity in the home country or locate it in a foreign country. **Configuration of value-adding activity** refers to the pattern or geographic arrangement of locations where the firm carries out value-chain activities.[4] Instead of concentrating value-adding activities in their home country, many firms configure them across the world to save money, reduce delivery time, access factors of production, or extract maximum advantages relative to competitors.

This helps explain the migration of manufacturing industries from Europe, Japan, and the United States to emerging markets in Asia, Latin America, and Eastern Europe. Depending on the firm and the industry, management may decide to concentrate certain value-adding activities in one or a handful of locations, while dispersing others to numerous countries. External suppliers are typically located in countries characterized by low-cost labor, competent production processes, and specific knowledge about relevant engineering and development activities.[5]

For example, DHL established offices in countries and cities worldwide to run its global network of package shipping. It also set up high-tech tracking centers in Arizona, Malaysia, and the Czech Republic. This configuration allows DHL staffers to track the locations of shipments worldwide, twenty-four hours a day. DHL management chose these specific locations for shipment tracking because, in a world of twenty-four time zones, they are each about eight hours distant from each other.

Global Sourcing

Global sourcing is the procurement of products or services from independent suppliers or company-owned subsidiaries located abroad for consumption in the home country or a third country. Also called *global procurement* or *global purchasing*, global sourcing amounts to importing—an inbound flow of goods and services. It is an entry strategy that relies on a contractual relationship between the buyer (the focal firm) and a foreign source of supply. Dell (www.dell.com) relies extensively on a manufacturing network, composed largely of independent suppliers located around the world. Exhibit 13.1 details how Dell assembles components from suppliers in numerous locations for its Dell Inspiron notebook computer.[6]

Global sourcing is a low-control strategy in which the focal firm sources from independent suppliers through contractual agreements, as opposed to the high-control strategy of buying from company-owned subsidiaries. Global sourcing frequently represents the firm's initial involvement in international business. For many firms, it increases management's awareness about other international opportunities. Based on experience it gains through such *inward internationalization*, the firm may progress to exporting, direct investment, or other forms of *outward internationalization*.

Global sourcing has been an established international business activity since the 1980s and has gained momentum in the current phase of globalization.[7] Three key drivers are especially responsible for the growth of global sourcing in recent years:

1. ***Technological advances in communications.*** This is seen especially in the Internet and international telephony. Access to vast online information means focal firms can quickly find and communicate with suppliers that meet specific needs, anywhere in the world.
2. ***Falling costs of international business.*** Tariffs and other trade barriers have declined substantially, while efficient communication and transportation systems have made international procurement cost effective and accessible to any firm.

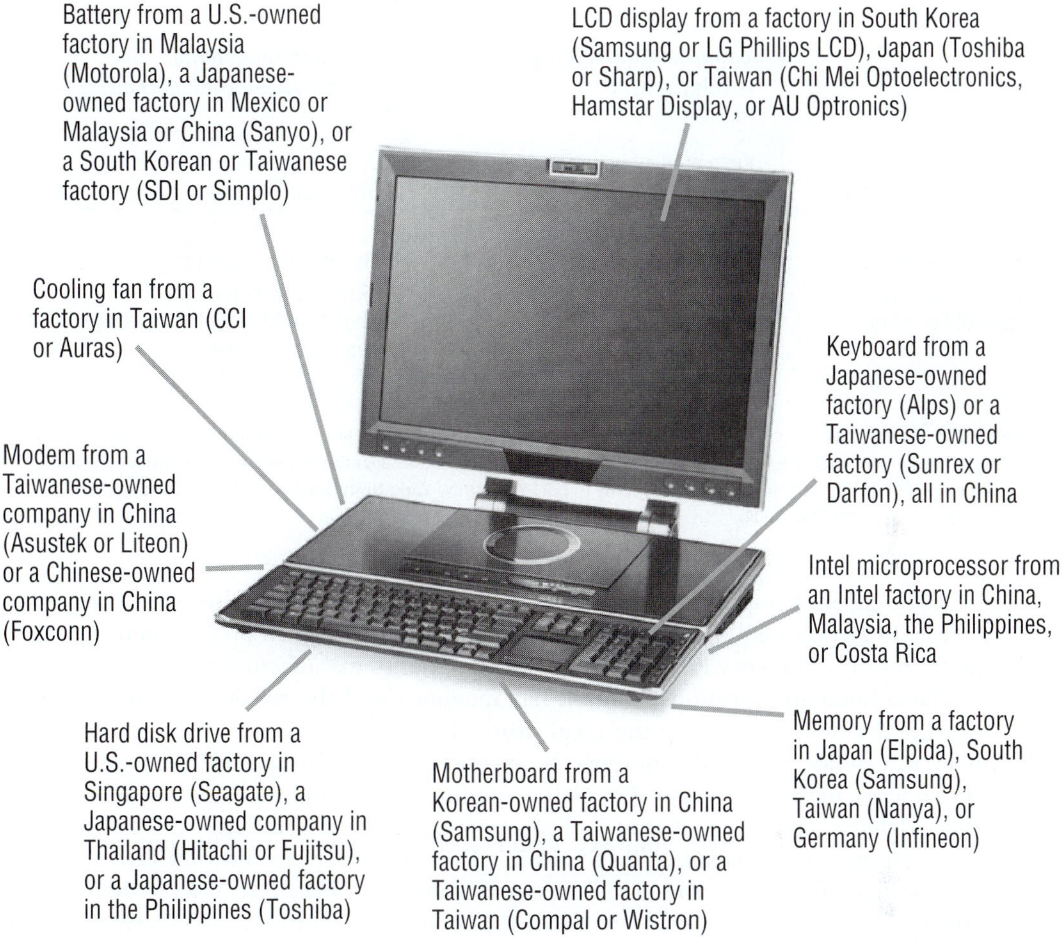

Battery from a U.S.-owned factory in Malaysia (Motorola), a Japanese-owned factory in Mexico or Malaysia or China (Sanyo), or a South Korean or Taiwanese factory (SDI or Simplo)

LCD display from a factory in South Korea (Samsung or LG Phillips LCD), Japan (Toshiba or Sharp), or Taiwan (Chi Mei Optoelectronics, Hamstar Display, or AU Optronics)

Cooling fan from a factory in Taiwan (CCI or Auras)

Keyboard from a Japanese-owned factory (Alps) or a Taiwanese-owned factory (Sunrex or Darfon), all in China

Modem from a Taiwanese-owned company in China (Asustek or Liteon) or a Chinese-owned company in China (Foxconn)

Intel microprocessor from an Intel factory in China, Malaysia, the Philippines, or Costa Rica

Hard disk drive from a U.S.-owned factory in Singapore (Seagate), a Japanese-owned company in Thailand (Hitachi or Fujitsu), or a Japanese-owned factory in the Philippines (Toshiba)

Motherboard from a Korean-owned factory in China (Samsung), a Taiwanese-owned factory in China (Quanta), or a Taiwanese-owned factory in Taiwan (Compal or Wistron)

Memory from a factory in Japan (Elpida), South Korea (Samsung), Taiwan (Nanya), or Germany (Infineon)

EXHIBIT 13.1 Sourcing for the Dell Inspiron Notebook Computer. *Source:* Adapted from Thomas Friedman, *The World a Flat 3.0: A Brief History of the Twenty-First Century* (New York: Picardor, 2007).

3. ***Entrepreneurship and rapid economic transformation in emerging markets.***
   Entrepreneurial suppliers aggressively pursue sourcing partnerships with foreign buyers in China, India, and other emerging markets.

The decisions about whether and where to outsource lead to the framework in Exhibit 13.2. The focal firm can source from independent suppliers, from company-owned subsidiaries and affiliates, or from both. In Exhibit 13.2, Cells C and D represent the global sourcing scenarios. While global sourcing implies procurement from foreign locations, in some cases the focal firm may source from its own wholly owned subsidiary or an affiliate jointly owned with another firm (Cell C). This is **captive sourcing**. Genpact was a captive sourcing unit of General Electric (GE), with annual revenues of more than $1 billion and more than 37,000 employees worldwide. Now an independent company based in India, Genpact (www.genpact.com) is one of the largest providers of business-process outsourcing services.[8]

	Value-adding activity is internalized	**Value-adding activity is externalized (outsourced)**
Value-adding activity kept in home country	*A* Keep production in-house, in home country	*B* Outsource production to third-party provider at home
Value-adding activity conducted abroad (global sourcing)	*C* Delegate production to foreign subsidiary or affiliate (captive sourcing)	*D* Outsource production to a third-party provider abroad (contract manufacturing or global sourcing from independent suppliers)

EXHIBIT 13.2   Nature of Outsourcing and Global Sourcing.   *Source:* B. Kedia and D. Mukherjee, "Understanding Offshoring: A Research Framework Based on Disintegration, Location and Externalization Advantages," Journal of World Business 44, no. 3 (2009): 250–261; Information Economy Report 2009 (New York: United Nations, 2009); World Investment Report 2004 (New York: UNCTAD, 2004).

The relationship between the focal firm and its foreign supplier (Cell D in Exhibit 13.2) may take the form of **contract manufacturing,** an arrangement in which the focal firm contracts with an independent supplier to manufacture products according to well-defined specifications. Once it has manufactured the products or components, the supplier delivers them to the focal firm, which then markets, sells, and distributes them. In essence, the focal firm rents the manufacturing capacity of the foreign contractor. Contract manufacturing is especially common in the apparel, shoe, furniture, aerospace, defense, computer, pharmaceutical, personal care, and automotive industries.

You may never have heard of Taiwan's Hon Hai Precision Industry Co., a leading contract manufacturer in the global electronics industry. Hon Hai (www.foxconn.com) works under contract for many well-known companies, churning out PlayStations for Sony; iPods, iPhones, and iPads for Apple; printers and PCs for Hewlett-Packard; and thousands of other products. In 2009, Hon Hai generated sales of $60 billion. The firm employs some 360,000 people in scores of contract factories worldwide, from Malaysia to Mexico.[9]

Offshoring

Offshoring is the relocation of a major business process or entire manufacturing facility to a foreign country. It is common in the service sector, including banking, software code writing, legal services, and customer service activities.[10] Large legal hubs have emerged in India that provide services such as drafting contracts and patent applications, conducting research and negotiations, and performing paralegal work, all on behalf of Western clients. With lawyers in Europe and North America costing $300 an hour or more, law firms in India can cut Western companies' legal bills by up to 75 percent.[11]

In each of the business functions—including human resources, accounting, finance, marketing, and customer service—certain tasks are routine and discrete, such as billing, credit card processing, managing databases, recording sales transactions, preparing payrolls, and administering benefits. Many are candidates for offshoring as long as their performance by independent suppliers does not threaten or diminish the focal firm's core competencies or strategic assets.

India is the current leader in the processing of advanced economies' relocated business services. Its market share grew dramatically in the 2000s and is expected to increase by several hundred percent between 2010 and 2020, thanks to India's huge pool of qualified labor working for as little as 25 percent of what comparable workers get in the advanced economies.[12] Firms in Eastern Europe perform support activities for architectural and engineering firms from Western Europe and the United States. Many IT support services for customers in Germany are actually based in the Czech Republic and Romania. Boeing, Nissan, and Nortel do much of their R&D in Russia. South Africa is the base for technical and user-support services for English-, French-, and German-speaking customers throughout Europe.[13]

Scope of Global Sourcing

Not all business activities or processes lend themselves to global sourcing. People normally do not travel abroad to see a banker, physician, or accountant.[14] Personal contact is vital at the downstream end of virtually all value chains. By 2010, fewer than 5 percent of jobs in the United States that require substantial customer interaction (such as in retailing) had been transferred to low-wage economies. Fewer than 15 percent of all service jobs have moved from advanced economies to emerging markets.[15]

Jobs most conducive to being sourced abroad tend to be in industries characterized by:

- Large-scale manufacturing whose primary competitive advantage is efficiency and low cost
- High labor intensity in product and service production, such as garment manufacturing and call centers
- Uniform customer needs and standardized technologies and processes in production and other value-chain activities, such as automobiles and machine parts
- Established products with a predictable pattern of sales, such as components for consumer electronics
- Information intensity whose functions and activities can be easily transmitted via the Internet, such as accounting, billing, and payroll
- Outputs that are easily codified and transmitted over the Internet or by telephone, such as software development, technical support, and customer service.

Diversity of Countries that Initiate and Receive Outsourced Work

Firms based in advanced economies outsource the most services by volume. U.S. firms have led by offshoring more than 50 percent of their service projects. More than 75 percent of major U.S. financial institutions send a portion of their IT work offshore. In Europe and Japan, the majority of large firms outsource some of their services, most often to China and India, followed by countries in Eastern Europe, Latin America, and the Middle East. In Asia, the Philippines is a successful recent entrant in global services sourcing. It draws on solid English skills and long-standing cultural ties with the West to attract call center work.[16]

	Central and Eastern Europe	Central and South Asia	Latin America and the Caribbean	Middle East and Africa
Top-Ranked Countries	Czech Republic, Bulgaria, Slovakia, Poland, Hungary	India, China, Malaysia, Philippines, Singapore, Thailand	Chile, Brazil, Mexico, Costa Rica, Argentina	Egypt, Jordan, United Arab Emirates, Ghana, Tunisia, Dubai
Up-and-Comers	Romania, Russia, Ukraine, Belarus	Indonesia, Vietnam, Sri Lanka	Jamaica, Panama, Nicaragua, Colombia	South Africa, Israel, Turkey, Morocco
Emerging Local Providers	Luxoft (Russia, software development); *EPAM Systems* (Belarus, software development); *Softengi* (Ukraine, software engineering)	NCS (Singapore, business processes); Bluem (China, IT services); *BroadenGate* (China, software development)	Softtek (Mexico, business processes); Neoris (Mexico, IT services); Politec (Brazil, IT services)	Xceed (Egypt, software development); Ness Technologies (Israel, IT services); Jeraisy Group (Saudi Arabia, IT services)

EXHIBIT 13.3 Key Players in Global Sourcing by Region. *Source:* Penny Crosman, "Worldsourcers," Wall Street & Technology, July (2008), p. 26; Pete Engardio, "The Future of Outsourcing: How It's Transforming Whole Industries and Changing the Way We Work," Business Week, January 30, (2006), p. 58.

Exhibit 13.3 identifies key players in global sourcing by four geographic regions. Russia is aiming at high-end programming jobs. With its strong engineering culture, it offers an abundant pool of talent at wages about one-fifth those of the United States. In Egypt, Xceed Contact Center (www.xceedcc.com) handles calls in Arabic and European languages on behalf of Carrefour, Microsoft, and Oracle.

Singapore and Dubai assert that their safety and advanced legal systems give them an edge in handling high-security and business-continuity services. Central and South American countries seek call center contracts for the Spanish-speaking Hispanic market in the United States.[17] With Europe as its largest export market, Vietnam dramatically increased outsourced production in the 2000s because it offers modern but low-cost operations, skilled but inexpensive labor, and access to local sources unburdened by trade restrictions.[18]

A. T. Kearney is a consultancy that produces an annual Global Services Location Index (www.atkearney.com), which identifies the best countries for outsourcing services. The index is topped by emerging markets and developing economies: India, China, Malaysia, Thailand, Indonesia, Egypt, Chile, and the Philippines. Canada and the United States are the only advanced economies in the top thirty destinations. In selecting locations, the index emphasizes various criteria: the country's financial structure (compensation costs, infrastructure costs, tax and regulatory costs), the availability and skills of its people (cumulative business-process experience and skills; labor force availability, education, and language; and worker attrition rates), and the nature of the business environment (the country's political and economic environment, physical infrastructure, cultural adaptability, and security of intellectual property).[19]

Strategic Choices in Global Sourcing

Exhibit 13.4 explains the strategic implications of the two choices firms face: whether to perform specific value-adding activities themselves or to outsource them, and whether to concentrate each activity in the home country or disperse it abroad. The exhibit portrays a typical value chain, ranging from R&D and design to customer service. The first row indicates the degree to which management considers each value-adding activity a strategic asset to the firm. The second row indicates whether the activity tends to be internalized inside the focal firm or outsourced to a foreign supplier. The third row indicates where management typically locates an activity.

In addition to large firms, global sourcing provides big benefits for small and medium-sized enterprises (SMEs). Main Street businesses from car dealerships to real estate firms increasingly farm out accounting, support services, and design work to suppliers in Brazil, Hungary, India, and other top destinations. Outsourcing brokers and international online sites such as www.guru.com and www.rentacoder.com do big business serving the global sourcing needs of countless SMEs. Internet search engines allow small firms to find service vendors anywhere in the world. A real estate agent in California uses suppliers in Hungary, India, and Portugal to design graphics, manage databases, and update online information.[20]

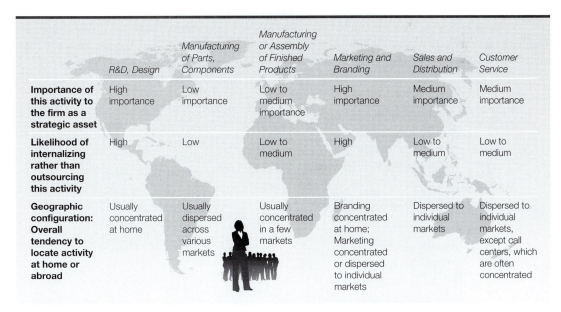

	R&D, Design	Manufacturing of Parts, Components	Manufacturing or Assembly of Finished Products	Marketing and Branding	Sales and Distribution	Customer Service
Importance of this activity to the firm as a strategic asset	High importance	Low importance	Low to medium importance	High importance	Medium importance	Medium importance
Likelihood of internalizing rather than outsourcing this activity	High	Low	Low to medium	High	Low to medium	Low to medium
Geographic configuration: Overall tendency to locate activity at home or abroad	Usually concentrated at home	Usually dispersed across various markets	Usually concentrated in a few markets	Branding concentrated at home; Marketing concentrated or dispersed to individual markets	Dispersed to individual markets	Dispersed to individual markets, except call centers, which are often concentrated

EXHIBIT 13.4 Typical Choices of Outsourcing and Geographic Dispersion of Value-Chain Activities among Firms.

BENEFITS OF GLOBAL SOURCING

Like other international entry strategies, global sourcing offers both benefits and risks. Exhibit 13.5 provides an overview. The exhibit lists two primary reasons to pursue global sourcing: cost efficiency and the ability to achieve strategic goals. Let's consider these in detail.

Cost Efficiency

Cost efficiency is the traditional rationale for sourcing abroad. One study found that firms expect to save an average of more than 40 percent off baseline costs as a result of offshoring, particularly in R&D, product design activities, and back-office operations such as accounting and data processing.[21] A worker in business process outsourcing in Egypt or the Philippines earns less than $5,000 per year. A call center worker in India earns roughly $500 per month, while the same worker in Europe or the United States earns $2,000 to $3,000 per month. This wage discrepancy explains why firms such as HP, Accenture, Dell, and HSBC grew their Indian operations 30 to 50 percent a year during the 2000s.[22]

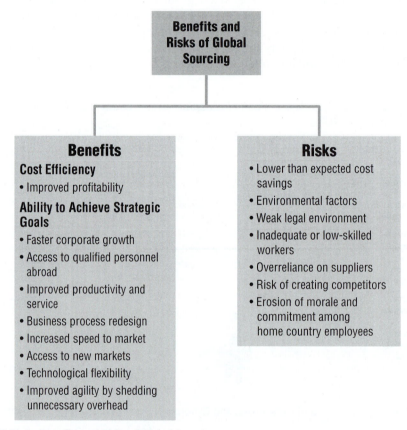

EXHIBIT 13.5   Benefits and Risks of Global Sourcing.

Ability to Achieve Strategic Goals

The strategic view of global sourcing—called *transformational outsourcing*—suggests that just as the firm achieves gains in efficiency, productivity, quality, and revenues by leveraging offshore talent, it also obtains the means to turn around failing businesses, speed up innovation, restructure operations, and fund otherwise unaffordable development projects.[23] Global sourcing allows the firm to free expensive analysts, engineers, and managers from routine tasks to spend more time researching, innovating, managing, and generally undertaking high-value-adding activities that contribute more productively to increasing company performance.[24] Global sourcing becomes a catalyst to overhaul organizational processes and company operations and increase the firm's overall competitive advantages.

The twin outcomes of cost efficiency and achieving strategic goals often are both present in any given sourcing activity. Global sourcing can provide other benefits as well, including:

- *Faster corporate growth.*   Firms can focus their resources on performing more profitable activities such as R&D or building relationships with customers.[25]
- *Access to qualified workers abroad.*   Countries such as China, India, the Philippines, and Ireland offer abundant pools of educated engineers, managers, and other specialists to help firms achieve their goals.
- *Improved productivity and service.*   Manufacturing productivity and other value-chain activities can be improved by suppliers that specialize in these activities. Global sourcing also enables firms to provide 24/7 coverage of customer service.
- *Business process redesign.*   By reconfiguring their value chains or reengineering business processes, companies can improve their production efficiency and resource utilization.[26]
- *Increased speed to market.*   By shifting software development and editorial work to India and the Philippines, for example, publisher Walters Kluwer now produces a greater variety of books and journals, and publishes them faster.
- *Access to new markets.*   Sourcing provides an entrée to the market, an understanding of customers there, and the means to initiate local marketing activities. Firms also can use global sourcing to serve countries that may be otherwise closed due to protectionism.
- *Technological flexibility.*   Leveraging independent suppliers abroad provides firms the flexibility to quickly change sources of supply, employing whichever suppliers offer the most advanced technologies.
- *Improved agility by shedding unnecessary overhead.*   Unburdened by bureaucracy and administrative overhead, companies can be more responsive to opportunities and adapt more easily to evolving threats, such as new competitors.

Combined, these benefits give firms the ability to continuously renew their strategic positions. Outsourcing specialists such as Accenture and Genpact meticulously dissect the workflow of other firms' human resources, finance, or IT departments. This helps the specialists build new IT platforms, redesign all processes, and administer programs, acting as virtual subsidiaries to their client firms. The specialists then disperse work among global networks of staff from Asia to Eastern Europe and elsewhere.[27]

RISKS OF GLOBAL SOURCING

In addition to potential benefits, global sourcing can also bring unexpected complications. Studies show that as many as half of all outsourcing arrangements are terminated earlier than planned. As summarized in Exhibit 13.5, global sourcing introduces the following major risks.[28]

- *Lower than expected cost savings.*   International transactions are often more complex and costly than expected. Conflicts and misunderstandings may arise from differences in the national and organizational cultures between the focal firm and foreign supplier. Establishing an outsourcing facility can be surprisingly expensive, due to the need to upgrade poor infrastructure or locate it in a large city to attract sufficient skilled labor.

- *Environmental factors.*   Environmental challenges include currency fluctuations, poor infrastructure, tariffs and other trade barriers, high energy and transportation costs, adverse macroeconomic events, and labor strikes. For example, if the Chinese yuan increases in value, then China's exports will likely decrease because it will be more expensive for foreign customers to buy Chinese products. In a similar way, firms that source from China will experience higher costs.

- *Weak legal environment.*   Many popular locations for global sourcing (for example, China, Mexico, Russia) have weak intellectual property laws and poor enforcement, which can erode key strategic assets. Inadequate legal systems, red tape, convoluted tax systems, and complex business regulations complicate local operations in many countries.

- *Inadequate or low-skilled workers.*   Some foreign suppliers may be staffed by employees who lack appropriate knowledge about the tasks with which they are charged. Other suppliers suffer rapid turnover of skilled employees. In 2009, customer complaints about the quality of service led Delta Airlines to move its corporate call centers from India back to the United States.[29]

- *Overreliance on suppliers.*   Unreliable suppliers may put earlier work aside when they gain a more important client. Suppliers occasionally encounter financial difficulties or are acquired by other firms with different priorities and procedures.

- *Risk of creating competitors.*   As the focal firm shares its intellectual property and business-process knowledge with foreign suppliers, it also runs the risk of creating future rivals. Schwinn, long the leader in the global bicycle industry, transferred much of its production and core expertise to lower-cost foreign suppliers, which acquired sufficient knowledge to become competitors, eventually forcing Schwinn into bankruptcy (from which it later recovered).

- *Erosion of morale and commitment among home country employees.* Global sourcing can leave employees caught in the middle between their employer and their employer's clients. When outsourcing forces retained and outsourced staff to work side by side, tensions and uncertainty may evolve into an us-versus-them syndrome and diminish employee commitment and enthusiasm.

Global sourcing is subject to global crises and natural disasters. As a result of the 2011 earthquake that struck Japan, for example, numerous industries that rely on Japanese suppliers suffered major interruptions. In the auto industry, a typical car contains about 15,000 parts, counting every last screw. If even one part is missing, car production must be halted. Following the Japan quake, General Motors temporarily stopped work at auto plants in Spain, Germany, and the United States. Ford was unable to obtain paint shades for some cars because of the loss of pigment production from plants in the earthquake zone. Toyota suspended operations in some plants that make car brakes and suspensions. As much as 30 percent of global car production was halted or interrupted in the months following the quake.

STRATEGIES FOR MINIMIZING THE RISKS OF GLOBAL SOURCING

Experience suggests seven managerial guidelines for achieving success in global sourcing:

1. ***Go offshore for the right reasons.*** Most companies cite cost cutting as the main reason for global sourcing, but such benefits quickly diminish over time. Longer term, the best rationale is strategic. To maximize returns, management should examine tasks and activities in each of the firm's value chains and outsource those in which the firm is weak, that offer little value to the bottom line, or that can be performed more effectively by others, yet are not critical to core competencies.

2. ***Get employees on board.*** Global sourcing can invite opposition from employees and other organizational stakeholders or create unnecessary tension and harm employee morale. Thus, management should seek employee support by reaching a consensus of middle managers and employees, developing alternatives for redeploying laid-off workers, and including employees in the selection of foreign partners. Managers can also seek the counsel of labor unions and incorporate their views.

3. ***Choose carefully between a captive operation and contracting with outside suppliers.*** Managers should be vigilant about striking the right balance between the organizational activities they retain inside the firm and those sourced from outside. Many companies establish their own sourcing operations to maintain control of outsourced activities and technologies.

4. ***Choose suppliers carefully.*** The focal firm may have limited influence over suppliers' manufacturing and processes. Suppliers may engage in opportunistic behavior or act in bad faith. To ensure the success of sourcing ventures, the focal firm must exercise great care to identify and screen potential suppliers and then monitor the activities of those suppliers from which it sources.

5. ***Emphasize effective communications with suppliers.*** A common reason for global sourcing failure is that buyers and suppliers spend too little time getting acquainted, which usually causes misunderstandings and poor results. Because production quality in an emerging market may vary over time, managers at the focal firm may need to closely monitor manufacturing processes, and partners must share necessary information.[30]

6. ***Invest in supplier development and collaboration.*** In the long run, benefits emerge when the focal firm emphasizes close collaboration with suppliers in codevelopment and codesign activities, and adjusts the firm's product and process requirements to match foreign suppliers' capabilities. Relationship-building efforts create a moral contract between the focal firm and the supplier, often more effective than a formal legal contract.

7. ***Safeguard interests.***   The focal firm should take specific actions to safeguard its interests in the supplier relationship. First, it should advise the supplier against taking any actions that jeopardize the firm's reputation. Second, it can escalate commitments by making partner-specific investments (such as sharing knowledge with the supplier) on an incremental basis. Third, it can build a stake for the supplier so that, in case of failure to meet expectations, the supplier also suffers costs or foregoes revenues. Fourth, it can maintain flexibility by keeping open its options for finding alternate partners if needed. Finally, the focal firm can keep the partner at bay by withholding access to intellectual property and key assets.

IMPLEMENTING GLOBAL SOURCING THROUGH SUPPLY-CHAIN MANAGEMENT

A key reason sourcing products from distant markets has become a major business phenomenon is the efficiency with which goods can be physically moved from one part of the globe to another.

A **global supply chain** is the firm's integrated network of sourcing, production, and distribution, organized on a worldwide scale and located in countries where competitive advantage can be maximized.

Global supply-chain management includes both upstream and downstream flows. Broadly, "upstream" refers to sourcing and production activities, while "downstream" refers to distribution and marketing activities. The concepts of supply chain and value chain are related but distinct. The value chain is the collection of activities intended to design, produce, market, deliver, and support a product or service. By contrast, the supply chain is the collection of logistics specialists and activities that provides inputs to the firm. Practically every company has a supply chain, including manufacturers, retailers, and even pure service-providing firms.

Sourcing from numerous suppliers scattered around the world would be neither economical nor feasible without an efficient supply-chain system. Casual observers are impressed by the vast collection of products in a supermarket or department store that originated from dozens of different countries. The speed with which these products are delivered to end users is equally impressive.

Boeing's new 787 Dreamliner is a fuel-saving, medium-sized passenger aircraft that uses carbon composite for the fuselage instead of aluminum. It is lightweight and has spacious interiors and better cabin pressure than other models, for a more comfortable journey. But Boeing (www.boeing.com) is responsible for manufacturing only about 10 percent of the jet's value—the tail fin and final assembly. Some 40 suppliers worldwide contribute the remaining 90 percent. The wings are built in Japan, the fuselage in Italy, and the landing gear in France. Global dispersion of manufacturing responsibility has transformed Boeing into a systems integrator, focusing on its core capabilities—design, marketing, and branding. However, launch of the 787 was delayed by more than two years, resulting in $10 billion of lost earnings. Many problems resulted from the complexity of coordinating a global supply chain network.[31]

Networks of supply-chain hubs and providers of global delivery service are an integral part of global supply chains. Many focal firms delegate supply-chain activities to independent logistics service providers such as DHL, FedEx, and TNT. Consulting firms that manage the logistics of other firms are called *third-party logistics providers (3PLs)*. Using a 3PL is often the best solution for international logistics, especially for firms that produce at low volumes or lack the resources and expertise to create their own logistics network.

The European Union provides a good example of evolving supply-chain management. The removal of border controls allowed supply-chain managers at many firms to redraw the maps of their sourcing and distribution activities throughout Europe. Warehousing and distribution centers were consolidated and centralized. Shipping costs were slashed by consolidating transportation into fewer suppliers. As a result, firms considerably improved on-time delivery and customer-service performance.[32]

Exhibit 13.6 illustrates the stages, functions, and activities in the supply chain. It reveals how suppliers interact with the focal firm and how these, in turn, interact with distributors and retailers.

Information and Communications Technology

Costs of physically delivering a product to an export market may account for as much as 40 percent of the good's total cost. Skillful supply-chain management reduces this cost while increasing customer satisfaction. Experienced firms use information and communications technologies (ICTs) to streamline supply chains, reducing costs and increasing

	Suppliers	Focal Firm	Intermediaries and/or Retailers
Stage in supply chain	Sourcing, from home country and abroad	Inbound materials; outbound goods and services	Distribution to domestic customers or foreign customers (exports)
Major functions	Provide raw materials, parts, components, supplies, as well as business processes and other services to focal firm	Manufacture or assemble components or finished products, or produce services	Distribute and sell products and services
Typical activities	Maintain inventory, process orders, transport goods, deliver services	Manage inventory, process orders, manufacture or assemble products, produce and deliver services, distribute products to customers, retailers, or intermediaries	Manage inventory, place or process orders, produce services, manage physical distribution, provide after-sales service

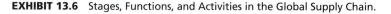

EXHIBIT 13.6   Stages, Functions, and Activities in the Global Supply Chain.

distribution efficiency. For example, *electronic data interchange (EDI)* automatically passes orders directly from customers to suppliers through a sophisticated ICT platform.

Specialized software enhances information sharing and improves efficiency by allowing the firm to track international shipments and clear customs. Many firms digitize key documents such as customs declarations and invoices, which improves speed and reduces order processing costs and shipping procedures. The most sophisticated supply chains are characterized by reliable, capable partners connected through automated, real-time communications. In an efficient system, the focal firm and its supply-chain partners continuously communicate and share information to constantly meet the demands of the marketplace.

Logistics and Transportation

Logistics physically moves goods through the supply chain. It incorporates information, transportation, inventory, warehousing, materials handling, and similar activities associated with the delivery of raw materials, parts, components, and finished products. Managers seek to reduce moving and storage costs by using just-in-time inventory systems. Internationally, logistics are complex due to wide geographic distances, multiple legal environments, and the often inadequate and costly nature of distribution infrastructure in individual countries. The more diverse the firm's global supply chain, the greater the cost of logistics.

Competent logistics management is critical, especially for just-in-time inventory systems, which are sensitive to unforeseen disruptions. For example, the California ports of Los Angeles (www.portoflosangeles.org) and Long Beach (www.polb.com) handle more than 40 percent of imports into the United States, processing 24,000 shipping containers per day. Strikes, the threat of terrorism, and infrastructure deficiencies occasionally produce transit delays. In Japan, concerns about radiation from nuclear plants damaged in the 2011 earthquake compelled some shipping companies to ban their ships from docking in Japanese ports, delaying delivery of parts and components to firms worldwide.

Transportation Modes

International logistics usually make use of multiple *transportation modes,* including land, ocean, and air transport. Land transportation is conducted via highways and railroads, ocean transport is via container ships, and air transport is via commercial or cargo aircraft. Transportation modes involve several trade-offs. The three main considerations are *cost, transit time* to deliver the goods, and *predictability*, the match between anticipated and actual transit times.

Land transport is usually more expensive than ocean transport but cheaper than air. Exporters often opt for ocean shipping even when land transport is available. For example, some Mexican firms send goods to Canada by ship. Ocean transport was revolutionized by the development of 20- and 40-foot shipping containers, the big boxes loaded onto seagoing vessels. The ability of a modern ship to carry thousands of containers yields economies of scale, making ocean transport very cost effective.

Given its high cost, air transport is used mostly to transport perishable products (like food and flowers), products with a high value-to-weight ratio (like fine jewelry and laptop computers), and urgently needed goods (like medicines and emergency supplies). It accounts for only 1 percent of international shipments.

GLOBAL SOURCING AND CORPORATE SOCIAL RESPONSIBILITY

The business community sees global sourcing as a way of maintaining or increasing business competitiveness. Others view it negatively, focusing on the loss of local jobs. When the state of Indiana awarded a $15 million IT services contract to a supplier that planned to use technicians from India to do some of the work, the Indiana Senate intervened and cancelled the deal. However, the state recently leased management of the Indiana Toll Road to an Australian-Spanish partnership for 75 years for $3.8 billion.[33]

Potential Harm to Local and National Economy from Global Sourcing

Critics of global sourcing point to three potentially major problems. Global sourcing can result in (1) job losses in the home country, (2) reduced national competitiveness, and (3) declining standards of living.

The number of jobs in the U.S. legal industry outsourced to foreign contractors now exceeds 25,000 per year.[34] Some estimate that more than 400,000 jobs in the United States IT industry have moved offshore.[35] Projections are that more than 3 million jobs will be outsourced from the United States by 2015.[36] Critics say this amounts to exporting jobs. Job losses are occurring in developing economies as well. For example, in the textile industry, El Salvador, Honduras, Indonesia, and Turkey have seen jobs gradually being transferred to China, India, and Pakistan.[37]

It takes considerable time for laid-off workers to find new jobs. According to one estimate, as many as one-third of U.S. workers who have been laid off cannot find suitable employment within a year.[38] Older workers in particular struggle to learn the skills needed for new positions. The rate of redeployment is likely to be even lower in Europe, where unemployment rates are already high, and in Japan, where employment practices are less flexible. In Germany, the percentage of workers who are not reemployed within a year of losing their jobs is as high as 60 percent. Under such circumstances, global sourcing may increase unemployment rates, reduce income levels, and harm the local community and national economy.

Public Policy on Global Sourcing

The consequences of global sourcing for the national economy and workers are not yet fully known. A recent comprehensive study carried out for the United States argues that official statistics understate the effect of offshoring on national economies.[39] The study concluded that more of the gain in living standards in recent years has come from cheap imports and less from increased domestic productivity.

Offshoring is a process of *creative destruction*, a concept first proposed by the Austrian economist Joseph Schumpeter.[40] According to this view, firms' innovative activities tend to make mature products obsolete over time: The introduction of personal computers essentially eliminated the typewriter industry, the DVD player eliminated the VCR, and so on. Just as offshoring results in job losses and adverse effects for particular groups and economic sectors, it also creates new advantages and opportunities for firms and consumers alike. New industries created through creative destruction will create new jobs and innovative products.

Public policy should strive to mitigate the potential harm global sourcing can cause.[41] Governments can use economic and fiscal policies to encourage the development of new technologies by helping entrepreneurs reap the financial benefits of their work and keeping the cost of capital for financing R&D low. Another useful policy is to ensure the nation has a strong educational system, including technical schools and well-funded universities that supply engineers, scientists, and knowledge workers. A strong educational system helps provide firms with pools of high-quality labor. And, as firms restructure through global sourcing efforts, flexibility acquired through education ensures that many who lose jobs can be redeployed in other positions.

Summary

Global sourcing refers to the procurement of products or services from suppliers or company-owned subsidiaries located abroad for consumption in the home country or a third country. **Outsourcing** is the procurement of selected value-adding activities, including production of intermediate goods or finished products, from external independent suppliers. **Business process outsourcing (BPO)** refers to the outsourcing of business functions such as finance, accounting, and human resources. Procurement can be from either independent suppliers or company-owned subsidiaries and affiliates. **Offshoring** refers to the relocation of an entire business process or manufacturing facility to a foreign country. Managers make two strategic decisions regarding value-adding activities: whether to *make or buy* inputs and where to locate value-adding activity— that is, the geographic **configuration of value-adding activity**. **Contract manufacturing** is an arrangement in which the focal firm contracts with an independent supplier to have the supplier manufacture products.

For some entrepreneurs, global sourcing has provided the means to turn around failing businesses, speed up the pace of innovation, or fund development projects that are otherwise unaffordable. Other benefits include faster corporate growth, the ability to access qualified personnel, improved productivity and service, redesigned business processes, faster foreign market entry, access to new markets, and technological flexibility.

Risks of global sourcing include failing to realize anticipated cost savings, dealing with environmental uncertainty, creating competitors, engaging suppliers with insufficient training, relying too much on suppliers, and eroding the morale of existing employees.

Firms should develop a strategic perspective in making global sourcing decisions. Global sourcing is a means to redeploy resources that improve long-term performance. To make global sourcing succeed, management should gain employee cooperation, emphasize strong supplier relations, safeguard its interests in the supplier relationship, and choose the right foreign suppliers.

Global supply chain refers to the firm's integrated network of sourcing, production, and distribution, organized on a world scale and located in countries where competitive advantage can be maximized. Global sourcing can contribute to job losses and declining living standards. Governments can encourage job retention and growth in the home country by reducing the cost of doing business, encouraging entrepreneurship and technological development, developing a strong educational system, and upgrading worker skills.

Key Terms

business process
  outsourcing
  (BPO) *239*
captive sourcing *241*

configuration of value-
  adding activity *239*
contract manufacturing, *242*
global sourcing *240*

global supply
  chain *254*
offshoring *242*
outsourcing *239*

Endnotes

1. Rupa Chanda, "India and Services Outsourcing in Asia," *The Singapore Economic Review* 53, no. 3 (2008): 419–47; Rahul Sachitanand, "IT Morphs Yet Again," *Business Today,* December 27, 2009, p. 7; Amol Sharma and Ben Worthen, "Indian Tech Outsourcers Aim to Widen Contracts," *Wall Street Journal,* October 5, 2009, p. B1; Ning Wright, "China's Emerging Role in Global Outsourcing," *The China Business Review,* November/December 2009, pp. 44–49.

2. Duke University CIBER/Archstone Consulting, *Second Biannual Offshore Survey Results,* 2005; UNCTAD, *World Investment Report 2005* (New York: United Nations, 2005).

3. "Outsourcing: Time to Bring It Back Home?" *Economist,* March 5, 2005, p. 63.

4. Michael E. Porter, *Competition in Global Industries* (Boston: Harvard Business School Press, 1986).

5. Benito Arrunada and Xose H. Vazquez, "When Your Contract Manufacturer Becomes Your Competitor," *Harvard Business Review,* September 2006, pp. 135–45.

6. Thomas Friedman, *The World is Flat 3.0: A Brief History of the Twenty-First Century* (New York: Picador, 2007).

7. Geri Smith, "Can Latin America Challenge India?" *Business Week,* January 30, 2006, Online Extra, retrieved from http://www .businessweek.com.

8. Andrew Baxter, "GE Unit Plugs into the Outside World," *Financial Times,* September 28, 2005, p. 8; Corporate profile of Genpact at http://www.hoovers.com.

9. Bruce Einhorn, "A Juggernaut In Electronics," *Business Week,* June 18, 2007, p. 46.

10. Masaaki Kotabe, Janet Murray, and Rajshekhar Javalgi, "Global Sourcing of Services and Market Performance: An Empirical Investigation," *Journal of International Marketing* 6 (1998): 10–31; Masaaki Kotabe and Janet Murray, "Outsourcing Service Activities," *Marketing Management* 10 (2001): 40–46.

11. "India: The Next Wave," *Economist,* December 17, 2005, pp. 57–58; Amy Kazmin, "Outsourcing: Law Firms Fuel the Demand for Offshore Services," *Financial Times,* January 30, 2009, retrieved from http://www.ft.com.

12. Institute for International Business, "Globalization of Work: Outsourcing and Offshoring," *Global Executive Forum,* Spring–Summer 2005, pp. 6–7; Niraj Sheth, "India Calls Are Now Taken at Home," *Wall Street Journal,* July 1, 2009, p. B6.

13. A. T. Kearney, "Geography of Offshoring Is Shifting, According to A. T. Kearney Study," May 18, 2009, retrieved from http://www .atkearney.com; "Is Your Job Next?" *Business Week,* February 3, 2003, retrieved from http://www.businessweek.com; Norihiko Shirouzu, "Engineering Jobs Become Car Makers New Export," *Wall Street Journal,* February 7, 2008, pp. B1–B2.

14. Murray Weidenbaum, "Outsourcing: Pros and Cons," *Executive Speeches* 19 (2004): 31–35.

15. Peter Marsh, "Foreign Threat to Service Jobs 'Overblown, Says Study,'" *Financial Times,* June 16, 2005, p. 12.

16. Chanda (2008); Penny Crosman, "Worldsourcers," *Wall Street & Technology,* July 2008, p. 26; Kazmin (2009); Everest Global, Inc., *Global Sourcing Market Vista,*

Everest Research Institute, 2009, retrieved from http://www.everestresearchinstitute.com.

17. *Business Week* (2003)

18. Patrick Burnson, "Strained," *Logistics Management,* May 2009, p. 36.

19. A. T. Kearney (2009).

20. Pete Engardio, "Mom-and-Pop Multinationals," *Business Week,* July 14 & 21, 2008, pp. 77–78.

21. Duke University CIBER/Archstone Consulting (2005).

22. James Hookway and Josephine Cuneta, "World News: Philippine Call Centers Ring Up Business," *Wall Street Journal,* May 30, 2009, p. A14; Paulo Prada and Niraj Sheth, "Delta Air Ends Use of India Call Centers," *Wall Street Journal,* April 18, 2009, p. B1; Sheth (2009).

23. *Business Week* (2003)

24. Pete Engardio, "The Future of Outsourcing," *Business Week,* January 30, 2006, pp. 50–64.

25. Duke University CIBER/Archstone Consulting (2005).

26. *Business Week* (2003)

27. Engardio (2006).

28. Masaaki Kotabe and Janet Murray, "Global Sourcing Strategy and Sustainable Competitive Advantage," *Industrial Marketing Management* 33 (2004): 7–14.

29. Prada and Sheth (2009); Jackie Range, "India Faces a Homegrown Staffing Issue: Not Enough Talent," *Wall Street Journal,* July 16, 2008, p. B8.

30. David Craig and Paul Willmott, "Outsourcing Grows Up," *The McKinsey Quarterly,* (February 2005), Web exclusive, retrieved from http://www.mckinseyquarterly.com.

31. Judith Crown and Carol Matlack, "Boeing Delays Dreamliner Again," *Business Week,* April 9, 2008, retrieved from http://www.businessweek.com; Dominic Gates, "Latest Delay of Boeing 787 Pushes Back First Delivery to Third Quarter of 2009," *Seattle Times,* April 10, 2008, retrieved from www.seattletimes.com; Jon Ostrower, "One Year On: The Story of the 787," *Flightglobal,* May 5, 2008, retrieved from www.flightglobal.com; Peter Sanders "Boeing Confronts New Woes in 787 Jet," *Wall Street Journal,* June 25, 2010, p. B1.

32. George Yip, *Total Global Strategy II* (Upper Saddle River, NJ: Prentice Hall, 2003).

33. Christopher Conkey, "Strapped Cities Outsource Transit Lines," *Wall Street Journal,* July 13, 2009, p. A6; Celeste Pagano, "Proceed with Caution: Avoiding Hazards in Toll Road Privatizations," *St. John's Law Review,* 83, no. 1 (2009): 351–94.

34. Eric Bellman and Nathan Koppel, "More U.S. Legal Work Moves to India's Low-Cost Lawyers," *Wall Street Journal,* September 28, 2005, p. B1; Kazmin (2009).

35. Weidenbaum (2004).

36. Chanda (2008); J. McCarthy, "3.3 Million U.S. Service Jobs to Go Offshore," *Forrester Research, Inc.,* 2002, retrieved from http://www.forrester.com.

37. John Thoburn, Kirsten Sutherland, and Thi Hoa Nguyen, "Globalization and Poverty: Impacts on Households of Employment and Restructuring in the Textiles Industry of Vietnam," *Journal of the Asia Pacific Economy* 12, no. 3 (2007): 345–62.

38. L. D. Tyson, "Offshoring: The Pros and Cons for Europe," *Business Week,* December 6, 2004, p. 32.

39. Michael Mandel, "The Real Cost of Offshoring," *Business Week,* June 18, 2007, p. 29.

40. Joseph A. Schumpeter, *Capitalism, Socialism, and Democracy* (New York: Harper, 1942).

41. Tyson (2004).

14

Marketing in the Global Firm

LEARNING OBJECTIVES
In this chapter, you will learn about:

1. Global marketing strategy

2. Standardization and adaptation of international marketing

3. Global branding and product development

4. International pricing

5. International marketing communications

6. International distribution

GLOBAL MARKETING STRATEGY

International marketing is concerned with identifying, measuring, and pursuing customer needs and market opportunities abroad. Exhibit 14.1 provides a framework for these activities and previews the topics of this chapter. The outer layer represents the cultural, social, political, legal, and regulatory environment of foreign markets. These environmental conditions constrain the firm's ability to price, promote, and distribute a product. For example, the firm will need to review prices frequently in high-inflation countries, adapt the positioning or selling propositions of the product to suit local customer expectations, and ensure products comply with mandated government standards.

The Environment of International Business

Diverse Cultural, Political, Legal, Monetary, and Financial
Environment of the Firm

Global Marketing Strategy

Targeting Customer Segments and Positioning

**International Marketing Program
Standardization and Adaptation**

Global Branding and Product Development	International Pricing
International Distribution	International Marketing Communications

EXHIBIT 14.1   Organizing Framework for Marketing in the International Firm.

The middle layer in Exhibit 14.1 represents **global marketing strategy**—a plan of action the firm develops for foreign markets that guides its decision making on (1) how to position itself and its offerings, (2) which customer segments to target, and (3) to what degree it should standardize or adapt its marketing program elements.[1]

Targeting Customer Segments and Positioning

Market segmentation is the process of dividing the firm's total customer base into homogeneous clusters in a way that allows management to formulate unique marketing strategies for each group. Within each market segment, customers exhibit similar characteristics, including income level, lifestyle, demographic profile, and desired product benefits.

In international business, firms frequently form market segments by grouping countries based on macro-level variables, such as level of economic development or cultural dimensions. For example, the MNE may group Latin American countries based on a common language (Spanish) or the European countries based on shared economic conditions. This approach has proven most effective for product categories in which governments play a key regulatory role (such as telecommunications, medical products, and processed foods) or where national characteristics prevail in determining product acceptance and usage.[2]

Today, firms increasingly target global market segments. A **global market segment** is a group of customers who share common characteristics across many national markets. Firms target these buyers with relatively uniform marketing programs. Frequent business travelers, for example, tend to be affluent, eager consumers of premium products that represent luxury and sophisticated style.

The firm's objective in pursuing global market segments is to uniquely position its offerings in the minds of target customers. *Positioning* is a marketing strategy in which the firm develops both the product and its marketing to evoke a distinct impression in the customer's mind, emphasizing differences from all competitive offerings. Positioning may also evoke the specific *attributes* consumers associate with a product. When Coca-Cola first entered Japan, for example, research revealed that Japanese women do not like products labeled "diet," nor is the population considered overweight. Thus, management altered the product's positioning in Japan by changing the name to Coke Light.

MNEs aim for a *global positioning strategy*, which positions the offering similarly in the minds of buyers worldwide. Sony, Starbucks, and Volvo successfully use this approach. Consumers worldwide view these strong brands in the same way. Global positioning strategy reduces international marketing costs by addressing the shared expectations of a global customer market segment.[3]

STANDARDIZATION AND ADAPTATION OF INTERNATIONAL MARKETING

In addition to guiding targeting and positioning, global marketing strategy also articulates the degree to which the firm's marketing program should vary between different foreign markets. With **adaptation** the firm modifies one or more elements of its international marketing program to accommodate specific customer requirements in a particular market. **Standardization** makes the marketing program elements uniform, with the goal of targeting entire regions, or even the global marketplace, with the same product or service.

In the innermost layer in Exhibit 14.1, we identify the key elements of the marketing program (also known as the *marketing mix*) affected by the standardization/adaptation decision. These are global branding and product development, international pricing, international marketing communications, and international distribution. In the international context, marketing strategy tackles the complexity of having both global and local competitors, as well as cross-national differences in culture, language, living standards, economic conditions, regulations, and quality of business infrastructure. A key challenge is to resolve the trade-offs between standardization and adaptation.

When they enter international markets, managers undertake broad corporate strategy in which they attempt to strike some ideal balance between *global integration* and *local responsiveness*. Global integration seeks cross-national synergy in the

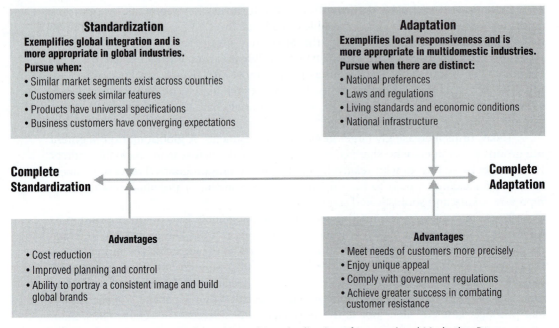

Standardization

Exemplifies global integration and is more appropriate in global industries.

Pursue when:
- Similar market segments exist across countries
- Customers seek similar features
- Products have universal specifications
- Business customers have converging expectations

Adaptation

Exemplifies local responsiveness and is more appropriate in multidomestic industries.

Pursue when there are distinct:
- National preferences
- Laws and regulations
- Living standards and economic conditions
- National infrastructure

Complete Standardization

Complete Adaptation

Advantages
- Cost reduction
- Improved planning and control
- Ability to portray a consistent image and build global brands

Advantages
- Meet needs of customers more precisely
- Enjoy unique appeal
- Comply with government regulations
- Achieve greater success in combating customer resistance

EXHIBIT 14.2   Trade-offs between Adaptation and Standardization of International Marketing Program.

firm's value-chain activities in order to take maximum advantage of similarities between countries, while local responsiveness aims to meet the specific needs of buyers in individual countries. How the firm resolves the balance between global integration and local responsiveness also affects how it makes standardization and adaptation decisions in its marketing program elements.

Exhibit 14.2 highlights the trade-offs between standardization and adaptation in international marketing. Let's examine the advantages of each approach.

Standardization

Representing a tendency toward global integration, standardization is more common in *global* industries such as aircraft manufacturing, pharmaceuticals, and credit cards. This marketing approach is most appropriate when:

- Similar market segments exist across countries
- Customers seek similar features in the product or service
- Products have universal specifications
- Business customers have converging expectations or needs regarding specifications, quality, performance, and other product attributes

Commodities, industrial equipment, and technology products lend themselves to a high degree of standardization. Automotive parts, building materials, dinnerware, and basic food ingredients are other products that require little or no adaptation. Popular consumer electronics such as Sony's PlayStation, Apple's iPod, and Canon digital cameras are largely standardized around the world. When managers build on commonalities in customer preferences and attempt to standardize their international marketing program, they can expect at least three types of favorable outcomes.

1. ***Cost reduction.***   Standardization reduces costs by making possible economies of scale in design, sourcing, manufacturing, and marketing. Offering a similar marketing program to the global marketplace or across entire regions is more efficient than adapting products for numerous individual markets.

2. ***Improved planning and control.*** Standardization provides for improved planning and control of value-adding activities. Having fewer offerings simplifies quality control and reduces the number of replacement parts a firm needs to stock. Marketing activities are also simplified—the firm can offer a largely standardized campaign for numerous countries.

3. ***Ability to portray a consistent image and build global brands.***   A brand is a name, sign, symbol, or design intended to identify the firm's product and to differentiate it from those of competitors. A **global brand** is one whose positioning, advertising strategy, look, and personality are standardized worldwide. Global branding increases customer interest and reduces the confusion that can arise when the firm offers numerous adapted products and marketing programs.[4]

Adaptation

While standardizing where they can, firms may also engage in adaptation when they consider local responsiveness a priority. Adaptation is useful in *multidomestic industries*, such as publishing and software, which tailor their offerings to suit individual markets. It may be as straightforward as translating labels, instructions, or books into a foreign language or as complex as completely modifying a product to fit unique market conditions. Managers consider several different rationales when adapting marketing program elements, which we explore next.

- ***Differences in national preferences.***   Adaptation may be carried out to modify the offering to the specific, unique wants and needs of customers in individual markets. When *The Simpsons* cartoon series was broadcast in Saudi Arabia, it was renamed *Al Shamshoon*, Homer Simpson's name was changed to Omar, and Bart Simpson became Badr. Producers translated the show into Arabic and modified the way the Simpson daughter and mother dress. Producers removed references to practices considered potentially offensive, such as consuming pork and beer. They changed Homer Simpson's Duff beer to soda, hot dogs to Egyptian beef sausages, and donuts to the popular Arab cookies called *kahk*. Moe's Bar was edited out of the show. As one Arab viewer told ABC News, "We are a totally different culture, so you can't talk about the same subject in the same way."[5]

- ***Differences in living standards and economic conditions.***   Because income levels vary greatly around the world, firms attempt to adjust both the pricing and the complexity of their product offerings for individual markets. Microsoft has lowered the price of its software for Thailand, Malaysia, and Indonesia to bring it in line with local purchasing power.[6] A recession signals a drop in consumer confidence and the firm may need to reduce prices to generate sales. High inflation can rapidly erode profits even as prices rise.

- ***Differences in laws and regulations.***   Germany, Norway, and Switzerland are among countries that restrict advertising directed at children. Packaged foods in

Europe are often labeled in several languages, including English, French, German, and Spanish. In Quebec, Canada's French-speaking province, local law requires product packaging in both English and French. In some markets, the use of certain sales promotion activities such as coupons and sales contests is restricted.

- *Differences in national infrastructure.* Infrastructure is especially poor in the rural parts of developing economies, necessitating innovative approaches for getting products to customers. Road and rail networks in western China are underdeveloped, so firms use small trucks to reach retailers in outlying communities. Undeveloped media also require substantial adaptations to carry marketing communications. In rural Vietnam, most consumers cannot access television, magazines, or the Internet. Firms advertise to low-income buyers via radio, billboards, and brochures.

In sum, we can identify four primary advantages of adapting an international marketing program to the local market:

1. Meet the needs of local customers more precisely
2. Create unique appeal for the product
3. Comply with local or national government regulations
4. Achieve greater success in combating local and global competitors

Adaptation also provides managers an opportunity to explore alternate ways to market the product or service. What they learn can guide R&D efforts, often leading to superior products for sale abroad and at home.

Standardization and Adaptation: A Balancing Act

A managerial decision about standardization and adaptation is not an either/or decision but rather a balancing act. It is up to senior marketing managers and the global new-product planning team to sort out the trade-offs in the distinctive environments in which the firm operates.

Perhaps the most important distinction in this balance is that standardization helps the firm reduce its costs, while local adaptation helps the firm more precisely cater to local needs and requirements, which tends to enhance revenues. Adaptation frequently requires adding marketing expertise in local subsidiaries. It is also time consuming and costly. It may require substantial redesign of products and modifications to manufacturing, pricing, distribution, and communications. Thus, managers usually adopt standardization because it is easier and less costly. Many firms adapt marketing program elements *only when necessary* to respond to local customer preferences and mandated regulations. Unilever (www.unilever.com) streamlined the number of its brands from more than 1,600 to about 400 and focused attention on a dozen or so global ones. However, in nutrition-conscious countries, it is adapting products by lowering the levels of sugar, salt, and saturated fats.[7]

Typically managers both standardize and adapt a given product or service in varying degrees. For instance, management might offer a standardized product worldwide but modify its pricing and advertising for different markets. Management decides not only *which* elements to adapt, but also *how much* to adapt them. IKEA maintains uniform product designs across markets while modifying, say, the size of beds or chests of drawers in individual countries.

individual markets. Honda and Toyota design models such as the Accord and Corolla around a standardized platform to which modular components, parts, and features are added to suit specific needs and tastes.

A *global new product planning team* is a group within a firm that determines which elements of the product will be standardized and which will be adapted locally. The team also decides how to launch products—with simultaneous release across countries or with sequential release. Sequential release implies launching a product one country at a time and is often preferred for products requiring substantial local adaptation.

Global new-product planning teams are assigned to formulate best practices the firm would implement in all its worldwide units. These teams assemble employees with specialized knowledge and expertise from various geographically diverse units of the MNE, who collaborate in a project to develop workable solutions to common problems.

INTERNATIONAL PRICING

Multiple currencies, trade barriers, extra cost considerations, government regulation, competitive reaction, and typically longer distribution channels make international pricing complex.[12] Prices can also escalate to unreasonable levels because of tariffs, taxes, and higher markups by foreign intermediaries. Price variations among different markets can lead to **gray market activity**—legal importation of genuine products into a country by intermediaries other than authorized distributors (also known as parallel imports). We discuss gray markets later in this chapter.

Prices influence customers' perception of value, determine the level of motivation of foreign intermediaries, affect promotional spending and strategy, and compensate for weaknesses in other elements of the marketing mix. Let's explore the unique aspects of international pricing.

Factors That Affect International Pricing

Factors that influence international pricing fall into four categories.

1. *Nature of the market.* Most countries are emerging markets or developing economies where the majority of consumers lack significant disposable income. Thus, prices must be set lower. Regulation, climate, infrastructure, and other factors in foreign markets can also impel the firm to spend money to modify a product or its distribution. Food items shipped to hot climates require refrigeration, which drives up costs. In countries with many rural residents or those with a poor distribution infrastructure, delivering products to widely dispersed customers necessitates higher pricing because of steeper shipping costs. Governments impose tariffs that lead to higher prices. They also enforce health rules, safety standards, and other regulations that increase the cost of doing business locally.

2. *Nature of the product or industry.* Products with substantial added value—such as cars or high-end computers—usually necessitate charging relatively high prices. A specialized product, or one with a technological edge, gives a company greater price flexibility. When the firm holds a relative monopoly in a product (such as Microsoft's operating system software), it can generally charge premium prices.

3. *Type of distribution system.* Exporting firms rely on independent distributors based abroad. Some distributors mark up prices to suit their own goals—up to 200

percent in some countries—which may harm the manufacturer's image and pricing strategy in the market. By contrast, when the firm internationalizes via FDI by establishing company-owned marketing subsidiaries abroad, management maintains control over pricing strategy. Firms that make direct sales to end users also control their pricing and can make rapid adjustments to suit evolving market conditions.

4. ***Location of the production facility.***   Locating manufacturing in those countries with low-cost labor enables a firm to charge lower prices. Locating factories in or near major markets cuts transportation costs and may reduce problems created by foreign exchange fluctuations. During the 1980s, Toyota and Honda built car factories in the United States, their most important foreign market. Mazda retained much of its manufacturing in Japan, exporting its cars to the United States. As the Japanese yen appreciated against the dollar, Mazda had to raise its prices, which hurt U.S. sales.

Exhibit 14.4 provides a comprehensive list of internal and external factors that influence how firms set international prices. Internally, management accounts for

Internal to the Firm
- Management's profit and market share expectations
- Cost of manufacturing, marketing, and other value-chain activities
- The degree of control management desires over price setting in foreign markets

External Factors
- Customer expectations, purchasing power, and sensitivity to price increases
- Nature of competitors' offerings, prices, and strategy
- International customer costs
  - Product/package modification; labeling and market requirements
  - Documentation (certificate of origin, invoices, banking fees)
  - Financing costs
  - Packing and container charges
  - Shipping (inspection, warehousing, freight forwarder's fee)
  - Insurance
- Landed cost
  - Tariffs (customs duty, import tax, customs clearance fee)
  - Warehousing charges at the port of import; local transportation
- Importer's cost
  - Value-added tax and other applicable taxes paid by the importer
  - Local intermediary (distributor, wholesaler, retailer) margins
  - Cost of financing inventory
- Anticipated fluctuations in currency exchange rates

EXHIBIT 14.4   Internal and External Factors That Affect International Pricing.

its own objectives regarding profit and market share, the cost of goods sold, and the degree of control desired over pricing of the firm's products abroad. Externally, management must account for customer characteristics, competitor prices, exchange rates, tariffs, taxes, and costs related to generating international sales, as well as transporting and distributing the goods. Many countries in Europe and elsewhere charge value-added taxes (VATs) on imported products. Unlike a sales tax, which is calculated based on the retail sales price, the VAT is determined as a percentage of the gross margin—the difference between the sales price and the cost to the seller of the item sold. In the EU, for example, VAT rates range between 15 and 25 percent.

A Framework for Setting International Prices

Managers examine the suitability of prices at several levels in the international distribution channel—importers, wholesalers, retailers, and end users—and then set prices accordingly. Exhibit 14.5 presents a systematic approach for setting international prices.[13]

Let's illustrate the international pricing framework with an example. Suppose a leading U.S. musical instrument manufacturer, Melody Corporation, wants to begin exporting electric guitars to Japan and needs to set prices. Melody decides to export its John Mayer brand of guitar, which retails for $2,000 in the United States. Initial research reveals that additional costs of shipping, insurance, and a 5 percent Japanese tariff will add a total of $300 to the price of each guitar, bringing the total *landed price* to $2,300. Melody has identified an importer in Japan, Aoki Wholesalers, which intends to add a 10 percent profit margin to the cost of each imported guitar. Thus, the total price once a guitar leaves Aoki's Japan warehouse is $2,530. This is the *floor price*, the lowest acceptable price to Melody, since management doesn't want Japanese earnings to dip below those in the United States.

Step 1. Estimate the "landed" price of the product in the foreign market by totaling all costs associated with shipping the product to the customer's location.

Step 2. Estimate the price the importer or distributor will charge when it adds its profit margin.

Step 3. Estimate the target price range for end users. Determine:
- Floor price (lowest acceptable price to the firm, based on cost considerations)
- Ceiling price (highest possible price, based on customer purchasing power, price sensitivity, and competitive considerations)

Step 4. Assess the company sales potential at the price the firm is most likely to charge (between the floor price and ceiling price).

Step 5. Select a suitable pricing strategy based on corporate goals and preferences from:
- Rigid cost-plus pricing
- Flexible cost-plus pricing
- Incremental pricing

Step 6. Check consistency with current prices across product lines, key customers, and foreign markets (in order to deter potential gray market activity).

Step 7. Implement pricing strategy and tactics, and set intermediary and end-user prices. Then, continuously monitor market performance and make pricing adjustments as necessary to accommodate evolving market conditions.

EXHIBIT 14.5   Key Steps in International Price Setting.

Next, market research on income levels and competitor prices reveals that Japanese musicians are willing to pay prices about 30 percent above typical U.S. prices for high-quality instruments. Given this information, Melody management believes Japan can sustain a ceiling price for the Mayer guitar of $2,600. Additional research provides estimates for Melody's sales potential at the floor price and at the ceiling price. Managers eventually decide on a suggested price of $2,560. Research has revealed this is the most appropriate price in light of factors in Japan such as local purchasing power, size of the market, market growth, competitors' prices, and Japanese attitudes on the relationship of price to product quality. Management also believes the price is reasonable given Melody's pricing in other markets, such as Hawaii and Australia. Accordingly, the firm implements the price level for end users and the corresponding price for Aoki, the importer. Melody begins shipping guitars to Japan and monitors the marketplace, keeping track of actual demand and the need to adjust prices in light of demand, economic conditions, and other emergent factors.

Let's review the three pricing strategies in Step 5 of Exhibit 14.5. *Rigid cost-plus pricing* refers to setting a fixed price for all export markets. In most cases, management simply adds a flat percentage to the domestic price to compensate for the added costs of doing business abroad. The export customer's final price includes a markup to cover transporting and marketing the product, as well as profit margins for both intermediaries and the manufacturer. A key disadvantage of this method is that it often fails to account for local market conditions, such as buyer demand, income level, and competition.

In *flexible cost-plus pricing*, management includes any added costs of doing business abroad in its final price. At the same time, management also accounts for local market and competitive conditions, such as customer purchasing power, demand, competitor prices, and other external variables, as identified in Exhibit 14.4. This approach is more sophisticated than rigid cost-plus pricing because it accounts for specific circumstances in the target market.

In highly competitive markets, the firm may set prices to cover only its variable costs, but not its fixed costs. This is known as *incremental pricing*. Here, management assumes fixed costs are already paid from sales of the product in the firm's home country or other markets. The approach enables the firm to offer competitive prices, but can also result in suboptimal profits.

When carried to an extreme, incremental pricing may invite competitors to accuse a firm of dumping. *Dumping* is the practice of charging a lower price for exported products, sometimes below manufacturing cost—potentially driving local suppliers out of business. The seller may compensate for the low price by charging higher prices in other markets. Many national governments regard dumping as a form of unfair competition and impose antidumping duties or initiate legal action through the World Trade Organization (www.wto.org).

Managing International Price Escalation

International price escalation refers to the problem of end-user prices reaching exorbitant levels in the export market caused by multilayered distribution channels, intermediary margins, tariffs, and other international costs (identified in Exhibit 14.4). International price escalation means the retail price in the export market can be significantly higher than the domestic price, creating a competitive disadvantage for the exporter. Corporations can use five key strategies to combat export price escalation abroad:[14]

1. ***Shorten the distribution channel.*** By bypassing some intermediaries, the firm establishes a more direct route to reach the final customer. A shorter channel implies fewer intermediaries to compensate, reducing the product's final price.

2. ***Redesign the product to remove costly features.*** Whirlpool developed a no-frills, simplified washing machine that it manufactures inexpensively and sells for a lower price in developing economies.

3. ***Ship products unassembled.*** Compared to final products, the parts and components used to assemble final products usually qualify for lower import tariffs. Thus, the firm should export basic inputs only and then perform final assembly in the foreign market. This approach works best when the firm can employ low-cost labor in the market or do assembly in a foreign trade zone where import costs are lower.[15]

4. ***Reclassify the exported product to qualify for lower tariffs.*** Suppose Nokia faces a high tariff when exporting telecommunications equipment to Bolivia. By having the product reclassified as computer equipment, Nokia might be able to export the product under a lower tariff because imported products often fit more than one product category for determining tariffs.

5. ***Move production or sourcing to another country.*** This can allow the firm to take advantage of lower production costs or favorable currency rates.

Managing Pricing under Varying Currency Conditions

In export markets, a strong domestic currency can reduce competitiveness, while a weakening domestic currency makes the firm's foreign pricing more competitive. Exhibit 14.6 presents various managerial responses to a weakening or appreciating domestic currency.[16]

Transfer Pricing

Transfer pricing, or intracorporate pricing, refers to the practice of pricing intermediate or finished products exchanged among the subsidiaries and affiliates of the same corporate family located in different countries.[17] For example, when the Ford engine plant in South Africa sells parts to the Ford factory in Spain, it charges a transfer price for this intracorporate transaction. This price generally differs from the market prices Ford charges its external customers.

MNEs attempt to manage internal prices primarily for two reasons.[18] First, it gives them a way to repatriate—that is, bring back to the home country—the profits from a country that restricts MNEs from taking their earnings out, often due to a shortage of its own currency. High prices charged to its foreign affiliate serve as an alternative means of transferring money out of the affiliate's country.

Second, transfer pricing can help MNEs shift profits out of a country with high corporate income taxes into a country with low corporate income taxes to increase companywide profitability. In this case, the MNE may opt to maximize the expenses (and therefore minimize the profits) of the foreign country affiliate by charging high prices for goods sold to the affiliate.

When the exporter gains a price advantage because its home country currency is WEAKENING relative to the customer's currency, then it should:	When the exporter suffers from a price disadvantage because its home country currency is APPRECIATING relative to the customer's currency, then it should:
Stress the benefits of the firm's low prices to foreign customers.	Accentuate competitive strengths in nonprice elements of its marketing program, such as product quality, delivery, and after-sales service.
Maintain normal price levels, expand the product line, or add more costly features.	Consider lowering prices by improving productivity, reducing production costs, or redesigning the product to eliminate costly features.
Exploit greater export opportunities in markets where this favorable exchange rate exists.	Concentrate exporting to those countries whose currencies have not weakened in relation to the exporter.
Speed repatriation of foreign-earned income and collections.	Maintain foreign-earned income in the customer's currency and delay collection of foreign accounts receivable (if there is an expectation that the customer's currency will regain strength over a reasonable time period).
Minimize expenditures in the customer's currency (for example, for advertising and local transportation).	Maximize expenditures in the customer's currency.

EXHIBIT 14.6   Strategies for Dealing with Varying Currency Conditions.

A subsidiary may buy or sell a finished or intermediate product from another affiliate below cost, at cost, or above cost. Suppose the MNE treats Subsidiary A as a favored unit. That is, Subsidiary A is allowed to *source at or below cost* and *sell at a relatively high price* when transacting with other subsidiaries. Over time, Subsidiary A will achieve superior financial results at the expense of other subsidiaries in the corporate family. A subsidiary would receive such favorable treatment if it is located in a country with one or more of the following features:

- Political stability
- High tariffs for the product in question
- Lower corporate income-tax rates
- Favorable accounting rules for calculating corporate income
- Little or no restrictions on profit repatriation
- Strategic importance to the MNE

Optimizing earnings of the MNE as a whole in this way frequently comes at a cost. First, manipulating transfer prices may make it more difficult to determine the true profit contribution of a subsidiary. Second, morale problems may arise at a subsidiary whose profit performance has been made to look worse than it really is. Third, some subsidiary managers may react negatively to price manipulation. Fourth, as local businesses, subsidiaries must abide by local laws and accounting rules, which may restrict transfer pricing.

Gray Market Activity (Parallel Imports)

What do companies such as Caterpillar, Duracell, Gucci, and Sony have in common? They are all MNEs with established brand names that have been the target of gray market activity, the emergence of unauthorized distributors for the firm's products.[19]

Consider a manufacturer that produces its products in Country A and exports them to Country B. If the going price of the product happens to be sufficiently lower in Country B, then gray market brokers can exploit arbitrage opportunities—buy the product at a low price in Country B, import it into the original source country, and sell it at a high price there.

In this scenario, the initial transaction is carried out by authorized channel intermediaries. The second transaction is carried out by unauthorized intermediaries. Often referred to as *gray marketers*, the unauthorized intermediaries are typically independent entrepreneurs. Because their transactions parallel those of authorized distributors, gray market activity is also called *parallel importation.*

In Canada, the government imposes price controls on medications. Consequently, drug prices are often lower there than in the United States. Because of this difference, some U.S. consumers purchase their prescription drugs from online pharmacies based in Canada, which may not be authorized to export the drugs.[20] Gray market activity is also common in automobiles, cameras, watches, computers, perfumes, and even construction equipment.

Gray market activity occurs mainly in the presence of a large price difference for the same product between two or more countries. Such price differences arise due to (1) the manufacturer's inability to coordinate prices across its markets; (2) deliberate efforts by the firm to charge higher prices in some countries when competitive conditions permit; or (3) exchange rate fluctuations that result in a price gap between products priced in two different currencies.

Managers worry about gray market activity because it can lead to:

- *A tarnished brand image.*   The brand image may suffer when customers realize the product is available at a lower price through alternative channels, particularly less-prestigious outlets.
- *Strained producer-distributor relations.*   Authorized distributors will be concerned and frustrated if parallel imports result in lost sales.
- *Disruptions in company planning.*   Gray market activity may negatively affect regional sales forecasting, pricing strategies, merchandising plans, and general marketing efforts.

Most governments have failed to take steps to prevent the occurrence of gray markets, or provide little enforcement of existing laws. Companies must develop their own solutions to combat such activity. Managers can pursue at least four strategies to cope with gray market imports.[21]

1. Aggressively cut prices in countries and regions targeted by gray market brokers.
2. Hinder the flow of products into markets where gray market brokers procure the product.

3. Design products with exclusive features that strongly appeal to customers.

4. Publicize the limitations of gray market channels and the possibility of counterfeiting.

INTERNATIONAL MARKETING COMMUNICATIONS

Companies use *marketing communications* (also known as *marketing promotion*) to provide information to and communicate with existing and potential customers, with the ultimate aim of stimulating demand. Let's examine international marketing communications in more detail.

International Advertising

Firms conduct advertising via *media*, which includes direct mail, radio, television, cinema, billboards, transit, print media, and the Internet. *Transit* refers to ads placed in buses, trains, and subways, and is particularly useful in large cities. *Print media* are newspapers, magazines, and trade journals. Managers assess the availability and viability of media by examining the amount and types of advertising spending already occurring in each market. In 2011, worldwide spending on advertising amounted to approximately USD $500 billion. In the United States, advertising expenditures exceeded $150 billion.[22] Five western firms—Yum Brands, Pernod Ricard, Avon Products, Colgate-Palmolive, and P&G—spend more than 10 percent of their ad budgets in just one country, China.[23] Smaller firms often lack the resources to advertise on TV or to develop a foreign sales force.

Literacy rates and the availability and quality of media determine the feasibility and nature of marketing communications. Exhibit 14.7 provides statistics on media for various countries. In developing economies, TV, radio, newspapers, and the Internet are often quite limited. Marketers in Peru and the Netherlands emphasize television advertising, in Kuwait and Norway they concentrate on print media, and in Bolivia firms use a lot of outdoor advertising on billboards and buildings. About half of all advertising funds in Italy are spent on television, more than double the figure for Britain, where newspapers attract the largest proportion of ad spending.[24]

Differences in culture, laws, and media availability mean it is seldom possible to duplicate in foreign markets the type and mix of advertising used in the home market. For example, the Italian government limits television advertising on state channels to 12 percent of airtime per hour and 4 percent per week. Culture determines buyer attitudes toward the role and function of advertising, humor content, the depiction of characters (such as the roles of men and women), and decency standards. Advertising conveys a message encoded in language, symbols, colors, and other attributes, each of which may have distinctive meanings. In China, Nike ran an ad in which NBA basketball star LeBron James battles—and defeats—a computer-generated Chinese Kung Fu master. Chinese consumers were offended and China's national government banned the ad.[25]

Many MNEs employ relatively standardized advertising around the world, an approach that simplifies communications strategy and saves money. Benetton, the Italian clothing manufacturer, has enjoyed much success by using essentially the same "United Colors of Benetton" ad campaigns in markets worldwide. The dialogue in

	Literacy Rate (percentage of population)	Televisions per 100 People	Radio Stations per one Million People	Daily Newspapers per one Million People	Internet Users (percentage of population)
Argentina	97%	21	32.4	4.8	66%
Australia	99	51	26.7	2.4	78
China	92	31	0.5	0.7	36
Ethiopia	43	1	0.1	0.1	1
India	61	6	0.2	3.8	9
Japan	99	68	9.1	0.9	78
Mexico	93	25	12.4	2.9	32
Netherlands	99	50	15.0	2.3	88
Nigeria	68	5	0.8	0.3	28
Saudi Arabia	79	23	2.7	0.5	42
United Kingdom	99	51	10.4	1.8	82
United States	99	75	44.0	5.0	78

EXHIBIT 14.7   Media Characteristics in Selected Countries.   *Sources: CIA World Factbook* at www.cia.gov; International Monetary Fund, at www.imf.org; United Nations, *International Human Development Indicators*, at http://hdrstats.undp.org; UNESCO Institute for Statistics, at http://stats.uis.unesco.org; World Bank, at www.worldbank.org Note: Data are for the latest year available.

Levi's ads is often in English worldwide.[26] The most effective ad campaigns are based on a full understanding of the target audience's buying motivations, values, behavior, purchasing power, and demographic characteristics.

Most MNEs employ advertising agencies to create promotional content and select media for foreign markets. The choice is usually between a home country–based agency with international expertise, a local agency based in the target market, or a *global advertising agency* with offices in the target market. Exhibit 14.8 identifies the leading global advertising agencies. These firms maintain networks of affiliates and local offices around the world. They can create advertising that is both global and sensitive to local conditions while offering a range of additional services such as market research, publicity, and package design.

International Promotional Activities

Promotional activities are short-term marketing activities intended to stimulate an initial purchase, immediate purchase, or increased purchases of the product and to improve intermediary effectiveness and cooperation. They include tools such as coupons, point-of-purchase displays, demonstrations, samples, contests, gifts, and Internet interfacing. Greece, Portugal, and Spain permit virtually every type of promotion; Germany, Norway, and Switzerland forbid or restrict some.

Rank	Agency	Headquarters	Worldwide Revenue, Millions of Dollars, 2008
1	Dentsu	Tokyo	$2,472
2	BBDO Worldwide	New York	1,986
3	McCann Erickson Worldwide	New York	1,741
4	DDB Worldwide	New York	1,509
5	TBWA Worldwide	New York	1,357
6	Euro RSCG Worldwide	New York	1,170
7	JWT	New York	1,157
8	Young & Rubicam	New York	1,100
9	Publicis	Paris	1,071
10	OgilvyOne Worldwide	New York	1,054

EXHIBIT 14.8   The Largest Global Ad Agencies.   *Source:* Advertising Age (2009). "Top 15 Consolidated Agency Networks," April 27, 2009, accessed at http://adage.com.

INTERNATIONAL DISTRIBUTION

Distribution is the process of getting the product or service from its place of origin to the customer. Distribution is the most inflexible of the marketing program elements—once a firm establishes a distribution channel, it may be difficult to change it. The most common approaches to international distribution are engaging independent intermediaries (for exporting firms) and establishing marketing and sales subsidiaries directly in target markets (an FDI-based approach). The exporting firm ships goods to its intermediary, which moves the product through customs and the foreign distribution channel to retail outlets or end users.

By contrast, the foreign direct investor establishes its own operations in the market, working directly with customers and retailers to move offerings through the channel into the local marketplace. Using this approach, the firm will lease, acquire, or set up a sales office, warehouse, or an entire distribution channel, directly in the target market. Direct investment provides various advantages. First, it helps ensure control over marketing and distribution activities in the target market. Second, it facilitates monitoring the performance of employees and other actors in the local market. Third, it allows the firm to get close to the market, which is especially helpful when the market is complex or rapidly changing. A key disadvantage of direct investment is that it is costly.

Some firms bypass traditional distribution systems altogether by using *direct marketing*—selling directly to end users. It typically implies using the Internet to provide detailed product information and the means for foreigners to buy offerings. Some firms such as Amazon.com are entirely Internet based, with no retail stores. Others, such as Coles, Tesco, and Home Depot combine direct marketing with traditional retailing.

Channel length refers to the number of distributors or other intermediaries that it takes to get the product from the manufacturer to the market. The longer the channel, the more intermediaries the firm must compensate, and the costlier the channel. For example, Japan is characterized by long distribution channels involving numerous intermediaries. High channel costs contribute to international price escalation, creating a competitive disadvantage for the firm.

Global Account Management

In a gradually globalizing world, foreign customers increasingly seek uniform and consistent prices, quality, and customer service. **Global account management (GAM)** refers to serving a key global customer in a consistent and standardized manner, regardless of where in the world it operates. Walmart is a key global account for Procter & Gamble, purchasing a substantial amount of P&G products. Walmart expects consistent service, including uniform prices for the same P&G product regardless of where in the world it is delivered.

Key accounts typically purchase from a collection of preferred suppliers that meet their specifications. Suppliers target these key customers by shifting resources from national, regional, and function-based operations to GAM, whose programs feature dedicated cross-functional teams, specialized coordination activities for specific accounts, and formalized structures and processes. Private IT-based portals facilitate the implementation of such systems. Each global customer is assigned a global account manager, or team, who provides the customer with coordinated marketing support and service across various countries.[27]

Summary

A **global marketing strategy** is a plan of action that guides the firm in how to position itself and its offerings in foreign markets, which customer segments to pursue, and to what degree its marketing program elements should be standardized and adapted. How management balances **adaptation** and **standardization** determines the extent to which the firm must modify a product and its marketing to suit foreign markets. Firms usually prefer to standardize their products to achieve scale economies and minimize complexity. A **global market segment** is a group of customers that shares common characteristics across many national markets. A **global brand** is perceived similarly in all the firm's markets and increases marketing strategy effectiveness.

In developing products with multicountry potential, managers emphasize the commonalities across countries rather than the differences.

A special challenge for exporters is **international price escalation**—the problem of end-user prices reaching high levels in the export market, caused by multilayered distribution channels, intermediary margins, tariffs, and other international customer costs. **Transfer pricing** is the practice of pricing intermediate or finished products exchanged among the subsidiaries and affiliates of the same corporate family located in different countries. **Gray market activity** refers to legal importation of genuine products into a country by intermediaries other than authorized distributors.

International marketing communications includes the management of advertising and promotional activities across national borders. Managers often must adapt their international communications due to unique legal, cultural, and socioeconomic factors in foreign markets. Firms also must accommodate literacy levels, language, and available media.

Firms usually engage foreign intermediaries or foreign-based subsidiaries to reach customers abroad. Long channels are relatively costly. In working with key business customers, firms may undertake **global account management (GAM)**—serving key global customers in a consistent and standardized manner worldwide.

Key Terms

adaptation *259*
global account
  management (GAM) *275*
global brand *261*

global market segment *259*
global marketing
  strategy *258*
gray market activity *265*

international price
  escalation *268*
standardization *259*
transfer pricing *269*

Endnotes

1. Shaoming Zou and S. Tamer Cavusgil, "The GMS: A Broad Conceptualization of Global Marketing Strategy and Its Effect on Firm Performance," *Journal of Marketing* 66 (2002): 40–56.
2. H. Gatignon, J. Eliashberg, and T. Robertson, "Modeling Multinational Diffusion Patterns: An Efficient Methodology," *Marketing Science* 8 (1989): 231–43.
3. George Yip, *Total Global Strategy II* (Upper Saddle River, NJ: Prentice Hall, 2003).
4. Roger Calantone, S. Tamer Cavusgil, Jeffrey Schmidt, and Geon-Cheol Shin, "Internationalization and the Dynamics of Product Adaptation—An Empirical Investigation," *Journal of Product Innovation Management* 21 (2004): 185–98.
5. J. Tapper and A. Miller, "'The Simpsons' Exported to Middle East," October 18, 2005, *ABC News,* retrieved from http://abcnews.go.com/wnt.
6. "Microsoft to Offer Budget Windows Program in Asia," *Wall Street Journal,* August 11, 2004, p. B2.
7. Gabriele Suder and David Suder, "Strategic Megabrand Management: Does Global Uncertainty Affect Brands?" *The Journal of Product and Brand Management* 17, no. 7 (2008): 436–45.
8. Janell Townsend, S. Tamer Cavusgil, and Marietta Baba, "Global Integration of Brands and New Product Development at General Motors," *The Journal of Product Innovation Management* 27, no. 1 (2010): 49–62; Yip (2003).
9. David A. Aaker, *Managing Brand Equity* (New York: The Free Press, 1991); James Gregory and Jack Wiechmann, *Branding Across Borders* (Chicago: McGraw-Hill, 2002).
10. Yip (2003).
11. *Ibid.*
12. Matthew B. Myers, "Implications of Pricing Strategy-Venture Strategy Congruence: An Application Using Optimal Models in an International Context," *Journal of Business Research* 57 (2004): 591–690.
13. S. Tamer Cavusgil, "Pricing for Global Markets," *Columbia Journal of World Business* (Winter 1996): 66–78.
14. S. Tamer Cavusgil, "Unraveling the Mystique of Export Pricing," *Business Horizons* 31 (1988): 54–63.
15. William McDaniel and Edgar Kossack, "The Financial Benefits to Users of Foreign-Trade Zones," *Columbia Journal of World Business* 18 (1983): 33–41.
16. Cavusgil (1988).

17. Thomas Pugel and Judith Ugelow, "Transfer Prices and Profit Maximization in Multinational Enterprise Operations," *Journal of International Business Studies* 13 (Spring–Summer 1982): 115–19.

18. Ralph Drtina and Jane Reimers, "Global Transfer Pricing: A Practical Guide for Managers," *S.A.M. Advanced Management Journal* 74, no. 2 (2009): 4–12.

19. S. Tamer Cavusgil and Ed Sikora, "How Multinationals Can Counter Gray Market Imports," *Columbia Journal of World Business* 23 (1988): 75–86; Reza Ahmadi and B. Rachel Yang, "Parallel Imports: Challenges from Unauthorized Distribution Channels," *Marketing Science* 19 (Summer 2000): 281; Matthew B. Myers, "Incidents of Gray Market Activity Among U.S. Exporters: Occurrences, Characteristics, and Consequences, *Journal of International Business Studies* 30 (1999): 105–26.

20. Ernst Berndt, "A Primer on the Economics of Re-Importation of Prescription Drugs," *Managerial and Decision Economics* 28 (2007): 415–35.

21. S. Tamer Cavusgil and Ed Sikora, "How Multinationals Can Counter Gray Market Imports," *Columbia Journal of World Business* 23 (1988): 75–86.

22. Michael Bush, "Global Ad Spending Growing Faster Than Expected," *AdAge Mediaworks*, December 6, 2010, at www.adage.com; Colin Macleod, "Global Economy and Adspend Prospects," *International Journal of Advertising* 28, no. 1 (2009): 187–89.

23. Laurel Wentz and Bradley Johnson, "Top 100 Global Advertisers Heap Their Spending Abroad," *Advertising Age*, November 30, 2009, pp. 1–2.

24. Macleod (2009).

25. F. Balfour and D. Kiley, "Ad Agencies Unchained," *BusinessWeek,* April 25, 2005, pp. 50–51.

26. Yip (2003).

27. Linda Shi, Shaoming Zou, J. Chris White, Regina McNally, and S. Tamer Cavusgil, "Executive Insights: Global Account Management Capability," *Journal of International Marketing* 13 (2005): 93–113; Sengun Yeniyurt, S. Tamer Cavusgil, and Tomas Hult, "A Global Market Advantage Framework: The Role of Global Market Knowledge Competencies," *International Business Review* 14 (2005): 1–19.

Human Resource Management in the Global Firm

LEARNING OBJECTIVES
In this chapter, you will learn about:

1. The strategic role of human resources in international business

2. International staffing policy

3. Preparation and training of international employees

4. International performance appraisal

5. Compensating employees

6. International labor relations

7. Diversity in the international workforce

THE STRATEGIC ROLE OF HUMAN RESOURCES IN INTERNATIONAL BUSINESS

Leading firms often refer to their employees as "human talent," "human capital," or "intangible assets," emphasizing that they represent a strategic investment rather than a cost. Without designers, problem solvers, knowledge workers, and other skilled people, Pixar, Gucci, Nokia, and many other firms likely could not compete globally.

Recruiting, managing, and retaining human resources is especially challenging in companies with global operations. In 2011, the German MNE Siemens (www .siemens.com) employed more than 400,000 people in some 190 countries: 240,000 throughout Europe, 91,000 in North and South America, 74,000 in the Asia-Pacific region, and 12,000 in Africa, the Middle East, and Russia.

International human resource management (IHRM) refers to the planning, selection, training, employment, and evaluation of employees for international operations.[1] Management grapples with a wide range of challenges in hiring and managing workers within the distinctive cultural and legal frameworks that govern firms worldwide. International human resource managers, usually located at corporate or regional headquarters, advise and support subsidiary managers by hiring, training, and evaluating employees for international operations and providing IHRM guidelines.

Three Employee Categories

In a firm with multicountry operations, international managers operate at three levels:

1. ***Parent country nationals.*** Citizens of the country where the MNE is headquartered. Also called "home country nationals."
2. ***Host country nationals.*** Citizens of the country where the MNE's subsidiary or affiliate is located. They typically constitute the largest proportion of workers hired abroad.
3. ***Third country nationals.*** Citizens of countries other than the home or host country. Most work in management and are hired because they possess special knowledge or skills.[2]

A Canadian MNE may employ Italian citizens in its subsidiary in Italy (host country nationals), send Canadian citizens to work in the Asia-Pacific region on assignment (parent country nationals), or assign Swiss employees to its subsidiary in Turkey (third country nationals).

Employees in any of the three categories assigned to work and reside in a foreign country for an extended period, usually a year or longer, are called **expatriates** (sometimes shortened to "expat"). A U.S. firm might employ a German manager in its subsidiary in France or transfer a Japanese executive to its U.S. headquarters.[3] Both these managers are expatriates.

For IHRM managers, the ultimate challenge is to ensure the right person is in the right position at the right location with the right pay scale. For example, the financial services and information technology sectors in southern India have experienced a shortage of mid- and senior level managerial talent. Consequently, managers from as far away as Eastern Europe are being posted to India to take advantage of compensation packages that are now competitive by advanced-economy standards.[4]

Differences between Domestic and International HRM

International human resource management is usually more complex than domestic human resource management. Driving this complexity are six key factors, which we examine next.[5]

1. ***New HR responsibilities.*** IHRM managers encounter various distinct responsibilities abroad, including taxation issues for expatriates, relocation and

orientation, administrative services for expatriates, host government relations, language translation services, and *repatriation* (returning the expatriate to his or her home country). An Australian national posted to Brazil can be subject to income tax by both governments. Thus, tax equalization—eliminating tax disincentives associated with an international assignment—is a complicating aspect of IHRM.

2. ***The need for an international perspective in compensation policy.*** Employees from parent, host, and third countries typically represent a wide range of nationalities. In an emerging market such as Vietnam, compensation may need to include allowances for housing, education, and other facilities not readily available there.

3. ***Greater involvement in employees' personal lives.*** Human resource professionals help expatriates and their families with housing arrangements, health care, children's schooling, safety, and security, as well as proper compensation given higher living costs in some foreign locations.

4. ***The mix of expatriates versus locals.*** Foreign subsidiaries are typically staffed from home, host, and third countries. The mix of staff depends on several factors, including the international experience of the firm, cost of living in the foreign location, and availability of qualified local staff.

5. ***Greater risk exposure for the firm.*** Adverse events—such as falling productivity, labor strikes, and the departure of key managers—are especially challenging when they occur in the firm's operations abroad. Exposure to political risk and terrorism are also potential problems, requiring greater compensation and security arrangements for employees and their families.

6. ***External influences of the government and national culture.*** Employees must be hired, evaluated, and compensated consistent with country and regional customs and regulations. Laws govern work hours, the firm's ability to dismiss or lay off employees, and severance pay. In many European countries, labor unions are active in managing the firm.

Key Tasks in International Human Resource Management

As outlined in Exhibit 15.1, international human resource managers are responsible for six major tasks:

1. International staffing policy—activities directed at recruiting, selecting, and placing employees
2. Preparation and training of international employees
3. International performance appraisal—providing feedback necessary for employees' professional development
4. Compensation of employees—pay and benefits packages vary greatly worldwide
5. International labor relations—interacting with labor unions and collective bargaining are often challenging
6. Diversity in the international workforce—especially as this relates to women and minorities.

The remainder of this chapter is devoted to examining these tasks.

Task	Strategic Goals	Illustrative Challenges
International staffing policy	• Choose between home country nationals, host country nationals, and third country nationals • Develop global managers • Recruit and select expatriates	• Avoid country bias, nepotism, and other local practices • Cultivate global mind-set
Preparation and training of international employees	• Increase effectiveness of international employees, leading to increased company performance • Train employees with an emphasis on area studies, practical information, and cross-cultural awareness	• Minimize culture shock and the occurrence of early departure by expatriates
International performance appraisal	• Assess, over time, how effectively managers and other employees perform their jobs abroad	• Establish uniform, organization wide performance benchmarks while remaining sensitive to customary local practices.
Compensation of employees	• Develop guidelines and administer compensation (e.g., base salary, benefits, allowances, and incentives)	• Avoid double taxation of employees
International labor relations	• Manage and interact with labor unions, engage in collective bargaining, handle strikes and other labor disputes, wage rates, and possible workforce reduction	• Reduce absenteeism, workplace injuries due to negligence, and the occurrence of labor strikes
Diversity in the international workforce	• Recruit talent from diverse backgrounds to bring experience and knowledge to the firm's problems and opportunities	• Achieve gender diversity

EXHIBIT 15.1   Key Tasks and Challenges of International Human Resource Management.

INTERNATIONAL STAFFING POLICY

One of the critical tasks for MNEs is to determine the ideal mix of employees in the firm's foreign subsidiaries and affiliates.[6] The optimal mix varies by location, industry, stage in the value chain, and availability of qualified local workers. Country laws may also dictate how many employees can come from nonlocal sources.

Exhibit 15.2 illustrates the criteria and rationale for hiring each type of employee.[7] Firms usually post parent country nationals abroad to take advantage of their specialized knowledge, especially in upstream value-chain operations, or to maintain local control over foreign operations. Parent country nationals can also help develop local managers.

Staff with Parent-Country Nationals When...	Staff with Host Country Nationals When...	Staff with Third Country Nationals When...
Headquarters wants to maintain strong control over its foreign operations.	The country is distant in terms of culture or language (such as Japan), or when local operations emphasize downstream value-chain activities such as marketing and sales, as host country nationals usually understand the local business environment best.	Top management wants to create a global culture among the firm's operations worldwide.
Headquarters wants to maintain control over valuable intellectual property that is easily dissipated when accessible by host country nationals or third country nationals.	Local connections and relations are critical to operational success (such as relations with the government in Russia).	Top management seeks unique perspectives for managing host country operations.
Knowledge sharing is desirable among headquarters and the subsidiaries, particularly for developing local managers or the host-country organization.	The local government requires the MNE to employ a minimum proportion of local personnel, or tough immigration requirements prevent the long-term employment of expatriates.	Headquarters wants to transfer knowledge and technology from third countries to host country operations.
Foreign operations emphasize R&D and manufacturing, because parent country nationals are usually more knowledgeable about such upstream value-chain activities.	Cost is an important consideration; salaries of parent country nationals, especially those with families, can be up to four times those of host country nationals.	The firm cannot afford to pay the expensive compensation typical of parent country nationals.

EXHIBIT 15.2 Criteria for Selecting Employees for Foreign Operations.

By contrast, firms prefer host country nationals when the host country environment is complex and their specialized knowledge or local connections are required in the local marketplace. Host country nationals often perform downstream value-chain activities, such as marketing and sales, which require extensive local knowledge.[8] They also usually require less compensation than parent or third country nationals.

Firms often prefer third country nationals when senior management wants to transfer specific knowledge or corporate culture from third countries to host country operations. Worldwide staffing with third country nationals helps firms develop an integrated global enterprise.

Recruitment refers to searching for and locating potential job candidates to fill the firm's needs. *Selection* is gathering information to evaluate and decide who should be employed in particular jobs. For most MNEs, finding talented managers willing and qualified to work outside their home countries is challenging. Schlumberger Ltd. (www.slb.com) is a Texas oil company with operations worldwide. To maintain a sufficient team of engineers, Schlumberger has turned its human resources department into a strategic asset for finding and developing talent worldwide. Schlumberger has assigned high-level executives as "ambassadors" to forty-four important engineering schools, such as Kazakhstan's Kazakh National Technical University, Beijing University, Massachusetts Institute of Technology, and Universidad Nacional Autónoma de México. IBM, Nokia, and Unilever employ similar approaches for finding and developing international talent.[9]

Developing talent is a multistep collaboration between human resource managers and executive management. Together, they need to:

- Analyze the firm's growth strategies and the mission-critical roles needed to achieve them.
- Define the desired skills, behaviors, and experiences for each role.
- Examine the firm's current supply of talent and create a plan to acquire needed talent.
- Develop talent internally and acquire existing or potential talent from outside the firm.
- Assess current and potential talent according to each individual's performance over time, willingness to learn, learning skills, and commitment to career advancement.[10]

Cultivating Global Mindsets

Ethnocentric headquarters staff may believe their ways of doing business are superior and can be readily transferred to other countries.[11] Sophisticated MNEs have a *geocentric orientation*—they staff headquarters and subsidiaries with the most competent people, regardless of national origin. Managers with a *global mind-set* are open to multiple cultural and strategic realities on both global and local levels.[12]

Those adept at working effectively in foreign environments tend to have the following characteristics:[13]

- *Technical competence.*   In distant locations, managers often take on several roles, and need sufficient managerial and technical capabilities to achieve company goals.
- *Self-reliance.*   Expatriate managers who are entrepreneurial, proactive, and innovative can function independently, with limited headquarters support.
- *Adaptability.*   The most important traits are flexibility, diplomacy, cultural empathy, and a positive attitude for overcoming stressful situations.
- *Interpersonal skills.*   The best candidates get along well with others. Building and maintaining relationships is key.[14]
- *Leadership ability.*   The most successful managers view change positively. They skillfully manage threats and opportunities that confront the firm.
- *Physical and emotional health.*   Adapting to life abroad can be stressful. Medical care is often different and may be difficult to access.
- *Spouse and dependents prepared for living abroad.*   The candidate's family must be willing and able to cope with unfamiliar environments and cultures.

Creating team consensus requires globally-minded employees who understand group and organizational dynamics.[15] *Global team* members benefit from specialized training that emphasizes working effectively with those from other cultures.

Cultural Intelligence

International human resource managers prepare expatriates and their families to live and work effectively in new cultural environments. Employees should be trained to understand local government regulations, cultural norms, and language differences, and to adapt to local customs such as gift giving and business dining.

Cultural intelligence is an employee's ability to function effectively in situations characterized by cultural diversity.[16] It has four dimensions: (1) *strategy* describes how an employee makes sense of cross-cultural experiences through her or his judgments; (2) *knowledge* is the employee's understanding of cultural dimensions such as values, social norms, religious beliefs, and language; (3) *motivation* measures the employee's interest in interacting with people from different cultures and confidence in doing so effectively; and (4) *behavioral flexibility* is the employee's ability to adopt verbal and nonverbal behaviors appropriate in different cultures.[17]

Expatriate Assignment Failure and Culture Shock

What happens when things go awry for the employee working abroad? **Expatriate assignment failure** refers to the unintended, premature return of an employee from an international assignment. It may occur because an employee is unable to perform well or because his or her family has difficulty adjusting. Such failure is costly to company productivity and goals. Failure also can affect expatriates themselves, leading to diminished careers or family problems. As many as one-third of foreign assignments end prematurely due to expatriate assignment failure. The rate is especially high among those assigned to countries with very different cultures and languages.

A leading cause of expatriate assignment failure is **culture shock**—confusion and anxiety experienced by a person who lives in a foreign culture for an extended period.[18] It can affect the expatriate or family members and results from an inability to cope with the differences experienced in a foreign environment. Inadequate language and cross-cultural skills tend to worsen culture shock, as the expatriate is unable to function effectively in the foreign environment or fails to communicate well with locals.[19] Most expatriates and their families who experience culture shock overcome it, usually within a few months. But a few give up and return home early.

PREPARATION AND TRAINING OF INTERNATIONAL EMPLOYEES

What can firms do to help employees better understand, adapt, and perform well in foreign environments?[20] Exhibit 15.3 highlights key features of preparation and training programs for international workers. Training consists of three components: (1) **area studies**—factual knowledge of the historical, political, and economic environment of the host country; (2) **practical information**—knowledge and skills necessary to function effectively in a country, including housing, health care, education, and daily living; and (3) **cross-cultural awareness**—the ability to interact effectively and appropriately with people from different language and cultural backgrounds.[21]

Goal	**Desirable employee qualities**	**Training emphasizes**	**Training methods**
Increase manager's effectiveness abroad; increase company performance	Technical competence, self-reliance, adaptability, interpersonal skills, leadership ability, physical and emotional health, spouse and dependents prepared for living abroad	• *Area studies*–host country historical, political, economic, and cultural dimensions • *Practical information*–skills necessary to work effectively in the host country • *Cultural awareness*–cross-cultural communication; negotiation techniques; reduction of ethnocentric orientation and self-reference criterion; language skills	Videos, lectures, assigned readings, case studies, critical incident analysis, simulations and role playing, language training, field experience, long-term immersion

EXHIBIT 15.3   Key Features of Preparation and Training for International Employees.

Employees benefit from training in the host country language and learning to communicate more effectively with local colleagues and workers, suppliers, and customers. Language skills allow them to monitor competitors, recruit local talent, and improve relationships with host country officials and organizations. Language ability also increases employees' insights into and enjoyment of the local culture.[22]

Cross-cultural awareness training increases intercultural sensitivity and helps avoid the *self-reference criterion*—the tendency to view other cultures through the lens of your own. It also guides managers in supervising and communicating with local employees, negotiating with customers and suppliers, and adapting to the local culture.

In order of increasing rigor, training methods include videos, lectures, assigned readings, case studies, books, Web-based instruction, critical incident analyses, simulations, role playing, language training, field experience, and long-term immersion. In role playing and simulations, the employee acts out typical encounters with foreigners. Critical incident analysis examines an episode in which tension arises between an employee and a foreign counterpart due to a cross-cultural misunderstanding. Field experience is a visit to the host country, usually for one or two weeks. Long-term immersion puts the employee in the country for several months or more, often for language and cultural training. In choosing training methods, the firm must strike a balance among cost, rigor, and the degree of interaction required abroad, as well as the distance between the employee's native and new cultures.[23]

Preparing Employees for Repatriation

Repatriation is the expatriate's return to his or her home country following completion of a foreign assignment. Like expatriation, it requires advance preparation, this time to help the employee avoid problems upon returning home. Some expatriates report financial difficulties upon returning, such as higher housing costs. Some find their international experience is not valued, and they may be placed in lesser positions than they held abroad. Others experience "reverse culture shock," difficult readjustment to home country culture. As many as one-quarter of expatriates leave their firm within one year of returning home. Others refuse subsequent international assignments.[24]

International human resource managers can provide counseling on the types of problems employees face upon returning home and monitor the expatriate's compensation and career path abroad. After repatriation, the firm can provide bridge loans and other interim financial assistance and ensure the expatriate has a career position equal to, or better than, the one held before going abroad.[25]

Charting Global Careers for Employees

As the firm generates an increasing proportion of sales and earnings from abroad, it needs globally experienced employees capable of managing company operations worldwide. Many firms establish career development programs that provide high-potential employees opportunities to gain experience both at headquarters and in the firm's operations worldwide. Career development broadens the pool of global talent for managerial positions and visibly demonstrates top management's commitment to global strategy.

For example, employees at the Anglo-Dutch firm Unilever (www.unilever.com) cannot advance far professionally without substantial international experience. Managers are rotated through various jobs and locations around the world, especially early in their careers. Human resource managers search the company's **global talent pool,** a database that profiles employees' international skill sets and potential for supporting the firm's global aspirations, regardless of where they work in Unilever's global network.[26]

INTERNATIONAL PERFORMANCE APPRAISAL

Performance appraisal is a formal process, typically annual, for assessing employee effectiveness, areas for improvement, and where additional training is needed. In appraising performance, managers compare mutually agreed-upon objectives with actual performance. MNEs devise diagnostic procedures to assess the performance of individual employees, see whether problems are attributable to inadequate skill levels, provide additional training and resources, and terminate employees who consistently fail to achieve prescribed goals.

Organizational goals vary from unit to unit. A new foreign subsidiary might be charged with establishing relationships with key customers and rapidly increasing sales. A manufacturing plant might be tasked with ensuring high productivity or maintaining high-quality output. Occasionally a subsidiary performs poorly, and the local manager's task is to resolve problems and get the unit back on track.

The following factors make performance evaluations more complex in the international context:[27]

- The problem of *noncomparable outcomes* arises because of differences in economic, political, legal, and cultural variables. For example, if worker productivity in a subsidiary is half the average of home country operations, top management should take into account local factors such as worker conditions and the quality of factory equipment.[28] Accounting rules can make financial results appear favorable if they are looser than rules applied at home.
- *Incomplete information* results because headquarters is separated from foreign units by time, distance, and cultural differences. Because headquarters staff usually cannot directly observe employees working in foreign subsidiaries, subsidiary managers may be assessed by two evaluators—one from headquarters and one based abroad.

- Performance outcomes may be affected by the *quality* of foreign operations. Older subsidiaries staffed with seasoned personnel often perform better than new subsidiaries with inexperienced workers. Alternatively, new, state-of-the-art factories can perform better than old plants with inferior equipment.

COMPENSATING EMPLOYEES

Compensation packages vary across nations because of differences in legally mandated benefits, tax laws, cost of living, local tradition, and culture. Employees posted abroad usually expect to be compensated at a level that allows them to maintain the living standard they enjoy at home. Managers typically consider four elements when developing compensation packages for employees working abroad: (1) base remuneration or wages, (2) benefits, (3) allowances, and (4) incentives.

The *base remuneration* represents the salary or wages the employee typically receives in his or her home country. A Japanese manager working in the United States would receive a base salary comparable to that paid to managers at the same level in Japan. Expatriate salaries are usually paid in the home currency, the local currency, or some combination of both.

Benefits include health care plans, life insurance, unemployment insurance, and a certain number of paid vacation days. They typically make up a third of the total compensation package but vary greatly as a function of local regulation, industry practice, and taxability. Expatriates usually receive the benefits normally accorded to home country employees.

Allowance is an additional payment that allows the expatriate to maintain a standard of living similar to that at home. It usually pays for housing, and sometimes food and clothing. Additional support may cover relocation, children's education, travel, and business-related entertainment. Hardship allowances compensate employees who work in countries with civil strife or other dangers, or in developing economies that lack essential housing, education, and other facilities.[29]

Given the potential hardships of working abroad, many MNEs also provide an *incentive,* or bonus, to motivate the employee to undertake extraordinary efforts to accomplish company goals abroad, particularly in new foreign markets. It is typically a one-time, lump-sum payment.[30]

We've seen above that expatriates may face tax bills from both the host and home countries. Most home country governments allow the expatriate to minimize this double taxation, and employers will usually reimburse any extra tax burden.

INTERNATIONAL LABOR RELATIONS

Labor relations is the process through which management and workers identify and determine job relationships that will apply in the workplace. *Labor unions* (also called trade unions) provide a means for **collective bargaining**—joint negotiations between management and hourly labor and technical staff regarding wages and working conditions. When the firm and labor union negotiate a relationship, they formalize it with a contract. Labor regulations vary substantially, from minimal rules in Africa and the Indian subcontinent to highly detailed laws and regulations in countries such as Germany and Sweden.

The percentage of workers who belong to labor unions varies by country. Membership has fallen to less than 15 percent of workers in France and the United States and less than 25 percent in Australia, Germany, Japan, and Mexico. However, union membership is relatively high in Belgium, Denmark, and Finland, where more than 50 percent of workers, mostly government employees, are unionized.[31] In many countries, younger workers are less interested in joining unions, and labor laws have become less union-friendly than in the past.[32] The trend toward outsourcing manufacturing and business processes to foreign suppliers also contributes to declining membership.

When management and labor fail to reach agreement, the union may declare a *strike*—an organized, collective refusal to work—with the aim of pressuring management to grant union demands. Though their incidence has declined, strikes remain a powerful weapon. In 2009, French transportation workers, automakers, oil workers, and even supermarket cashiers shut down trains and air travel, halted work in key industries, and forced closure of numerous schools throughout the nation. In 2011, miner strikes in Chile and Indonesia substantially affected the world price and supply of copper, a vital input for many industrial firms.[33]

If a strike lasts more than a few days, a *mediator* or an *arbitrator* may be called in to negotiate between labor and management in an attempt to end the dispute. A mediator is an expert in labor–management relations who brings both sides together and helps them reach a mutually acceptable settlement. An arbitrator is an expert third party who delivers a judgment in favor of one side or the other, after assessing arguments by both sides.

Distinctive Features of Labor around the World

Union membership in the United States peaked in the 1950s, and the unionized labor force in various traditional industries such as automobiles and steel has shrunk in recent decades through globalization, capital mobility, and mass migration from Mexico. Nevertheless, U.S. labor unions remain an important political force. Their activities center on collective bargaining over wages, benefits, and workplace conditions.[34]

Given close ties between Chinese labor and government, Western managers usually deal extensively with China's national and local governments in managing labor relations. China also has a developing independent labor movement. Unions are a factor in reducing the occurrence of sweatshops and other poor working conditions in China.[35] A campaign by the All-China Federation of Trade Unions (ACFTU), the world's largest labor federation, is seeking to unionize workers at all foreign firms operating in China to bridge labor demands and the interests of the Chinese government.[36]

Unions in Europe often represent not only factory workers but white-collar workers such as physicians, engineers, and teachers. A unique feature in Europe, especially in Germany and the Scandinavian countries, is labor union participation in determining wage rates, bonuses, profit sharing, holiday leaves, dismissals, and plant expansions and closings. In 2006, the European Union passed new legislation that requires even small enterprises to consult employees about a range of business, employment, and work organization issues.[37] In Sweden and Germany (in contrast to the United States), labor participation in management may be mandated, and workers often sit on corporate boards, a practice known as **codetermination.**[38]

Cost, Quality, and Productivity of Labor

Worker wages vary greatly worldwide. So do the quality and productivity of worker efforts. Advanced economies tend to pay high wages. Hourly wages are particularly high in Northern Europe. Lower wages in emerging markets and developing economies are commensurate with the lower costs of living in those countries; firms typically pay wages consistent with local living standards and market conditions.

Quality and trainability of labor vary substantially around the world. Well-educated and skilled labor pools are scarce in some countries. Low productivity, poor work quality, and the cost of training offset some of the benefits of paying low wages. Firms must consider wages in the context of worker productivity. All else being equal, a worker in Romania who is paid half the wage of a comparable worker in Germany but is only half as productive provides no additional value. When outsourcing work to foreign suppliers, managers must ensure worker productivity in the host country meets acceptable levels. Firms may outsource or offshore work abroad only to discover the local productivity level is less than expected.

Workforce Reduction

In the recent global financial crisis, deteriorating economic conditions forced countless firms to lay off workers around the world. In 2010, General Motors closed its plant in Antwerp, Belgium, as part of a restructuring of global operations and announced plans to lay off 4,000 employees in Germany. During the recession, many advanced-economy firms shifted work to countries with low labor costs to compensate for falling revenues.[39]

Laying off workers (or making them *redundant*, as it is called in some countries) requires management to consider local norms, regulations, and the presence of strong labor unions. Local custom obligates firms in Japan to avoid layoffs or find positions for dismissed workers in supplier organizations. Most European countries have regulations that restrict management's ability to lay off workers.

Many countries require *just cause* to terminate an employee. In most cases, just cause is satisfied if the employee becomes permanently disabled, is terminated within a probationary period (usually one to six months), or is found guilty of incompetence, theft, or disclosure of confidential information. If the firm cannot demonstrate just cause, local courts may require it to pay an indemnity, a sum of money upon termination that can be substantial. In most countries, ambiguous cases are usually settled in the employee's favor.[40]

Trends in International Labor

Labor is increasingly mobile across national borders thanks to the growing integration of national economies, the rapid expansion of multinational firms, the rise of international collaborative ventures, and the loosening of protectionist policies that restrict work permits for foreigners.[41]

Some nations, particularly those with labor shortages or rapidly growing econo- mies, encourage immigration. Several million Polish workers have sought jobs in Britain since Poland became a member of the European Union. By contrast, Japan discourages worker immigration, a policy that, combined with a low birth rate, will produce labor shortages in the future.

Formation of global alliances by national labor unions is another recent trend. To help counter weakening union power, labor organizations have lobbied suprana- tional organizations, such as the International Labour Organization (www.ilo.org; a United Nations agency), to require MNEs to comply with labor standards and prac- tices worldwide. Some national labor unions are joining forces with unions in other countries, forming global labor/trade unions.[42] Subsidiaries of European firms in the United States have signed union-organizing agreements that compel their U.S. units to comply with European labor standards.[43] A few unions have succeeded in creat- ing global agreements that affect all the subsidiaries of numerous MNEs. The Union Network International (UNI) represents 900 unions with 15 million members around the world. Firms that have signed global agreements with the UNI include Carrefour (France), H&M (Sweden), Metro AG (Germany), and Telefonica (Spain).[44]

Firm Strategy in International Labor Relations

MNEs frequently delegate the management of labor relations to their foreign subsid- iaries. However, this can be a mistake because of the potential *global* impact of labor relations in any one country. Labor agreements made by foreign subsidiaries can cre- ate precedents for negotiations in other countries, and wage levels or labor unrest in one country affect the firm's activities in other countries. For example, a strike by 1,800 workers at an auto component factory in India caused a parts shortage that temporarily closed Ford and General Motors factories in North America.[45] Thus, it is critical to maintain cohesive labor relations.

A centralized information system, ideally on the company's intranet, can provide continuous data on labor developments among subsidiaries to help managers antici- pate employee concerns and resolve potential threats in cross-national labor relations. The intranet is also useful for communicating with employees worldwide and regu- larly informing them of the firm's mission, objectives, ongoing challenges, and future threats. It is often easier to negotiate with labor unions when they understand what confronts the firm.

DIVERSITY IN THE INTERNATIONAL WORKFORCE

Female managers in international business are still relatively uncommon.[46] Consider the proportion of women in top management positions.[47] Representation by women in senior management is relatively low in Belgium and Japan. It is highest in the Philippines and Russia. Women's rights are not generally contentious in the Philippines, where religious practices do not clash with a woman's right to work out- side the home, and women have refined their entrepreneurial and leadership skills over many decades.

Although evidence suggests just as many women seek international positions as men, relatively few are asked to fill expatriate positions.[48] Senior managers may assume women do not make suitable leaders abroad or that foreign men do not like reporting to female managers. Firms are reluctant to send women to locations where the demarcation between male and female roles is sharp. Some women may feel uncomfortable in all-male settings.[49] Although flexible and part-time work policies are often beneficial to women's progress up the corporate ladder, not all companies provide them. Finally, because women currently occupy relatively few top management positions (in Europe, they hold only 15 percent of such posts), fewer women have sufficient experience to be sent abroad for important jobs.[50]

Today, women account for about one-third of students in MBA programs in Europe and the United States. About one-half of recruits who join European firms are female university graduates.[51] In the United States, 140 women enroll in higher education each year for every 100 men; in Sweden, the rate is as high as 150.[52]

In 2003, females accounted for only 6 percent of seats on Norwegian boards of directors. Under an initiative by the Norwegian government, however, public and state-owned companies were required to ensure that women hold at least 40 percent of seats, and they now hold 45 percent in such companies. New companies also must comply with the rules, and the government is considering extending them to family-owned companies as well. Spain has since followed suit with rules for female board representation, and France has proposed similar laws.

About half the firms in a survey by Mercer Human Resource Consulting (www .mercer.com) believe the number of female expatriates will continue rising in the future. At the same time, 15 percent of companies said they would not send women to hardship locations such as the Middle East. The survey included more than 100 multinational companies with nearly 17,000 male and female expatriates.[53]

Success Strategies for Women Managers in International Business

In many countries, being a female expatriate can be an advantage for developing and leveraging strengths as a woman and as a manager. In the long run, managerial competence wins out over prejudice.

Many women have found it is easier to get foreign assignments if they speak a foreign language or have other international skills. Gaining substantial experience as a domestic manager or in short international assignments can greatly improve prospects for working abroad. Garnering strong support from senior management increases credibility. Once abroad, most women report the initial reaction of surprise is often replaced by professionalism and respect.

Firms can ensure women achieve greater equality in international business. They can provide training programs to develop female managerial talent. They can fill leadership roles in foreign assignments with qualified women. They can fill a minimal percentage of senior executive posts with female employees. They can set targets for the number of women on executive boards. Many female executives are now serving as mentors and role models for aspiring women. Leading firms understand the need to forge a new paradigm of diverse and internationally successful female managers. Organizations such as Accenture, Ernst & Young, and Vinson & Elkins sponsor programs that assist women to advance in the global workplace. The Association of Women in International Trade is a U.S. organization that promotes the interests of women working in international business (www.wiit.org).

Summary

International human resource management (IHRM) is the selection, training, employment, and motivation of employees for international operations. IHRM is more complex than its domestic counterpart. The firm must develop procedures, policies, and processes appropriate for each country where it does business. A **parent country national** (also called a "home country national") is an employee who is a citizen of the country where the MNE is headquartered. A **host country national** is an employee who is a citizen of the country where the MNE subsidiary or affiliate is located. A **third country national** is an employee who is a citizen of a country other than the home or host country. An expatriate is an employee who is assigned to work and reside in a foreign country for an extended period, usually a year or longer. There are six key tasks in IHRM: staffing; training and development; performance appraisal; compensation; labor relations; and achieving diversity in the workplace.

Managers best suited for working abroad typically have technical competence, self-reliance, adaptability, interpersonal skills, leadership ability, physical and emotional health, and, if present, a family prepared for living abroad. **Expatriate assignment failure** is the unplanned early return home of an employee or the failure of an expatriate to function effectively abroad. Many expatriates experience **culture shock**.

Training for foreign assignments covers **area studies, practical information,** and **cross-cultural awareness.** Acquiring language skills provides managers with numerous advantages. Repatriation is the return of the expatriate to the home country and requires advance preparation.

International performance appraisals offer feedback on employee effectiveness, identify problems, and provide a basis to reward superior performance. Firms must develop systems to fairly measure the performance of foreign units.

Expatriates expect to be compensated at a level that allows them to maintain their usual standard of living. Typical expatriate compensation includes base salary, benefits, allowances, and incentives.

Many nonmanagerial employees abroad are represented by *labor unions.* Management must ensure effective labor relations and take care when reducing the workforce. Along with labor costs, the quality and productivity of the workforce are important considerations. Leading MNEs establish an information system on labor developments, communicate with all employees, and formulate a standard policy on employment and working conditions worldwide.

Sophisticated MNEs include people from diverse backgrounds, nationalities, and gender who bring experience and knowledge to addressing the firm's problems and opportunities. Firms can take several steps to ensure women achieve more equality in international business.

Key Terms

area studies *284*
codetermination *289*
collective bargaining *287*
cross-cultural awareness *284*

cultural intelligence *284*
culture shock *284*
expatriate assignment
    failure *284*

expatriates *279*
global talent pool *286*
host country
    national *279*

Endnotes

1. Peter Dowling, Marion Festing, and Allen Engle, *International HRM: Managing People in a Multinational Context,* 5th ed. (London: Thomson Learning, 2008).
2. *Ibid.*
3. *Ibid.*
4. Jo Johnson, "More Westerners Take Top Posts in India as Locals' Pay Demand Soars," *Financial Times,* May 30, 2007, p. 1.
5. Dowling, Festing, and Engle (2008).
6. James Neelankavil, Anil Mathur, and Yong Zhang, "Determinants of Managerial Performance: A Cross-Cultural Comparison of the Perceptions of Middle-Level Managers in Four Countries," *Journal of International Business Studies* 31, no. 1 (2000): 121–41.
7. Dowling, Festing, and Engle (2008); Anne-Wil Harzing, "Of Bears, Bumble-Bees, and Spiders: The Role of Expatriates in Controlling Foreign Subsidiaries," *Journal of World Business* 36, no. 4 (2008): 366–79.
8. Anne-Wil Harzing, "Who's in Charge? An Empirical Study of Executive Staffing Practices in Foreign Subsidiaries," *Human Resource Management* 40, no. 2 (2001): 139–45.
9. Debbie Lovewell, "Employer Profile: World Order," *Employee Benefits*, September 2009, p. 50.
10. Nanette Byrnes, "Star Search," *Business Week,* October 10, 2005, p. 68; David Pollitt, "Unilever 'Raises the Bar' in Terms of Leadership Performance," *Human Resource Management International Digest* 14, no. 5 (2006): 23–25; Philip Harris, Robert Moran, and Sarah Moran, *Managing Cultural Differences,* 6th ed. (Burlington, MA: Elsevier Buttermann-Heinemann, 2007).
11. Robert T. Moran and John R. Riesenberger, *The Global Challenge* (London: McGraw-Hill, 1994).
12. Ben L. Kedia and Akuro Mukherji, "Global Managers: Developing a Mindset for Global Competitiveness," *Journal of World Business* 34, no. 3 (1999): 230–51; Orly Levy, Schon Beechler, Sully Taylor, and Nakiye Boyacigiller, "What We Talk about When We Talk about 'Global Mindset'— Managerial Cognition in Multinational Corporations," *Journal of International Business Studies* 38, no. 2 (2007): 231–58.
13. Dowling, Festing, and Engle (2008).
14. Harris, Moran, and Moran (2007).
15. Jeanne Brett, Kristin Beyfar, and Mary Kern, "Managing Multicultural Teams," *Harvard Business Review* 84, no. 11 (2006): 84–92.
16. S. Ang, L. Van Dyne, and C. K. S. Koh, "Personality Correlates of the Four Factor Model of Cultural Intelligence," *Group and Organization Management* 31 (2006): 100–23.
17. *Ibid.*
18. Dowling, Festing, and Engle (2008).
19. Anne-Wil Harzing and Claus Christensen, "Expatriate Failure: Time to Abandon the Concept?" *Career Development International* 9, no. 6/7 (2004): 616–20.
20. M. Mendenhall, E. Dunbar, and G. Oddou, "Expatriate Selection, Training and Career Pathing: A Review and Critique," *Human Resources Management,* 26 (1987): 331–45.
21. Harris, Moran, and Moran (2007).
22. Stephen Rhinesmith, *A Manager's Guide to Globalization* (Homewood, IL: Business One Irwin, 1998).
23. Rosalie Tung, "Expatriate Assignments: Enhancing Success and Minimizing Failure," *Academy of Management Executive* 1 (1987): 117–26.
24. J. Black, H. Gregersen, and M. Mendenhall, "Toward a Theoretical Framework of Repatriation Adjustment," *Journal of*

International Business Studies 23 (1992): 737–60.

25. Harris, Moran, and Moran (2007).

26. George Yip, *Total Global Strategy II* (Upper Saddle River, NJ: Prentice Hall, 2003).

27. Peter Dowling, Denice Welch, and Randall Schuler, *International Human Resource Management,* 3rd. ed. (Cincinnati, OH: South-Western, 1999).

28. *Ibid.*

29. Richard Hodgetts and Fred Luthans, *International Management: Culture, Strategy, and Behavior,* 5th ed. (Boston: McGraw-Hill Irwin, 2003).

30. *Ibid.*

31. David Blanchflower, "International Patterns of Union Membership," *British Journal of Industrial Relations* 45, no. 1 (2007): 1–28.

32. *Ibid.*; Guglielmo Meardi, "Multinationals' Heaven? Uncovering and Understanding Worker Responses to Multinational Companies in Post-Communist Central Europe," *International Journal of Human Resource Management* 17, no. 8 (2006): 1366–78.

33. "Paris in the Spring; Unrest in France," *Economist,* March 21, 2009, p. 52; Li Xiaowei, "Chinese Copper TC/RCs Plunge to $50/5 Cents on Mining Strikes," *Metal Bulletin Daily*, July 29, 2011, p. 250.

34. M. Dubofsky and F. R. Dulles, *Labor in America: A History,* 7th ed. (Wheeling, IL: Harlan Davidson, 2004).

35. "Business: Membership Required; Trade Unions in China," *Economist,* August 2, 2008, p. 55; Charles Umney, "The International Labour Movement and China," *Industrial Relations Journal* 42 no. 4 (2011): 322-338.

36. Jian Qiao, "Between the State and Market: Multiple Roles of the Chinese Trade Unions from the Perspectives of Shop Stewards," *Employee Relations* 32, no. 1 (2010): 28–41; Umney, 2011; Victorien Wu, "Labor Relations in Focus," *The China Business Review* 33, no. 6 (2006): 40–44.

37. John Gennard, "Development of Transnational Collective Bargaining in Europe," *Employee Relations* 31, no. 4 (2009): 341–46; Stephen Hardy and Nick Adnett, "Breaking the ICE: Workplace Democracy in a Modernized Social Europe," *The International Journal of Human Resource Management* 17, no. 6 (2006): 1021–31.

38. Alberto Alesina and Francesco Giavazzi, *The Future of Europe: Reform or Decline* (Boston: MIT Press, 2006).

39. Randal Archibold, "Despite Violence, U.S. Firms Expand in Mexico," *New York Times,* July 10, 2011, accessed at www.nytimes.com; Stanley Pignal, John Reed, and Daniel Schafer, "GM Opel Confirms Antwerp Factory Will Shut," *Financial Times,* January 22, 2010, p. 24.

40. Lawrence Koslow and Robert Scarlett, *Global Business* (Houston, TX: Cashman Dudley, 1999).

41. Dominique Gross and Nicolas Schmitt, "Low- and High-Skill Migration Flows: Free Mobility versus Other Determinants," *Applied Economics,* 12, no. 44 (2012): 1–20.

42. C. Mako, P. Csizmadi, and M. Illessy, "Labour Relations in Comparative Perspective," *Journal for East European Management Studies* 11, no. 3 (2006): 267–87.

43. Jessica Marquez, "Unions' Global End Run," *Workforce Management,* January 30, 2006, pp. 1–4.

44. John Gennard, "A New Emerging Trend? Cross Border Trade Union Mergers," *Employee Relations* 31, no. 1 (2009): 5–8.

45. Krishna, Thoppil, and Guha (2010).

46. Dowling, Welch, and Schuler (1999); "The Conundrum of the Glass Ceiling," *Economist,* July 23, 2005, pp. 63–65; Price Waterhouse, *International Assignments: European Policy and Practice 1997/1998* (London: Price Waterhouse, 1997).

47. Grant Thornton International Ltd., *Privately Held Businesses: The Lifeblood of the Global Economy, International Business Report 2009,* retrieved from http://www.grantthorntonibos.com.

48. Nancy Adler, *International Dimensions of Organizational Behavior,* 4th ed. (Cincinnati, OH: South-Western, 2002; Harris, Moran, and Moran (2007).

49. Robert T. Moran, Phillip R. Harris, and Sarah V. Moran, *Managing Cultural*

Differences, Global Leadership Strategies for the 21st Century, 7th ed. (Oxford, UK: Elsevier, 2007); Jeanine Prime, Karsten Jonsen, Nancy Carter, and Martha Maznevski, "Managers' Perceptions of Women and Men Leaders: A Cross Cultural Comparison," *International Journal of Cross Cultural Management* 8, no. 2 (2008): 171–80.

50. Georges Desvaux, Sandrine Devillard-Hoellinger, and Mary Meaney, "A Business Case for Women," *McKinsey Quarterly* September, 2008, retrieved from www .mckinseyquarterly.com; Lynda Gratton, "Steps That Can Help Women Make It to the Top," *Financial Times,* May 23, 2007, p. 13.

51. *Ibid.*; "Conundrum of the Glass Ceiling" (2005); Ruth Simpson and Afam Ituma, "Transformation and Feminisation: The Masculinity of the MBA and the 'Un-Development' of Men," *Journal of Management Development* 28, no. 4 (2009): 301–16.

52. "Women and the World Economy: A Guide to Womenomics," *Economics,* April 12, 2006, p. 80; Matthew Brannan and Vincenza Priola, "Between a Rock and a Hard Place: Exploring Women's Experience of Participation and Progress in Managerial Careers," *Equal Opportunities International* 28, no. 5 (2009): 378–97.

53. Mercer Human Resource Consulting, "More Females Sent on International Assignment Than Ever Before, Survey Finds," October 12, 2006, retrieved from http://www.mercerhr .com.

GLOSSARY

Absolute advantage principle. A country benefits by producing only those products in which it has an absolute advantage or that it can produce using fewer resources than another country.

Acculturation. The process of adjusting and adapting to a culture other than one's own.

Acquisition. Direct investment to purchase an existing company or facility.

Adaptation. Firm's efforts to modify one or more elements of its international marketing program to accommodate specific customer requirements in a particular market.

Advanced economies. Post-industrial countries characterized by high per-capita income, highly competitive industries, and well-developed commercial infrastructure.

Agent. An intermediary (often an individual or a small firm) that handles orders to buy and sell commodities, products, and services in international business transactions for a commission.

Antidumping duty. A tax imposed on products deemed to be dumped and causing injury to producers of competing products in the importing country.

Arbitragers. Currency traders who buy and sell the same currency in two or more foreign-exchange markets to profit from differences in the currency's exchange rate.

Area studies. Factual knowledge of the historical, political, and economic environment of the host country.

Balance of payments. The annual accounting of all economic transactions of a nation with *all* other nations.

Barter. A type of countertrade in which goods are directly exchanged without the transfer of any money.

Bond. A debt instrument that enables the issuer (borrower) to raise capital by promising to repay the principal along with interest on a specified date (maturity).

Born global firm. A young entrepreneurial company that initiates international business activity very early in its evolution, moving rapidly into foreign markets.

Build-operate-transfer (BOT). Arrangement in which the firm or a consortium of firms contracts to build a major facility abroad, operate it for a specified period, and then hand it over to the project sponsor, typically the host-country government or public utility.

Business process outsourcing (BPO). The outsourcing to independent suppliers of business service functions such as accounting, payroll, human resource functions, travel services, IT services, customer service, or technical support.

Buy-back agreement. A type of countertrade in which the seller agrees to supply technology or equipment to construct a facility and receives payment in the form of goods produced by the facility.

Capital flight. The rapid sell-off by residents or foreigners of their holdings in a nation's currency or other assets, usually in response to a domestic crisis that causes investors to lose confidence in the country's economy.

Captive sourcing. Sourcing from the firm's own production facilities.

Central bank. The monetary authority in each nation that regulates the money supply and credit, issues currency, and manages the exchange rate of the nation's currency.

Codetermination. An industrial relations practice in which labor representatives sit on the corporate board and participate in company decision making.

Collective bargaining. Joint negotiations between management and hourly labor and technical staff regarding wages and working conditions.

Commercial risk. Firm's potential loss or failure from poorly developed or executed business strategies, tactics, or procedures.

Common market. A stage of regional integration in which trade barriers are reduced or removed, common external barriers are established, and products, services, and *factors of production* are allowed to move freely among the member countries.

Company-owned subsidiary. A representative office of the focal firm that handles marketing, physical distribution, promotion, and customer service activities in the foreign market.

Company sales potential. An estimate of the share of annual industry sales that the firm expects to generate in a particular target market.

Comparative advantage. Superior features of a country that provide unique benefits in global competition, typically derived from either natural endowments or deliberate national policies.

Comparative advantage principle. It can be beneficial for two countries to trade without barriers as long as one is relatively more efficient at producing goods or services needed by the other. What matters is not the absolute cost of production but rather the relative efficiency with which a country can produce the product.

Compensation deals. A type of countertrade in which payment is in both goods and cash.

Competitive advantage. Distinctive assets or competencies of a firm that are difficult for competitors to imitate and are typically derived from specific knowledge, capabilities, skills, or superior strategies.

Configuration of value-adding activity. The pattern or geographic arrangement of locations where the firm carries out value-chain activities.

Consortium. A project-based, nonequity venture initiated by multiple partners to fulfill a large-scale project.

Contract manufacturing. An arrangement in which the focal firm contracts with an independent supplier to manufacture products according to well-defined specifications.

Contractual entry strategies in international business. Cross-border exchanges where the relationship between the focal firm and its foreign partner is governed by an explicit contract.

Corporate governance. The system of procedures and processes by which corporations are managed, directed, and controlled.

Corporate social responsibility (CSR). A manner of operating a business that meets or exceeds the ethical, legal, commercial, and public expectations of stakeholders, including customers, shareholders, employees, and communities.

Corruption. The abuse of power to achieve illegitimate personal gain.

Counterpurchase. A type of countertrade with two distinct contracts. In the first, the seller agrees to a set price for goods and receives cash from the buyer. This first deal is contingent on a second wherein the seller agrees to purchase goods from the buyer for the same amount as in the first contract or a set percentage of same.

Countertrade. An international business transaction where all or partial payments are made in kind rather than cash.

Countervailing duty. Tariff imposed on products imported into a country to offset subsidies given to producers or exporters in the exporting country.

Country risk. Exposure to potential loss or adverse effects on company operations and profitability caused by developments in a country's political and/or legal environments.

Critical incident analysis (CIA). A method for analyzing awkward situations in cross-cultural encounters by developing objectivity and empathy for other points of view.

Cross-cultural awareness. Ability to interact effectively and appropriately with people from different language and cultural backgrounds.

Cross-cultural risk. A situation or event where a cultural misunderstanding puts some human value at stake.

Cross-licensing agreement. A type of project-based, nonequity venture where partners agree to access licensed technology developed by the other on preferential terms.

Cultural intelligence. An employee's ability to function effectively in situations characterized by cultural diversity.

Cultural metaphor. A distinctive tradition or institution strongly associated with a particular society.

Culture. The learned, shared, and enduring orientation patterns in a society. People demonstrate their culture through values, ideas, attitudes, behaviors, and symbols.

Culture shock. Confusion and anxiety experienced by a person who lives in a foreign culture for an extended period.

Currency control. Restrictions on the outflow of hard currency from a country or the inflow of foreign currencies.

Currency option. A contract that gives the purchaser the right, but not the obligation, to buy a certain amount of foreign currency at a set exchange rate within a specified amount of time.

Currency risk. Potential harm that arises from changes in the price of one currency relative to another.

Currency swap. An agreement to exchange one currency for another, according to a specified schedule.

Current rate method. Translation of foreign currency balance sheet and income statements at the current exchange rate—the spot exchange rate in effect on the day or for the period when the statements are prepared.

Customs. Checkpoints at the ports of entry in each country where government officials inspect imported products and levy tariffs.

Customs brokers. Specialist enterprises that arrange clearance of products through customs on behalf of importing firms.

Customs union. A stage of regional integration in which the member countries agree to adopt common tariff and nontariff barriers on imports from nonmember countries.

Debt financing. The borrowing of money from banks or other financial intermediaries, or the sale of corporate bonds to individuals or institutions, to raise capital.

Devaluation. Government action to reduce the official value of its currency, relative to other currencies.

Developing economies. Low-income countries characterized by limited industrialization and stagnant economies.

Direct exporting. Exporting that is accomplished by contracting with intermediaries located in the foreign market.

Direct quote. The number of units of domestic currency needed to acquire one unit of foreign currency; also known as the normal quote.

Distribution channel intermediary. A specialist firm that provides various logistics and marketing services for focal firms as part of the international supply chain, both in the home country and abroad.

Documentation. Official forms and other paperwork required in export transactions for shipping and customs procedures.

Dumping. Pricing exported products at less than their normal value, generally less than their price in the domestic or third-country markets, or at less than production cost.

Economic exposure. The currency risk that results from exchange rate fluctuations affecting the pricing of products, the cost of inputs, and the value of foreign investments.

Economic union. A stage of regional integration in which member countries enjoy all the advantages of early stages, but also strive to have common fiscal and monetary policies.

Emerging markets. Former developing economies that have achieved substantial industrialization, modernization, and rapid economic growth since the 1980s.

Equity financing. The issuance of shares of stock to raise capital from investors and the use of retained earnings to reinvest in the firm.

Equity joint venture. A type of partnership in which a separate firm is created through the investment or pooling of assets by two or more parent firms that gain joint ownership of the new legal entity.

Equity participation. Acquisition of partial ownership in an existing firm.

Ethics. Moral principles and values that govern the behavior of people, firms, and governments, regarding right and wrong.

Ethnocentric orientation. Using our own culture as the standard for judging other cultures.

Eurobond. A bond sold outside the issuer's home country but denominated in its own currency.

Eurocurrency. Any currency deposited in a bank outside its country of origin.

Eurodollars. U.S. dollars held in banks outside the United States, including foreign branches of U.S. banks.

Exchange rate. The price of one currency expressed in terms of another; the number of units of one currency that can be exchanged for another.

Expatriate. An employee assigned to work and reside in a foreign country for an extended period, usually a year or longer.

Expatriate assignment failure. An employee's premature return from an international assignment.

Export control. A government measure intended to manage or prevent the export of certain products or trade with certain countries.

Export department. A unit within the firm charged with managing the firm's export operations.

Export management company (EMC). A domestically based intermediary that acts as an export agent on behalf of a client company.

Exporting. The strategy of producing products or services in one country (often the producer's home country), and selling and distributing them to customers located in other countries.

Extraterritoriality. Application of home country laws to persons or conduct outside national borders.

Facilitator. A firm or an individual with special expertise in banking, legal advice, customs clearance, or related support services that assists focal firms in the performance of international business transactions.

Family conglomerate. A large, highly diversified company that is privately owned.

Focal firm. The initiator of an international business transaction, which conceives, designs, and produces offerings intended for consumption by customers worldwide. Focal firms are primarily MNEs and SMEs.

Foreign bond. A bond sold outside the issuer's country and denominated in the currency of the country where issued.

Foreign direct investment (FDI). An internationalization strategy in which the firm establishes a physical presence abroad through acquisition of productive assets such as capital, technology, labor, land, plant, and equipment.

Foreign distributor. A foreign market-based intermediary that works under contract for an exporter, takes title to, and distributes the exporter's products in a national market or territory, often performing marketing functions such as sales, promotion, and after-sales service.

Foreign exchange. All forms of money that are traded internationally, including foreign currencies, bank deposits, checks, and electronic transfers.

Foreign exchange market. The global marketplace for buying and selling national currencies.

Foreign trade zone (FTZ). An area within a country that receives imported goods for assembly or other processing and re-export. For customs purposes the FTZ is treated as if it is outside the country's borders.

Forward contract. A contract to exchange two currencies at a specified exchange rate on a set future date.

Forward rate. The exchange rate applicable to the collection or delivery of a foreign currency at some future date.

Franchising. Arrangement in which the firm allows another the right to use an entire business system in exchange for fees, royalties, or other forms of compensation.

Franchisor. A firm that grants another the right to use an entire business system in exchange for fees, royalties, or other forms of compensation.

Free trade. Relative absence of restrictions to the flow of goods and services between nations.

Free trade agreement. A formal arrangement between two or more countries to reduce or eliminate tariffs, quotas, and barriers to trade in products and services.

Free trade area. A stage of regional integration in which member countries agree to eliminate tariffs and other barriers to trade in products and services within the bloc.

Freight forwarder. A specialized logistics service provider that arranges international shipping on behalf of exporting firms.

Fronting loan. A loan between the parent and its subsidiary, channeled through a large bank or other financial intermediary.

Functional structure. An arrangement in which management of the firm's international operations is organized by functional activity, such as production and marketing.

Futures contract. An agreement to buy or sell a currency in exchange for another at a specified price on a specified date.

Geocentric orientation. A global mind-set in which the manager is able to understand a business or market without regard to country boundaries.

Geographic area structure. An organizational design in which management and control are decentralized to the level of individual geographic regions.

Global account management (GAM). Serving a key global customer in a consistent and standardized manner, regardless of where in the world it operates.

Global bond market. The international marketplace in which bonds are bought and sold, primarily through bond brokers.

Global brand. A brand whose positioning, advertising strategy, look, and personality are standardized worldwide.

Global capital market. The collective financial markets where firms and governments raise intermediate and long-term financing.

Global equity market. The worldwide market of funds for equity financing—stock exchanges around the world where investors and firms meet to buy and sell shares of stock.

Global financial system. The collective of financial institutions that facilitate and regulate investment and capital flows worldwide, such as central banks, commercial banks, and national stock exchanges.

Global industry. An industry in which competition is on a regional or worldwide scale.

Global integration. Coordination of the firm's value-chain activities across countries to achieve worldwide efficiency, synergy, and cross-fertilization in order to take maximum advantage of similarities between countries.

Global market opportunity. Favorable combination of circumstances, locations, and timing that offers prospects for exporting, investing, sourcing, or partnering in foreign markets.

Global market segment. A group of customers who share common characteristics across many national markets.

Global marketing strategy. A plan of action for foreign markets that guides the firm in deciding how to position itself and its offerings, which customer segments to target, and the degree to which it should standardize or adapt its marketing program elements.

Global matrix structure. An arrangement that blends the geographic area, product, and functional structures to leverage the benefits of a purely global strategy while keeping the firm responsive to local needs.

Global money market. The collective financial markets where firms and governments raise short-term financing.

Global sourcing. The procurement of products or services from independent suppliers or company-owned subsidiaries located abroad for consumption in the home country or a third country.

Global strategy. An approach where headquarters seeks substantial control over its country operations in order to minimize redundancy and maximize efficiency, learning, and integration worldwide.

Global supply chain. The firm's integrated network of sourcing, production, and distribution, organized on a worldwide scale and located in countries where competitive advantage can be maximized.

Global talent pool. A searchable database of employees, profiling their international skill sets and potential for supporting the firm's global aspirations.

Global team. An internationally distributed group of employees charged with a specific problem-solving or best-practice mandate that affects the entire organization.

Globalization of markets. Ongoing economic integration and growing interdependency of countries worldwide.

Gray market activity. Legal importation of genuine products into a country by intermediaries other than authorized distributors (also known as parallel imports).

Greenfield investment. Direct investment to build a new manufacturing, marketing, or administrative facility, as opposed to acquiring existing facilities.

Hedgers. Currency traders who seek to minimize their risk of exchange rate fluctuations, often by entering into forward contracts or similar financial instruments.

Hedging. Using financial instruments and other measures to reduce or eliminate exposure to currency risk by locking in guaranteed foreign exchange positions.

High-context culture. A culture that emphasizes nonverbal messages and views communication as a means to promote smooth, harmonious relationships.

Home replication strategy. An approach in which the firm views international business as separate from and secondary to its domestic business.

Horizontal integration. An arrangement whereby the firm owns, or seeks to own, the activities performed in a single stage of its value chain.

Host-country national (HCN). An employee who is a citizen of the country where the MNE subsidiary or affiliate is located.

Idiom. An expression whose symbolic meaning is different from its literal meaning.

Import license. Government authorization granted to a firm for importing a product.

Importing or global sourcing. Procurement of products or services from suppliers located abroad for consumption in the home country or a third country.

Incoterms. Universally accepted terms of sale that specify how the buyer and the seller share the cost of freight and insurance in an international transaction and at which point the buyer takes title to the goods.

Indirect exporting. Exporting that is accomplished by contracting with intermediaries located in the firm's home market.

Indirect quote. The number of units of foreign currency obtained for one unit of domestic currency.

Individualism versus collectivism. Describes whether a person functions primarily as an individual or as part of a group.

Industrial cluster. A concentration of businesses, suppliers, and supporting firms in the same industry at a particular location,

characterized by a critical mass of human talent, capital, or other factor endowments.

Industry market potential. An estimate of the likely sales for all firms in a particular industry over a specific period.

Infringement of intellectual property. Unauthorized use, publication, or reproduction of products or services protected by a patent, copyright, trademark, or other intellectual property right.

Intellectual property. Ideas or works created by individuals or firms, including discoveries and inventions; artistic, musical, and literary works; and words, phrases, symbols, and designs.

Intellectual property rights. The legal claim through which the proprietary assets of firms and individuals are protected from unauthorized use by other parties.

Internalization theory. An explanation of the process by which firms acquire and retain one or more value-chain activities inside the firm, minimizing the disadvantages of dealing with external partners and allowing for greater control over foreign operations.

International business. Performance of trade and investment activities by firms across national borders.

International collaborative venture. Cross-border business alliance whereby partnering firms pool their resources and share costs and risks to undertake a new business venture; also referred to as an "international partnership" or an "international strategic alliance."

International division structure. An organizational design in which all international activities are centralized within one division in the firm, separate from domestic units.

International human resource management (IHRM). The planning, selection, training, employment, and evaluation of employees for international operations.

International investment. The transfer of assets to another country or the acquisition of assets in that country.

International Monetary Fund (IMF). An international agency that aims to stabilize currencies by monitoring the foreign exchange systems of member countries and lending money to developing economies.

International monetary system. Institutional framework, rules, and procedures by which national currencies are exchanged for one another.

International portfolio investment. Passive ownership of foreign securities such as stocks and bonds for the purpose of generating financial returns.

International price escalation. The problem of end-user prices reaching exorbitant levels in the export market caused by multilayered distribution channels, intermediary margins, tariffs, and other international customer costs.

International trade. Exchange of products and services across national borders, typically through exporting and importing.

Intracorporate financing. Funds from sources inside the firm (both headquarters and subsidiaries) such as equity, loans, and trade credits.

Investment incentive. Transfer payment or tax concession made directly to foreign firms to entice them to invest in the country.

Joint venture. A form of collaboration between two or more firms to create a new, jointly owned enterprise.

Joint venture partner. A focal firm that creates and jointly owns a new legal entity through equity investment or pooling of assets.

Know-how agreement. Contract in which the focal firm provides technological or management knowledge about how to design, manufacture, or deliver a product or a service.

Legal system. A system for interpreting and enforcing laws.

Letter of credit. Contract between the banks of a buyer and a seller that ensures payment from the buyer to the seller upon receipt of an export shipment.

Licensing. Arrangement in which the owner of intellectual property grants a firm the right to use that property for a specified period of time in exchange for royalties or other compensation.

Licensor. A firm that enters a contractual agreement with a foreign partner to allow the partner the right to use certain intellectual property for a specified period of time in exchange for royalties or other compensation.

Local responsiveness. Management of the firm's value-chain activities on a country-by-country basis to address diverse opportunities and risks.

Logistics service provider. A transportation specialist that arranges for physical distribution and storage of products on behalf of focal firms, and also controls information between the point of origin and the point of consumption.

Long-term versus short-term orientation. Refers to the degree to which people and organizations defer gratification to achieve long-term success.

Low-context culture. A culture that relies on elaborate verbal explanations, putting much emphasis on spoken words.

Management contract. Arrangement in which a contractor supplies managerial know-how to operate a hotel, hospital, airport, or other facility in exchange for compensation.

Manufacturer's representative. An intermediary contracted by the exporter to represent and sell its merchandise or services in a designated country or territory.

Maquiladoras. Export-assembly plants in northern Mexico along the U.S. border that produce components and typically finished products destined for the United States on a tariff-free basis.

Masculinity versus femininity. Refers to a society's orientation based on traditional male and female values. Masculine cultures tend to value competitiveness, assertiveness, ambition, and the accumulation of wealth. Feminine cultures emphasize nurturing roles, interdependence among people, and taking care of less fortunate people.

Master franchise. Arrangement in which an independent company is licensed to establish, develop, and manage the entire franchising network in its market and has the right to subfranchise to other franchisees, assuming the role of local franchisor.

Mercantilism. The belief that national prosperity is the result of a positive balance of trade, achieved by maximizing exports and minimizing imports.

Merger. A special type of acquisition in which two firms join to form a new, larger firm.

Monetary intervention. The buying and selling of currencies by a central bank to maintain the exchange rate of a country's currency at some acceptable level.

Monochronic orientation. A rigid orientation to time, in which the individual is focused on schedules, punctuality, and time as a resource.

Multidomestic industry. An industry in which competition takes place on a country-by-country basis.

Multidomestic strategy. An approach to firm internationalization in which headquarters delegates considerable autonomy to each country manager, allowing him or her to operate independently and pursue local responsiveness.

Multilateral development banks (MDB). International financial institutions owned by multiple governments within world regions or other groups.

Multilateral netting. Strategic reduction of cash transfers within the MNE family through the elimination of offsetting cash flows.

Multinational enterprise (MNE). A large company with substantial resources that performs various business activities through a network of subsidiaries and affiliates located in multiple countries.

National industrial policy. A proactive economic development plan initiated by the government, often in collaboration with the private sector, that aims to develop or support particular industries within the nation.

New global challengers. Top firms from emerging markets that are fast becoming key contenders in world markets.

Nontariff trade barrier. A government policy, regulation, or procedure that impedes trade through means other than explicit tariffs.

Normativism. The belief that ethical behavioral standards are universal, and firms and individuals should seek to uphold them around the world.

Offshoring. The relocation of a business process or entire manufacturing facility to a foreign country.

Organizational culture. The pattern of shared values, behavioral norms, systems, policies, and procedures that employees learn and adopt.

Organizational processes. Managerial routines, behaviors, and mechanisms that allow the firm to function as intended.

Organizational structure. Reporting relationships inside the firm that specify the links between people, functions, and processes.

Outsourcing. The procurement of selected value-adding activities, including production of intermediate goods or finished products, from independent suppliers.

Parent-country national (PCN). An employee who is a citizen of the country where the MNE is headquartered.

Performance appraisal. A formal process for assessing how effectively employees perform their jobs.

Political system. A set of formal institutions that constitute a government.

Polycentric orientation. A host-country mindset in which the manager develops a strong affinity with the country in which she or he conducts business.

Polychronic perspective. A flexible, nonlinear orientation to time, whereby the individual takes a long-term perspective and emphasizes human relationships.

Power distance. Describes how a society deals with the inequalities in power that exist among people.

Practical information. Knowledge and skills necessary to function effectively in a country, including housing, health care, education, and daily living.

Privatization. Transfer of state-owned industries to private concerns.

Product structure. An arrangement in which management of international operations is organized by major product line.

Project-based, nonequity venture. A collaboration in which the partners create a project with a relatively narrow scope and a well-defined timetable, without creating a new legal entity.

Protectionism. National economic policies designed to restrict free trade and protect domestic industries from foreign competition.

Quota. A quantitative restriction placed on imports of a specific product over a specified period of time.

Regional economic integration. The growing economic interdependence that results when two or more countries within a geographic region form an alliance aimed at reducing barriers to trade and investment.

Regional economic integration bloc. A geographic area consisting of two or more countries that have agreed to pursue economic integration by reducing barriers to the cross-border flow of products, services, capital, and, in more advanced states, labor.

Relativism. The belief that ethical truths are not absolute but differ from group to group.

Repatriation. The expatriate's return to his or her home country following the completion of a foreign assignment.

Royalty. A fee paid periodically to compensate a licensor for the temporary use of its intellectual property, often based on a percentage of gross sales generated from the use of the licensed asset.

Rule of law. A legal system in which rules are clear, publicly disclosed, fairly enforced, and widely respected by individuals, organizations, and the government.

Self-reference criterion. The tendency to view other cultures through the lens of our own culture.

Small and medium-sized enterprise (SME). A company with 500 or fewer employees (as defined in Canada and the United States).

Socialization. The process of learning the rules and behavioral patterns appropriate to one's given society.

Sovereign wealth fund (SWF). A state-owned investment fund that undertakes systematic, global investment activities.

Special Drawing Right (SDR). A unit of account or a reserve asset, a type of currency used by central banks to supplement their existing reserves in transactions with the IMF.

Speculators. Currency traders who seek profits by investing in currencies with the expectation their value will change in the future.

Spot rate. The exchange rate applied when the current exchange rate is used for immediate receipt of a currency.

Standardization. Firm's efforts to make its marketing program elements uniform, with a view to targeting entire regions, or even the global marketplace, with the same product or service.

Strategy. A planned set of actions that managers employ to make best use of the firm's resources and core competencies to gain competitive advantage.

Subsidy. Monetary or other resources that a government grants to a firm or group of firms, usually intended to encourage exports or to facilitate the production and marketing of products at reduced prices, to ensure the involved firms prosper.

Sustainability. Meeting humanity's needs without harming future generations.

Tariff. A tax imposed on imported products, effectively increasing the cost of acquisition for the customer.

Tax haven. A country hospitable to business and inward investment because of its low corporate income taxes.

Temporal method. Translation of foreign currency balance sheet and income statements at an exchange rate that varies with the underlying method of valuation.

Tenders. Formal offers made by a buyer to purchase certain products or services.

Third-country national (TCN). An employee who is a citizen of a country other than the home or host country.

Trade deficit. A condition in which a nation's imports exceed its exports for a specific period of time.

Trade surplus. A condition in which a nation's exports exceed its imports for a specific period of time.

Trading company. An intermediary that engages in import and export of a variety of commodities, products, and services.

Transaction exposure. The currency risk firms face when outstanding accounts receivable or payable are denominated in foreign currencies.

Transfer pricing. The practice of pricing intermediate or finished products exchanged among the subsidiaries and affiliates of the same corporate family located in different countries.

Transition economies. A subset of emerging markets that evolved from centrally planned economies into liberalized markets.

Translation exposure. The currency risk that results when a firm translates financial statements denominated in a foreign currency into the functional currency of the parent firm, as part of consolidating international financial results.

Transnational strategy. A coordinated approach to internationalization in which the firm strives to be relatively responsive to local needs while retaining sufficient central control of operations to ensure efficiency and learning.

Transparency. The degree to which companies regularly reveal substantial information about their financial condition and accounting practices.

Turnkey contracting. Arrangement in which the focal firm or a consortium of firms plans, finances, organizes, manages, and implements all phases of a project abroad and then hands it over to a foreign customer after training local workers.

Turnkey contractors. Focal firms or a consortium of firms that plan, finance, organize, manage, and implement all phases of a project and then hand it over to a foreign customer after training local personnel.

Uncertainty avoidance. The extent to which people can tolerate risk and uncertainty in their lives.

Vertical integration. An arrangement whereby the firm owns, or seeks to own, multiple stages of a value chain for producing, selling, and delivering a product or service.

Visionary leadership. A quality of senior management that provides superior strategic guidance for managing efficiency, flexibility, and learning.

Wholly owned direct investment. A foreign direct investment in which the investor fully owns the foreign assets.

World Bank. An international agency that provides loans and technical assistance to low- and middle-income countries with the goal of reducing poverty.

AUTHOR INDEX

SUBJECT INDEX

This index included terms and topics. For authors cited, see the Author Index. Page numbers with "e" refer to exhibits.